The Films of Oshima

The Films
of Oshima Nagisa

Images of a Japanese Iconoclast

Maureen Turim

UNIVERSITY OF CALIFORNIA PRESS

Berkeley   Los Angeles   London

Although the publisher has endeavored to maintain the highest possible resolution for the original images provided, frame enlargements reproduced in this book may appear in less than optimal form.

University of California Press
Berkeley and Los Angeles, California

University of California Press
London, England

Library of Congress Cataloging-in-Publication Data

Turim, Maureen Cheryn, 1951-
    The films of Oshima Nagisa : images of a Japanese iconoclast / Maureen Turim.
        p.   cm.
    Includes bibliographical references and index.
    ISBN 0-520-20665-7 (cl : alk. paper). — ISBN 0-520-20666-5 (pbk. : alk. paper)
    1. Ōshima, Nagisa, 1932- —Criticism and interpretation.
    I. Title.
PN1998.3.O84T87   1997   96-39466
791.43'0233'092—dc21   CIP

Printed in the United States of America

1 2 3 4 5 6 7 8 9

The paper used in this publication meets the minimum requirements of American National Standard for Information Sciences—Permanence of Paper for Printed Library Materials. ANSI Z39.48-1984 ⊚

To my mother, Ruthanne Cherin Turim,
and to the memory of my sister, Dona Jean Turim

CONTENTS

ACKNOWLEDGMENTS / *ix*

1. Cultural Iconclasm and Contexts of Innovation / *1*

2. Cruel Stories of Youth and Politics / *27*

3. Rituals, Desire, Death: Leaving One's Will on Film / *61*

4. Signs of Sexuality in Oshima's Tales of Passion / *125*

5. Warring Subjects / *157*

6. Popular Song, Fantasies, and Comedies of Iconoclasm / *185*

7. Documents of Guilt and Empire / *215*

8. Feminist Troubles on a Map of Split Subjectivities / *246*

Conclusion: Whither Oshima? / *269*

FILMOGRAPHY / *274*
BIBLIOGRAPHY / *291*
INDEX / *299*

ACKNOWLEDGMENTS

This book was written over a number of years with the help of many individuals and institutions whom I wish to thank. First I wish to acknowledge gratefully the help of Oshima Nagisa, who upon reading my early essays on his work was eager to discuss the theoretical, aesthetic, and ideological issues I raised at length in an extended interview in Tokyo in 1986. My exchanges with Oshima, not only during that research trip to Tokyo but also at screenings in which he was present in Paris, Athens, Ohio, and New York, have always been rewarding, challenging, and provocative; he welcomes debate and hard questions. I wish to thank Oshima also for access to and permission to publish the images used to illustrate this volume. In conjunction with this, I wish to thank Shimuzu Akira of the Japan Film Library Council in Tokyo who provided a personal introduction to Oshima and arranged for screenings of films not only at the Library Council but also, with Oshima's permission and help, at the Kyoto prefecture at Shochiku, and through Ushiyama Junichi Productions. Donald Richie was also welcoming and helpful when I arrived in Tokyo, and Kyoko Hirano, now of the Japan Society, has been continuously helpful.

I wish to thank Scott Nygren as well who shared this trip to Japan with me, and my personal and professional life then and since. Our mutual interest in Japanese culture, creative filmmaking, cultural theory, and child rearing has been a source of renewable pleasure and sustenance. Many thanks to my husband and colleague.

Earlier versions of some of the writing in this book appeared in *Wide Angle, Journal of Film and Video, Iris,* and *Enclitic.* These include an essay coauthored with John Mowitt, whom I wish to thank for that collaboration. In retaining aspects of that earlier essay here, I do so with the full acknowledgment that the exchanges that went into writing collectively were fundamental to the thoughts I had then and now about this film. That collaboration was presented first in a seminar on filmic modernism offered by David Bordwell at the University of Wisconsin–Madison, which I remember most fondly as a dynamic intellectual experience, due to David's vitality as a teacher and to the participation of other graduate students including Diane Waldman, Fina Bathrick, and Edward Branigan. In returning to writing on Oshima after my other book projects and the essays published earlier, I can never forget those early years in Madison, or my studies and professors in Paris, for those were the years in which the theories that inform this book began to assume their importance in my life. French sources on Oshima figure prominently in this book, as his work is perhaps best appreciated in France, due to the theoretical junctures I explore.

I thank Dana Polan and Bill Haver for their superb suggestions and encouraging comments on the manuscript and my colleague at the University of Florida, Joseph Murphy, for his help with sources, close reading, and comments. I am grateful to David Desser, whose own book so clearly maps the relationship of Oshima to the rest of Japanese New Wave that I did not repeat his work here, for his generous reading and useful comments on this book. I am also grateful to New Yorker Films for permitting me to rescreen a film in New York.

During my years at the State University of New York at Binghamton, I received a grant for research that went into this volume and benefited from great exchanges with colleagues John Chaffee and Bill Haver as well as other members of the East Asian Program there. In addition, the Women's Studies Program there provided a forum for my presentation of gender in Oshima's films, and discussion with colleagues, particularly Jane Collins, Catherine Lutz, and Sidonie Smith, was useful. I wish to thank also the Cornell University East Asian Program for visits there as an honorary fellow, and especially Tim Murray, Brett du Bary, and Naoki Sakai for their comments on papers on Oshima I delivered at Cornell. Similarly, let me thank Wimal Dissanayake and the East-West Center at the University of Hawaii for discussions there.

I want to thank the University of Florida for its summer support grant that aided completion of this book and all my colleagues and students in the English Department and the Film Studies Program who provide a vibrant theoretical base from which to work. Thanks to my editor, Edward Dimendberg, for his interest in and support of this book and to Michelle Nordon for her caring work on this manuscript.

Thanks to my mother, Ruthanne Turim, to my sister, Shereen Turim Rahamim, to Scott, and to my daughter, Mika Turim-Nygren, for love and support.

CHAPTER ONE

Cultural Iconoclasm
and Contexts of Innovation

The film career of Oshima Nagisa spans the years 1959 to the present. Coinciding with Japan's reemergence after its World War II defeat and the Occupation as a major global economic power, Oshima's films represent a running commentary, direct and indirect, on the intellectual and political life of postwar Japan. This volume analyzes the films' engagement in that history, seeking a multiplicity of meanings they evoke in context.

As important as the social and political stances represented in these films are, they are of equal interest for their formal innovations. Form and structure are integral to the meanings of these films, in very subtle and complex ways. Oshima uses patterns of editing and narrative development that simultaneously interlace mutually impossible story lines and interpretations of events. These techniques invoke the functioning of the unconscious and desire. Innovative use of zoom lenses, camera movements, and conflicting camera angles mold a vision of subjectivity quite different from that seen in other films. This unique application of filmic technique aims at presenting the internal conflicts of the individual psyche. Psychoanalytic theory helps us understand these perceptual and enunciative elements.

This form of representation is particularly striking in a Japanese artist, as much of Japanese literature and art has traditionally limited the exploration of the psyche and interior thought. Modernism in Japan, however, introduces subjectivity, in part as an absorption of Western influences, a history explored in more detail later in this chapter.

Oshima's films therefore demand a dual context: the specificity of Japan and the international arena. We must consider not only how Oshima blends Japanese and non-Japanese elements but also how the Japan of the postwar period is already an international culture. Then there is another sense in which Oshima's films demand being seen in an international context: while his earliest films were distributed at first primarily in Japan and other Asian countries, eventually these films and most of his later ones received international distribution. His most recent films were not only made for an international audience, they were financed by non-Japanese sources. Oshima's career corresponds to the period in which Japanese film has received recognition from the rest of the world, which had previously been relatively unaware of the rich history of cinema in Japan.

Oshima's films call many theories into play. Narratives are fractured, events are presented ambiguously, modes of representation conflict with each other. In fact, paradoxical logic that allows for a multiplicity of truths is key to understanding the constant variation, the different approaches, the changes in the films. Some films even make "bibliographical" references to such key Western theoreticians as Bertolt Brecht, Friedrich Nietzsche, and Wilhelm Reich. Japanese writers and philosophers also resonate through these films, in ways that have been perhaps less apparent to European and American audiences. Like his "Shinjuku Thief" in his film *Shinjuku dorobo nikki* (Diary of a Shinjuku Thief, 1969) Oshima has performed acts of borrowing that we now associate with postmodernism, the piling together of fragments of thoughts and sources to reshape ideas and create stories. His aim is often to shape history, for more than most filmmakers, Oshima saw film as an activist intervention in a global culture.

A NOTE ON THE AUTEUR

Any study of the works of an individual director faces questions of the debts it owes to auteurism, the methodology of film history and analysis that developed in the fifties and sixties which privileges the director as the "author" of his or her films. The function of the director as creative consciousness, shaping a film's artistic purpose and merit, was central to auteurism's concerns. Auteurism construed itself as a remedy to the studio system and the industrialization and standardization of film production. It was also a response to film histories that concentrated on the role of producers, actors, national industries or studios, and even the audience, rather than on the films' directors. Auteurism quickly became an assumption in the writing of film history. It has subsequently been challenged on a number of grounds, mainly for its excessive supplanting of alternative approaches, for its biographical fixations on "great, individual artists," and for its factual errors (faulty assumptions of directorial responsibility for elements in a film that other talents initiated).

Oshima emerged as a filmmaker when auteurism was among the newest and most dynamic concepts in film criticism internationally. His career is marked by claims for his prominence as a filmic auteur, as a director who had vision, wrote many of his own scripts, and worked with teams made up of many of the same actors and "creative" personnel—camera persons, set designers, and so on—from film to film. Oshima certainly thought of himself in auteurist terms and marketed his works that way, especially when he also established his own production company. So if for no other reason than historical context, auteurism drifts, more or less consciously, through any study of Oshima.

There are many forms of auteurism. Some forms of auteurist film criticism borrow heavily from biographical methodologies in literary criticism, art and music history, the history of science, and other disciplines. In film studies the biographical is amplified by journalistic coverage. Film journals such as the French *Cahiers du Cinéma,* the Japanese *Kinema Jumpo,* the British *Sight and Sound,* and the American *Wide Angle* covered Oshima by offering interviews in which he was asked, or volunteered, to present his films autobiographically.

Yet we should question the romantic tendencies of the practice of auteurism in film studies and recognize its debt to traditions of literary criticism, as Ed Buscombe points out in his 1973 essay, "Ideas of Authorship." This essay comes on the heels of much debate in France over the larger issues of authorship, historically, and its relationship to modernity and contemporary theory that we will turn to momentarily; for now let us consider that one danger some saw in auteurism was its tendency in many cases to remove films from discussion of ideology. When a filmmaker declared a goal other than social commentary, be it aesthetics, entertainment, or the search for universal truths, such stated intentions could be used to restrict investigation of other issues. Even those auteurist studies that avoided focus on a filmmaker's statements could end up extrapolating a restricted sense of purpose from the films themselves, using such arguments to foreclose social inquiry.

In Oshima's case, however, auteurism clearly does not preclude sociological and historical correlations, since Oshima himself foregrounds this aspect of his work. Thus the biographical framework in Oshima's work produces interpretations open to social history, but it introduces some other problems that we will examine. Even an auteurism open to social history may tend to assure a set of authorized meanings, limiting exploration of the modernity and complexity of the works.

The most unquestioned approach to biography as a framework for an auteurist approach to Oshima's films is offered by Louis Danvers and Charles Tatum, Jr. (1986). The first chapter establishes Oshima's biography, and his presence as personality and artist is foregrounded throughout. There is much that is valid in the biographical approach to authorship, but methodological questions arise. First, we must ask whether the biography presented is accurate. Second, we must ask on what interpretive assumptions biographical explanation rests.

Before sorting through the many issues that these questions pose, let us note that besides the auteurist and biographical tendencies of the foreign press and film scholarship, the focus on the director accrues specific meaning in the Japanese context. The arts in Japan have traditionally been the province of artisan families; since the Tokugawa period, birth into a family of crafts people or artists gave one access to an apprenticeship that constituted the precondition of artistic production (though adoptions could augment such lineages). Within this control of access to specific lineages, the notion of the "great artist" plays a central hierarchical role. In fact, at present the throne bestows the title "great national living treasure" to artists of special talent and renown. Certainly there were moments in the history of the arts in Japan where new directions emerged both from outside influences (such as the forcible importation of Korean ceramists by Toyotomi Hideyoshi following his invasions of Korea in 1592 and 1597) (Mikami 1981: 36–47) and through the long history of aesthetic dissent and splinter groups within Japan, many of which helped to reformulate a tradition. Arts that we now associate with traditional Japan, Kabuki and Ukiyoe, originated as subversive manifestations of popular culture associated with the "water trade," the sexual entertainment districts of Edo (Tokyo) and Kyoto. Yet the strength of hierarchical tradition and aesthetic doctrine in Japan is such that even these arts evolved into codified traditions, many, such as Kabuki, developing strict familial lineages limiting entrance to the sons of performers and those adopted into the familial system.

The modern culture industries have opened up this tradition of inherited right to cultural expression in the newly emerging technological arts. Even some of the closed traditional arts, such as Nō and Kabuki theater or pottery, are now less completely circumscribed to "outsiders." Yet many of the assumptions of inherited status persist in Japanese notions of artistic genius; though modern theater, films, modern dance, oil painting, sculpture, and so on, may have been an artistic outlet for a new group of artists, the traditions of acclaim surrounding the great artist were readily transferred to these new and Western-influenced disciplines. This includes the artistic position of film director. At Japanese studios, directors historically wielded great authority as artists. Apprenticeship as assistant director was the customary way to learn this art and accede to the status of film director (Anderson and Richie 1982: 346–351, 495).

Similarly, Japanese film criticism is often director centered. Sato Tadao in *Oshima Nagisa no Sekai* (1973) reflects the tendency toward auteurist approaches in Japanese film criticism. Yet in Sato's work on Oshima, we find a contradiction that is itself quite illuminating, as Sato is also one of the most sociological of Japanese film critic-scholars. He makes a great effort to place Oshima in a larger cultural and political frame, similar to his more general tracing of the cultural meanings in his historical essays in *Currents in Japanese Cinema* (1982).

Oshima even becomes useful as an emblem of a whole period to David Desser in his book, *Eros plus Massacre,* which he supports by citing other critics' similar moves (1988: 13–36, 46–59). In the structure of this book, Oshima not only plays the role of key participant in a period of filmic production, but his ideas and themes are used to coordinate the disparate tendencies of the period and derivations of his film titles name several chapters. Two of Oshima's early films, *Cruel Story of Youth* and *Night and Fog in Japan,* are presented as "paradigmatic" of the New Wave movement in Japan (Desser 1988: 25, 48, 236). Perception of paradigmatic status and even of this leadership role may be partially due to foreign reception; none of the other figures that Desser is identifying with the New Wave were known outside Japan until years later. Oshima, as well as the other directors, as Desser (1988: 46) points out, sees the movement as less unified than this. We will reconsider interpretations of the historical changes in the Japanese film industry later. For now, let us note that, arguably, both the role and the legend of Oshima in the history of contemporary Japanese film and culture are large. A direct, critical look at the issues raised by what we know of his biography and how that informs his explorations of subjectivity is most relevant to the films and their history of reception.

BIOGRAPHY AND SUBJECTIVITY

So here is the trouble with which we are faced. We have a series of films made by a filmmaker, Oshima Nagisa, whose biography is hard to ignore when looking at his films, even if one's methods of film analysis make one wary of such a biographical, auteurist approach. First, Oshima, as a part of a modernist practice in Japan and in film, creates his films drawing not only on his immediate personal experience but also on his self in the more extended sense of his feelings, his psyche, his unconscious. Second, he covers his films with his "self." By this I mean that he writes about his films extensively. The writings are themselves often brilliant; Oshima is not only articulate on his strategies but also a powerful theorist and critic of his own work as well as the works of others. With his writings, I would include the form of "writing" that we call the "interview," which I have already placed as overdetermined by an auteurist historical moment. Of course, interviews are mediated not only by the other's questions and reporting of answers but also by expectations of what the other might want to hear, or to which she or he might be provoked to respond. In all his pronouncements Oshima was a particularly gifted publicist; he brings to interviews great intelligence, strong political opinions, and complex interpretations of his own films, which he is able to express in accessible terms. He seems to reach a most intriguing balance of saying what his audience might respond to well while still introducing elements meant to shock or provoke.

Yet Oshima's very success in expressing his ideas about his films seems to cause a certain journalistic dependence on his ideas, a tendency to substitute for analysis of the films themselves mere juxtaposition and collation of his quotes. His films are read biographically or as the accomplishment of the author's intentions more often than they are read as in any way venturing beyond the self and intentions (and the projected self and stated, conscious intentions, at that) that Oshima's writings express. Oshima warns about the dangers of insularity and literal "self" reflection in his essays "The Laws of Self-Negation" and "Beyond Endless Self-Negation" (the title of the latter is mistranslated: it should be "From an Endless Self-Negation"), indicating that self-negation is a positive term in Oshima's lexicon, one that indicates not self-effacement but the willingness to engage subjectively in a dialectical relationship with one's preconceptions (Oshima 1992: 47–48, 52–53).

Oshima advances a kind of auteurism—"films must first and foremost, express the filmmaker's *active involvement as an individual*" (my emphasis)—but it is one tempered by restraints on ego investment (1988: 47). The Japanese word that has been translated as "active involvement" is *shutaiteki,* which means the direct exteriorization of inner subjectivity, a nuance that is combined with suspicion of any reified notion of singular and sacrosanct intentionality. On the contrary, Oshima simultaneously advocates a willingness to change one's approach in response to a reality that is "always changing" (1992: 53). Methodologically, for him, this means that creating a film "must be a reality-based negation of the images expressed in the script" (1992: 52). This is a demand for improvisation, but improvisation in response to important preplanning. Spontaneity and fluidity that negate the preestablished conception allow for the discovery of "new images." We will return to what Oshima might mean by "reality" here, for it is a term he uses frequently in a specifically political, as well as an aesthetic, sense. What I wish to highlight is that involvement "as an individual" is not for Oshima a simple championing of the artist's selfhood.

Further, there is the sense in which subjectivity is a radical concept in the Japanese context, in opposition to a Buddhist and Confucian focus on collectivity and on the effacement of individual needs and desires. This may even be the reason why the translator chose the mistranslation "beyond," assuming that "self-negation" would have to be a concept Oshima, as a critic of Japanese traditions, would hold in contempt; it is clear from the context of both essays, however, that self-negation for him is not negation of subjectivity but rather a dialectics of the inner, anterior self with the social and artistic circumstance.

Similarly we need to look at the specifics of the question of biography. The major biographical elements in Oshima's case, as presented in his writings, his interviews, and the critical works that draw on these sources, investigate just these boundaries of self and history. I will examine four elements often taken as mythic keys to Oshima in a manner that looks at biography self-consciously. Interest in social context and psychoanalysis makes this material highly relevant, but our readings of it cannot be a merely direct causal transference of biographical statements as explanations of works of art. These key instances still need to be examined in a larger context and read for the conflicting and ambivalent narratives they represent.

Consider Oshima's family background. He is said to be from an "aristocratic" background as well as a "descendant of a Samurai family" (Danvers and Tatum 1986: 19). His father is also identified as a government official who kept a large library. Each of these carries various meanings, especially in contemporary Japanese society; the samurai were a privileged class of warriors who emerged in the eleventh and twelfth centuries and whose codification in the Tokugawa period gave them privileged status in the shogunate; the terms, "aristocrat" and "samurai," while not entirely consistent with one another, taken together connote a tradition of education, privilege, and self-esteem, which, since the Meiji restoration, would find its most likely equivalent in government service, the higher echelons of the military (with right-wing associations, particularly in memory of the thirties and World War II), or in established intellectual activity such as that of a university professor. So in this view Oshima becomes the rebellious son whose rebellion is nonetheless informed by his inherited sense of power and will to action. Another version of this background is offered in a quote from Imamura Shohei with which Audie Bock (1978: 309) introduces her chapter on Oshima: "I'm a country farmer; Nagisa Oshima is a samurai." Some might take Imamura to mean he is the simpler and more passive of the two and Oshima is the more aggressive fighter. One of the connotations of Imamura's opposition, however, is that between peasant as "outcast" *(hani)*, inherently critical of Japanese official culture, and samurai, which in this context emphasizes a historical role as both privileged and loyal servant of the Tokugawa shogunate, or at the very least to the daimyo, the local retainer. If Oshima is still marked as a "samurai" long after the demise of this official class, what are we to make of the successful government servant who was Oshima's father but apparently widely enough read to be familiar with Marx?

Whatever we might postulate is conditioned by absence, as the father died when Oshima was only six years old. Oshima marks this as the most significant factor in his childhood, in his essay "My Father's Non-existence: A Determining Factor in My Existence" (Oshima 1992: 201–202). He even counsels other parents that such absence is preferable to more attentive and controlling parenting, advising them to create parental time away from the child as "true discipline and education." This statement is perhaps to be understood in the context of his rebellion against conformity, for what he praises in his own formation is his acceptance and even desire to be out of the ordinary. Yet what Oshima seems to forget is both how many Japanese boys lost their fathers (and mothers) during the Pacific War and how absent many living Japanese fathers are, with their long hours at work and their evenings at bars with colleagues. Given their numbers, the children of these absent fathers are among the conforming children. We might also recognize how symptomatic the essay's rejection of nurturing as "overprotective" is, as it is divorced from any larger perspective. Oshima holds his protective mother in contempt, blaming women in general for conformity. "I resented my mother's existence; it made my life merely average, relatively speaking, as opposed to extraordinary" (1992: 201). Lacking an analysis of female dependency and limitations within Japanese society, or other, institutional pressures toward conformity, the essay singles out overprotective, dominant mothers. It is all too reminiscent of U.S. attitudes toward motherhood in the late forties and fifties, following the lead of Philip Wylie's *A Generation of Vipers* (1942), in which mothers, themselves oppressed by a patriarchal limitation on their lives, were accused of stifling the lives of their sons. Yet even if we read such an essay critically, we should remember that such revelations of self and psyche are not common in Japanese culture. The attempt to look at personal psychology, to examine the workings of one's family, is to be read as an act of nonconformity and an attempt in itself to escape tradition and reinvent Japanese identity.

Oshima also speaks of resentment and longing for his dead father. He tells of his attempt to hide his father's books during the war, only to watch them disintegrate. It is through such metaphors that this story of Oshima's family background gains special significance in the context of the Pacific War, the next key instance often cited in renderings of Oshima's biography. The Pacific War was a time of extreme political repression in Japan, during which the mere possession of leftist literature was a crime. To watch the destruction of the legacy of the period in which leftist social thought flowered among the Japanese intelligentsia is for Oshima to learn of his nation's intellectual and moral somnambulance.

As he tells us in an autobiographical essay, "My Adolescence Began with Defeat," Oshima had a Pacific War childhood (Oshima 1992: 195–200). Born in 1932, the year before the invasion of Manchuria, Oshima's early life and schooling were colored by his nation's militarism and imperialist expansion. He was thirteen years old at the time of surrender, and therefore his adolescence was a coming to terms with the nation's fallibility and the deceit practiced by the powerful and the respected. The realization *après-coup* of the Japanese propaganda machine having been a false foundation of childhood truth is what coming of age meant for much of his generation. His image in the essay is of playing Go all day on the day the defeat was announced, but not remembering whether he won or lost the game (1992: 195).

Thus the father's Marxist texts are a trace of a schism in twentieth-century Japanese culture between tradition and the impulse for social change stimulated by revolutionary ideas from the West. Yet the father continued to serve the nation through the invasion of Manchuria and the growth of militarism, to die from natural causes rather than from resistance, abandoning the son to simply shared faith in Japan's actions and demoralization at Japan's defeat. As Oshima has said in an interview with this author in 1984, his generation came of age through a realization of their being duped to follow an ill-conceived and immoral militarism and patriotism. These biographical elements place Oshima on a broad cultural and historical map in which those who previously enjoyed privilege and believed in the Japanese nation are caught culturally between nostalgic longing and rejection of the past. They help to explain the emotional charge that interlaces nation and father under patriarchal systems.

Oshima's involvement, beginning in high school and then later when he was a student at the Law Faculty of Kyoto University, in left-wing student movements and drama groups is another aspect of his life that is a touchstone for interpretation of his films. In his account published in *Sekkai no eiga sakka 6* (Film Directors of the World) as well as his essays, he tells of his leadership role as vice president of the student association and then president of the Kyoto Prefecture student alliance. A key demonstration took place in 1951, when protests surrounding a visit by the emperor resulted in banning the student organization. Then in 1953 the students held a demonstration over the right of the group to meet, known as "the KU incident," which led to violent confrontations with the police. These years were an extraordinary period in which Japanese students were still reacting to Japan's wartime militarism, its defeat, and the U.S. occupation, as well as events such as the revolution in China, the war in Korea, the Soviet Union's increasing postwar power, and the war against the French in Vietnam. Oshima's account gives us his concern with what he calls the "logic of organized struggle," given his growing critique of Communist party cell operation within the student movement, Stalinist tactics, and the dynamics of factional infighting.

Oshima's biography does find reflection in his *Nihon no yuro to kiri* (Night and Fog in Japan), a film I will discuss in chapter 2; it is a surprisingly direct representation of the sort of intellectual theoretical debate that characterizes the Japanese student left, colored by the vicissitudes of personal desires and jealousies. What is interesting to note here is Oshima's processes of fictionalization, even when he draws on the personal. First, this film concerns students organizing in opposition to the 1960 security pact treaty. While Oshima's involvement in political groups of this sort was in the fifties, his films represent a younger generation of sixties protests. Rather than work from the directly autobiographical, he applies his analysis to what is immediate and topical at the time of the film's making, which is already removed from his experience, filtered analytically from his perspective at a distance. Political groups, protests, and student interaction figure in many of the films, but the representations of the participants, the characters, are not only fictional, they are allegorical abstractions imbued with heightened dramatic power within a theoretical frame. Even when the filmmaker's life intersects so closely with his subject matter, his subjectivity as an artist is rarely as direct as the correlation of life incidents with filmic statements would imply. Yet in a filmmaker whose own life is so clearly a source and reference point, we need to bring this material to bear on the works, knowing that they are insufficient explanations of the films but rather elements in what can be conceived as a poststructuralist view of the artwork. They are elements that filter through the individual artist, along with elements gathered through him or her from a much broader cultural frame. The student demonstrations of the fifties and sixties are one instance in which Oshima shows us the artistic psyche in history, gathering, focalizing, theorizing, and reacting to circumstances that are much larger than the personal.

THE AUTHORIAL SUBJECT IN THE FILM INDUSTRY

Oshima's biographical material also gives us an entrance into Japanese film industry history at a critical juncture. We have seen earlier how Oshima is often taken as the defining presence in Japan's New Wave. However important his role and however valid it may be to speak of a distinct cinematic movement in the early sixties in Japan paralleling that of France, the convention of simply centering this "New Wave" on Oshima inevitably distorts aspects of film history and our understanding of its place in a larger social history. I wish now to take a view that considers these phenomena as less directly or even causally connected a priori. My purpose is to show how the authorial subject, Oshima, both fits into and shapes film history in the pivotal years that mark his entrance as director.

His biographical writings touching on his six-year filmmaking apprenticeship and subsequent promotion to director at Shochiku Ofuna are numerous—and somewhat contradictory. Reading Oshima's film criticism from this period indicates that it might be understood as the story of a newly graduated student radical moving into the heart of the corporate establishment, bringing to this move highly critical creative aspirations, yearnings to put his aesthetic theories into practice. However, retrospectively remarking that "there is no youth without adventure," he then reminisces on this period with ironic antiheroic detachment: "I entered a film company for the simple reason that it was difficult to find a job at that time, and due in part to my activity in the student movement, I couldn't find anything else" (Oshima 1992: 205). This contradictory presentation of self in history, and the irony of its presentation, is characteristic of Oshima and his view of subjectivity as expressed in his films and his writing. He is deeply aware of unconscious motivations both underlying and raging against consciousness, of splits within the subject, of multiple determinations of history.

Placing Oshima's biography within Japanese film industry history demands that we see this story as just that complex. As background, it is important to recognize Shochiku as one of Japan's oldest surviving studios, the twenties' cinematic offshoot of a company whose roots were as a theater monopoly, owning both Kabuki and Shimpa companies (Anderson and Richie 1982: 40). According to Joseph Anderson and Donald Richie, Shochiku at first sought its inspiration in Hollywood, seeking to replace "old-style Japanese movies" with "only the latest ideas" (1982: 41). Evidence of this is its production of such features as *Rojo no reikon* (Souls of the Road, Minoru Murata and Osanai Kaoru, 1921) (Burch 1979: 100–107). This beginning seems like a prefiguration of events at the studio surrounding the promotion of Oshima to director in 1959, which also sought the "latest ideas" to renew cinematic style in order to secure its economic future. While the studio perhaps was launched on a program of innovation, by 1924 Shochiku had secured a place within the Big Four monopoly that formed the Japan Motion Pictures Association (Anderson and Richie 1982: 60). At this point it displayed many of the conservative traits one might expect from an industry giant, and these policies continued throughout the thirties and forties. Shochiku introduced a sound-on-film system that was instrumental in the Japanese industry's transition to sound (Anderson and Richie 1982: 77; Bordwell and Thompson 1994: 228). The studio head, Kido Shiro, became involved in the expansion of the Japanese industry into newly occupied countries during the Pacific War, and the studio later made wartime national policy films (Anderson and Richie 1982: 142). During the Occupation it specialized in melodramas and women's films (Anderson and Richie 1982: 142). Throughout its history Shochiku could at times support artistic innovations in contexts of audience acceptance and financial gain. It was the studio at which Ozu Yasujiro made all his films, and during wartime it produced such films as *Genroku chushingura* (Forty-seven Ronin, 1941–1942) by Mizoguchi Kenji.

The fifties were a period of artistic and financial flourishing for Japanese cinema, marked by a string of internationally acclaimed films by Kurosawa and the later films of Naruse, Mizoguchi, and Ozu, as well as the general financial health of commercial narrative filmmaking through lucrative "program" pictures, the Japanese term for predictable genre features. If the Japanese industry in the late fifties was at its height, if Shochiku had huge commercial successes with such films as Kinoshita's *Nijushi no hitomi* (Twenty-four Eyes, 1955), a sentimental melodrama of a rural schoolteacher's relationship to her pupils, Shochiku was feeling the competition both from other Japanese studios and from an ever-increasing U.S. and European penetration of the Japanese film exhibition market. The growth of Japanese television was substantial in the late fifties. Film studios in Japan, as worldwide,

needed to position themselves to compete with and infiltrate television production. One weapon would be the widescreen image ratios of Shochiko
Grandscope and Tohoscope used in many fifties and sixties films. Shochiku
undoubtedly felt pressure to transform its style to rival Nikkatsu, which was
scoring huge market successes with its new "sun tribe" genre (films of juvenile rebellion or delinquency) made by a group of young directors.

In 1958, Oshima, then an assistant director at Shochiku, wrote "Is It a
Breakthrough? The Modernists of Japanese Film" for the widely read Japanese journal *Eiga Hihyo* (Film Review). It opens:

> In July 1956, Nakahiro Ko breezed onto the scene with *Crazed Fruit,*
> boasting "*Season of the Sun* glorified the sun tribe and *Punishment Room*
> criticized it; I sneer at the sun tribe." In the rip of a woman's skirt and the
> buzz of a motorboat, sensitive people heard the heralding of a new genera-
> tion of Japanese film. Then in May of the following year, with *The Betrothed,* a
> wholesome, rational depiction of adolescence, Shirasaka Yoshio proved that
> scripts of exceptional style can transcend the weaknesses of the director and
> determine the style of the entire film. At the same time, even more people
> became aware that this new element could not be ignored when talking
> about Japanese film. In September of that year, when Yasuzo used a freely
> moving camera to depict a pair of young motorcycle-riding lovers in *Kisses,*
> this new generation had assumed a place in Japanese Cinema as an intense,
> unstoppable force that could no longer be ignored. (Oshima 1992: 26; my
> translation correction)

All of the films mentioned in this passage, those in the internal citation of
Nakahiro and those added by Oshima, were produced by Shochiku's rival
studios, either by Nikkatsu or, in the case of Ichikawa's *Punishment Room* and
Masumura's *Kisses,* Daiei. Note that Oshima's phrase "In the rip of a woman's
skirt and the buzz of a motorboat" prefigures his citation of Ko in his use of
these elements in a crucial scene in his 1960 *Cruel Story of Youth.* Note also
his emphasis on script writing as a source of cinematic exuberance. The article goes on to place these modernists within an assessment of Japanese film
history, continuing to praise works by Nakahiro and Masumura in detail. It
advocates a more politically informed use of the *taiyo-zoku* (usually translated
as "sun tribe" and indicating hedonist youth culture) genre and filmmaking
in general, avoiding the potential for sheer exploitation by the industry of
the youth audience. Among the several goals of this essay Oshima sought implicitly to confront his employer, Shochiku, with neglecting to support similar cinematic innovation.

A subsequent article does this more directly. "A Review of 'Sleeping Lion':
Shochiku Ofuna" was Oshima's answer in *Eiga Hiyoron* (Film Criticism) to a
June 1959 article, "Sleeping Lion: Shochiku Ofuna," in *Eiga Hihyo* (Film Review) by Noguchi Yuichiro and Sato Tadao. Oshima complains that the article is too gentle in its criticism and its appeal to management to be a little

smarter; he would have had them call the studio a "dead lion" and demand a turning over of production to "a new class of directors whose inner consciousness is not yet completely dominated by the old Ofuna framework." He goes on to say, "Not only the directing department, but every department involved in making films must give the postwar generation, which is capable of establishing the content and method of new works, the opportunity for self-expression" (Oshima 1992: 41). Yet Oshima notes in this piece that management at Shochiku has been discussing the Noguchi and Sato article.

His arm twisted in print, Shochiku's studio head, Kido, responded by designating Ofuna Studios as a unit devoted to tapping a new consumer market, competing in the youth film cycle that had made the career of Masumura. Besides this internal competition in the Japanese market, Kido was likely to have been aware that production was shifting internationally from studio sound stages to independents using equipment that could make increasing use of lighter, more mobile camera and sound equipment. The Italian neorealist movement was clearly affecting Japanese film, as was the first entrance into feature production in 1957–1958 of Jean-Pierre Melville, Louis Malle, and Claude Chabrol, the filmmakers who, along with others still making shorts at this time, would later be seen as precursors of a movement and called the *nouvelle vague* (the French New Wave).

It makes sense that these foreign filmmakers would, in addition to domestic rivals, spur Shochiku heads to pay attention to the young assistant directors in their own ranks who were not only proving themselves in their apprentice production jobs but also, in Oshima's case, writing for film journals and praising works at rival studios. However, it seems that the often-assumed direct influence of Jean-Luc Godard on Oshima at this stage may be exaggerated (stated, for example, in Anderson's 1982 addendum to his and Richie's *Japanese Film* [1982: 465]). If one considers only the years before Godard's first feature, *A Bout de souffle* (Breathless), was released in Japan in 1960, there seem to be certain problems with holding that Oshima's or Shochiku's motivation was to imitate Godard, though it was clear that Oshima admired Godard on viewing his first film and said so in print (Oshima 1992: 46). At this point, however, *Seishun sankoku monogatari* (Cruel Story of Youth), Oshima's second film, was already in production. It is probable that Oshima knew earlier of Godard's film criticism in *Cahiers* and his late fifties shorts; though Oshima's ability to speak French is minimal, *Cahiers* was followed in film circles in Tokyo, and surely the long talks at bars characteristic of the film world at this time provided some exposure. Further, one is struck by the similarities between the two directors' careers in the late fifties, as both were known as critics before becoming directors. However, close attention to the dates does not support Godard as a motivating figure for Oshima's filmmaking, or for his studio head's financing; it is probably better history to posit that both directors were being affected by similar forces in quite separate circumstances than to see Oshima as from the start modeled after Godard. Once their film careers were both under way in the early sixties, Shochiku marketed Oshima as the "Japanese Godard," a phrase that continues even today in reviews and advertisements for revivals of Oshima's films. Certainly throughout the sixties and particularly at the point Oshima comes to Cannes and Paris, the filmmakers are engaged in a kind of filmic dialogue, perhaps between themselves, but certainly in the minds of critics and audiences.

The forces shaping Oshima's entry into the film industry are those of a generalized move toward independent production in the postwar period, with the studios scrambling to co-opt the independents, either by making at least some of their features look like independents, by buying independent companies, or by hiring the independent directors. Cinema as an industry must renew itself as it confronts a crisis; at Shochiku Ofuna, Oshima and an extraordinary collection of other talented assistant directors were able to seize this opportunity, to market their will to innovation and artistic expression, in some cases joining this with political expression that pushed at the limits of what that industry would allow. We might also remember in looking back at this history Oshima's admonition to critics more interested in codifying film history than in responding actively to the politics of industry production and their relation to national politics; in calling for protests to the shelving of his fourth feature, *Nihon no yoru to kiri* (Night and Fog in Japan, 1960), he vented his anger over the publicity myth of Shochiku Ofuna as home to a cinematic movement of quasi-independents, telling critics, "Stop using the term 'New Wave' once and for all! Evaluate each film on its merits!" (Oshima 1992: 57).

Some practitioners of auteurist criticism see Oshima as a director remarkable for his lack of stylistic consistency, his lack of a coherent style from film to film; Peter Lehman (1987: 28) suggests that if one were to show *Burial of the Sun* and *Night and Fog in Japan* without the credits, "it is almost inconceivable that the viewer would guess that the same filmmaker made both films, much less in direct succession in the same year." He also argues that "Oshima does not have a style which he develops, and his work does not break down into the conventional early, middle and late periods" (p. 28). If these points seem telling in a conventional auteurist framework, they are debatable depending on the parameters one might adopt for establishing recurring concerns and stylistic gestures; Lehman focuses on shot duration and montage, which admittedly are the formal parameters that vary the most from film to film in Oshima's works. I would rather read such pronouncements as symptomatic of a methodology imposing its own assumptions even as it points toward recognizing something of what I am calling Oshima's iconoclasm. Other methodologies for looking at a corpus of films will avoid the tangle of such assumptions and more clearly present Oshima's contribution to filmmaking. As Lehman goes on to suggest, "Although it is entirely beyond the scope of this paper, the significant question to me seems to be: What is the relationship between Oshima's paradoxical abandonment of an individual style and his nearly compulsive pursuit of deeply personal issues? Oshima's radical pluralism rejects the individual and personal at one level and reinscribes it at another" (p. 31). What I hope to do here is answer just such questions about repetition and variation, style and "concerns," the "personal" and the political, using methodologies open to seeing the subject Oshima in history.

AUTHOR-FUNCTIONS, STYLE, AND A CORPUS OF FILMS

The issues raised by Oshima and auteurism are even larger and more theoretical than this critical recognition of his biography and its relationship to industry history indicates. For if Oshima is the product of a certain period of auteurism's flowering, he is also contemporaneous with, and arguably a part of, a deconstructive investigation of auteurism. As we shall see later, Oshima's film *Tokyo senso sengo hiwa* (The Battle of Tokyo, or the Story of the Young Man Who Left His Will on Film, 1970) addresses the issues of authorship and collective expression in highly theoretical and engaged ways. It is arguably a deconstructive work of fiction, pointing to the theoretical issues that make auteurist approaches problematic. While Oshima's works self-consciously raise issues of authorship, these theoretical issues were being debated in the years 1968–1972 in France as structuralists extended earlier Russian formalists' critique of biographical fallacies through emphasis on textual construction.

Thus we have Roland Barthes's monumental essay "The Death of the Author," first published in 1968. In this short, concise, and often elliptical essay, Barthes presents the author as a "modern" concept emerging from the Middle Ages and beginning to flower in the Renaissance. Despite the work of formalists, Barthes tells us, "The Author still reigns in histories of literature, biographies of writers, interviews, magazines, as in the very consciousness of men of letters anxious to unite their person and their work through diaries and memoirs" (1977: 143). The "allegory of the fiction" is largely interpreted by the reading public as the "author confiding in us" (1977: 143).

Modern writing, for Barthes, with its attention to language, calls that notion of the author into question; Mallarmé serves Barthes (1977: 143–144) as an author who begins pointing to the forces in language that supersede a myth of authorial and poetic voice. Barthes is arguing not only for a self-consciousness concerning allegorical readings of literature as authorial confidences but also for a special recognition that modern literature cannot be understood in these terms, as its purpose lies elsewhere.

Michel Foucault indirectly responds to Barthes and goes a few steps further, or perhaps in another direction, when he proposes the "author-function" in his essay "What Is an Author?" published the next year. As Barthes introduced a sort of "Foucaultian genealogy," in tracing the development of the author to Renaissance impulses, it seems Foucault wants to put that historical tracing of the author as function precisely in his genealogical framework of discourses. He wants to exceed the literary realm, referencing authors of nonfiction, particularly those who write theory. The author-function then becomes a way of addressing texts as discourses in circulation, stimulating Foucault to summarize what would be the positive changes in methodology to replace recourse to authorial construction as four suggested questions:

> What are the modes of existence of this discourse?
> Where does it come from; how is it circulated; who controls it?
> What placements are determined for possible subjects?
> Who can fulfill these diverse functions of the subject? (Foucault 1977: 138)

These questions turn out to be very useful for examining the works of Oshima, in particular, as works that clearly have preexisting discourses circulating through them and place spectators in multiple and troubled positions.

However, the misinterpretations of Barthes's and Foucault's essays, their caricature as refusals to consider authorship at all, rather than as proposals of methodologies that would avoid the limits of an author-constricted allegory, have had a life of their own. Foucault's provocative ending to his essay contributes to such misinterpretations when he suggests that behind the questions he proposes lies a murmured indifference to "who's speaking" (1977: 138). This is a provocation, whose emphasis on the metaphor of a murmur and an ironic use of "indifference" now seems doomed to have not been heard in its subtlety. Rather than being taken as an acknowledgment that current intellectual thought was ready to speak of cultural forces, instead of attaching fictions only to individuals, it was doomed to be heard as flamboyant antihumanism, even as inhuman. Let me emphasize here that despite their differences, Barthes and Foucault were part of a new intellectual history that would trace the force and signification of concepts and paradigms rather than offer chronicles of the lives of thinkers. Their essays were a part of a movement toward a literary history that would be about narrative representation and language, an art history that would be about visual representation and its reception, film histories that would be less about directors and more about the representation in and circulation of a corpus of films. Thus in *Language and Cinema*, Christian Metz revisits auteurism by giving it a most concise structural definition as authorial corpus; the films are worthy of study together to investigate the ways they may be linked by a notion of enunciation or forms of representation.

Film theorists responded to these propositions by incorporating the notion of author-functions into auteurist study. Jean-Pierre Oudart proposed work on authorship and style from a theoretical perspective in his 1971 essay, "Le sujet Bresson." Oudart tries to deconstruct an earlier *Cahiers* notion of authorship, one that revered Robert Bresson as a cinematic stylist but viewed his work hermetically. He introduces psychoanalytic and Marxist concepts to interrogate the author as subject and to address something parallel to what Foucault called "placements for possible subjects." Ultimately the nouvelle vague, the group of filmmakers so closely linked to an earlier *Cahiers*, are the subject of this deconstruction, for whom Bresson is a slightly displaced (historically his career predates that movement), specific, and yet emblematic example.

Oudart's audacious piece was part of the ongoing incorporation of structuralism and ideological critique into film theory and analysis in which *Cahiers* was joined by film journals devoted editorially to such an approach, the more radical *Ça* and *Cinétheque*. However, filmmakers whose work was already more in line with such theories and approaches were less likely to see their place as "authorial subjects" deconstructed; in these cases, influences and conscious intentions, ironically, still could be subjected to the auteurist focus. Thus in a *Cahiers* essay from the same period, Jacques Aumont contrasts Oshima to filmmakers he terms "monothématiques," Miklos Jansco and Glauber Rocha, whose single themes were those of the political histories of their countries and whose innovative formal composition was more uniform from film to film. Still operative is the concept of auteur who chooses to switch approaches and styles, as well as concerns, from film to film. This variation of topics and filmic techniques is not necessarily at odds with auteurism; Howard Hawks was seen by the fifties *Cahiers* as just such an author, whose range from comedy to action-drama already demanded the auteur theory to account for a set of differences within its notion of repeated explorations of a distinctive approach to filmmaking. If we do not get a deconstructive piece on "le sujet Oshima," it is in part due to the tendency at that time to read politically motivated directors as more coherent masters of the forces circulating through their works. In retrospect, there is an irony to this omission, as intentions and expression were seen as unified by alternative or contestatory theories when they were suspect in other contexts.

Feminist film theory long has been cognizant of the gender factors in analyzing the author as subject as evidenced through his or her fictions and been more willing to question this implied restriction on deconstructive criticism to the politically unselfconscious. Recently, Kaja Silverman, in *Male Subjectivity at the Margins* (1992: 157–162, 214–217), speaks of "authorial subjectivity," reviving Oudart's early seventies approach to the subjectivity of auteurism, infusing it with a strongly psychoanalytic perspective on gender in her look at Henry James and filmmaker Rainer Werner Fassbinder. "Authorial subjectivity" replaces "author-function" in her terminology, a move greatly indebted to Oudart, though not in her work infused with as much economic and class analysis as was Oudart, who in turn was deeply indebted to Lucien Goldmann and Pierre Macherey as well as to French psychoanalysis.

I want to keep deconstructive strategies foregrounded in examining the works of Oshima, even while I hold on to Oshima's material intervention in the production and reception of film in Japan and the particularity of his writing, organizing, directing, and producing a series of films. These are films laced with obsessions, of repetitions and variations from film to film, that await a grouping as corpus, a comparative viewing and reading. Oshima as subject is an emblem in which we can see a response to the iconographic traditions of Japan, to the visual influences of the United States and Europe, to theories of the social and of psychoanalysis, to women and to men in their social and sexual interactions. So emblematically, I will call the author-function of Oshima "iconoclast."

OSHIMA, ICONOCLAST

"Iconoclast" describes this filmmaker's ongoing assault on cherished beliefs and traditional institutions. It recalls Oshima's statement, "My hatred for Japanese cinema includes absolutely all of it" ("Interview," 1970). Perhaps this term will give us a fresh way to look at how his films challenge Japanese beliefs about themselves and their culture and also challenge Western beliefs about Japan.

It may seem odd to choose the term "iconoclast" in the Japanese context; perhaps it would be more appropriate to introduce a Japanese term. Yet if it is useful, it is to accentuate Oshima as not simply a Japanese filmmaker, but an international voice issuing from and formed by a Japanese context. His rejection of cherished beliefs extends beyond those of the Japanese canon to many Western and other non-Japanese notions. His works call for a comparatist methodology, a reading across cultural borders. Perhaps the notion of iconoclasm signals this will on my part to a comparative method and an international context.

Iconoclasm carries with it an association with the Judeo-Christian tradition, but a specific one. It names historic contestations of that tradition. From the Greek *eikonoklastes,* literally, breaker of icons, it came to us most directly from the Latin. If the Greeks were to establish the gods as statuary in idealized human form for the Romans to follow, their word migrated to European Christianity to apply to the Christians of the eighth and ninth centuries who objected to the worship of icons, as embodiments of Christ, the Virgin Mary, and the saints.

Yet this instance is one of a cross-cultural recall of earlier Old Testament prohibitions on icons. The prohibition on imagery finds its Judaic meaning in the story of Moses and Aaron, their conflict over the golden calf versus a restriction to the abstraction of the word and the idea as specified by one of the Ten Commandments, "Thou shalt not have false gods before thee." The prohibition becomes interpreted as not only applying to images of God, but, by extension of the belief that God created mankind in God's image, to any human representation. This leads to the medieval devices of Hebrew illuminated manuscripts, where illustrations substitute animal heads for human representations, a practice that coincidentally produces an iconography overlapping with a tradition in Japanese scroll painting and later Zen painting. As concerns the Judaic prohibition against the figurative human body, it gives way in 1913, as a young generation of Jews meet in Paris to practice a new expressionist iconography. With Chagall, Soutine, and Lipchitz, Jewish figural art, expressionism of body, broke a religious tradition that had effectively foreclosed Jewish painters. They, in turn, became iconoclasts, dissenters from their tradition, by forming icons. This paradox of Judaic iconoclasm illustrates how iconoclasm inevitably traffics in paradoxes. Iconoclasts produce other images. If I have reviewed this history here, it is because I wish to apply this aspect of iconoclasm to Oshima as well, to see him as a generator of new and hybrid imagery.

In filmmaking, iconoclasm has never been so directly expressed as by the Soviet filmmakers Sergei Eisenstein and Dziga Vertov, who each created memorable sequences in their films by borrowing and elaborating through their montage the images created by Bolshevik revolutionaries tearing down the architectural icons of the Russian Orthodox church. Again, filmmakers who are iconoclasts work through substitution; they create icons to attack other icons. These sequences are as much icons of a revolutionary spirit as the spires and symmetrical portraits of saints were icons for Russian Orthodoxy. If our discourse can be permitted a return to biography, Oshima's university studies concentrated on Russian revolution.

It is with these connotations in mind that, despite all the specifically Western associations of the word, *iconoclast* is rich in its implications for Oshima. Not only does he provoke one to critically assess traditions, but like other aesthetic iconoclasts, he is a filmmaker of paradox and contradiction. The assault may be directed at specific traditions, but it produces a new iconography, as we shall see.

What traditions does Oshima attack? In his writings, notably his essay "To the Critics, Mainly, from Future Artists," the object of attack seems very specific. He opposes what in Japan are termed "program pictures" (Oshima 1992: 21), meaning the melodramas, both historical and contemporary, and other genre films that the large Japanese studios produced. It might even seem as if he is establishing a simple opposition between the hackneyed films of generic traditions and what he might offer as an alternative, "art films," "auteur films," or "idea films." But read carefully, the essay does not so much attack genre films as the policies of mass production that limit innovation within filmmaking as well as the critics who in turn fail to laud instances when studio-produced genre films display innovative cinematic ideas that transcend the limitations. He speaks on behalf of film crews attempting to be creative in a difficult context and closes the essay by saying that future artists "will not be satisfied by a situation in which one outstanding director shoots masterpieces while all others listlessly make program pictures," instead calling on critics to fulfill their responsibility by "furnishing the audience with technical criticism of program pictures, . . . [which] would foster a desire for better films."

This 1956 plea for recognition was to give way to a much harsher condemnation a few years later, taking such form as the statement "My hatred for Japanese cinema includes absolutely all of it," cited earlier ("Interview," 1970). Here Oshima seems to attack not only the entire film industry, including its most renowned directors, but also something like Japanese national identity. In response to a question proclaiming admiration for the films of Kurosawa and Mizoguchi, Oshima gave this reply: "In Europe, you always speak of the formal beauty of Japanese cinema, but you are wrong to not speak sufficiently of the content. . . . [F]orm is something one can always borrow, and from which, one can always make something passable. But with content you have to work with things that are important to you" ("Interview," 1970).

There are several issues here. Oshima wants first of all to emphasize his critique of the Japanese film production system, as discussed above. He may also be reacting to Europe's ignorance of Japanese film history. When his French interviewers single out only these two famous directors whom Oshima realizes caught the European imagination for their shot composition, editing, camerawork, and, in Mizoguchi's case, long takes, this may have struck Oshima as too naive a reaction to their films. He admits he has learned from Japanese film but refuses to discuss this further, as if negating an implicit desire on the part of *Cahiers* staff to have him say he borrowed his long takes from Mizoguchi or that *Cruel Story of Youth* could be seen as a remake of *Crucified Lovers*. Further, he jokes that his hatred for Japanese film includes his own works.

There is something of the ploy operating here. It is interesting to consider that on another occasion, Oshima expressed his admiration for Kurosawa's *Waga seishun ni kui nashi* (No Regrets for Our Youth, 1946), which is, among other things, a trenchant look at the Japanese government's suppression of free speech at Kyoto University prior to the war and its subsequent arrest and murder of dissenters during the Pacific War ("Interview," 1978). However, he has also offered a negative critical assessment of this film, stemming in part from his disillusionment with the historical figure of Professor Takikawa at Kyoto University. If under repeated questioning by the *Cahiers* interviewers he refuses to relent on his condemnation of Japanese film, if he answers the question, "But this hate, is there really no exception?" with an adamant "No" that, in fact, ends the interview, what he achieves by this is the stance of iconoclasm.

Implicit here is the idea that beauty is a reified value among the Japanese, and what Europe most appreciates in Japan; therefore, beauty is despicable. As Annette Michelson (1992: 1–2) has pointed out, Oshima's essay "Banish Green," written for *Kyosenyui,* a periodical devoted to ikebana (flower arranging), develops this critique. Oshima voices his disgust with "tear-jerking melodramas and flavorless domestic dramas" set in rooms that "contain such symbols of family stability as tea cabinets" and have a traditional garden in the background (Oshima 1992: 208) The Japanese film, in confirming an aesthetics of the beautiful, confirms "Japan" as cultural identity. "I hated those characters, rooms, gardens from the depths of my being. I firmly believed that unless the dark sensibility that those things engendered was completely destroyed, nothing new could come into being" (p. 208).

I am reminded here of another scene in Kurosawa's *No Regrets for Our Youth,* where the young heroine who has been studying ikebana tears her creation apart. Hers is a gesture possible to interpret as an attack on a Japanese aesthetics of the everyday, given the political context of fascism. The garden, ikebana, haiku, the elements of traditional Japanese aesthetics and ritual, in a certain sense, are fundamental to an understanding of the specificity of Japanese culture. Values such as subtlety of suggestion, mutability or perishability, irregularity or asymmetry, and simplicity are embodied by these ritual and aesthetic practices (Keene 1988). "The green of pines is particularly bad. When that irregularly shaped green comes in, everything becomes ambiguous, neutral," Oshima adds slyly, implying a critique of the landscape scroll and the symbolic stage decor of No theater as well as explaining why he "didn't shoot the roof of the houses or the sky outside windows at all" (Oshima 1992: 210). Those very elements seem to fix a national identity that covers over the questions individuals need to pose concerning which directions leaders take the nation. These are the kinds of questions Sakai Naoki poses concerning national cultural identity, both theoretically and in the tradition of Japanese writing during the Tokugawa period, in his book, *Voices of the Past.*

Oshima's attack on green's suggestion of tranquility is more nuanced than it first might appear. It is at once an attack on traditional Japanese aesthetics and on Western audiences' admiration for the films born of these aesthetics and of the value systems they may reinforce. While it seems to ignore that many earlier Japanese films had embraced an "ashcan" aesthetic, it would be a mistake to see this as a counterargument to Oshima's position, as he does not limit his purview simply to the display and choice of objects in filmic mise-en-scène. There may be little green in Kurosawa's *Ikuru* with its open sewers and ugly bureaucracy. However, one could argue that when the dying hero manages to build a park at the end, the humanist value of green is ultimately recuperated. Oshima realizes that removing icons from the mise-en-scène only to symbolically restore them through the movement of the narrative would negate the negation. Hence his narratives sometimes end in death or introduce circularity to suggest the full force of his critique. Oshima is not using the representation of green solely and exclusively in its literal sense, though that is where he starts; it is a symptom of and a metonymy for Japanese humanism.

Second, Oshima finishes the essay by exploring a certain naïveté in his original proposition, an aspect of the essay that Michelson does not address but that indicates how he frames his approach as filmmaker as one that has its own evolution in relationship to a changing Japan as well as his own subjective changes. The desire to banish green led him to instead place his hopes (and his person) in a "high-rise development of reinforced concrete," only to find that his lived reaction to such architecture made him "barely able to resist the temptation to throw myself out the window." This story seems to parallel the allegory that he will take up in his *Battle of Tokyo,* a film we will discuss in chapter 4, where architecture, the window, and the suicidal fantasy figure large. The modern, brutalist alternative to the tradition, particularly as it coincides with a modernity bureaucratized by the state, is equally insupportable. Rebellion as negation perhaps creates its own imprisonment, one that mimics the architectural lines of an urban adaptation, a placement the state is preparing for its modern subjects. By 1974 when this essay appeared, the redesign of Tokyo as ongoing postwar project had reached the dimensions of a new cityscape that was already bewildering in its replacement of all that is traditional within Japanese aesthetics with the bright artificial angularity that Oshima once hoped would wake the Japanese. It seems he is no longer sure that the modern (or perhaps the emerging postmodern) landscape is preferable to the nostalgic tradition. He is at least wondering if his own unconscious will provide access only to an iconography based primarily on negation.

As I said earlier, iconoclasm is clearly not only a negation but a creative replacement of signifiers as well. Oshima comes to reflect on the limits of his early negations, his alternative images, his positions; as we shall see, from film to film, the strategy does not remain the same. The windows are opened, their vision on the landscape self-consciously interrogated. Some green is even seen in *Ai no borei* (Empire of Passion, 1998), though vastly reframed. This sense of change within the corpus of films, as within the authorial subject, is another reason why we should, as Oshima said, "evaluate each film on its merits!" We might also see in this process that more "green" than he originally imagined is retained throughout, that his intentions to break with his cultural traditions could never eliminate all reference and even reverence that filters through a subject for the culture he inhabits.

Another way of putting this is that the traditional and the modern, Japanese and the West, are less antithetical than much theorization might pretend. Karatani Kojin, in *The Origins of Modern Literature,* discusses the need to think of Japanese literature beyond these oppositions. We may need to think of Oshima's works, retrospectively, as carrying with them much more intertextual Japanese iconography, perhaps much more humanism, than is first apparent, in spite of his intentions. Further, Japanese tradition is one of incorporation, blending. The Japanese nation is a forged homogeneity, syncretic and complex. The tea ceremony that the banished tea cabinet represents is itself a mix of Shinto-Buddhist ritual, while its contemporary vestiges are perhaps quite removed from these significations, increasingly signifying class, spectacle, and even tourism. Icons are themselves mutable in a changing Japan, meaning that the work of the iconoclast could never simply repeat.

While Oshima's iconoclasm wants to displace Japanese aesthetics, one of his tropes for what will replace them is a mirror. This mirror will be held up to the Japanese, as a mirror in which they could see their faces, their beings, and the unjust aspects of Japanese culture. "The Japanese don't want to look in the mirror. I want to force the Japanese to look in the mirror" ("Interview," 1978). One way of reading this proclamation is that Oshima wants the Japanese to see their responsibility for whatever attraction or tolerance they have for fascism, for xenophobia, for racism.

Let us pause for a moment on this mirror image. It brings to mind three quite separate concepts we might associate with the mirror, whose refraction might further develop Oshima's imagery. Oshima's metaphor of film as an alternative mirror held up to a people might also be seen in reference to Marxist reflection theory, which holds that films and other cultural artifacts reflect not social reality but class interests in the mythologies they present. Reflection theory proposes readings that analyze these class interests in bourgeois fiction. As an antidote to the growth and dominance of such myths, reflection theory often proposes a critical proletarian realism, reflecting instead the interests of the working class to build proletarian consciousness. However, Oshima needed another strategy to avoid both the emotional appeal of the Japanese leftist film and Stalinist appropriations of proletarian realism. Oshima's mirror metaphor might be seen as breaking with reflection theory's strategies, to reformulate a more critical impetus in which the film as mirror is staged. The kind of mirror the film becomes is not simply a reflection of a presumed reality but a mirror of cultural heritages and attitudes that includes an analysis of their consequences. The emphasis is not on a mirror that reflects but on a mirror that shows, forms, and instructs, a kind of performative mirror in which looking and identifying are the central issues; rather than being givens, looking and identifying are the processes called into question. It is both through Japanese cultural specificity and psychoanalysis that we can understand Oshima's mirror metaphor.

In a directly Japanese context, mirrors have an ancient and rich cultural history. Bronze mirrors of Han dynasty China found their way to Japan in the Yayoi period, 200 B.C.–A.D. 300. "From the middle of the period, bronze objects, primarily swords, spears and mirrors, are imported from the continent and used as symbols of wealth and authority" (Amakasu 1978: 166). These mirrors were quickly incorporated into Japanese imperial symbolism, where the mirror is a token, along with the sword and jewel, of the authority of the emperor (Singer 1973: 25, 27, 117). In Shinto shrines, mirrors never reflect worshipers but stand for the *shintai*, the god body, a luminous perfection. Such distinctive symbolism supplies the ancient mirror with specific cultural values. In practical life owning a mirror would be an element of class; wives and daughters of shogun and samurai would have mirrors in their elaborate lacquer grooming sets. Oshima's erecting of alternative image–mirrors is a way of breaking through the symbolism fixed in a mirror, a complacency with rituals of power and exterior decorum, by supplanting it with other images.

Significantly, a Japanese folktale, "The Mirror of Matsuyama," supplies another association with the mirror, this time linked to commoners and fully psychoanalytic in its symbolism. Variations on this folktale all involve the gift of a mirror in a village that has never seen a mirror before. In one variation the gift is from a father to his wife; as a mother years later, she gives the mirror to her beloved daughter on her deathbed. She tells her daughter that as the years pass, the daughter may look at it to see once again her mother's face, and this promise is narrated as the specular fulfillment of residual desire for the mother:

> Poor child, she longed just for one glimpse of the loved face, one sound of the voice calling her pet name, or for one moment's forgetfulness of the aching void in her heart. . . . Behold, her mother's words were true! In the round mirror before her she saw her mother's face; but, oh what a joyful surprise! It was not her mother thin and wasted by illness, but the young and beautiful woman she remembered far back in the days of her own childhood. (Ozaki 1967: 130–131)

The mirror is thought by the daughter to supernaturally communicate with her mother's ghost spirit, which guides her. However, after her stepmother arouses the father's suspicion that in her private rituals the daughter is cursing the stepmother's image, the secret of the mirror is revealed as reflecting her own image that has grown into the likeness of the cherished deceased mother. There are many variations of this tale, including a son who buys a mirror because he sees in it the likeness of his dead father (Yanagita 1986: 253)

Examined theoretically, this Japanese folktale, like Oshima's mirror metaphor, displays particular alignment with the mirror stage of Lacanian psychoanalytic theory. In Lacanian theory, the mirror stage is a complex theorization of development of a sense of autonomous self in relation to a specular image of the body *and* in relation to separation from the body of the mother. In referring to the mirror stage here, I mean not only the early formulations of it in *Ecrits* but its reworking in *Le Séminaire livre I* and *Le Séminaire livre XI*. In full elaboration, as Mikkel Borch-Jacobson (1991: 45) reminds us, the mirror stage includes not only the role of the mirror in psychoperceptual formation of the imaginary and the symbolic but also links to a nexus of representations of the self, including "the image, the double, narcissism, imaginary fragmentation (and by implication castration) and death." While film theory has made frequent reference to the mirror stage to explain a spectator's captivation by the image, my reference here highlights the way film imagery can be used to expand and comment on a mirror-function of representations.

In the folktale, the child's mirror stage is represented as extending into young adulthood; extended mourning that never reconciles to the loss of the mother as well as particularly strong identity bonds with the parents condition separation as unfinished. Rather than simply separate from the mother or father, the child assumes the spirit and the face of the beloved parent. Japanese closeness to parents, particularly the mother, has led Japanese psychoanalysts to posit a specificity to separation and identity problems among the Japanese, exacerbated by the abruptness with which modernity has wrought extreme transformations on contemporary urban Japanese and roles within the family. In Japanese fiction, a modernist concern with identity produces such "mirror stage" fiction, as epitomized by the 1965 Abe Kobo novel, *Tanin no kao* (The Face of Another), whose contemporary crisis of identity was given filmic shape by Teshigahara Hiroshi (1966) from a script by the author. Whereas others see such modernist concerns as Abe's as "Western" (Desser 1988: 77), we can see how the imagery also reacts to a Japanese heritage of the mirror and to Japanese psychoanalytic specificity.

Many of Oshima's films stage such imagery and identity concerns. Notably, *Koshikei* (Death by Hanging, 1968), *Shonen* (Boy, 1969), *Tokyo senso sengo hiwa* (The Battle of Tokyo, or the Story of the Young Man Who Left His Will on Film, 1970), *Gishiki* (Ceremonies, 1971), and *Natsu no imoto* (Dear Summer Sister, 1972) all present characters whose selves dissolve in mirrored images that others assume or supply. If I have not called the mirror a "theme" or spoken of "mirror symbolism," but rather a trope at once of the self and of representations, it is to avoid a tradition of labeling meanings rather than exploring structures. It is important to remember that we are speaking of signifiers here whose meanings are always multiple, evocative, and in question, or there would be little purpose to the complexity of the structures in which they are embedded. This fragmentation of the self in its complicated association with others is a structure that Oshima's films repeat. The repetitions are emphatic, even obsessive, but each turns on difference and variation to create a weave of challenging textual associations. So throughout this book we will return to the mirror metaphor in its psychoanalytic dimensions. Narrative film becomes for Oshima an alternative mirror in which the subject is confronted with images, reflections that are meant to reshape identity and the psyche.

I have noted, then, in this chapter that the notion of Oshima as an auteur figures strongly in previous criticism of his work for several reasons: 1) the historical conjuncture of his career with auteurist criticism; 2) Oshima's role as writer–critic drawing on his biography for theoretical reflections lends itself to critical writing that explores his intentions; 3) Oshima's political engagement helps to exempt his work from critiques of an auteurism that avoids the social; and 4) Oshima himself exploits auteurist myths to publicize his films as part of a strategy to change the film industry. In the course of establishing these points, I have shown that the questions of biography might be part of a less unified notion of subjectivity. Biographical elements of a social and psychoanalytic history of the author as subject remain greatly significant for works like Oshima's that explore the fragmented subject in history as a kind of parallel to the representations of the films. Oshima's writings about his films will be cited but not necessarily seen as privileged keys to decipherment. I have begun to articulate the ways in which this book will propose seeing Oshima's films through the trope of a specifically defined iconoclasm, one that proposes new images containing a critique of traditional iconography. In a more figurative sense, I have explored how the films hold up an active mirror through which the subject might examine the self. Throughout the rest of this book, I will address these films as a corpus, as Oshima's films, in order to analyze their intertextuality. I will use the name *Oshima* to possess, to claim, and to designate this corpus, keeping in mind that the term *corpus* is one of a fictional extension and the site of collective participation. Oshima's films are more than his, yet they are his, and they are usefully grouped together. Such is the nature of this project.

CHAPTER TWO

Cruel Stories of Youth and Politics

In one shot that punctuates Oshima's *Taiyo no hakaba* (Burial of the Sun, 1960), Osaka castle, a symbol of Japan's military heritage, is romantically silhouetted against the sunset. In another parallel punctuation shot later in the film, factory smokestacks become a similar silhouette marking Osaka's choking industrial sprawl. These two shots stand out as tableaus indicating the visual force of Oshima's films, evident from the very beginning of his career. This force draws into the cinematic frame the ironic and complex dynamics of a political critique that weaves the intrapsychic with the sociological, the historical with the interpersonal. Oshima's first four films, *Ai to kibo no machi* (A Town of Love and Hope, 1959), *Burial of the Sun*, *Seishun sankoku monogatari* (Cruel Story of Youth, 1960), and *Night and Fog in Japan* (1960), were made in a two-year period at Shochiku studios in Tokyo. Each already displays the innovative structural weave of a politicized desire and a fiction of the imaginary that pinpoints real crises.

These wide-screen features all focus on contemporary Japanese youth. They are indeed "cruel tales," to cite the title of one, antihumanist and antirealist, in which romantic figuration is systematically decentered. The "towns" that Oshima depicts, Osaka, Kyoto, Tokyo, have no love or hope suspended as false promises before the contemporary spectator. Instead, Oshima moves us through a night and fog specific to a Japan whose rising sun has been buried in the future of its illusions. This dystopic rage fills the long horizontals of Oshima's films. It is my purpose to show how Oshima builds this raging expression through allegorical visual configurations and transformations of narrative structure. By carrying allegory beyond its limits as a symbolic representation in which elements suggest another level of meaning— a limit precisely formed by this other level being accessible, singular, free from internal contradictions—he will push allegory toward increasing mul-

27

1. A punctuation shot in *Taiyo no hakaba* (Burial of the Sun, 1960) of factory smokestacks becomes a silhouette similar to an earlier shot of Osaka castle, but this shot marks Osaka's choking industrial sprawl. Still courtesy of Oshima Productions.

tiplicity where play with ambiguity and dialectics eventually leads to mutually impossible representations.

ALLEGORY

Oshima's first film was released under the title *Ai to kibo no machi,* evidently imposed by the studio against Oshima's wishes. This title amounts to nothing less "than a reversal into the opposite," to borrow a phrase Sigmund Freud (1900: 5:326) used to describe certain representations in dreams. Reversal into the opposite, as the section of Tokyo depicted in the film has none of the sentimental optimism this title indicates. This reversal can be seen as an attempt on the part of the studio to retain the film within the very genre of humanist poetic realism that this film ever so slyly seeks to renounce.

Oshima's preferred title, "The Boy Who Sold His Pigeon," is simply a straightforward summary of the major action of the film—boy sells pigeon. This title immediately brings to mind the titles of the films it foreshadows, *Shonen* and *Tokyo senso sengo hiwa.* In all three of these films protagonists simply act, but their actions are to be construed in other registers. The codes of action (proairetics) are transformed into symbolic codes. The pigeon acts as a device in the formalist sense of the word, an object that circulates, initiating, binding, and closing the narrative, linking its parts. In addition, the pigeon permits certain kinds of symbolic exchanges.

Significantly, the pigeon circulates between classes. The boy who sells the pigeon is lower class; his mother is the lone head of the household and works, when she is well enough, as a shoeshine lady on the street. Their poor household includes a retarded sister and is a one-room shack in a slum. The boy's schoolmate who purchases the pigeon is from a family of new industrial wealth; her father is a television set manufacturer. Their house is Western-style and luxurious. The film is constructed out of this visual contrast of sites, a microcosm of contemporary Japan. Creating the father as a head of a television manufacturing company is meant to represent the Zaibatsu, industrial giants who were restored in the latter half of the Occupation (1948–1952) in an effort to stimulate the economy (Varley 1984: 269–270).

The liaison between these households, initiated by the pigeon sale, is continued by the efforts of a schoolteacher, a young woman who has both the poor boy and the rich girl in her class. This teacher behaves virtually as a social worker, intervening on behalf of the boy in an effort to keep him from descending further into juvenile delinquency. In the process of appealing to the girl's wealthy father to help poor students find jobs with his firm, she becomes romantically involved with the girl's older brother, who works at the family firm. Both households are headed by a single parent, a mother in the case of the poor family, a father in the case of the rich, with no explanation in either case for the other parent's absence. These interactions between the households create the teacher as liaison between the parallel configurations of father-brother-girl in the rich family and mother-sister-boy in the poor one. The pigeon can be seen as occupying the same place as the teacher, an element that connects the familial configurations. We can also see that the mentally retarded sister who plays with rats and adores the pigeon is more isolated than any other character; she interacts with her mother and brother, but her most significant role seems to be one of contrast with the girl and the teacher, who desire that the boy reform. The sister is at home in the squalor of the slums and is never happier than when the pigeon returns after being sold. She represents an alternative logic to that of the bourgeois society, one that the boy comes to defend in his refusal to let go of his scam.

Scams will become a trope in many of Oshima's narratives. They will become textual devices to display logical, if perverse, extensions of capitalist systems of exchange. The scams' illegality is coupled with their outrageous circularity, their overwhelming and exploitive laws of return that violate capitalist exchange systems but simultaneously expose how such systems easily accommodate and even encourage abuse. Here the pigeon scam consists of selling something that shortly thereafter returns to the seller on its own accord. Its power as metaphor lies in the way it violates the basic laws of the circulation of capital and commodities, and does so quite "innocently," as it is in the bird's instinct to return home.

As a device the pigeon allows for a series of philosophical arguments on

Japanese postwar morality between the teacher and the boy. For example, the teacher argues in the name of equality that the boy cannot bring a pigeon to school because none of the other students have pigeons. This principle of equality, however, thinly disguises a conformist imperative. The pigeon becomes marked as excess, as an object that signifies differentiation in a conformist democracy. Further, the teacher and the girl both try to teach the boy that the pigeon scam is wrong, immoral. To the end, he resists their moralizing, claiming that he never did anything wrong. He ruins his chances at advancing socially by refusing to apologize, refusing to promise never again to conduct the scam, that is, refusing to submit to the teacher's view of his behavior and benefit from her efforts on his behalf.

In the final scene of the film, the symbolic use of the pigeon device culminates in a scene on the girl's elegant, modern balcony in which her brother shoots the pigeon with a rifle as she urges him to do so. With the pigeon destroyed, the film simply ends, leaving us to wonder exactly what it means for these two characters to be the assassin of the boy's object of desire and rebellion. Two earlier scenes set up the context of this violent repression. One is the meeting of the teacher and brother in a fancy restaurant whose picture windows provide a distanced rooftop view of the factories below. The couple discuss social philosophy, and the brother seems drawn to the reform spirit of this woman. This communion is short-lived, however, and it is the difference in class affiliations and politics that separates them. The second scene is a street fight initiated when poor youths from the boy's neighborhood attack the boy and girl as the couple head toward his house, apparently because they resent the upper-class girl invading their territory. It is the girl who fends off their attackers with her umbrella, a demonstration that gains her new respect from the boy.

These two scenes set up cross-class romances as sites of resentment. The violence that destroys the pigeon is the culmination and release of resentment and frustration. This violent release, finally, annihilates the possibility of such desire.

A Town of Love and Hope operates against a background of various genres of realism. While the Japanese genre of *shomin-geki* (family dramas) is the most direct antecedent (Burch 1979: 358), both the film's realist aspects and its class awareness recall tendency films, such as those of Shimazu in the thirties. In fact, Sato Tadao makes the point that studio head Kido Shiro may have been expecting a more optimistic portrayal of the love affair but found that Oshima's film, through its insistence that there was no basis for a bond between the bourgeoisie and the proletariat, "might as well be a tendency film" (Sato 1973: 38–39). The film also incorporates aspects of neorealism, in its gritty depiction in black and white of the slum neighborhood. It is reminiscent not only of the Italian genre embodied in Vitto-

2. In the final scene of the film, the symbolic use of the pigeon device culminates in a scene on the girl's elegant, modern balcony in which her brother shoots the pigeon with a rifle as she urges him to do so. Production still, *Ai to kibo no machi* (A Town of Love and Hope, 1959). Still courtesy of Oshima Productions.

rio de Sica's *Sciuscià* (Shoeshine, 1946), for example, but the Japanese one as well, characterized by the immediate postwar films of Kurosawa, such as *Subarashiki Nichiyobi* (One Wonderful Sunday, 1947) or *Yoidore tenshi* (Drunken Angel, 1948). The more recent *Doro no kawa* (Muddy River, Oguri, 1984), in its return to neorealism to trace the lives of the underclass children growing up on a river barge, also makes a fascinating comparison. In both Italian and Japanese films of this genre, realism is coupled with leftist sentiments.

A *Town of Love and Hope* does differentiate itself from neorealist films by refusing to allow the attachment of humanist sentiments to class consciousness. Even so, it remains closer to the Marxist realist tradition than Oshima's later films. If ideological critique and social commentary never leave Oshima's films, never again will his filmmaking be so close to the tendency film of Japan or the neorealist evocations. This explains why a critic looking for more traditional Marxist humanism and clearly drawn class oppositions, such as Paul Coates, finds it preferable to Oshima's later works whose greater narrative complexity and structural repetitions provoke ambiguity and polysemy.

The allegorical mode associated with poetic realism appears in *A Town of Love and Hope,* but the function of allegory is decentered from an expected reading. Sympathies do not align romantically. Not even melancholy or nostalgia is evoked when characters are torn apart by class and circumstance. Whereas at the end of *Muddy River* the boy runs desperately along the river to wave good-bye to his departing friends, at the end of Oshima's film two characters kill a pigeon and then the screen goes blank. We are left with a representation of the misunderstanding of the other's desire and the determination to maintain the order of things.

The pigeon, the object that circulates between classes, that cheats the desire for exchange by returning back to the sender, invites theoretical comparison to a slew of recent meditations on objects sent. Beginning with critical response to Edgar Allan Poe's "The Purloined Letter," the debate by theorists, including Jacques Lacan, Jacques Derrida, and Barbara Johnson (1988), focuses on the act of narrating the exchange, concealment, and search for the letter; at the core of this debate resides the letter's status as allegorical emblem of the signifier (the semiotic term for any unit potentially bearing meaning). Another striking aspect of the debate is that various parties place the circulation of this signifier in different contexts at different moments: in everyday operations, in literary structures, or in the unconscious. Many of the theorists slide the letter qua signifier from one context to another. By this I mean that sometimes the theorist, while referring to one context, actually directs us to another, as when literary structure is perceived as revealing the unconscious. Some of the debate hinges on the meaning of the phrase, introduced by Lacan at the conclusion of his essay, "a letter always arrives at its destination." Yet as Johnson points out, this phrase is not nearly as self-evidently determinist as it might appear, nor as sure of which destination the letter should have, as might first be implied; rather, as Lacan makes clear from the outset, it means to indicate the persistence of, the insistence of, signifiers in the unconscious, tied to Freud's notion of the return of the repressed.

Another fascinating aspect of the debate is the way it has positioned speech and writing both in relationship to each other and in relationship to technology. For Derrida, it has afforded the story through which to retell at various junctures his insistence on writing and on chance as overturning communication models and the certainty of fixed meanings or truths. Technologies such as telephones, televisions, recording devices, and computers, increasingly linked technologies at that, facilitate speech and writing in new interchanges, the rethinking of theories of exchange (Ronnell 1989)—how meanings (more commonly, "information") are sent and how humans perceive and receive it, the basic lines of the argument that rest on Poe's antiquely sealed letter, explode into a questioning of the parameters of language and desire.

Given this theoretical background, it is intriguing to see the film's pigeon as a signifier guaranteed to return. The pigeon is a device that carries no specific or intrinsic message—this is not a carrier pigeon bearing letters. Always, it returns to its sender; as a homing pigeon, it ventures out only to return to a symbolic home. In a narrative in which the Japanese home is in question, this return is only to a character who is never at home, who will never be allowed into the bourgeois family. That is why the pigeon must pay with its life, why the signifier must meet death, becoming in the process the "dead letter" Derrida introduces into the theoretical debate, the letter stuck in the postal system, the signifier that never arrives and may be lost. Yet the pigeon paradoxically allows the hero to communicate with others, creating their increased awareness of him, of his suffering, so in another sense the pigeon always arrives, always brings home its message. To display such paradoxes is to push representation into unsettling territory, where the evident allegory does not simply hold. The struggle of Oshima's films will be to more convincingly maintain an allegorical paradox, to more successfully turn genres inside out to send forth philosophical letters.

DISPLAYS OF DESIRE

If *A Town of Love and Hope* breaks with certain conventions of neorealism and poetic realism, while borrowing others, the two films that follow perform a similar shifting of genre conventions for ideological ends. The two genres that provide the ground for *Cruel Story of Youth* and *Burial of the Sun*, both made and released in 1960, are the taiyo-zoku and *yakuza* (ganster) films. Both genres, even in their most commercial and apolitical manifestations, represent a cultural resistance to the Occupation and monopoly industrialization of Japan. In Chapter 1 we saw how as a film critic Oshima championed the taiyo-zoku films of the mid-fifties such as *Kurutta kajitsu* (Crazed Fruit, aka *Juvenile Passion*, 1956) by Nakahiro Ko, *Nagasugita haru* (The Summer That Was Too Long, aka *The Betrothed*, 1957) by Shirasaka Yoshio, and *Kuchisuke* (The Kiss, 1956) by Masumura Yasuzo. In fact, his commentary on Masumura shows clearly the formation of his own future path, as he praises him for "turning his back on the atmosphere and lyricism dominant in Japanese society and cinema" and approvingly quotes Masumura, who says his "goal is to paint in all their excess, the desires and passions of human beings" (Oshima 1992: 30).

In this quote, one can read an admiration for the break implied in Japanese popular culture with principles dear to the humanist left. Its emphasis on social environment in a sentimental appeal to understanding delinquency yields to an attraction to displays of desire. Displays of desire are attractive to a Japanese critic of his own society, as they cut through prohibitions in Japanese custom against directly expressing personal preferences. They are the assertion of individuation unchecked by expectations of adapting inconspicuously to circumstances often ruled by hierarchies, of accepting what is offered rather than requesting what one would like.

"Displays of desire" has psychoanalytic and poststructuralist resonances. Rather than direct influence, the question is one of confluence, in which theoretical principles developing elsewhere help us to understand Oshima's impulses, as well as those generalized in Japanese popular culture. Later, this confluence will be acknowledged equally in Europe and in Japan, with Oshima's other films, and will become central to *Ai no korida* (In the Realm of the Senses, 1976), as we shall see in chapter 4.

For now, let us simply consider how the issues addressed in Lacan's 1959–1960 seminar on the ethics of psychoanalysis form a fascinating reference through which to read Oshima's gratitude for a subcultural display of desire. Lacan clarifies questions of the subject's relationship to desire and display that had been circulating in his work and that of others. Posing desire as a metonymy for the subject him- or herself, Lacan plays with the notion that those seeking power over the subject deny the subject his or her desire. Then he introduces the notion that the only thing of which one can be guilty, at least in a psychoanalytic perspective, is "to have given ground relative to desire" (*d'avoir cédé sur son desir*) (1992: 319). Yet before reaching this point, he remarks on the failure, which he takes to be inevitable, of any libertine project of freeing desire, and he explores what the writings of de Sade tell us of an unmitigated acting on desire in its relationship to suffering. He is aware that desire inhabits a paradox: "On the far edge of guilt, insofar as it occupies the field of desire, there are the bonds of a permanent bookkeeping, and this is so independently of any particular articulation that may be given of it" (Lacan 1992: 318).

Lacan struggles with ethics even as he wishes to wrest desire from its limitation as the subject who is told "as far as desire is concerned, come back later" (1992: 319). A similar paradox of wishing to act on desire and knowing the limits of acting on desire manifests itself in Oshima's admiration for libertine youth heroes of the taiyo-zoku, despite his call for something like social responsibility on the part of filmmakers displaying these characters' displays of desire.

As a result, there is a difference between Oshima's incursions into the taiyo-zoku and yakuza genres and those of the filmmakers he admired, even as Masumura's own self-conscious project and Oshima's readings of certain of his predecessors' films try to bring out a nascent use of paradox and political purpose that marks this difference. Shochiku publicity (1960) tried to market Oshima's films by erasing this difference, glorifying their lead characters as antiheroes. Yet the films are systematically lacking in such glorification or even empathy. The gangs that clash in *Burial of the Sun* and the young couple in *Cruel Story of Youth* inhabit realms devoid of romanticism. If for a moment idealism or hope seems to rise to the surface, it is quickly washed away not only by external forces but also by interiorized imperatives. In other words, characters do not divide into heroes and villains, innocents and forces of evil; the flow of energies, positive and negative, is shared.

CRUEL TALES: REPETITION COMPULSIONS AND SPATIAL LACK

In *Cruel Story of Youth,* the imagery is again suggestive symbolically, this time of foreclosed spaces and sadistic, violent conflict delimiting the desire for human interaction. The credits present blood-red letters over a background of spread-out newspapers. The very first scene of the film follows a young woman past several large cars on the side of a busy nighttime street as she seeks a ride from a businessman, only to be beckoned by a girlfriend who has found a better offer, a signal that the camera sweeps to view with a swish pan left.

Accompanied by a percussive jazz strain, this opening suggests a citation of the dynamic opening in Marseilles of Godard's *Breathless,* with its newspapers, women, and signals surrounding Michel's car theft, liberally blended with later scenes from that film of young women hitchhiking (on the highway to Paris and its memorable footage of Montparnasse at night). The music certainly is so similar to the theme from *Breathless* that it seems to mark more than coincidental resonance; if so, the citation is made with incredible rapidity, as Godard's film only premiered March 16, 1960, in Paris, though there was a sneak preview four months earlier and release of a recording of the music and much press in the intervening four months (Moullet 1960). By June 1960 Oshima made a glowing reference to Godard's film in an article, but how direct his knowledge and citation is in this instance is less the issue than is recognizing the common strains in the two films and knowing that viewers would come to see the comparison. Oshima, like Godard, practices a citational filmic writing, one that loves reference and resonance and that begs for comparative readings.

The hitchhiking scene is a prelude to an incident that establishes circumstantially the "innocent" version of what will later become an aggression/rescue scam repeated throughout the film. The two women sitting in the backseat of the car are asked by the driver about the advisability of hitchhiking; a jump cut switches the image to Makoto at some later time being picked up hitchhiking by a man in a business suit. This car pulls up to a "love hotel," one of the new, garish Western architectural structures that offer their rooms by the hour, here indicated only metonymically by signs. Unwilling, she exits the car and attempts to get away, but the businessman backs her up against a wall on the street opposite the hotel. The wall fills the background of the widescreen frame, whose narrow horizontals follow the action of the ensuing struggle. She slaps the man, but he returns the violence twofold, then presses an embrace. Then a young man, in a typical student's blue uniform, fights off the aggressor, throwing him to the ground. The threat to turn him in to police leads the businessman to toss bills at the young man, who is, in fact, Kiyoshi, the male protagonist. We are to understand that this incident is how Makoto and Kiyoshi meet. It is presented as innocent and circumstantial, but its structural overdetermination comes to mock the narrative's recourse to chance encounters.

In a controversial scene that follows, Kiyoshi, a college student, takes Makoto, a naive high school student, to a section of Tokyo bay dominated by the lumber industry, thus filled with logs. The rape scene that ensues is introduced by a speedboat slicing the frame; the Cinemascope elongated rectangle is traversed from left to right and at an angle by the boat, then the frame moves to follow the boat's trajectory until it is moving left to right in the extreme distance of the shot along the right frame line. This movement is echoed in the shot that follows, framing Kiyoshi chasing Makoto as she runs down a "pier" of tied logs. Setting the young man's violence in this bizarrely literalized "floating world" is an invitation to remember Oshima's praise, cited in chapter 1: "In the rip of a woman's skirt and the buzz of a motorboat, sensitive people heard the heralding of a new generation of Japanese film." These are the elements he cites and reworks here; the possible citation of Godard mentioned above is joined with a citation of taiyo-zoku, as Oshima begs the "sensitive" viewer to read these images as heralding a self-conscious framing of a new filmmaking practice.

The rape is first indicated metonymically, as the pan that follows a chase across the logs gives way to a series of jarringly angled shot-reverse shots depicting Kiyoshi's kiss, Makoto's slap, and Kiyoshi's double slap back that repeats the businessman's aggression. Kiyoshi assumes the violent male role even more fully, by the perverse act of throwing Makoto in the water, then pushing and later kicking her hands away as she tries to pull herself back on the log while still refusing to yield to his desire. The dialogue marks his demand for submission, in the language of male self-centered subjectivity, but the mise-en-scène indicates that Kiyoshi meets his objective, not by the strength of argument, but by a torturous exhaustion of his victim's ability to resist. Once his prey is subdued, Kiyoshi embraces her virtually lifeless body, as the camera pans to the sky.

After the graphic scenes of torture and forced submission, the sexual act is indicated only by elision; the white that fills the screen is joined by an airplane sound off, while the image dissolves to another pan of the logs, this

3. Kiyoshi, the male protagonist, takes Makoto, a female high school student, to a section of Tokyo bay dominated by the lumber industry. This bizarrely literalized "floating world" evokes the history of the pleasure quarters of Edo (Tokyo). *Seishun sankoku monogatari* (Cruel Story of Youth, 1960). Still courtesy of Oshima Productions.

time with clothes scattered, followed by a pan across Makoto's body alone, exhausted after the violent scene. Still in the same panning shot, Kiyoshi dives into the water, swims vigorously away from the logs, then back. The logs float as the site of a perverse Eros, providing a scenography dense in metaphor. This site plays on the Japanese term "floating world," the phrase used to designate the historical pleasure districts of Edo and Kyoto in which prostitution promised a transient and ephemeral sexual pleasure. The film's contemporary refiguration places the sexual in Japan in a floating world that, unlike the pleasure quarters of the past, is literally offshore. In this new culture, intercourse is conceived in violence.

On returning to the logs after his swim, Kiyoshi finds Makoto has covered her face with his shirt, which he seemingly had draped over her body. He lovingly caresses her, but her response to this affection is to question. "Then you don't hate me? You didn't do that just for kicks?" He answers by explaining the displacement of violence that erupted at her: "I hated something, but it wasn't you." And when she questions what, he responds, "Everything."

If this scene seems to transform a rape into a seduction in a manner common in melodrama and romance fiction, it could suggest an effort to justify male violence through a necessary and ultimately welcome breakdown of female resistance. However, this dialogue, its structuration, and its context suggest that this reading is not simply given or left uncontested by the film; rather, the image of violent sexuality that was presented in a close-up of the couple on the edge of the logs needs to be seen in its embedding in representations of violence throughout the film. Particularly significant is Makoto's admonishment of Kiyoshi much later, a point we will examine later as we look at Oshima's use of the female voice in chapter 8.

This rape not only doubles the violence of their first meeting, it is presented in the context of the sexual scam that the young couple later devises. Midway through the film the repetition of this scheme, now organized as extortion, becomes the way the young couple finances their union. The scheme exploits the "love hotel" tryst fantasies of Japan's business class; these hotels are frequented not only by prostitutes and clients, as are "hotels de passe" in France, but by couples seeking clandestine liaisons, making them a site that blurs the borderline between prostitution, seduction, and liaison. The couple's scam entices the businessmen with the implied promise of such an encounter on the part of the girl. It then forces the businessmen to pay for a commodity, sex, that remains undelivered, as the boy shows up to fend off the middle-aged sexual aggressor who pays to protect his anonymity or to appease the couple. With money as incentive, the repetition of this scam becomes compulsive, broken only by one businessman who refuses to perform his role as sexual aggressor.

The repetition of the extortion is mirrored by Makoto's repeated pyromaniacal acts of burning liquor in an ashtray, which can also be seen as a delayed response to the logging rape. These repetitions form the psychoanalytic dimension of the narrative's form; like the involutions of *The Battle of Tokyo, or the Story of the Young Man Who Left His Will on Film* or the repeated self-annihilating staged accidents in *Boy,* which I will discuss in chapter 3, this narrative is energized by compulsive structures.

To understand these repetitions, we need to consider their relationship to the psychoanalysis of obsession. The first time we see Makoto light such a fire, she is admonished by Kiyoshi for doing it again, the repetition already inscribed. She retorts, "You taught me to do this." The dialogue itself wants to point to the figure of the displaced sexuality in pyromania. Freud's theorization of the compulsion to repeat posits that repeated acts or representations are the subject's means of discharging material that through repression is located in the unconscious. Neither this material nor its potential emotional charge is integrated into consciousness. Pyromania is a particularly vivid form of such obsessional behavior. The fire in the ashtray displays such "senseless" combustion. It is also, in a sense, purely erotic. The ashtray pyromania is the film's means of displaying the condensation of eroticism and obsessional repetition in a culture not at all at ease with sexuality.

Jean-François Lyotard (1986) suggests another view of pyrotechnics, perhaps just as suggestive for the film's repeated ashtray-fire imagery, but on a different level, one that looks at metacinematic functioning. Explosive visual manifestations provide a pure delight in energy expended, Lyotard suggests, and he uses this assertion as a metaphor for the pleasure that similar explosive visual poetics have in avant-garde films whose imagery and montage create incendiary moments stimulating the viewer. The ashtray fires provide in wide-screen extreme close-ups a visual punctuation of vivid color and kinetics, a moment in a narrative film in which cinematic montage achieves attraction by a sensual, immediate visual explosion. This metacinematic consideration of pyrotechnics does not contradict consideration of their psychosymbolic function; rather, it suggests a powerful means by which levels of filmic articulation are brought together in a repeated image. Indeed, the pyrotechnics here neither function in abstraction, as they do in avant-garde films that absent the figuration of characters, nor are they motivated and overdetermined by plot circumstances such as the explosions of cars, buildings, gunfire, and bombs in chase and suspense action genres. They are instead a middle instance in which narrative motivation plays its role, but the excess of filmic figuration takes on a life of its own. The spectator shares in the pyrotechnic fascination with the characters, and is asked to understand the displacement symbolized.

Early in *Cruel Story of Youth,* before the harbor rape scene, there is an insert, a direct reference to the political events of 1959 that places this nihilistic tale in a specific context. The insert begins as an interruption after the harbor scene, a cut to a sequence beginning with a title in a black-and-white newsreel of violent student demonstrations in South Korea. We see shots of a tanker truck on fire, Korean women in traditional white robes on a flatbed truck cheering the demonstrators, and militant street confrontations with police. A direct cut takes us out of this newsreel scene, to the outside of a movie theater where Makoto stands as Kiyoshi exits. "You didn't wait for me," she says, disappointed, to which he replies simply, "You were late." Their romance, born of violence, remains surrounded by violence, and in addition, becomes troubled by missed communications and an inability to be in the right place on time. The Korean newsreel returns in the real, immediately, as next the young couple enter a street filled with AMPO (as the U.S.–Japanese security treaty was known) demonstrators, at first like a peaceful parade. Another group in formation, forming zigzag lines with their bodies connected by linked arms, runs aggressively through the street. Kiyoshi and Makoto are outside the demonstration, on the sidelines, and not much interested. However, Kiyoshi is recognized by one of the militant demonstrators, which leads him to explain to Makoto that this demonstrator was an old

friend who joined the Zengakuren (the large national militant student organization formed in the postwar period and at this time engaged in protests
against the U.S.–Japanese security treaty). Makoto and Kiyoshi represent distanced observers of both student demonstrations, the militant and violent
South Korean one and the more pacifist Japanese demonstration that are
collaged together by the cinematic drifting of this couple. As is the case with
the right-wing agitators in *Burial of the Sun,* to be discussed later, Oshima offers us the point of view of characters whose vantage point departs from his
own. This couple constitutes Oshima's attempt to offer a view of those who
were bystanders in the student protests, indifferent to the issues and to social engagement. If they greet with disinterest the context that surrounds
their motorboat rides, pyromania, and sexuality, they manifest similar anx-
ieties and contradictions. While their peers devote their energies to demonstrations, these youths displace their alienation into empty but powerful
and poetic displays.

Later in the film, we learn that Makoto's older sister, Yuki, met her lover
during similar demonstrations in 1952. This insert and reference contextu-
alizes these sixties youths as those whose desires are too personal and self-
involved to participate. The older sister and her former lover, who came of
age in the radicalism of the fifties, have lost all motivation whatsoever, political and erotic. Oshima thus examines both generations, that which
formed in the Communist party-dominated radicalism of the Bloody May
Day of 1953 (his own generation) and that which should be interested in the
AMPO demonstrations of 1959–1960 but isn't (a portion of the youth at the
time the film was made).

Sexual relations among these youths take the form of moving in and out
of a shared space. We learn that Kiyoshi lends his room to his male friends
for encounters with their female lovers when he takes Makoto there after the
Tokyo bay scene, only to find it occupied by another couple. Later, the interchangeability of these encounters is marked when Makoto searches for
Kiyoshi. Her knock is answered by Kiyoshi's friend from behind the door with
a dismissal, "Go away, we're through," but the friend thinks he is speaking
to his girlfriend.

We may read this as a reference to Tokyo's housing shortage, parallel to
the market for love hotels at which one can rent privacy by the hour. Space
in which one can have intercourse is at a premium. The offshore site in
which rape acts as initiator of sexual relations is another means by which the
negation of a space of intercourse, its absence and violence, is represented.

The virtual space of a telephone call, significantly, links and explains what
was so enigmatically left dangling at this juncture in the narrative. Making
the call is suggested to Makoto by Kiyoshi's apartment-sharing friend; this call
supplies us with the other, older woman referred to earlier in a bar scene by

two men who asked Kiyoshi about his new conquest, Makoto, and requested rights to take over his lucrative relationship with an older woman. The telephone is answered by the woman who will shortly be identified as this person, but at first all this kimono-clad woman does is peek into a room to call "Sensei" to the telephone—from this and the scene in the interior, we understand that Kiyoshi is tutoring her daughter. The following shot of Kiyoshi on the phone frames this older woman, on the stairs above him, listening to him speak to Makoto.

We cut to an extreme close-up of Kiyoshi's chest as the introduction of a conversation between them in bed. Such cuts occur regularly in this very fragmented and sparse exposition. Transitions and narrative "dead" time are eliminated, giving us only three scenes collaged together: tutoring, phone call, discussion of phone call afterward. In this case the cut takes us to the naked images of the affair, the smooth chest of Kiyoshi contrasted with the aging face of his older lover, framing their dialogue on the future of their relationship in this context.

Structurally, a parallel between Makoto's encounters with older men and Kiyoshi's affair with an older woman laces the film. We come back to this structure of pairing across generations in *Realm of the Senses;* in both instances it links desire and sexuality to a system of perverse exchange, where the need for money makes the young subject to unequal power relations. Vitality touches mortality through such pairings, significant in the narrative movement toward death that propels the symbolic registers of both films.

As in *Burial of the Sun,* gangs and bars figure prominently here. When Kiyoshi fails to show up for a date, Makoto goes drinking with the gang from the bar. When Kiyoshi returns, the bar owner referees a fight over her. This fight is the first in a series of encounters between Kiyoshi and the gang. The terms of the owner's rescue of Kiyoshi from a knife-wielding gang member is a promissory note of 5,000 yen. A motorcycle borrowed on the pretense of securing the money only accumulates a further debt, until by the film's end Kiyoshi is haunted by the threat of the gang's retaliation as collection on these debts.

Added to these debts is the financial cost of an abortion. Yuki's former lover is now an abortion doctor. In chapter 8 we will explore the abortion scene in greater detail in looking at the sexual politics of Oshima's representation of women; here I want to stress how it becomes one of a series of scenes amassing a discourse on political failure.

First Makoto's father has a monologue on his generation's increasing disillusionment after the initial hopes of the postwar period. "Times were hard after the war, but we thought we had a better way of life, that we were reborn as a democratic nation, that responsibility went hand in hand with freedom, but what can I say to this child now? What have we to offer?"

Later Makoto's sister Yuki and the doctor reflect on the failure of their generation. It is their dialogue that is heard as voice-over as the young couple finds a moment of comfort and tenderness in the abortion clinic. Such brief moments of happiness are rare in the film; there will be but one other, a scene in which Makoto and Kiyoshi return to the sea by motorcycle, driving straight into the waves and then making love in the surf. The moment of tender happiness at the abortion clinic through crosscutting becomes ensconced in the context of historical forces and reflections on those forces that engulf such isolated attempts at happiness. Contrast and contextualization then show youth's fantasies of detached personal contentment to be empty wishes.

The foreclosure of possibilities of escape or happiness culminates as their final attempt at the scam fails. Makoto is picked up by Horio, a man even richer and higher placed than the others. First he acts fatherly and takes her home, after she, inexplicably, fails to pursue the scam. When they meet another night, Horio comforts her, then takes her to a hotel room. Her phone call to Kiyoshi from this hotel room is blocked, a busy signal; it actually crosses with Kiyoshi's call to his other lover. The scam and the relationship are no longer unfolding as planned. But the variation seems at first simply a displaced insistence, as Kiyoshi confronts Horio separately, this time not as a mock rescuer but as a full-fledged pimp and blackmailer, demanding money for Horio's sexual encounter with Makoto.

This variation culminates in the couple's arrest, represented in its doubleness. Both get arrested, shown in parallel editing initiated by two black-and-white photographs developing in a police laboratory. Their separate freedoms are bought; they have one last moment together on a night street, after Makoto again flees her house and they evade Kiyoshi's older woman friend who follows them, attempting to use her money to entrap Kiyoshi.

A further cinematic doubling, this time of death at the film's end, unites the couple in an involuntary "double suicide." After they have broken apart from each other, crosscutting not only shows us events that lead to the doom of each protagonist, but it suggests a psychic link between the two, with visual montage showing us Makoto's apparent reactions to the violent beating of Kiyoshi and sound bleeds linking the two series of shots. Here is how the crosscutting series unfolds:

> Kiyoshi, after being rescued from jail by his other lover, the older woman who has been supporting him, is beaten to death by the gang from whom he previously rescued Makoto.
> Makoto is seen in two shot, from behind, in the front seat of the car of a man who has picked her up. She turns over her shoulder to the left, her eyes seemingly searching for Kiyoshi, as if she wishes to verify the image of his beating we have just seen which is appearing to her as premonition. Such premonition visualizations were a trope of early

cinema melodrama, here renewed by the startling context of extreme violence and the brilliance of the sound montage.

Cut back to Kiyoshi being beaten and strangled by a boot. Makoto opens
the door, apparently to jump, but her high heel lodges in the car
door, and we see her being dragged along as the car continues to
speed along, only to have her body drop from sight, as the shot continues on the high angle on empty asphalt as the car continues. The
sequence ends with a slow pan up her body, capturing one last
movement as she dies, terminating on a close-up of her face on the
left of the image joined by a fade-in of a close-up of Kiyoshi's dead
face, dripping blood from his mouth.

The poetic of the rendering of death in parallel sequences that eventually join in superimposition demonstrates through graphic violence another
logical possibility that had not yet been played out in the variation of the
aggression/rescue scam: Makoto's death. Without a rescuer, the flirtation
with male sexual violence doesn't pay. The violence is not left as gratuitous,
sexualized instances of conflict from which heroic or antiheroic figures
emerge unscathed.

The split-screen images of deaths leave no one to save or be saved; the
compulsive narrative goes beyond the symbolic murder of *A Town of Love and
Hope*. Preternatural communication (borrowed from early film melodrama)
and the moments offered of the couple's attainment of sympathy and even
love across a tortured relationship are perhaps vestiges of a romanticism
reemerging from underneath Oshima's dark social critique and his prevailing antihumanism. What Catherine Russell calls Oshima's "narrative morality" is perhaps best illustrated by this film (1995: 105–123).

Oshima's impulse to look at the political other is here pursued with characters who come close to the filmmaker himself, but the story remains one
of a youth whose detachment, self-destruction, and hopelessness the film
questions. Here the characters of the older sister and a cynical doctor directly
represent a vantage point from which to view this other. The view is filled with
ambiguity. There is criticism, some pity, some anger, but also some admiration and envy.

OSHIMA'S ANTECEDENTS: MEYERHOLD, BRECHT, AND JAPANESE LEFTIST THEATER

Burial of the Sun seems to eliminate audience empathy and identification with
characters in the traditional sense. We have, at least in part, a Brechtian strategy of *Verfremdung*: the term translated as "alienation" or "distanciation"
which means a theatricality aimed at breaking spectators' emotive identification in favor of a more analytic mode of active participation in and thought

about theater. Brecht (1964: 91–100, 104–105) meant "alienation" in the sense of a making different or strange, through rendering events outside of their naturalistic context and heightening their theatricality. Key to this, as Walter Benjamin (1974: 4–12) reminds us, is a notion of the social *geste,* the gesture or action represented in what I would like to call both its symbolic and economic social functions, its functions of exchange.

However common it has been to call Oshima's strategies Brechtian, as with many other modern and postmodern filmmakers, the designation needs several qualifications. The tendency to call Oshima 'Brechtian' is clearly overdetermined by European and U.S. critics and audiences for whom Brecht is the clearest referent; my position is that those techniques have multiple historical explanations, and the label "Brechtian" could conceal a fascinating history of cross-cultural theoretical exchange that I will try to explicate without reduction to a story of influences.

First, Brecht must be seen as only one source of Oshima's strategies of reshaping cinematic representation. Brechtian theories are combined with other sources, notably Soviet and Japanese. The Soviet agit-prop theater of Vsevolod Meyerhold, itself an influence on Brecht, was a particularly strong presence in modern Japanese theater history. We have to keep in mind the domination of the modern theater movement in Japan by left-wing troupes in the 1920s such as the Tuskiji Little Theater Group, the Vanguard Troupe, and the Japan Proletariat Theater League, which saw theater as an organ of social reform. The latter even had an offshoot in Japan called the Korean Proletariat Theater Group, devoted to issues of those of Korean ancestry living in Japan, of particular interest here as this group becomes a focus in Oshima's films. The year 1931 marks the formation of the International Arbeiter Theatre Bund, a leftist union of directors, actors, and actresses and other production personnel associated with several theaters throughout Japan; the German nomenclature comes from marked affinities with the German left, not the as-yet-nascent Nazi party. Banned in 1937, such leftist theater was to enjoy a resurgence after the war in conjunction with the Communist party, labor unions, and children's theater (Bowers 1982: 214–216, 230–233). As we know, Oshima's artistic background as a student was in theater groups that were inheritors of this leftist tradition. So we might view the history of leftist theater in Japan as struggling against its early ties to *shingeki,* the turn-of-the-century modernist theatrical form characterized by realism and naturalism. It turns first to the Soviet innovators like Meyerhold and later to the Germans such as Brecht. Recently the significance of Brecht for all of modern East Asian theater has been the subject of study (*Brecht and East Asian Theatre* 1982). Yet these influences need to be seen as balanced and transformed by the subtending Japanese context. Further, the ongoing ideological debate within the Japanese left, including shifts in positions of the Japanese Communist party, concerning Marxist aesthetics means that the history of assimilation and reference to and reaction against figures like Meyerhold and Brecht is extremely complex in itself (Ortolani 1990: 219–251).

Second, we should consider how components of a "Brechtian" strategy might be hard to distinguish from a specifically Japanese theatricality. This is for good reason, historically, as Western avant-gardists in theater drew on traditional Japanese theater, especially Kabuki, for inspiration (Song 1977; Tatlow 1977). Meyerhold, Eisenstein, and Brecht all sought techniques in Japanese and Chinese theater traditions that would, on being introduced in Western theater, produce a new theatrical mode, in Brecht's terms, Verfremdung (Eaton 1985).

Another historical matter that is less than clear is *when* Oshima moves from the will to negate melodrama, present from his first film, *A Town of Love and Hope,* to a self-consciously "Brechtian" mode, if such a distinction can be made. Oshima's reactions against both commercial film and the left's naturalist melodrama parallel Brecht's critique of the emotional appeals of identification in the theater and the commercial imperatives of the film industry, but how much is a parallel and how much conscious, concerted theoretical application at this point cannot be decided, nor is it all that germane. The point is that one process, the attack on melodrama, overlaps with the other, a search for theoretical techniques of cinematic transformations, and the films and writings at various points mark this trajectory. One can certainly term later Oshima films, particularly *Death by Hanging,* which I will discuss in depth in the next chapter, Brechtian, particularly close to Brecht's *The Rise and Fall of the City of Mahogany* in aspects of structuration, including its use of written intertitles and a segmented narrative molded as a "learning play." There is little doubt that his essay protesting the censorship of *Realm of the Senses* parallels, and is perhaps modeled on, Brecht's protest of Georg Wilhelm Pabst's adaptation of *Die Dreigroshenoper* (The Threepenny Opera). Oshima's background of student involvement in political theater is most evident in his films in his inclusion of Juro in *Diary of a Shinjuku Thief;* this character and his theater group are incorporated into the narrative, Oshima's nod to the modern political Japanese theater. This signals that Oshima wishes to foreground the relationship of his cinematic strategies to those of the avant-garde theater.

All of this must also be placed in the context of a sixties resurgence of theoretical debate on how Brecht's theories of theater can be transferred to cinema (Lellis 1982). Most theories of radical cinema incorporate some ideas borrowed from Brecht. Jean-Luc Godard, Alexandre Kluge, Rainer Werner Fassbinder, and Jean-Marie Straub and Danielle Huillet were seen as central examples of cinematic borrowers from and translators of Brecht. While theorists such as Dana Polan insisted Oshima's films should play a key role in this debate, the European focus of those looking for a Brechtian cinema sometimes overlooked the contribution of his films.

Let me caution that Oshima's Brechtian strategies are not completely Brechtian, for Oshima differs from Brecht in several significant ways. Most important, Oshima seems to embrace selectively Brecht's dictum of depriving the scene of its "sensationalism." As we have seen, he will use sex and violence sensationally, only to create a critical edge to such depictions. Oshima's depiction of the slums may be seen as inscribing codes of naturalism or, alternatively, may be read as so extreme as to exaggerate and theatricalize both poverty and bawdy nightlife. Certainly, Brecht's own *Threepenny Opera* and *Mahogany,* in lurid language and display of prostitution and female sexuality, had their own sensational aspects. Yet the question of visual sensational appeal goes to the heart of differences between theater and film, differences that along with film's scale of financing and concomitant obligation to equally large-scale profit led to Brecht's own distrust of film.

Even if Oshima were a faithful Brechtian, one senses that *Burial of the Sun*'s reception might indicate that Brechtian strategies are far from infallible given the context of viewer identification with character. This fallibility is tied to the persistence of romantic identification on the part of spectators, the will to read films through experiences of identification. Some readings of *Burial of the Sun* romantically identify with the lead characters as a violent couple and then proceed to read Oshima's foregrounding of criminality as a break with conventional ethics that should be considered a necessary first stage of a transformational politics (Knee 1987: 51–52). Such readings depend on the polarity of criminality being villainous *or* antiheroic but never see its use in a symbolic context as a device through which to organize a series of *social gestes,* to display contradictions without bringing the audience over to rooting for the criminal.

The tableaus mentioned at the outset of this chapter are one key to Brechtian readings of the film that would trouble such identificatory readings. Cityscapes in these tableaus are foregrounded rather than used as backdrop, reversing the tradition of setting action in a scene that supports it. The tableaus help Oshima to pursue the goals he spoke of in admiring the taiyo-zoku, to display a cityscape while "avoiding the myth of the environment, eliminating all atmosphere, cutting all bridges to sentimentalism." Here the scene acts as frame and as picture in itself, an actant, not merely motivating or affecting characters, but an element of central focus. The tableaus constitute both the citation and *the negation* of what Noël Burch (1979) termed the "pillow shots" in Ozu. Looking at other aspects of structure and scenography in the film will show that we are in a strange and forceful framework, where our place and our placement is not taken for granted at any level.

4. Widescreen framing allows for the grouping of the characters against the neon-lit street in the poorest section of Osaka, Kama-ga-saki. Note that the young couple are framed back to back at some distance from each other while an older man solicits her. *Taiyo no hakaba* (Burial of the Sun, 1960). Still courtesy of Oshima Productions.

SCENOGRAPHY OF *BURIAL OF THE SUN*

In *Burial of the Sun* the central female character, Hanako, structurally links two groups of men, the *shinai-kai*, a street gang of unemployed young men who pimp and steal for a living, and a group composed of middle-aged right-wing agitators and petty yakuza. Hanako's father, Yosematsu, is a member of the second group. He is involved first in the junk trade but graduates with his other right-wing collaborators, including a ringleader known as the "Agitator," to an immigration scam. They convince Japanese workers to sell their passports to Koreans, thus exploiting the needs of both groups and symbolically depriving both of their identities. Both groups, the shinai-kai and the right-wing profiteers, operate in the shadows of real yakuza led by Ohama, with whom Hanako also has somewhat mysterious connections.

Hanako's own moneymaking schemes are prostitution and selling plasma to cosmetics firms. We see her first in the opening blood-gathering sequence, in a dirty and dilapidated shack dressed only in a long-line bra and panties. Her trade in blood includes a young assistant who lures fishermen into her portside operation, where a partner assists her by drawing the blood. When the operation closes for the night, the partner swigs a drink, then lurches across the long, narrow wide-screen frame, right to left, to attack her, only to be fought off by a knife-wielding Hanako who calls him a fool for thinking that theirs is anything more than a business partnership. As the tawdry shack marks the distance of this makeshift operation from a legitimate blood bank, this scene of lurching, unwelcome sexuality combines with later comments on the questionable legality of gathering human blood for cosmetics to set the scene of Hanako as a daring female entrepreneur within the harsh rules of this marginal social order. These aspects of Hanako's gender and sexual representation will be the subject of further exploration in chapter 6. As representation, she is both an image to be exploited by the film and a self-conscious critique of female positioning in Japanese society; profligate, her complete lack of ethics is contextualized not simply as a "fault" of her gender but as a rebellion against her treatment.

The film revels in images of the daytime muddy squalor and neon-lit nightlife of the poorest section of Osaka, Kama-ga-saki. Here fifties American fashion is emblematic of a desperate renunciation of traditional Japanese culture, the codes of polite, subservient, and honest behavior. Hanako walks these streets in her ponytail and print full skirts or pedal pushers, not as the dignified and sympathetic prostitute that one might encounter in a Mizoguchi film, but as an aggressively self-enterprising woman whose lack of concern with the feelings of others is the key to her survival. In fact, the narrative seems to be conditioned by the production of images that evoke the nihilistic despair of this environment, such as a body being tossed in the river by the junkman in the middle of the film; he unloads the body not methodically, with suspense and stealth, but as a simple, paid act of garbage disposal. This image of body disposal and others of bombed ruins remind us of an atmosphere that seems almost immediately postwar, though of course the fifties styles mark the intervening Occupation and the beginnings of a consumerist economic regrowth.

Complicated narrative threads receive a fragmented exposition parceled out over several sequences. For example, consider the carefully interlaced introduction of two newcomers to this scene, young men named Takeshi and Tatsu, whose assimilation into the shinai-kai comprises one of the motor forces for narrative. As the first bloodletting sequence ends with Hanako walking down the street with her entourage, this segues into two of the gang shaking down two strangers for a "loan." A fight ensues, sirens are heard off-screen, and the four men retreat to an alleyway, then a shot-reverse shot pattern links this shot with another in which Shin, the gang leader, converses with this group. Only retrospectively do we realize the shift to another location, the gang's hideout, when the new sequence continues in what is this new space. There we learn of the interest of the gang leader Shin in his new recruits. Such editing between scenes in different locations gives a false sense of spatiotemporal continuity, then shatters that continuity by revealing its falseness. This staging of scenes as fragments, coupled with tricky transitions marked by graphic matches, forms a compositional experimentation with visual narrative structure. While we are able to follow, we are engaged

5. Takeshi takes on Shin, his attack occurring along the railroad tracks; this violence belies a homoerotic bond between the gang members. *Taiyo no hakaba* (Burial of the Sun, 1960). Still courtesy of Oshima Productions.

in and disconcerted by a world full of spatial and temporal surprises. The film becomes an uncertain environment, a quality that can be seen as one means of translating Brecht's alienation effect to cinema.

The induction of Takeshi and Tatsu takes them through a hallway, where the camera pauses to frame their witnessing a scene of a gang member disciplining the prostitutes whom the gang controls and pimps. One woman is tortured with a crutch for becoming pregnant. Her captor chides her for becoming pregnant as another abortion will waste the gang's money. Such staged voyeurism, in which we watch characters watching sex, or in this case, violence staged sexually as sadism, is a recurring figure in Oshima's films that garnered theoretical attention for its use in *Realm of the Senses* (Heath 1976–1977: 145–153). Here voyeurism is framed both as initiation and as ethical dilemma: Having seen, what will be the response of these two young men? Will they behave as they have been shown?

A triangular relationship develops when Takeshi and Tatsu both attract Hanako's sexual interest; complicating this triangle is both men's subservience to Shin, whose own relationship to Hanako will become pivotal.

Hanako not only links all groups but specifically these three men in a bond that would otherwise be purely homoerotic; she becomes object of desire, sister-self, mother, judge—myriad roles in their gang interactions.

To see how this works, let us look at the staging of initiation rites and betrayals across the film. As part of their initiation to the gang. Takeshi and Tatsu are to rob a young couple. The scene takes place in a graveyard in ruins, with Hanako acting as lookout and thus voyeur, watching them from a distance. When Tatsu proceeds to rape the girl, Takeshi returns to Hanako, asking, "Did you see what Tatsu is doing?" This question of course doubles the earlier voyeuristic witnessing of the prostitute's torture.

While Hanako observes this initiation ritual devoid of emotions, Takeshi is haunted by guilt afterward. Hanako urges him to simply forget, even though they hear that the girl's lover has committed suicide out of humiliation. Later in the film Takeshi returns to the graveyard, haunted as a Japanese character should be in a traditional tale. However, this traditional response is eventually undone. The rape victim comes after Takeshi with a knife at a construction site, and it is Hanako's quick defensive moves that save him, momentarily illustrating the practical worth of her every-man-for-himself ethics (I retain the masculine to underline the absence of feminism in such ethics).

The narrative generates more symbolic, violent encounters, as Takeshi takes on Shin, his attack occurring along the railroad tracks. When both are killed, Hanako continues alone, now turning against her father, burning down the shacks in which his group operates. Against the flames that engulf her world, Hanako simply moves on, remarking to her quack business partner that they still have their work.

The film seems to be almost a parody of the violent narratives of films like Nicholas Ray's *Rebel Without a Cause* (1955), on one hand, and the sun tribe exploitation films, on the other. Instead of pleading for a social and psychoanalytic explanation of juvenile delinquency as Ray's film does, Oshima's film presents the violence not as romantically rebellious but as detached; there is no character development spurred by tragedy of the sort that allows *Rebel*'s defiant and alienated son to assume responsibility within his peer group and reconcile with his parents. The climactic violence in *Burial of the Sun* merely annihilates instead of re-forming a young couple in the shadow and acceptance of their parents. Extremes of character representation and the framing of events render identification far more complex. If Hanako's survival motive and Takeshi's struggle with guilt undermine any simple rejection of them, they are never presented as admirable.

Nor does the film exploit its explosive violence as youth exploitation films do by urging imaginary emulation of its youthful delinquents. Its aesthetics frame the violence in the reds and yellows of neon and flames, but these are set against the metaphor of the sunset and burial, as well as the cool blues of other scenes. The widescreen framing maintains an aesthetic distance. Not only does no rapid editing excite the pacing, but the emphasis on composition becomes in itself a signifier. Shots, whether in long shot or extreme close-up, sustain the quality of a composed tableau image. The imagery is visually lush without being romantic and participatory. This is accentuated by the punctuation shots described at the beginning of this chapter; images in *Burial of the Sun,* as in all Oshima's films, function with an emphatic presentation of themselves as signs, to be understood emblematically.

In this case, the allegory generated by this tale of right-wing gangs and their antiheroine survivor can be understood in the context of an implicit contrast between the slums of Osaka and the privileged world of Kyoto University. Kyoto, the traditional cultural center of Japan and the site of one of Japan's great universities, is just a short train ride away from Osaka, a fact that helps us to understand the implications of a statement made by the right-wing Agitator late in the film. He speaks of his desire to become a policeman in order to be sanctioned to beat up the protesting students in Kyoto. By crossing the border that separates one community from another, Oshima explores the logic of survival in this other scene as not simply indicative of its own dynamics but rather as a commentary on contemporary Japan in general. If Japan's rising sun is pictured in the process of being buried in 1960, the funeral is conditioned by the right wing first having driven the country to self-annihilation in the war, then trying to profit on the aftermath. It is symbolically important that while the scene of profiteering burns at the end, even the antiheroic survivor has nowhere to escape. The film ends on the promise of a repetition of the scene and a savage refusal of heroism as a structure for allegory. Instead of a complete and logical system of equivalencies, allegory here takes the shape of fragmented images: a setting sun, self-annihilation, pimping, commerce that steals identities and traffics in human blood.

THE POLITICAL SELF

In contrast, *Night and Fog in Japan* is a direct look at the political self. Even so, the film is hardly autobiographical; instead it represents the self through a highly fictionalized and restructured allegory. It draws directly on Oshima's experience with oppositional theater groups, through the use of actors he knew from his days in the theater and through staging that is highly theatrical. It draws equally on Oshima's experience with political movements on the left, presenting dialogues filled with direct citations of typical political arguments, specific political and rhetorical references to factional debates between the Communist party and other leftist groups. In this rhetoric lies a will toward theoretical analyses, containing much of the same terminology and style of argumentation one finds internationally in Marxist and post-

Marxist debates. In that way it is similar to *The Battle of Tokyo, or the Story of the Young Man Who Left His Will on Film,* to be discussed in the next chapter, which also uses "political" language. In both cases, Oshima does not simply reproduce this language but mines the poetic ironies of such dialogue, forming a critique out of situating language exchanges in verbal montage. The dialogue is not one's usual concept of film dialogue (immediate, action- and object-oriented, direct). Sato Tadao (1973: 72, 89 ff.) has called the style Oshima adopts in this film by the anglicized term, *diskasshon-dorama,* discussion-drama, a term that I think demonstrates how dialogue debate here is given an intense dramatic investment. Yet if this debate rivets our attention, it is not only through the design of the language and arguments alone but also in their filmic rendering, the images that frame, punctuate, and comment on the movements of the verbal exchanges.

The cinematic techniques that Oshima has been developing as a characteristic use of panning and framing of the widescreen image, a particular rhythm of editing, intensify in this film as a concentration on the long take. The film is composed of forty-three shot sequences, a unique formal constraint that couples with the film's pursuit of ideological and political discussions rare in a commercially released feature film of any country. Oshima was able to pursue this use of formal experimentation, combined with highly political material, because of the box office success of the previous features and by concealing from his studio heads certain elements of the script until after the film was completed. Shochiku wanted to profit from the new directions of its young filmmakers, whom it was promoting as the "Shochiku-Ofuna new wave," but the studio, as we shall see, was not prepared to launch a film so politically avant-garde as *Night and Fog in Japan.* Censorship, in the form of pulling the film from distribution after only three days of limited release in Tokyo and shelving it in their archives for the next four years, was Shochiku's response to the daring film Oshima presented on October 9, 1960.

If retrospectively one can only be amazed that Oshima attempted commercial production of this film, one can also see it as precisely where Oshima had been aiming, as the logical goal set by the earlier films. If the preceding three films were in their own ways a compromise between his impulses toward subjective expression and political engagement, on one hand, and strategies aimed at establishing himself in the industry, on the other, this film would favor the subjective, political impulses, even though, as Sato Tadao (1973: 87–89) suggests, others warned him on seeing the script that its determined pursuit of political material would come at the cost of his newly established commercial success.

To understand Oshima's determination to make this film, we must consider the significance both the formal and the political elements held for him. The title is a clue, as the film is named after *Nuit et bruillard* (Night and Fog), a brooding essay-documentary made by Alain Resnais in 1957. Resnais's

6. Camera movement creates a theatricality that is spatial and subject to reframing, a blocking of character interaction that is specifically visual and cinematic. *Nihon no yoru to kiri* (Night and Fog in Japan, 1960). Still courtesy of Oshima Productions.

film uses long takes, extended traveling shots of the concentration camp, and extensive voice-over to situate philosophically the Holocaust within memory. In montage, documentary images of the atrocities confront the viewer with the evidence of what seems unimaginable. Oshima's film has entirely different subject matter; the link seems to be more in the stylistic daring and the visual and voiced confrontational style Resnais brought to the film essay.

Of course, the long take and shot sequence have another heritage in Japan, as they were brought to an apex by Mizoguchi Kenji. Mizoguchi's long takes are elegant tools of a visual narration. Camera movement and framing in Mizoguchi beg comparison with brushstroke and scroll composition in Japanese painting, or with the rhythmic flows and punctuations of Japanese music. Yet in many ways Oshima's long takes in *Night and Fog in Japan* strive more for the dramatic tension of the closed mise-en-scène of a single space that Alfred Hitchcock achieves in *Rope*. Convergence in the fifties of theories of the long take set the stage for Oshima's effort, theories expounded in an essay by Alexandre Astruc, "What Is Mise-en-Scène?"

Night and Fog in Japan's minimalism and rigor, its extreme emphasis on the long take, are coupled with an equally important emphasis on theatricality. Theatricality in the film includes the concept of a topical theater, one that can risk direct political reference and intervention. It is a theater that thrives on the tension between improvisational and scripted elements. The film's theatricality includes restricted spatiality; the "action" is mainly statically located in a set of rooms in the present and past. Gesture, lighting, and spatial alignment color the dialogue exchanges; while verbal signifiers are, in a sense, highly privileged in a film displaying such theatricality, it is cinematic form that shapes the reception of these words. Sato (1973: 87–89) presents the film as so concerned with the rendering of dialogue and conveying a political message that formal concerns were treated as insignificant, as its topicality and timeliness demanding a rushed production schedule. In contrast, Polan (1983: 104–107) presents the film as one in which form intricately effects a political purpose, masterfully developing a "political language of film."

I agree with Polan, and with others such as Danvers and Tatum (1986), that the camera work here is graphically fascinating, a new form of cinematic theatricality. Yet Sato's view of the film as one made under severe temporal constraint and with an emphasis on verbal debate to the detriment of careful composition or montage is historically important as an indication of how the film was received, at least by some, in Japan.

Let me suggest that the shot, its framing and changeability, can be seen as the index of the film's theatricality. The studied quality of Oshima's shots up until this point continues here and becomes even more pronounced in the sense that given a primarily dialogic form, we are much more attentive to uses of framing. Camera movement creates a theatricality that is spatial and subject to reframing, a blocking of character interaction that is specifically visual and cinematic. This kind of filmic theatricality and compositional insistence has much in common with the cinematic strategies of Straub and Huillet, particularly their *Othon* and *Moses and Aaron* (Turim 1984, 1986). Oshima's swish pan movements do suggest a greater improvisational, or more random, element to framing than Straub and Huillet's combination of static shots and deliberate slow camera movements, but this difference need not be determinate. The element I wish to compare is attention to the frame and composition as regards the utterance and dramatic confrontations. In both cases, spoken lines are construed as framed, placed, and composed in a textual order, a semiotic order. The cinema becomes a device for redefining theatrical language.

The film is set in 1960, the year it was made and the time of the defeat of the protests against the security treaty. It opens with a shot sequence lasting for the first ten minutes of the film, beginning with an image filled with fog and moving into the space of a wedding ceremony, then panning in response to dialogue exchanges. Nozawa (Watanabe Fumio), a journalist and former member of the Zengakuren, is marrying a young student, Reiko (Kuwano Miyuki), who was a participant in the most recent demonstrations. The reception is attended by his former comrades, many of whom also have become professionals somewhat distanced from political struggles, and by her young female friends. Also in attendance are an older liberal professor, Utakawa (Akutagwa Hiroshi), and his wife and another married couple of the groom's generation, Nakayama (Yoshizawa Takao) and his wife, Misako (Koyama Akiko). The attributes of these various characters and others are learned in the course of the ceremony and its disruption by two uninvited guests, Oota (Tsugawa Nasahiko), who is actively being pursued by the police as a result of his participation in last June's political demonstration, and Takumi (Hayami Ichiro), who has taken the identity of a friend of Nozawa's who died during an earlier political struggle and serves to initiate a ghostly haunting of the past.

Weddings were configured by the new left, not only in Japan but also in the United States and elsewhere at this time, as bourgeois and traditional ceremonies much at odds with "the movement" (Bates 1992). Staging such a ceremony's disruption, especially through the haunting of a fallen comrade, becomes a brilliant means of condensing the conflicts of the period. As he will in *Ceremonies,* Oshima makes much of the formal staging typical of a Japanese wedding, using exaggerated symmetrical configurations to heighten the artificiality of the tradition. In contrast, the entrance of the disruptive figures interrupts the symmetry, pointing to the fog and the memories of events occurring in the past and outside this ritually organized space (Turim 1980, 1981–1982).

This haunting is accomplished by a series of flashbacks to two prior time periods: one series covers a period ten years earlier in which the first AMPO demonstrations took place and the Zengakuren were formed; the second series chronicles the recent protests of the renewal of the treaty on its tenth-year expiration. Also at issue is the history of the Zengakuren; in the fifties, when Nozawa belonged, student protest was dominated by Communist party directives, despite much autonomous feeling and dissension by many students. By 1960 the Zengakuren again tried to assert autonomy, but internal conflicts, intensified by the failure of the protest to stop the treaty, hampered this effort. Since Nozawa represents the Communist party affiliation of the Zengakuren and Reiko those who tried to break with this affiliation, their marriage represents, on an allegorical plane, the reconciliation of factions on an institutional basis, without any resolution of the issues. Professor Utakawa's initial speech at the marriage ceremony expresses this symbolic reading of the intergenerational alliance and introduces his preoccupation with a united-front politics. Nakayama joins him in denying both defeat and disunity.

In my book, *Flashbacks in Film* (1989), I present this film as part of a modernist cinematic redefinition of the flashback. Linked to an earlier flashback preoccupation of the cinema as a device to represent both memory and history, modernist instances of the flashback dissect both terms. Some fragment memory processes, exploring the complexity of memory traces and unconscious images, while others self-consciously focus on historical memory, its meaning, interpretation, and ideology. In *Night and Fog in Japan* some memories are given as stories told, the illustrations of internal narrators' interventions. They are stories used to raise questions of political ethics and theory, or as Oshima put it, to "offer a revolutionary critique of revolutionary practice" (interview with author). If they, like psychological flashbacks, give us the return of the repressed, the repressed they bring back are historical events as the object of a political repression, as it occurs in a collective consciousness. Oota and Takumi are accusing the guests at the wedding of both having forgotten and having betrayed the past, by refusing to learn from it.

Other flashbacks to the June demonstrations surge forth as memory associations. The two intruders each insist that the unresolved issues of the past be remembered and faced. This insistence takes the form of recalling two figures from the past. One is Takao (Sakonji Hiroshi), a Zengakuren from the fifties who committed suicide after being accused by the Communist party faction of helping an informer escape; the alleged informer is accused also as a Trotskyite, and Takao in turn is called "imperialist." The accuracy of the accusation should be unquestioned according to the party. Raising questions, as Takao did, violates the necessity of following party discipline and accepting its positions as absolute truth. Forcing Nozawa, Professor Utakawa, and Nakayama to remember Takao is asking them to face their Stalinist pasts. The young need to learn about those pasts and understand how their new Zengakuren is not so different, even if it is professed to be anti-Stalinist.

The other figure, Kitami (Ajioka Toru), is addressed to this younger generation, as he was a friend of Reiko's who was wounded in the June demonstrations. Kitami is presented by Oota as having disappeared after Reiko abandoned him at the hospital on meeting Nozawa. These two figures, each a comrade who has disappeared, one through suicide and the other mysteriously, illustrate the mistakes and callousness of the movement. Political movements can engender such sacrifices, martyrs who die directly in the line of fire or people like these whose demise is more foggy. In forcing Nozawa, Reiko, and their guests to remember Takao and Kitami, Takumi and Oota recall how the personal betrayals are linked to the political issues.

This linking of the personal and the political seems to me to be one of the film's greatest strengths. It evokes the slogan introduced by feminists in

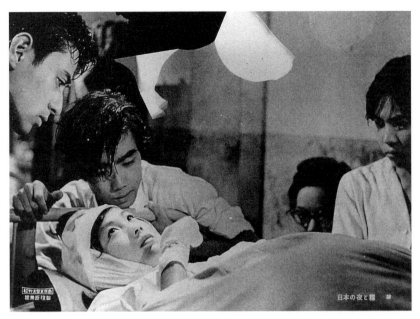

7. Reiko, wounded in the hospital following the June demonstrations, will be charged by her former comrades with abandoning Oota on meeting the journalist Nozawa, one of the ways the film links the personal and the political. *Nihon no yoru to kiri* (Night and Fog in Japan, 1960). Still courtesy of Oshima Productions.

the United States, "the personal is political," while it simultaneously infuses the political intrigue with subjective intrigues of jealousy and ambition. For example, several of the men were attracted to Misako, while she chose Nakayama, the leader and the most Stalinist of the group. This colors the anti-Stalinist attacks on Nakayama with residual personal jealousies, and even suggests that Takao's suicide and Nozawa's marriage to Reiko are to some extent motivated by their loss of Misako.

The wedding of Nozawa and Reiko in the present is doubled by that of Nakayama and Misako in the flashback. This is a major key to the narrative structure, a parallel marked by a graphic match from one wedding to the other. The film's dual weddings raise issues of women's role in the political struggle; here women are mainly marginalized, with Misako representing the passive wife of the older-generation militants while Reiko, initially more active and self-defined, marries as a gesture away from this active role, into the older generation. The marriages also display the relationship of political struggle to desire, weaving this through other questions.

8. Three freeze-frames mark the demonstration flashbacks: in this one, the frame is filled with red flags against a night sky. *Nihon no yoru to kiri* (Night and Fog in Japan, 1960). Still courtesy of Oshima Productions.

Late in the film, Oota's use of Kitami's story is challenged by another militant who says he not only knows where Kitami is but spoke with him recently. He adds that Kitami does not think at all like Oota. Here we flash back to images of Kitami rising from his hospital bed to address Reiko. Kitami's bandages from head to foot become symbolic of those sacrificed in a movement and then abandoned by comrades. His bandages begin to represent the illness of the movement itself.

Night and Fog in Japan ends with the arrest of Oota, followed by a debate on the response to this event by all present. The last words are a droning denunciation of Oota's radicalism by Nakayama in favor of Communist party fidelity. Visually, the film ends on the dark fog clouding the exterior, visually commenting on the voice-over to which no one any longer listens.

Oshima's *Night and Fog in Japan* echoes Kurosawa's *No Regrets for Our Youth* in its flashback structure and concerns; it differs in its treatment of political involvement and memory. Oshima breaks with Kurosawa's humanism that salutes the courage of the righteous in the past and reinscribes that respect in another form in the present. If Oshima is concerned with presenting the issues that led to political involvement through retrospection, this is coupled with a harsh critique of political motivations and organizations. Memory sequences are sites of reexamination, and the angles on the past are not defensive or celebratory but sharp and analytical. Even more negative is his ending on the fog of betrayal and uncertainty (Polan 1985: 107).

This dark fog gains its full visual impact in reference to the tableau shots elsewhere in the film. There are three other freeze-frames, each in a demonstration flashback: in one, the wide-screen frame is filled with red flags against a night sky; another has torches against the sky; and the third is a high angle on a pavement flowing with blood. The banners summon comparison with Eisenstein's *October* (1929), in which the framing of angular banners in montage is so characteristic of the dynamic editing of that film. Here the homage is not without irony, as Eisenstein's Leninist film is here echoed in a film highly critical of the Japanese Communist party. The euphoria and promise Eisenstein emphasized in celebrating the Bolshevik Revolution is remembered here in images diachronically counterposed and metaphorically covered with images of fog and bloody defeat.

THE REAL OFFSCREEN AND THE WIDESCREEN TABLEAUS

Three days after the film's release, on October 12, 1960, the president of Japan's Socialist party, Asanuma Inejiro, was assassinated by a young right-wing nationalist. The next day Shochiku pulled Oshima's film from distribution. Oshima's wedding to Koyama Akiko took place shortly thereafter and the groom used the occasion to stage a protest mirroring the mise-en-scène of *Night and Fog in Japan,* delivering a blistering address in protest of the film's shelving to the Shochiku management among the guests. In light of the questioning treatment of autobiographical and auteurist criticism discussed in chapter 1, this marriage ceremony stages an answer to industry mistreatment by borrowing its mise-en-scène from the fictional universe the censorship of which was the issue of the hour; it envelops the real with the theatricality of fiction, just as the fiction reaches out to pierce itself with references to reality.

One is struck by the symmetry and interpenetrability of offscreen politics and those contained and dissected within the frames of the widescreen tableaus. If I began this chapter speaking of Oshima's Eastmancolor widescreen tableau images, just as I have closed it, it is for a purpose. To me they signify the traumatic and ambiguous inscription of these four important films within a specifically Japanese history of production at the Shochiku Ofunu, that is to say, as innovative gestures within a commercial and conservative production system. For just as the challenge of working against a system from within invigorates the films, so does working with such resources as widescreen and color and such collaborators as Uno Koji (set decoration), Ishodo Toshiro (script collaboration), Manabe Riichiro (music), and Kawamata Takashi (camera) give to the project of a cinema of contestation an aesthetic vitality, a grand palette of sounds and images selected and ordered with innovative significance.

We remember, in watching them now, the history of Oshima's tenure at Shochiku, ending so abruptly when the management of the studio pulled *Night and Fog in Japan* from distribution a mere three days into its theatrical release (Oshima 1992: 54–58; Sato 1973: 87–89). All four films can be read retrospectively from that moment of political censorship. In doing so, one remembers images from across the films, one puzzles out their allegorical meanings and ruminates on their visual power, completely taken with the way they speak of a subjective attitude on the situation in Japan in 1959–1960.

CHAPTER THREE

Rituals, Desire, Death
Leaving One's Will on Film

Between 1968 and 1971, Oshima made the five films that are responsible for the growth of his international reputation. This period of intense artistic activity comes after a period in which financing for feature production proved less certain and Oshima alternated between documentary work and feature production in various genres that will be the subject of other chapters. If we now turn to these films from this three-year period of intense political, intellectual, and artistic upheaval for Japan and the world at large, it is to group together films as a larger ensemble that have been heralded as heteroclitic and unique masterpieces. Indeed, each one tempts a critic-theorist to evoke superlatives, and each presents different commentary on the charged political scene of these years. Yet it is their common historical and artistic engagement that I wish to investigate here. While recognizing the obvious stylistic differences, the focus here will be on the dialogue these films establish on philosophical and cinematic issues.

Narrative and filmic expression are interrogated in new, complexly innovative ways. Philosophically, the films address a common issue, the nature of consciousness and its virtual antithesis, the unconscious, evoking a post-Nietzschean and post-Freudian meditation on subjectivity, will, and values. Rarely has such seriousness of purpose been coupled with aesthetic success for such a sustained series of works while increasing the audience, internationally, from film to film.

Let us put this in historical context. First, the mid-sixties were the most hospitable moment historically for the distribution of what is known as "art cinema," the term that covers all cinematic expression exhibited within a commercial circuit that demands of its audience openness to different of modes of expression, to foreign cultures, or to political engagement. Many national cinemas began to thrive in a context where they were able to compete suc-

cessfully for an audience with Hollywood production, many through government subsidies, though this was not the case in Japan. Production budgets for these films are often comparatively small, but their market is global,
rather than merely national. Increased distribution aided by international festivals where companies can hook up to foreign distributors are key. Portions
of the audience for these films are intellectually or aesthetically versed, but
others are young, open to the "newness" of this cinema or drawn by its breaking of sexual mores. This vitality for national cinemas reached the crest that
Oshima and the rest of the Japanese New Wave rode in the years 1968–1971.

This vitality was matched by lively activity in Japanese art and left-wing
political movements. During these same years, an explosion of creativity
and political engagement occurred, mainly in Tokyo, but not exclusively.
This newly invigorated activism drew on earlier leftist movements, including
those surrounding the AMPO demonstrations. Earlier artistic avant-gardes
such as Butoh (an expressionist dance-theater movement) (Munroe 1994b)
and Gutai (abstract expressionist painting) (Munroe 1994c) offered their expressionism and emphasis on subjectivity as models, though sometimes as
negative models to inspire a dialectical opposition, an embrace of objec-
tivity, conceptual projects, and intellectual rigor. Late sixties activism had a
distinctively new flavor, blending politics and culture. Student strikes at the
University of Tokyo and Nihon University began with issues specific to reg-
ulations at these campuses but quickly expanded into a Maoist-inspired
questioning of Japan's industrial, technological, and financial recovery.
While the recovery was increasingly successful in economic terms, the next
generation began to question its dutiful function in an economic machine
that had developed since 1945 with Japan's emergence as a renewed capitalist power at the brink of sharing with the United States and Europe an international dominance that was facing off with an increasingly divided communist coalition of the USSR and the People's Republic of China.

Artists responded to this changing environment within Japanese culture.
Termed "obsessional," on one hand, and "conceptual," on the other, art took
to the streets and took on theory and ideas, though in different measures.
Oshima's films from this period play a leading role in this energy and activity crossing politics and art. The films often include references to the movements, or characters modeled after artists and student leaders. Beyond the
specific references, one senses the shared zeitgeist and the continuation of
the works discussed in the last chapter, but without the constraints of studio
control and the need to fit commercial genres. These films allow themselves
the same freedom of expression and conception that *Night and Fog in Japan*
had sought. Unlike the censorship that kept that film from reaching its audience, these films reached theirs, with great impact.

The first of these, *Death by Hanging*, takes on the theater of justice in contemporary Japan. It is Oshima's most Brechtian film, the embodiment of the

blending of Brecht with elements specific to Japanese theater that I discussed in relationship to Oshima and the Japanese theatrical avant-garde in chapter 2. Not only is *Death by Hanging* a strategic readjustment of Brechtian devices of distanciation to cinematic form, it invites specific comparison in its treatment of the hanging to that at the end of Brecht's *The Threepenny Opera* (1928). It also invites comparison to his *Caucasian Chalk Circle* (1948). Justice is on trial. For this reason and for its dark humor, its theoretical connections to Brecht are significant.

The necessity to repeat a hanging that fails to kill the condemned man as prelude to an interrogation of justice uses a reflexive strategy similar to the self-conscious "Finale" of *The Threepenny Opera* that announces its deus ex machina in the form of the savior on horseback who brings Macheath a reprieve after the condemned man has already mounted the gallows. Peachum's speech announces this in the famous verses that emphasize religion's complicity with the state and the ironies of a vengeful justice:

> Dear audience, we now are coming to
> The point where we must hang him by the neck
> Because it is the Christian thing to do
> Proving that men must pay for what they take
>
> But as we want to keep our fingers clean
> And you're the people we can't risk offending
> We thought we'd better do without this scene
> And substitute instead a different ending.
>
> Since this is opera not life, you'll see
> Justice give way before humanity.
> So now, to stop our story in its course
> Enter the royal official on his horse. (P. 140)

Similarly, in scene five of the *Caucasian Chalk Circle,* Brecht establishes a tone of repartee that sets the stage for the one Oshima adopts in *Death by Hanging*. Brecht's stage directions establish an intricate tableau in which characters who will soon exchange barbed comments are arranged:

> (Azdak is sitting on the seat of justice, peeling an apple. Shauva is sweeping the courtroom. On one side an invalid in a wheelchair, a doctor who is the defendant, and a lame man in rags. On the other side a young man accused of blackmail. An Ironshirt bearing the banner of the Ironshirt cops, stands at the door)

Quoting just from the first of these exchanges, we see how replete with social criticism they are, while their jocular tone in contrast to the high seriousness of the issues sets the irony:

> *Adzak:* Today, in view of the large number of cases pending, the court will hear two cases at once. Before I begin, a brief announcement: I take. (He

holds out his hand. Only the blackmailer takes out money and gives it
to him) I reserve the right to punish one of the parties here present (He
looks at the invalid) for contempt of court. (To the doctor) You are a
doctor, and you (to the invalid) are the plaintiff. Is the doctor to blame
for your condition?

The Invalid: He is. I had a stroke because of him.

Adzak: That would be professional negligence.

The Invalid: Worse than negligence. I loaned him money for his studies.
He's never repaid a cent, so when I heard he was treating patients for
nothing, I had a stroke.

The scene continues in this vein, until all the elements of the original tableau
are imbricated in complex relationships, each of which inverts the expectations previously established. Finally, Adzak's judgments are announced together, paralleling and providing closure to his opening remarks, and a
singer with his musicians enters to provide further commentary in verse:

Every pleasure costs full measure, funds are rarely come by squarely,
Justice has no eyes in front or back.
That is why we ask a genius to decide and judge between us
Which is done for half a penny by Adzak.

We will see how similar this is to Oshima's strategy in his extended sequences
interrogating the judgment of officials as they consider procedure after
their condemned Korean prisoner fails to be executed.

The ironic twists of fate *Death by Hanging*'s accused criminal faces before
a judicial apparatus also recall Franz Kafka's *The Trial,* particularly the long
exchange between Joseph K. and the priest in chapter 10, "In the Cathedral."
The debate on the "doorkeeper to the Law" parable ends with lines ironically reinscribing the parable and its dismissive attitude toward all plaintiffs:

"You must first see who I am," said the priest. "You are the prison chaplain,"
said K., groping his way nearer to the priest again. . . . "That means I belong
to the Court," said the priest. "So why should I want anything from you?
The Court wants nothing from you. It receives you when you come and
it dismisses you when you go." (Kafka 1968: 278)

In addition, *Death by Hanging* shares many qualities with works of the theater
of the absurd. It uses laughter to the philosophical ends sought by absurdist
comedy, extending the verbal and situational ironies of Brechtian theater and
Kafka into a more slapstick humor of absurd actions, amplified by repetitions.
What emerges is a truly unique film, whose use of cinematic expression as-
tounds at each turn, as it blends work on distanciation with an appreciation
and exploration of the unconscious not often directly found in Brecht,
though sometimes implied in Brecht's depiction of raging jealousies and
greed. *Death by Hanging,* in its continual play with fantasy and the unconscious

of representation, conjoins Brechtian and Freudian thought to generate a complex image of racism, repression, and contestatory consciousness.

The premise of *Death by Hanging* is that a man, sentenced to death, identified only by the letter "R," is rendered amnesiac through a failed hanging and thus unconscious of his crime. The simple remedy for the Japanese officials would be to rehang the condemned man, but according to at least some interpretations of Japanese law presented in the film, a man who has no memory cannot be legally punished, as he is neither cognizant of his crime nor able to understand its punishment. This creates a situation in which the embarrassed officials assembled must reawaken the conscious knowledge of identity, and thus the past and guilt.

Yet the film does not simply tell the story of this process. Rather, it explores contradictions in it. It is not simply a film against capital punishment, even though that is its seeming point of departure. Critics who desire a film focusing on capital punishment alone, such as Keiko McDonald, charge the film with not clearly developing this issue: "We feel somewhat oversaturated by his overt attack on Japanese imperialism and are discouraged from a more serious intellectual reflection upon capital punishment that a less 'belligerent' film might have made possible" (McDonald 1983: 149). Such criticism seeks a simpler message from the film than its open-ended exploration of situational contradictions implies. The film is polyvalent, exploring issues and statements through their logical incompatibilities, especially when these propositions are projected to their "logical" conclusions. The film plays with if-then suppositions juxtaposed to each other in a constant challenge to a stable and conclusive center, or end point. The state's ability to achieve justice is the question on which these suppositions pivot.

Oshima's concern with issues of justice and the state are grounded in reference to a "real" incident, even if he addresses them in a mode that defies realism. The script is indeed inspired by an actual incident that occurred in 1958, the murder of two Japanese schoolgirls by a Korean named Ri Chin'u. This murder preoccupied the Japanese press and public. According to Sato (1973: 285–287), Ri called the newspapers, talked about how the victims had been killed, and gave details of clothing as a tease to the investigation. His taped telephone conversations were broadcast. After his arrest, he wrote a fictional story about the murders for a short story competition. He displayed no regret or wish to reform. Ri corresponded with a female journalist, a pro-Pyongyang Korean, named Bok Junan. San-ichi Shabo press published these letters as a volume entitled *Crime, Death and Love*. Several writers and filmmakers adapted this story, including an Ishihara Shintaro segment of a compilation film called *Love of a Twenty-Year-Old*. Given the way the case presented from the outset a perpetrator of a crime whose compulsions included seeking publicity, and given the mythologizing by the media that preceded the work of Oshima and his collaborators, the film flirts with romanticizing criminality, as Adam Knee (1987) suggests of this and other Oshima films.

Yet *Death by Hanging* does not simply present R's crimes as "political in origin," though at one point in the film such a statement is made. The film treats the rape not as a political act, per se, but as a *displacement,* in the psychoanalytic sense. Instead of acting politically and consciously, the oppressed subject acts out a displaced anger and frustration. In the analysis that follows, I will show how this focus on displacement occurs and what its value is in negating the criminal as object of fascination. This negation allows directly ideological questions about justice and judgment, rather than antiheroic identifications.

The story of the script's genesis is particularly intriguing in this light. According to Sato, Oshima solicited a script from Fukao Michinori, which took a more straightforward narrative approach. This script was a more direct account of Ri's motivations as a murderer, ending with the moment of his arrest. Sato contends that a radically austere budget imposed by the production companies, ATG and Sozosha, necessitated changes (1973: 290–291). Oshima demanded rewriting and four men collaborated on a new script: Oshima and Fukao were joined by Tamura Takeshi and Sasaki Mamoru. It was this economically conditioned rewriting, according to Sato, that gave the film its present form of beginning with R's failed hanging and staging the attempts of the state to reestablish his identity to permit a rehanging; this form gave the script a great economy of location, with many scenes confined to the prison execution chambers (Sato 1973: 292–293). Oshima tells a different story of the genesis of the script. He begins, "I'd been thinking of devoting a work to Ri ever since he committed his crime in 1958. I wrote one script in 1963, the year after the execution." Oshima goes on to emphasize the importance of Ri's letters in sparking his interest, as well as the collaborative participation of many in attaining the film's final innovative form (Oshima 1992: 168–169). What is clear despite the discrepant accounts is that ten years after the occurrence of the murder, a group of scriptwriters and actors collaborated to create a film that treats this incident conceptually and presents a major innovation in film by so doing. Writing and rewriting moved *Death by Hanging* to a vantage point in history where theoretical concerns could blossom.

One clue to the conceptual tone that comes to fruition in *Death by Hanging* lies in a series of seven intertitles that punctuate segments of the film. Each punctuating statement begins with R as subject, but each states the conditions under which R as subject is uncertain, in ways we will explore in detail. Each of these seven segments of the film takes a decidedly different tack, shifting the conception and depiction of R. While the intertitles, written in Japanese characters on large-grid graph paper, could be interpreted as being from R's own hand, they function similarly to the verbal placards Brecht used in staging, announcing the action to come to create distance and to emphasize the literary chapter markings over theatrical flows of "real" action. The use of R instead of the actual Korean name, Ri Chin'u, lends to these statements the quality of logical or even mathematical propositions. R's identity becomes, metaphorically, a "variable" in an equation. Associations here include Ludwig Wittgenstein's philosophical investigation of language that produces such statements as "Thus the propositions 'A has a gold tooth' and 'A has a headache' are not used analogously" (Wittgenstein 1958: 53). The use of "R" also evokes French postwar literature, both the existential novel where the protagonist can be designated as simply "the stranger" in Albert Camus's *L'Etranger* and the *nouveau roman* where the abstraction of character gives us "A" and "X" in Alain Robbe-Grillet's *L'Année dernière à Marienbad*. Calling his protagonist "R," Oshima not only marks this character's abstraction and distance from the real Ri Chin'u, he also focuses on language and its relationship to sentences and therefore to truth and judgment. This prefigures and illustrates many of the issues that will later be taken up by Lyotard in *The Differend* and *Au Juste,* works themselves indebted to Wittgenstein. Consider the section "Stakes" in Lyotard's *The Differend* as a commentary on Oshima's R as a variable whose identity is in political dispute, and on statements made throughout the film's dialogues (A. stands for author):

> To convince the reader (including the first one, the A.) that thought, cognition, ethics, politics, history or being, depending on the case, are in play when one phrase is linked onto another. To refute the prejudice anchored in the reader by centuries of humanism and of "human sciences" that there is "man," that there is "language," that the former makes use of the latter for his own ends, that if he does not succeed in attaining these ends, it is for want of good control of language by means of a better language. To defend and illustrate philosophy in its differend with its two adversaries: on its outside, the genre of economic discourse (exchange, capital); on its inside, the genre of academic discourse (mastery). By showing that the linking of one phrase onto another is problematic and that this problem is the problem of politics, to set up a philosophical politics apart from the politics of "intellectuals" and politicians. To bear witness to the *differend.* (1988: xii–xiii)

Oshima's argument with humanism may not be as absolute and vociferous as Lyotard's, a question we will examine repeatedly in this chapter. Empathy for others and respect for individual rights remain a concern for a filmmaker who grew up under the dissolution of individual rights by the Japanese militarist government engaged in the Pacific War. Oshima wants to locate his critique of language much more firmly as one opposed to the official language of the state. Yet the dialogue of his film and the naming strategy that gives us "R" should be heard as bearing witness to the *differend,* demonstrating that as Lyotard suggests, "The possibility of reality, including the reality of the subject, is fixed in networks of names 'before' reality shows itself and signifies itself in experience" (1988: 46).

SEEING AN EXECUTION: THE TABOO AND THE FAILED ACTION

We will look first at the "false" documentary opening that precedes the film's central exploration of R's uncertain recovery of subjectivity. The documentary tone here is a ruse that provides entrance into the film's narrative, allowing for a shift in filmic address and in spectator positioning that can be quite disconcerting. The film posits a documentary on capital punishment interrupted by the failure of the execution that was to provide its typical example; the real is to be derailed from the start. This documentary opening is similar to that in *Hiroshima, Mon Amour,* but whereas Alain Resnais and Marguerite Duras mix the documentary with a poetic voice-over of lovers, the ploy of Oshima's pseudodocumentary is different. The paradox of Oshima's overture is to mimic "the real" as it is coded by documentary and yet to diverge radically as the rupture produced by the false hanging breaks away from any documentary coding. The result is that any fictional coding of reality is also troubled.

In this pseudodocumentary beginning, before the rupture, the singular issue *is* capital punishment. Graphics introduce a poll dated June 1957 that gives Japanese attitudes toward capital punishment: 71 percent for the abolition of capital punishment, 16 percent against the abolition, and 13 percent undecided. While these numbers look refreshing from a U.S. standpoint nearly forty years later, with large numbers of the population clamoring for more death sentences, they are even more impressive as a measure of Japan's postwar antiviolence, its aversion to its traditional military and state codes of punishment.

When the narrator of the embedded documentary asks, "Did you ever see an execution or an execution chamber?" he provides the lead, reiterated graphically in a set of intertitles, into the first representation of hanging in the film. The aerial long shot of the prison that opens the pseudodocumentary and subsequent shots of the prison execution chamber inscribe the cinematic panopticon overview of modern institutional architecture. Within an edifice primarily devoted to modern incarceration, the persistence of the death sentence can be seen as a sign of the atavistic desire to see punishment, even though actual viewing is limited in the United States and Japan. "Seeing punishment" and "seeing an execution" are phrases for which it is useful to evoke how Foucault looks at the justice system in his *Discipline and Punish.* In this groundbreaking work, first published in France in 1975, Foucault traces the historical movement from the spectacle of punishment to incarceration based on surveillance and on the panopticon as a model of prison architecture. Similarly, in Oshima's film the spectacle of punishment is coupled with an opening sequence that visually explores the architectonics of the prison as a site of punishment. So witnessing an execution is rife with contradictory potential; on one hand, the spectator might feel repulsion in viewing an act that the society commits in a newly sanitized and secretive manner, and on the other, the film addresses self-consciously a darker impulse, the desire to see and to celebrate a retaliatory, spectacular killing, a primitive spectacle that has now become virtually taboo to actual vision. While the question "Did you ever see an execution?" is pronounced in the pseudodocumentary with the implication that witnessing an execution would evoke one's conscience, this question bears the titillating promise of violating the taboo, offering the state execution as forbidden spectacle. The sanitized execution chamber that opens to a cutaway spectacle for the film's viewers is watched through a picture window by the gallery of invited official guests within the film, doubling the gaze on the scene. Anachronistically, for all its architectural modernism, the facility features a simple rope noose. By making the most visually of the doubling of the gaze and the anachronistic noose, the scenography emphasizes the contradictions of the forbidden spectacle.

The sound mix provides other interpretive challenges. Cymbal-like metallic echoes punctuate the film's titles, as they will key other moments in the film, as hushed voices gathered from some extrafilmic space provide low echoes of words; we hear "Germany" and "United States" pronounced in English in this low babel. Breaking with documentary coding, this sound mix paradigm will recur at other crucial junctures in the film, introducing another audial space, entirely imaginary. In this space we hear echoes of other nations where the state has murdered with racist motivations under the guise of law, if not justice; just the country's names evoke official lynchings in the United States and the Holocaust gas chambers in Germany. Arguments that will later be raised comparing Koreans sentenced to death in Japan to U.S. blacks historically are only suggested here through fragmented litotes. Characteristically, in such sound mixes, the film exposes more signifiers than will be understood on a first viewing, or by all viewers.

The voice-over also plays a crucial role in similarly amplifying and complicating the images of this pseudodocumentary. Voice-over description fills in colors for the black-and-white image, describing "salmon walls" and telling us the "curtains are dark yellow." Such decorator details are superfluous in one sense, unless one reads the obsessive detail of this descriptive voice ironically, as a semiotic joke on metacommentary, on establishing the scene. Then the voice makes good on this joke, commenting on religious ceremonies afforded prisoners and contrasting its general description with the images' specific representation, their narrative. The voice says that the "Prison Chaplain will perform his last role," and goes on to point out the Buddhist altar used for a last blessing, but tells us that "if the prisoner is Christian, the doors remain closed." The image shows us closed doors, our first indication of R's religion, and an indication of R's possible Korean ethnicity, although there are, of course, Japanese Christians and Korean Buddhists. Still, it is this sly and oblique aporia opened between a distanced and general voiced commentary and the concreteness of the image representing R's execution that first indicates R's religion and ethnicity. Similarly, the omissions of this detailed voice speak volumes. We note that the image shows R struggling furiously against his captors and protesting physically his pending hanging, while the voice methodically stays with the general case. The film demands attention to such discursive details, ironies embedded in just such discrepancies between sound and image.

"R's Body Refuses Capital Punishment" introduces a segment in which the body acts out resistance to the state. The intertitle emphasizes the "body," through this phrase separating the physical body from a notion of unified subjectivity. As Pascal Bonitzer (1970: 31) notes, what is at stake in the failed hanging is the hole opened in the fiction by an impossible representation. That which logically cannot happen, is represented as happening even so.

We might also make the connection to the notion of the "failed action" in Freud, an action that derails due to the force of unconscious desires that have not been addressed by the subject. Here the narrative rather than the subject is at stake; the narrative itself performs as if it were governed by an unconscious, a prior repression overdetermining the representation and sequence of events. This explosive unconscious "erupts" through a self-consciously designed organization, of course; the "failed action" is a theoretical ploy.

The "farce" that ensues, first in this segment, then repeated across the various segments, is a highly structured dialogue investigation of all the issues surrounding justice and the past. This farce is staged as chaotic and often hilarious, playing with the surface interaction between the officials and their condemned man. The ensemble acting is caught in mobile long takes that glide gracefully around the movements of the characters. Tight framing on the exchanges between the officials invigorates the lines of their debate, while R's body remains impassive among them.

The refrain for this first interchange among the officials is "I am not responsible." R's heartbeat fills the sound track, as a low, rhythmic reminder that despite R's stillness, he is not dead. The officials discuss the time allotted the prisoner to die and the meaning of "Section 479," with its exclusion of corporal punishment for incompetent offenders. Desperately they attempt artificial respiration in an attempt to get out of the double-bind situation presented by their impassive, but not-yet-dead prisoner.

Revealing lines connect the officials to their prior service in the Pacific War, and thus their current philosophy of punishment to the Japanese militarist tradition: "During the war, in the colonies, we used to have to wake the nearly dead in order for their executions to take place. Death only has meaning if you know it's coming." This offers a latent and much more negative, because less humanitarian, version of the logic behind forbidding execution of the incompetent. The link to colonial occupation presents another means of preparing the emergence of the Korean issues, paradigmatically. Thus, later on, R will be accused of faking his amnesia, backed by the comparison to "war criminals who used that trick," and eventually, as we shall see, the agony of the war in the memories of these officials will explode from its repression to dominate a scene later in the film. A psychoanalytic structure underlies this Brechtian film at every level. Not restricted to the psyches of individual characters, psychic mechanisms inform representation and narrative structure.

ACTING OUT IN THE THEATERS OF MEMORY

"R does not accept being R" announces segments that obliquely investigate the nature of consciousness and the unconscious, deconstructing in the process what we might mean by a whole or unified identity. Memory must be reawakened through such strategies as reading the narrative of the crime from the trial transcript. When this fails, the officials try "to communicate through the senses." Gestural communication fails, too. First they maintain a choke hold on R, then R mimics the gesture at their urging. Not only does the physical, the gestural, fail to provoke memory, the mirroring is nearly lethal, as the Education Officer admonishes R, "Not so hard." The Education Officer's telling R "This is about you" restores only R's recent, friendly memory of the Education Officer himself and not the victim he is playing, as R says, "Haven't seen you in a long time. How are you doing?" Representation itself seems to fail, but nonetheless, as the officials need representation to work, they seek other strategies.

Their next step is the theatrical presentation, leading to a series of increasingly more complete reenactments. The first reenactment takes place in the corridor of the prison, performed by the Education Officer. He offers an evocative description: "The spring breeze is wonderful. You pedal harder, hair blowing in the breeze. You sense an exciting smell, you wonder, 'Will she sleep with me?'" Then the officer comically adds, "I'm only guessing what you felt." Imagining the other proves no easy task, for it inevitably involves projecting from a self inadequate to the task. So a minute later, when the Prison Doctor tries to play the rape victim, his effort is undone by a physical discrepancy, as he touches himself, noting, "I do not have soft breasts." And then the reenactment itself comically falls apart, pressed by the immediacy of the moment, with the ironically self-incriminating statement by the doctor, "I don't feel like rape *all of a sudden.*"

What this moment emphasizes is that when the officers play the parts, they display a virtual inability to stay identified with the victim. Instead, they exhibit a male predisposition to identify with the rapist. If they try to do both, they are unable to play the parts at all. These failures introduce gender positioning as key to the theatrics of memory and identification, as well as issues of justice, again preparing for the later sequences when the two female victims and the sister are introduced. The absurdist comedy is based not only on an inversion of roles but also on an inversion of processes; rather than evoke R's memory and guilt, the officers keep revealing their own.

"R Acknowledges the Existence of R as a Stranger," the title of section three, resonates with existentialism and the foreigner as other, or stranger. It is full of irony. It presents the important context of these issues in Japan, reminding the viewer, through the dialogue, that there is no naturalized citizenship in Japan, nor are the children of noncitizen residents eligible for citizenship. In fact, a more recent case in which a Japanese couple sought citizenship for a child of Korean immigrant parentage whom they adopted emphasizes how adamant Japanese law has been in enforcing the pretense of "Japanese ethnicity" as a prerequisite for Japanese citizenship. This section of the film also looks at the specificity of Koreans in Japan as an immigrant minority group, focusing on their forced immigration under Japanese occupation. The information concerning the Korean context in Japan is fully theatricalized in the Brechtian learning-play mode.

This staging begins with the reciting of the verdict of the second crime, the rape of a second girl, who had been reading near her high school. The officers pantomime to the recited narration, then begin repeating lines the narrator says that R said, a doubling that gives us in microcosm the repetitions of reenactments that are the motor force driving much of the film. In explaining this crime, the officer introduces R's Korean heritage, his Chosen-jin (Korean) name. R's response, "What is a Korean?" leads to another attempt at reeducation. Subsequently, this is temporarily deferred as a too-complicated history of races and nationhood. A comic irony grows from all responses, as, for example, an officer alludes regretfully to the physiognomic similarity between Koreans and Japanese, and indicates the racial prejudice underlying their assumptions by saying, "I wish his skin were black, it would be easier." Unsuccessful with the Korean question, they continue with the crime narrative, only to have R stop them with other basic questions, such as "What is rape?" (comic response: "For me it's pure theory, I haven't felt that way in a long time. Perhaps the younger men can explain"), but this only leads to the more basic "What is carnal desire?" (comic response: "What is not permitted between some men and women").

Next they try to reestablish the scene of his family background. Their version of a scene from Korean family life is a compendium of stereotypes of the underclass, including argumentative siblings, a drunken father, a passive mother, a deaf-mute. Their "stage" directions to each other reveal the depth

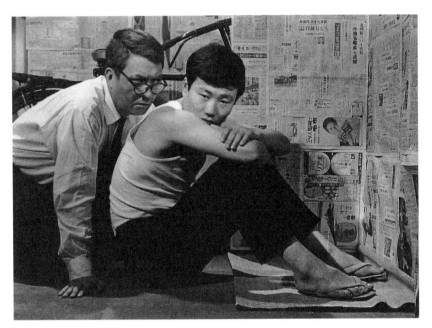

9. The newsprint wallpaper provides a brilliant stroke of mise-en-scène, for in addition to connoting a poor environment, it places the Korean family in a space of public discourse and current events. *Koshikei* (Death by Hanging, 1968). Still courtesy of Oshima Productions.

of their prejudice, as the admonition "Do it more like a Korean" invokes a switch to broken grammar. Yet even *they* know the contradictions in this portrayal, as they include mention of R's evening school and his reading of Dostoyevsky and Goethe as their evidence of his frustration with his upbringing. This staging of family background and the more complete version that follows undercut criminology's standard explanations for crimes of violence; the assumptions surrounding a criminal's motivation are shown to be not only standard templates, but ones constructed with prejudice.

The next section, "R Tries to Be R," takes place in a room at the prison that is now dressed for this scene by the addition of newspaper wallpaper. It is a brilliant stroke of mise-en-scène, for besides connoting a poor environment, it places the Korean family in a space of public discourse and current events. A picture window off to one side provides a "viewing room" for the officials assembled in front of the Japanese flag, while a U.S. flag is hung on the side. The officials' verbal "stage" directions continue to reveal their racism, as an officer is urged to "be more vulgar" in playing the father. He complies by parading around with his hands pointing from his crotch in simulation of an erect penis. R follows the urging of the Education Officer

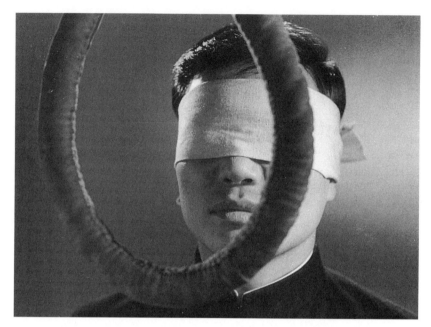

10. Framed in close-up by the noose still hanging in the prison's execution chamber, R "acts out" embracing the register of the imaginary within representation. *Koshikei* (Death by Hanging, 1968). Still courtesy of Oshima Productions.

and for the first time plays himself in this continuation of the scene of family life that the various officials create for him. He does so quite passively at first. Then an Eisensteinian montage similar to the sailor's breaking of the plate in *The Battleship Potemkin* is used to show R's reactions. First used as R slowly turns his head away from the scene in long shot, then repeats the move in close-up, such emphatic temporal repetition montage becomes more active as it shows him forming a fist and standing up in protest after the officials mix a traditional song about the Yalu River and a reference to the North Korean leader Kim Il Sung into their representation.

This montage represents a break in register, an entrance into R's subjectivity. His response can be understood as a dramatic overidentification with their degraded view of what it means to be a Korean. R *acts out* seeing himself as excrement in a most vivid way.

To act out (*mise-en-acte, agieren*) is a psychoanalytic construct indicating actions taken by a subject in the grip of his or her unconscious wishes and fantasies. These repetitive gestures return from a repressed past that is precisely not remembered; *agieren* is to be contrasted to *erinnern*, to remember, as a different way of bringing the past into the present. The gestures appear absurd until the underlying psychoanalytic logic is revealed. This film introduces a theoretical tension between acting out and remembering that will inform several of the Oshima films from this period; we shall see similar play in *Diary of a Shinjuku Thief* and *Ceremonies*. The tension here is heightened by juxtaposition to acting out in the theatrical sense of the term, the repetitive performance of scenes by the officers.

Through the introduction of "acting out" the film fully embraces the register of the imaginary within representation, first introduced in the failed hanging. Framed in close-up by the noose still hanging in the prison's execution chamber, in pantomime R turns the noose into a toilet pull and the trapdoor beneath his feet into a floor toilet. In this imaginary position he invents a further cycle of degradation, scatalogically eating tapeworms from his excrement. The psychoanalytic logic of a failure at identification is thus superseded by an imaginary acting out that is in fact an overidentification with the judgments implicit in the earlier scene; he is absorbing himself as excrement. The film's representation of the psychoanalytic failure to identify and of imaginary acting out forms a sublime representation of R's rejection of the consciousness being imposed on him.

Exploration of the filmic register of R's imaginary continues through his response to a question from his younger siblings; they seek money for an escapist adventure, and he provides an imaginary tour of Tokyo, evoking their imaginary activities through his voiced narration. It is a powerful fantasy of happiness that, in its evocation of a visit to the zoo at Ueno Park, places the young Koreans as simply children of Tokyo, capable of enjoying everyday life, but a life fantasized as having "everything free, no shopkeepers," with "everyone having a TV and refrigerators," the dream of a postscarcity anarchy, consumerism without and beyond capitalism that echoes a dream typical of some radical writings in the late sixties.

Yet the goals of the officers remain, and their solution is to again increase the quotient of realism in the setting, moving their mise-en-scène via a transition shot in the slum neighborhood R's family inhabited to the first actual scene of his crime, a "real" setting, the edge of a river where the crime is said to have occurred, to stimulate the role playing and R's memory through greater verisimilitude. A bicycle prop is added, since the victim was riding one when attacked. This is the segment Stephen Heath analyses in detail in his essay "Narrative Space" (1981: 64–69) for the manner in which the reenaction creates a metacommentary on spatial representation. Heath emphasizes two elements, the first being the voice of the Education Officer indicating R's place in the scene, a place that R does not fill. Actually, when Heath makes this point, he refers to all scenes of reenactment in the film, including ones in which the "Sister" later appears and R stands in for himself, but in this one the question of the stand-in is particularly intriguing for it will be given alternatively to two of the officials, a point I will return to shortly. Second, Heath describes in detail an editing pattern in which a glance at a cat is used to emblematize R's distraction as the Education Officer speaks to him. Heath shows that the cutaways to the cat are used to pivot the space, until finally the space the cat occupies is impossible, entailing a disappearance of a wall that should be, according to earlier shots, in the line of sight from camera to the cat. In this final shot, as the cat gazes out at the viewer, Heath says the cat "says something," as it functions as metacommentary on narrative spatial representation.

Here I would like, in addition, to extend Heath's deciphering of reflexive representation of space and events into a specific reflection on how reenactment, as strategy, is itself critiqued for the manner in which it allows us to understand history. It is the genre of docudrama with its pretense of understanding historical reality that is critiqued here, especially as it attempts to create emotional identification as a fictionalized document of the real. The question of who stands in for R here is significant. First the doctor is R's stand-in, but he quits, saying he doesn't feel that *acting* allows him to feel the desire to rape (echoing an earlier line); this failure of "method" acting is overcome by the next R stand-in, the prison's Chief of Security. However, even his zealous participatory representation stirs no identification on R's part. This sequence stages the limits of memory and identification. It implies that film should not try to be an "Education Officer," not because it could not teach, but because what it teaches through identification is suspect. If film fulfills a "duty" in re-creating the real and forcing identification with a predetermined notion of the subject, the suggestion is that such "teaching" through identification does not necessarily provoke consciousness.

That is why Oshima's film did not choose to be a direct reenactment of the life of Ri Chin'u, unlike the earlier versions of the scripts discussed above, any more than *Realm of the Senses* is a direct reenactment of the life of Abe Sada. *Death by Hanging* is rather a dissection of a reenactment at the very places that are the "scenes of crime." Oshima overcomes Brecht's own doubts that distanciation could be performed by film as a medium by employing reflexive stagings of scenes, each variation marking its distance from anything like the real past. The cat seems also, then, to mark a temporal, historical distinction, as its wandering, innocent, and impassive presence shows that the scene of the crime is at present *no longer* the scene of crime. The only scene that contains that crime is one of memory. That memory remains stubbornly unrecoverable; for the moment, though, the film will continue to pursue the real sites as a key to R's identification with the officers' reconstruction of his self.

Across a number of sites in quick succession, the film takes a visual tour permitting brief episodic encounters that ostensibly are motivated by a search for R's high school. They prefigure a strategy used in the mapping sequences of *The Battle of Tokyo*, which we will look at later in this chapter, of structural repetition and variation whose uncanny elements mimic dream

imagery. A train station and a pay telephone begin this series, suggesting failures at communication, while a shot of the group running across a bridge
in a distorted telephoto view that echoes itself through a temporally repetitive montage suggests a struggle to traverse space. Then an ice cream shop
and an empty classroom of the high school become sites that do not fulfill
their promise to bring back memory association. Finally we arrive at another
reenactment of the murder, on the rooftop of the high school. This time,
the Education Officer, carried away by *his* imagination in a kind of psychoanalytic countertransference, strangles the schoolgirl. Or perhaps we should
say, the representation bifurcates, as the play-acting divides into cross-pur-
poses. The Education Officer and R see the girl's corpse, but the others are
unable to see her. Instead of evoking R's memory and guilt for an earlier
crime, an official has now fully acted out his potential to commit the same
crime, a potential foreshadowed by the previous invocations of the perverse
desires and the war crimes of the officers.

THE DESIRE TO COMBINE THE REAL AND THE IMAGINARY

"R Was Proven to Be a Korean," the fifth segment, introduces the idea of
proof, reminding us that these mathematically constructed statements have
been leading to the conclusion of a "syllogism." Retrospectively, the perverse
logic by which the preceding sequences can be understood becomes clear
and R (or "non-R" as he is once called) is seen as a variable in an equation
of elusive identity. If R had indeed recognized R as a stranger, if he had
learned what a Korean is, and if he tried hard enough to be R, it might be
hoped that something like the desired reeducation would occur. Yet each of
the segments has failed to affect R as intended by the Japanese officials. So
even though R was *not* proven to be R by *them*, in this segment he will accept
external confirmation of his Korean identity as a first step toward effectively
becoming R, the sequence that will follow.

   The external force (in the sense that she is outside the officer's plan) is
a Korean woman, who suddenly appears, substituting herself for the
"corpse" of the schoolgirl who was "strangled" in the previous segment of
reenactment. She identifies herself as R's "sister," as she stands up from a
coffin. This new apparition is an ethereal, angelic presence and R's double.
She is at first only seen by R and the Education Officer (as was the corpse
she replaced), but gradually other of the officials see her, a device the film
uses to once again shift its register of representation into what now is no
longer an acting out of what the officials believe to have been R's thoughts
and actions, no longer R's imagination either, but a free-floating imaginary
with a life of its own. This Korean "sister" is Oshima's means of incorporating into the film the journalist Bok Junan and some of the political and
philosophical debates of her correspondence with Ri Chin'u. Prior to this

we have heard only the accusation directed at R: "You had been proud of yourself. You had phoned the police claiming to have turned killing into a high art."

One significance of the "sister" is to introduce the oppression of Korean women historically; this places R's acts of violence against women in a new context, not justifying them, but showing them to be not only a displacement of his discontent but also, ironically, a reenactment against others of the violence done to his own people. The sister taking his victim's place represents this symbolic linkage, so important to the functioning of the film.

It would be easy for the film to simply end at this point. The Korean sister would be a political redeeming angel, R would be R, the Korean, but a new R, conscious of his identity and able to expiate his crime that belonged to a less politically conscious R of the past. However, the exchanges continue, and the justifications and explanations of the sister are both logically refuted by the officials and simultaneously rejected by R. Like other scenes of political debate in Oshima's films, this one will be given no righteous central figure, and is instead ascribed an absurdist logic, where individuals talk past each other and rebuttal of each point is always possible. Such scenes usually are played for a wry and ironic humor. Finally this absurdist bent must once again be acted out, as even the officials who cannot see her demand that the "invisible woman" be executed; she is hanged at the end of the segment precisely as R was to have been hanged.

This execution initiates a celebration by the police officers, introducing the sixth section, bearing the title "R Finally Becomes R." Organized as crosscuts between shots of the drunken officials and another series of shots in which R kneels over the Korean "sister" lying on the floor, this section continues the direction taken in the previous one, but now instead of the sister talking to R as the officials overhear and even interrupt, there is a radical disjunction between the two separate sets of crosscut images and events. The comic, absurdist, satirical elements are all contained in the official's interaction, which allows the dialogue between R and the sister to not only progress seriously but call up images of illustration from R's past. It is as if the sister is analyst and R is reviewing his past with her, understanding for the first time his motivations. Passages here are taken directly from the letters of Ri Chin'u and Bok Junan, with the montage of images from R's memory projected on the scene becoming some of the most elegant of Oshima's filmwork, comparable to the film-within-the-film projections of *The Battle of Tokyo*.

Meanwhile, the officers' drunken party yields a surprising confession; the doctor, in a broken and inebriated stream-of-consciousness ramble, tells first of cutting off a woman's finger during an interrogation-torture, then of being tried and imprisoned for the murder of Pierre, his prisoner in Saigon at the end of World War II; in the throes of this memory, he speaks in

French, uttering an ambiguous "Non, je ne sais pas," either indicating the refusal of his victims to speak, which evokes his frustration, or presenting his own denial, his refusal to know what he is doing as torturer. He speaks of being abandoned by his fellow soldiers and even by the emperor after the incident and Japan's defeat. In exploring this psychology of guilt and loss, the inability of this torturer to mourn his victims, Oshima has shifted the focus from the psychology of R to that of his executioners. The doctor regrets his prison job, linking it to the tarnished record of being a convicted war criminal; he presents his role in executions as costing him twenty-nine girlfriends, as "when the trapdoor springs, the girls run away." Later the doctor will return to this incident when another of the officials confesses his wartime erotic obsession with executions: "The firing squad really stimulated me." The doctor responds, ironically, "And I was called a war criminal!"

Such scenes are crosscut with R and the sister, in changing poses that serve to support their dialogue, yielding to R's discourse on the imaginary. Taken from letters, these passages are not only psychoanalytic but also have specific Lacanian resonance, as did an image earlier in the street sequence when a store window becomes a mirror image for R searching for his identity. Consider also these passages collected here from their fragmentation as crosscut with the officials' dialogues: "When I play with myself I look at a photo of an actress, and though only a photo, my imagination begins spreading. Soon imagination has no limits. When my imagination doesn't satisfy, I begin to steal. These thefts excite my imagination. In my imagination I have done my crimes over and over again." R describes both confidence and hesitation about assuming his past given his imaginary obsessions, saying, "I only have the desire to combine the real and the imaginary," to which the sister-analyst responds, symbolically, "A dream as always."

Running parallel to this discourse on the imaginary in which "people are so vague and misty, I can't imagine them being real," is the ongoing presentation of the sister as object lesson on the real consequences of victimization of others. Early on the sister says, "When history is sad, women are sad. We women are beaten by our husbands, we bear scars, suicide scars." Much later, R makes the connection between Korean sister and Japanese victims implied both in the film's substitution of one for another and the sister's remarks on women. He asks, "What if you were raped or killed like I did to them?"

Still, R's moment of self-recognition, his "Now I can think as R," is made possible by his private exchanges with the "sister." This self-recognition launches a lyrical sequence in which R and the sister revisit the river, as she rides the bicycle. Dreamlike transformations of this image ensue, including an image of the bicycle wheel turning, the two of them in an embrace rolling down a hill, the two of them on a boat drifting down the river, first assuming a Pietà pose, then an erotic embrace. The lyricism here suggests the polysemy of their relationship, its poetry. While the theatrics of the officers in the plays within the film attempt to force memory through visual associations to the past, these images replete with references to a diverse cultural past suggest a possible future, if the context of the past could be elided.

This dreamlike moment ends as the title "R Accepts Being R for the Sake of All Rs" introduces R's statement to the officials, "I understand that I am R." This of course allows for the repetition of R's execution, after renewed debate on capital punishment, in which R proposes that in taking his life his executioners will commit murder and thus deserve the same punishment. The film ends with the noose image repeated, the trapdoor opening, the body disappearing, the same sequence as in the "documentary" overture. The circular imagery of noose, Japanese flag, and spinning bicycle wheel is complemented by a narrative looping, an ending that fulfills the film's opening by circling back to the hanging. After so many reenactments we are finally left with a reexecution, a virtual oxymoron, and the film ends with a flourish of self-conscious theatricality as the narrator thanks the spectators for watching the film.

The title "R Accepts Being R for the Sake of All Rs" has of course a ring of martyrdom, a Christian resonance (augmented by the Pietà pose), but a Christian resonance in Japan bears with it the traces of Japan's oppressed Christian minority and the larger Korean Christian community discussed earlier in relationship to the film's opening sequence. Read more theoretically, this phrase suggests that a postcolonial identity is fraught with difficulty, becoming a task to accept.

R's desire to combine the real and the imaginary is Oshima's self-conscious inscription of his own theory of film. In exploring the real, dialogue references are key indicators; they point toward the events of history and the codes of sociology and law. Dialogue is crucial throughout, especially in the first part of the film, and it is why I have quoted dialogue extensively in the above analysis, for much of the humor and irony is a matter of verbal repartee, presented in exquisite timing and visual framing. This said, the visual dimensions of the film lend themselves particularly to an opening to the imaginary; the luxuriant imagery of sensuous affinity between R and the "sister" and its visual contrast in the noose/Japanese flag imagery that pervades the film create an appreciation, even a demand for the appeal to the force of the imaginary within political consciousness. The sound track in its insertion of extradiegetic noise and music (coming from sources outside the story and in this case often beyond codes of verisimilitude) sparsely, but effectively, punctuates the dialogue, pointing also to a space of reception not limited to the scene, a space that refers to a world beyond the prison, beyond this fictional world. This imaginary space is linked to R's imagination. In this the imaginary reaches out to touch the real in the Lacanian sense of the "touché," the selective but critical points in which one recognizes how the imaginary itself is affected by a real it never directly exposes, that it is indeed unable simply to expose. This is why combining the imaginary and the real remains "a dream" to which R gives voice, necessarily a goal desired, but never entirely fulfilled or even capable of fulfillment. Marked as dreamwork, only possible through a free play and the open logic of imaginary processes, this space is deftly crafted by cinematic signifiers combined to create fiction beyond its expected limits. If the bounds of fiction are delimited by narrative, the folds, curves, and involutions of this film keep straining for a greater inclusiveness. Far-reaching allusions to dream fragments stretch the very notion of diegesis and narrative logic, reshaping them as part of a treatise on the interactions of psyche and politics.

BIBLIOPHILIA AND OTHER PERVERSIONS

Oshima's next film, in a sense, continues the investigations opened here. *Diary of a Shinjuku Thief* has a connection to Ri Chin'u. As Sato (1973: 283) explains, Ri Chin'u, like the protagonist thief in *Diary*, stole books from the library, primarily books of foreign literature, and was especially engrossed by the works of Dostoyevsky.

Oshima works this idea extracted from the letters of Ri Chin'u into a film that uses the Shinjuku Kinokuniya bookstore as a repeated setting. This multistory bookstore, relatively new at the time this film was made, is one of the largest in Tokyo, a mecca for intellectuals and students, but also for the young who collect comic books. Along with this space, the film locates itself more generally in the postwar architectural reconstruction of the Shinjuku district of Tokyo, its station, concrete plaza, high-rise buildings, and multistory restaurants and bars as the ironic site for the emergence of a youth culture ghetto; here street culture and leftist political culture mix with capitalism into a new amalgam for which the bookstore becomes the microcosm.

A visual poetics and a collage structure characterize the film; from the outset we will be challenged by imbricated sequences that choose a modernist theatrical mode and at times employ a most Eisensteinian form of montage. This visual poetics and collage combination is introduced in the first shots that offer us the time in various cities, a reference to Eisenstein's *October* (1927). This reference suggests a parallel between the montage of Oshima's film and Soviet editing theory, later amplified in other montage patterns. It also sets up a comparison between the Soviet revolutionary movements of the teens and leftist culture and protests of the sixties, in Japan, specifically, and internationally. Then a hand intervenes, breaking the clock, only to become moments later a "thief's" hands, stealing the hands of the clock. Intertextual reference, documentary riot footage, and surrealism are all presented in this short, dreamlike montage of shots, as they will be throughout the film. Oshima is playing with the modalities of representation again, fast and loose, in a manner that challenges the audience.

This act of "stealing time" gives way to the oblique entrance of an actual Japanese theater group, the Juro Karo Situation Players. This group, one of the important postwar troupes of the modernist theater movement, will set the theatrical, performative tone of the representation. However, they are introduced without a frame in which to place them, at first not even the "frame" of "street theater." Their stage is simply a staging, a sliding into the filmic frame, infusing and abusing its "realism." By this I mean that Juro himself runs into an image of Shinjuku station's cement plaza, chased by others, their shouts on the sound track introducing him as a thief. He stops, questions, "What do you think I took?" Then he takes his pants off, revealing a Japanese loincloth and a further question, "What do you think I have in here?" His stripping then exposes a rose tattoo, the symbol of the Juro theater. His pursuers, members of his troupe, stand on their hands and apologize. This "performance art" sequence, or in sixties terminology, this street theater or "happening," is a key to the modal ambience of the film. It will be further collaged with Juro appearing as a folksinger, introducing the first verse of a song that will periodically punctuate the film:

> This is Ali Baba, town of mystery
> someone asks you, morning in the sea, noon on the hill, night in the river
> Who is it? Bero, Bero, a little boy, . . .

As the refrain begins to repeat, so do the written titles, collaged with a group of three of the performers, walking rhythmically and singing along the brick wall near Shinjuku station.

This montage introduction with its inscription of song and theatricality gives way, we think, to more clearly narrative sequences. A spectator of the street theater seems to emerge as our main character, Birdy Hilltop, our Shinjuku thief whose diary this film is supposed to be. Bibliophilia is his perversion, as the film works with the eroticization of the book and with the bookstore as the erotic temple of the book, as exemplified by three sequences early in the film that use Kinokuniya as their set.

The first of these sequences traces, voyeuristically, Birdy Hilltop's bookstore stealth. Birdy is caught in the gaze of a female clerk, Suzuki Umeko, as a subjective camera lingers momentarily on his fingering books on the shelf. Her gaze follows him down a bookshelf aisle, then as he descends the staircase to exit the store, never having stopped by the register to pay for his selections. Another metonymic hand shot, this time the clerk's hand on the staircase rail, derails the theft.

The first shot of the sequence immediately following the staircase apprehension of the thief gives us a close-up on the Japanese title of the book topping the pile Birdy has attempted to steal: *Dorobo nikki*. This is the Japanese translation of Jean Genet's *Journal d'un voleur,* which lends its name to the film, a self-conscious naming retained across translations both of the film and of the book title, not only in Japanese but also in French, English, German, and so on. Like *Night and Fog in Japan, Diary of a Shinjuku Thief* demonstrates through Oshima's reflexive naming his use of French culture and theory in a specifically Japanese context. The importing of ideas is one way the iconoclast breaks with the doxa of his culture by introducing a breach of Japanese merchant-consumer faith. The break is with the famous *idée reçu* that has some basis in everyday reality, that Japanese consumers and shopkeepers are scrupulously honest as a result of a respect system that deeply inscribes reputation and face-saving as significant values within the culture. Shoplifting is the type of crime, like pickpocketing and mugging, that is supposedly not common in Japanese society, even though larger yakuza operations and official corruption may flourish. The thief violates the Japanese honor system.

The owner of the bookstore, Tanabe, becomes a father figure presiding like a judge over this violation. The law of this father is hardly an impartial ruling, as signaled by the *Dorobo nikki* shot. He is prejudiced by his own fascination with Genet, and the other books that are the objects of the thief's larceny. If his response is to forgive the violation, his presents are offered not simply as a measure of magnanimity, but as self-interested investment.

The psychoanalytic triad in which the father identifies with the young couple, becoming a facilitator rather than a barrier to their coupling, is the motor force of these three bookstore sequences. The second scene of book theft repeats the earlier scene, but this time with greater elaboration of all elements, embellishing each gesture with new meanings. The young female clerk eyes the male thief from the moment of his first entrance into this space, their coupling fraught with tensions of all sorts. An open book is visually presented in close-up, held open on its binding, showing itself symbolically as a slit; stacks become seductive places for tracking the gaze and movements of the other. In this maze, the spectator is a privileged observer of stolen objects and stolen glances, of libidinal energy circulating.

The apprehension scene for this second strike again begins with a pan of the desktop in Tanabe's office, providing a survey of the variety of texts stolen. Tanabe, the owner–father figure, is reluctant to make another gift of "so much merchandise," instead substituting his own book, "which doesn't sell," *Conversations with a Naked Figure.* This gift is dedicated and autographed, eliciting a further joke on the *kanji,* the Chinese written characters in Birdy Hilltop's name. Names as puns, poetic and figural slidings, and the riddles of Juro's song lyrics give us parts of the puzzle, but for the time being there is but a loose association of the disparate sequences with one another, with

11. Umeko is isolated with the dropped books against a background of the rectangular lines ruling the contemporary redesign of Tokyo's governmental and office buildings. *Shinjuku dorobo nikki* (Diary of a Shinjuku Thief, 1969). Still courtesy of Oshima Productions.

an "unsolvable, solvable riddle" (in the words of the song) mysteriously ruling this fantasy. Tanabe is fascinated with his errant "son" and, subsequently, the couple formed by the thief and the clerk. Instead of punishment, he offers rewards, supplementing the gift of the books with money for a date. Rather than follow through with the consummation of a paternally blessed desire, however, the couple part on a bridge. Negation, perversion, fetishism rule; Birdy says he ejaculated when stealing the books, but the couples' sexual interaction is blocked. A book falls open to a crucial illustration, a transection of a penis.

Birdy has already heard Umeko's whispered confidence that thieves receive three strikes before being called out; his third attempt is delayed. In the interim, the film proposes five related sequences, each a response to the liaisons made between stealing as an act of displaced intercourse and intercourse as subject to theft, in the form of rape and voyeurism. These five sequences develop images of voyeurism, gender uncertainties, and violence against women. The third bookstore sequence can only take place following them, for it uses the previous propositions on these issues as matter for its development, but first five other sequences intervene.

PSYCHOSEXUAL NEGATIONS AND NEGOTIATIONS

These five sequences slide from shoplifting to voyeurism, from unsuccessful sex therapy to rape. Birdy and Umeko, together, "on the outside," where books give way to more direct action, are doomed to misadventure across these sequences. The theater of sexuality is here perverse and unable to achieve coital satisfaction, except as violence and aggression:

1. "Fashion Village"—This sequence takes place in a boutique called the Fashion Village (in English). The sequence places the store window between the couple, to serve as their "looking glass." Birdy has Umeko steal clothes, so that she can experience the sexuality of thievery, but Birdy's vantage point as voyeur watching through the store's window allows her action to mirror his. Lacan's suggestive connection of the vitrine (the store window) as a supplement to the mirror in his mirror stage theory suggests this framing might be seen figuratively, as a "mirror-stage" inspired exchange of identities. Later in the bookstore, gender ambiguity will again be manifest through cross-dressing, as Birdy will put on Umeko's skirt.

2. "Sex therapy"—At the urging of the bookstore-owner "father," the young couple visit a sex therapist, Takahashi Tetsu. The film here glosses a tradition in which sex therapy replaces or supplements psychoanalysis, ranging from the writings of Reich, in which sex therapy serves as a reinvigoration of Freud, to U.S.-inspired practical therapy applications. Takahashi offers a quick opinion on the couple's dysfunction, claiming that it is caused by androgyny and gender ambiguity. This continues references made to gender ambiguities in the preceding "Fashion Village" sequence and along with it anticipates the third bookstore segment.

3. "Voyeurism at a Japanese inn"—Here the characters seem to have entered another movie. From the garden they view a sexual act at a traditional Japanese inn. The open shoji through which they watch acts as a "Cinemascope" frame within the image. The film frames cinematic voyeurism, reflexively, prefiguring *Realm of the Senses* (see chapter 4). By framing such a traditional setting as a film within the film, this sequence provides a metacommentary suggesting the period drama, the *jidai-geki*, as a setting for lessons in sexual seduction.

4. "Cinema verité discussion of sex"—The film crew's drunken sexual thoughts are documented in this scene, as a cinema verité interlude of Oshima, actors, and crew discussing the meaning of sex while drinking begins as intercutting with the end of the previous sequence. Like drinking scenes in Oshima's other films, this one allows a group discussion, the difference being that the lines are spoken extradiegeti-

cally and, in the case of the actors, "out of character." At the heart of
the debate is whether males and females merge in coitus, or feel entirely differently about the experience.

5. "Chase-rape sequence"—Two actors from the cast scene appear on a
wall overlooking the garden, following up on the third sequence by
chasing and raping Umeko, while Birdy is helpless to defend her. This
brings about a negation of Umeko and Birdy's sexuality from the outside, by mysterious figures. It is as if these male attackers are refugees
of the drunken male exchange, embodying the forces and attitudes
that violate women and consequently deform this couple. All negotiations have led to further negation. Umeko and Birdy find their way
back to the Shinjuku station plaza, and then to the bookstore, their
date a hopeless misadventure in which the "real" world conspires
against them.

These five disjointed sequences, grouped together, explore issues of sexuality, voyeurism, gender shifting, and violence as a loose episodic excursion into
a fictional world marked by reflexivity and metacomedy. In a sense they form
a journey, a quest that returns to the bookstore with all questions unresolved.

THEATERS OF SEXUALITY

Umeko, who has been locked in the Kinokuniya bathroom, comes out after
hours, entering a frame that is extremely dark, a space that is deserted. She
comes out announcing herself as the active performer, selecting books from
the shelves, then piling them into a loose mound on the floor of the central
aisle, where they are illuminated with a theatrical stage spotlight. Textual readings fill the sound track with different voice-overs during this action, as if the
books were speaking themselves. This scene bears comparison with the "Bouvard et Pécuchet" scene in Jean-Luc Godard's *Deux ou trois choses que je sais d'elle*
(Two or Three Things I Know about Her, 1966), in which we briefly meet
characters in a café bearing the same names as the main characters of
Flaubert's novel. *Bouvard et Pécuchet* is Flaubert's satire on the *Encyclopedists*,
on books taken as unquestioned authority. In the Godard scene, M. Bouvard
reads random passages from books of various sorts in several different languages, while M. Pecuchet notes down what he reads. Similarly in the Oshima film, characters undertake a surreal, theatrical action as they sculpt a pile
of books, some passages of which are read aloud accompanying visual textual
inserts from the books. In both cases, these scenes serve to introduce a collage textuality into a filmic space, a visual trope of reading and textuality as
varied, full of strange juxtapositions and linkages, and, finally, cacophonous.

Beginning with Genet, the texts include passages from Yanagida Kunio,
Yoshimoto Ryumei, Hagiwara Sakutaro, and Tomioka Taeko as well as from
Muhammad Ali on the African-American reclaiming of names and cultural

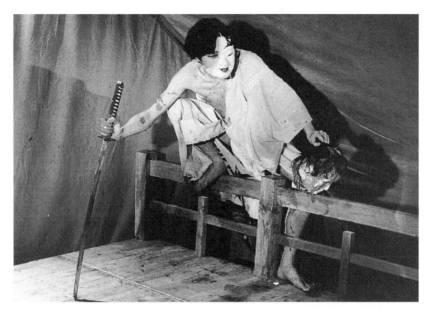

12. Another theater of sexuality intercedes with the Juro Karo Situation Players performing *Yui shoshetsu,* as the mise-en-scène of the play within the film blends reinterpretations of the Japanese traditional arts with radical principles of restaging or refiguration. *Shinjuku dorobo nikki* (Diary of a Shinjuku Thief, 1969). Still courtesy of Oshima Productions.

identity, Stalin on women's liberation, Henry Miller sanctioning incest and bestiality as methods to free the human race, and a text describing a clitorectomy. Rather than a unified discourse, this collage of texts is filled with internal contradictions, uneasy fragments of selves positioned vis-à-vis sexuality, gender, and social change.

This is the game toward which the bookstore sequences have been heading, as the final play occurs once the books have become a mound, and Birdy grabs Umeko in an awkward embrace on top, then tries briefly to pull Tanabe in to replace him. "I knew you were never my employee" is Tanabe's ejaculation, while sex has become associated with fascism, in a position called "the Swastika," which Tanabe denounces as hurting the books and therefore himself. This violent negation brings the game to an end. Yet it is but prelude to another theater of sexuality, this time the Juro Karo Situation Players performing *Yui shoshetsu,* with Birdy in the lead role of the son of a shogun in the Tokugawa period who is beheaded for staging a revolt.

It is in this final theatrical sequence that the film's drawing on Japanese sixties theater and art movements is at its height. Juro explains how Kabuki means to "act in a wild manner," giving us a succinct example of how many

Japanese artists at this time began blending reinterpretations of the Japanese traditional arts with radical principles of restaging or refiguration. The fragments of the play we see are preoccupied with the beheading. A montage gives us a shot of a sword, a close-up on a cracked mask, then the half mask falls away to reveal a bloody face. This violence recalls the song Juro has been singing at intervals throughout the film, which culminates in the narrative of a razor murderer, slashing his victims behind Izetan, a large department store near the Kinokuniya bookstore. In the play, a woman calls out, "Heads for sale."

Throughout the fragmented play, Umeko's interaction with Birdy doubles the play from the "wings" as interwoven montage. Umeko's period is given as the exaggerated image of blood flowing between her legs, then Birdy uses this blood to trace a wound on her stomach, evoking seppuku, Japanese ritual suicide by disembowelment. From this traced scar, we move to an actual scar near her nipple; Birdy asks her to tell the story of this wound. She says she received it when attacked in Shinjuku when she was eighteen. With this revelation, the razor of Juro's song has become "real," just as the imaginary scar evoked disclosure of a real one. Like the sister in *Death by Hanging*, Umeko faces down the male fantasy of violence with the scar she as victim bears from an actual, haunting instance of male violence. This scar bears witness to the male sexual violence that culminates Juro's song and the earlier rape-chase sequence.

The sexual dysfunction diagnosed in the earlier sex therapy sequence with Takahashi Tetsu is displaced as violence; dysfunction is never resolved. Instead the play ends in a depiction of the historical revolt, which in turn segues into footage of a riot in Shinjuku. The theatrical celebration of a revolt cedes the screen to the theatrics of a contemporary revolt, as at the Shinjuku police station windows and the clock are shattered. This returns us to the opening clock-smashing sequence. It also demonstrates Oshima's willingness to mark the difference of this student revolt from the October Revolution, to mark his difference in approach with Eisenstein's montage of clocks marking the time of revolution in all the major capitals. There is finally much that compares in *Diary of a Shinjuku Thief* to Godard's *Masculin-Feminin* and *La Chinoise,* films that in their analytical view of the sixties youth movements are fascinated with the psychosexual dimensions of this discontent. If Oshima is a little closer in spirit to the rioters than was Godard before his transformation post-1968 into the production of agit-prop films, both directors charted how revolt in a postmodern moment is bound to sexual energies and tied to theatrics. If rebellion explodes onto the street, it is likely to be the crossroads of a commercial center such as Shinjuku that provides the backdrop, while confrontations with police become a target, a goal.

Watching *Diary of a Shinjuku Thief* now one is struck by the topicality of its obsession with androgyny in light of current gender theory, though the film wavers between celebrating androgyny and treating it as symptom. The loose structure of this film allows powerful tableaus to be juxtaposed. An aesthetics of collage supersedes principles of coherence and development. The film is not the polished gem of construction and contradiction characteristic of many of the other films in this chapter. Its unrestrained and playful gestures grasp the topical as street theater.

HUMANISM, REVISITED

If *Death by Hanging* was seen as Oshima's most Brechtian film and *Diary of a Shinjuku Thief* reaches toward a Japanese avant-garde situationist fragmentation, *Boy*, in contrast, was seen as the most "humanist," particularly among the films of this period. Some critics decried the film as a step backward, but others, and apparently much of the public, found it more palatable, precisely because its focus on a youthful protagonist and its linear narrative construction made it both easier to understand and more emotionally involving.

Boy's reworking of the family melodrama is perhaps less of a dramatic departure from convention than many of Oshima's works. We have been analyzing how previous Oshima films render a split subject through innovative filmic form, refracting the debates then beginning to take shape between humanism and poststructuralism. Deconstruction emerges within this debate as a desire to decenter the subject, rather than straightforwardly embracing self-other connections. *Boy* does not abandon all the distanciation techniques of Oshima in favor of humanism; the montage is as precise as ever, in its covering a series of automobile accidents and using surprising angles, framings, sounds, and cuts in shifting variations on a pattern. *Boy* is as attentive as the previous films of Oshima to the imaginary register of the character's psyche and of representation. The film does evoke empathy for a young Japanese boy caught in familial traps of crime, scam, ritual abuse, and imaginary escape. The young Boy is played by Abe Tetsuo with great subtlety; the range of his emotions is often suggested through reaction shots that give us but minimal gestural information, his eyes alone, wide, taking in events. One is struck by the similarity of these shots to the documentary images of the street kids in *Diary of Yunbogi*.

It is no directly humanist melodrama. Given the internal frames, repetitions, and formal, strategic shifts, the film is not as straightforward as might first appear, despite its linearity. It remains a look at "the subversion of the subject and the dialectic of desire," to borrow a phrase from Lacan's essay on the Freudian unconscious. It is through this look at family, objects, and fantasy that the film appears to still have much vested in decentering the subject, but in a specifically psychoanalytic view.

Boy is a film centered on the repetition of a scam, like *A Town of Love and Hope, The Burial of the Sun,* and *Cruel Story of Youth;* but we should also note that like *Death by Hanging, Boy* finds its source in a real event and its news

13. Mise-en-scène depicts the shifts of affinities and antagonisms within the family, as here, where the father is distanced from the mother and sons. *Shonen* (Boy, 1969). Still courtesy of Oshima Productions.

coverage, in this case what the French call a "fait-divers" source, a "human interest" story of strange dimensions, a family engaged in extortion of damages for faked accidents. This family traversed Japan, bilking numerous motorists before being caught. It is this contact with the real, the actual, and its resonance of family drama that seems to have inspired Oshima to rework the scam structure; the "true story" becomes a source that, as Aumont (1970: 35) has put it, has "just enough of the unbelievable in it—exterior signs of strangeness necessary to be taken as believable." Once again the film is structured on the repetition of an act, the faked accidents, each time filmed differently.

It has an almost musical structure of theme and variations. The sound track complements this richly with musical motifs, some of which are concrete music, others, songs sung. By the end of the film the sounds of brakes and cars crashing become autonomous sound track figures, punctuating scenes as an audial reminder of the repetitive "accidents" so much more frequent at the film's beginning.

FEAR OF ABANDONMENT

The entire scam takes place against a backdrop of familial strife, in which the Boy's fear of abandonment alternates with his desire for evasion. The fa-

ther is a World War II veteran with a lingering war disability, but the film indicates that the extent of his wound may be exaggerated. It may be his alibi
for his refusal to work to support his family, either consciously or unconsciously. While the stepmother originally performs the scam, the Boy takes
over, substituting his body for hers. This act of substitution implies a rivalry
between them for the father's gratitude and attention that eventually gives
way to a complicity, as they both react against the father.

The condition of enslavement the Boy faces is orchestrated by the father's
manipulation. First the father threatens to send him away to his grandmother's; then he later refuses to let his son return. In a shot that shows father and son standing at a urinal, the father tells the Boy that his grandmother wouldn't want him, that his friends have forgotten him. By framing
the father's verbal abuse at a specifically male site, the film implies a phallic
joke that undermines the power imperatives of phallic control.

Abortion figures in this context. With the family around a table, the
younger brother screams for his mother's attention, until she deposits him
in an adjoining room, as prelude to her question of whether she really must
go through with "it," meaning the abortion the father pressures her into having on discovering she is once again pregnant. The Boy witnesses the argument between his parents, which includes intimations of jealousy about the
stepmother's past connected to this town of Fukui where they have come to
seek the abortion, and perhaps a past use of the abortion clinic itself. The
Boy's knowledge of the pending abortion remains indirect at this juncture,
but he is charged by the father to ensure his mother's entry into the clinic.

The two shots that show the Boy and the stepmother approach the clinic
offer images in which the complicity of the stepmother and Boy are marked,
as they were in an earlier arcade walk marked by a hat purchase that I will
discuss shortly. In this moment of complicity, stopped in front of the clinic,
she confides more than she should: "I came here with a man, once. Do you
understand such things?" This question will remain suspended, as the Boy
is told to go play, and dutifully departs. The film simply shows his return at
an unspecified time to watch from a nearby bridge.

The boy is caught between regimes of knowing and not-knowing, of split
loyalties between father and mother, of being exposed to far more than he
should be expected to understand. Yet clearly he witnesses everything, takes
in all the threats posed by cheating and being-cheated-on in adult relationships. This is part of the larger nexus of knowledge, duping others and being duped, that informs this view of familial relations, certainly accentuated
here as this family has as its source of income its collaboration in the performance of a scam. Though perhaps the Boy was only obeying her commands,
the stepmother, on seeing him, rushes toward him, accuses him of spying for
his father, and brutally slaps him. His response to this confrontation is a
telling denial of bearing witness: "I don't think anything about anything."

14. Throughout the film circulation is graphically presented in images of the traffic, the cars that pass through the frame as the family stages, or contemplates staging, another of their "accident" scams. *Shonen* (Boy, 1969). Still courtesy of Oshima Productions.

As she has not come from the clinic, but from farther down the street, the Boy is bribed to keep her secret. He asks for a watch that will tell not only the time but also the date. Then as the stepmother and Boy swing together in a small park, he is told to keep the watch secret. However, they are unable to set the date, implying that their lives are so devoid of scheduling and routine that neither one knows. "Every day is like Sunday," the stepmother offers, but this is no wonderful freedom from time, only a drifting lack of purpose. The stepmother then reveals the impending birth of a new baby, giving another secret away, and promising a more regulated life after its birth, though acknowledging that the need for money will be even greater.

In choosing the park swings for this scene, the film lingers on a familiar neorealist space in Japanese film, the space of the park swing on which the elderly hero, Watanabe, sits in the final flashback in *Ikiru* by Kurosawa Akira (1952). In that film a bureaucrat's funeral becomes the site of speculation as to why he was transformed into an activist, advocating the draining of an open sewer and the construction of a neighborhood park. The shot on the swing shows Watanabe singing a song whose lyrics call for the devotion to love, as "life is so short." The line in the park scene in *Boy*, "Every day is like

Sunday," similarly recalls Kurosawa's *One Wonderful Sunday,* in which a young couple who have no money and are unable to afford their dream apartment nonetheless make the best of a rainy day bolstering each other's spirits as they wander through a Tokyo in which wartime destruction is in evidence. The park scene of *Boy* alludes to such promises to rise above or change unpleasant conditions, to such hopeful commitment to a better future, but the scene is ironically inscribed into a larger paradigm of wandering and circularity. I will call this the film's circulation metaphor, its insistence on a journey on a map, without time as a marker.

Throughout the film circulation is graphically presented in images of the traffic, the cars that pass through the frame as the family stages, or contemplates staging, another of their "accident" scams. This circulation couples with their voyage, across the map of Japan, a map that is repeatedly seen as an insert in segments in which we hear the Boy narrating his view of their journey. If we link this journey, apparently circular but eventually reaching "the edge of Japan" (or the even more poetic "end of Japan" in the English subtitle's rendering), to the question of knowledge, we see that the film is a devastatingly critical coming of age story, in which the young subject comes to know that there is no evasion by imaginary means.

RED OBJECTS: THE FORMAL AND THE PSYCHOANALYTIC

The film's contact with realist modes is enmeshed with formal devices that immediately call our attention to the artificial, the contrived, the structured. In an expansive wide-screen frame, the composition is as deliberate and the montage as precise as ever in Oshima's films. Within the color image, red becomes a selected focal point, an exaggerated instance of repetition and displacement across frames, as red or other formal elements often do in the film of Ozu Yasujiro. In Ozu these elements vary and construct formal composition (Bordwell 1988: 83). Oshima's red objects beg the comparison to Ozu, asking that we see this family melodrama in reference to Ozu's corpus. When later we even have transitional series of shots of "empty space" so characteristic of Ozu's "pillow shots" between scenes, the Ozu comparison is made even stronger.

Yet Oshima's use of red, as one might expect of a filmmaker whose formal concerns are far more invested with exploration of psychoanalytic excess, does more than refer to or parallel Ozu's strategies. He takes this device more in the direction it is used in Hitchcock's *Marnie,* into the realm of the psychoanalytic. Remember that the objects in question are a baseball hat, the stepmother's suit, a boot, and blood; they come to form a paradigm by virtue of their color association, a paradigm associated with the mother and loss, or the mother as lost object, reflecting the child's own self-disintegration.

This all begins with the hat given to the Boy as a present from his stepmother. The hat is yellow with red piping, and to be more precise on its status as present as well, it is a gift given only after the demand "Buy me that" is made by the Boy walking with his stepmother down the street of an enclosed shopping arcade. Seen in the store window displayed on a robot, this automaton origin of the hat inaugurates the Boy's Andromeda fantasy, his dreams of evasion to outer space. Markedly, the hat is central to the first time the Boy actually runs away. While on his own, he witnesses an extortion scene, in which two older boys shake down a victim for his pocket money. When the Boy approaches the victim afterward, this stranger responds by throwing the Boy's hat in a mud puddle. The boy methodically washes it in a rain gutter, then dries it over a steam vent. His hat becomes an object through which he demonstrates his self-reliance, ingenuity, and self-worth after an experience in which the world of his peers mimics the cruelty of the world of adults to which he has been subjected. Just as the hat is once again clean, his stepmother finds him and throws the hat back onto the street pavement in disgust. A high angle close-up shows a car wheel rolling over the hat, once again squashing it.

The hat as object is invested with symbolizing the self. Similarly, the red objects throughout link one subject to another, and violence to the very nature of being. For example, the stepmother's suit is another red object, soon echoed by the blood that trickles down her face when the father beats her, beating her in fact for a missed menstrual cycle. The red here links the stepmother to the Boy and both to another victim, the girl who will be introduced and killed in Hokkaido; it is a red shared by victims of circumstances, surely, but also clearly victims of a patriarchal imperative that commands circumstances that they cannot hope to control.

Finally a red boot is introduced when they reach "the end of Japan," their phrase for the northern island of Hokkaido. It is in Hokkaido that the last accident in the series takes place, at the point that they are circumscribed in their scam as the police now possess their photo and knowledge of their previous extortions. This time the accident is truly accidental, caused by the little brother running out in front of a jeep in deep snow. A young girl's head smashes against the jeep's window, and the Boy, who stays behind transfixed while other family members flee, sees a trickle of red blood that marks her wound as she is carried away by an ambulance. The Boy finds one of her red boots dropped in the snow, which he carries back as a reminder and presents as a challenge to his father.

The boot comes to adorn a "snowman" made for his little brother. This "snowman" is a triangular mound, visually echoing a cemetery mound on which the Boy plays in the beginning of the film. Here the film relies on an architectural shape, the triangular mound, to create a circularity and closure of the childhood play in the context of death. The snowman becomes a funeral ceremony for the dead girl, linking the younger brother for whom the snowman was originally constructed and the girl victim of the car crash. They represent the Boy's commitment to dreams and to his generation, as well as his fantasy of escape from a Japan of his father's generation. The fantasy of the space alien is an ego-ideal projection fantasy on the Boy's part, in which he sees himself as both alien (alienated, otherworldly) and savior. Instead, circumstances conspire to force blood into this scene; instead of becoming a savior, a hero, the Boy sees himself as guilty, complicit, unable to escape.

In a voice-over narrative interlude the Boy tells us they have given up the scam and moved into "one of those new houses in Osaka." Suddenly, we are bombarded with news stories montaged to show the police unraveling of the scam, followed by brief newsreel-style biographies of both mother and father. The distanced media descriptions of these characters, including details of their pasts (divorces, remarriages, the stepmother's stint as a bar hostess), are never exposed in the film to this point. The arrest itself is told in just two shots. In one, the police confront the mother first as the boys watch television; the police disrupt a scene of utter domestic normality. The shot that follows visually matches the first, as the Boy screams out "Run away" before his father enters the doorway; the police who have been waiting struggle to subdue him. A poetics of simplicity and variation couples with formal departures that become quite pronounced at the end of the film.

The interrogation of each of the parents is shown with no diegetic sound. The Boy is shown alone with protective prison officials, resisting their questions, giving responses that deny all aspects of the family's history. Instead of offering us the Boy's feelings through dialogue, the film subsequently presents his thoughts as flashback imagery, in just four shots: the boot on the "snowman" altar, followed by the girl's head bleeding, then another shot of just the boot, and another of the dead girl. These four shots are reiterative, representing the Boy's regret. They present with poignant minimalism the film's insistence on the Boy's disjuncture from his father. He acknowledges responsibility for a crime, though one of a different order and magnitude from the series of scams for which the family is arrested. The crime that haunts him is less actual; it is one of contingent circumstance, one that brings to the fore that playing with accidents and injury risks a confrontation with death. He sees the death of another as if it were his responsibility, and as if it were his own.

Early in the film, as part of his space-alien fantasy, the Boy declares to his younger brother that he is a visitor from the nebula Andromeda, "come to save the world." The images of the young girl in death speak of the failure of this fantasy, and of a concomitant failure to make the intentions visited in fantasy match the real.

Boy is a far more complicated film than it might first appear. Its linearity and its openness to humanist readings disguise the depth and the rupture of its treatment of fantasy and the psyche. There is a great and subtle variation to each series of like images; each time not only do framing and sound vary, but the mode of expression differs as well. We journey across representations that mix realist codes with stylized departures from realism in a carefully crafted setting of one scene in relation to another. The enigmatic and engaging lead character, the Boy, is given an imaginary life and a quiet knowing quality as witness. Both what he sees and what he imagines are presented as laments for a Japan that does not normally see its own journey with the Boy's acuity. In a sense, I like to think of the character, Boy, as a younger version of the character Motoki in Oshima's next film, linked as the two are by maps, by regrets for lost childhoods and uncertain identities, and by subjective shots in each film that emblematize their poetic witnessing of this world, such as a framing of the tiled rooftops characteristic of urban Japan.

THE FALSE BEGINNING OR THE POSTMODERN CHASE FILM

The puzzling opening frames of *The Battle of Tokyo, or the Story of the Young Man Who Left His Will on Film* are a clue that the first sequence of the film will be extraordinary and that the film to follow will challenge the viewer with images and dialogue difficult to decipher. It starts with shaky subjective images lurching forward on a boulevard in Tokyo. A voice-off admonishes, enigmatically, "You should have brought it back this morning." As the sequence progresses, the shaky camera is coded as handheld, and the voice-off, as well as the "it" (the camera) is identified. Yet if I insist on how the signifiers here are presented to the spectator without clear meaning, it is to introduce how the entire film will pursue disconcerting strategies undermining our expectations of narrative and logic, supplanting them with surprises. Synopses of this film have a tendency to present it as far more linear and simple than it is. To respect its strategies of complication, I will analyze the film's poetics of form and treat the contradictions as they appear.

The image frame is first presented as the equation of our vision with the vision of an imaginary filmmaker in the process of filming. The spectator's eye is identified with the eye pressed against the viewfinder, reflexively mirroring the camera lens as recording device and apparatus of representation. We see fragmented images of a chase, a street filled with signs, oncoming traffic, a bit of tower to the left. The image burns to a white absence, then returns.

So far, an opaque projection. The voice-off adds, "You could take landscapes anytime." This interjection implies that these landscape images by an artist-filmmaker are less urgent than some other implied task due the camera. What task? For the moment there is no answer. Which landscapes? Perhaps those we will come to understand as the landscapes of narration, brought to our attention, and placed under siege. We as spectators must struggle, as if with an indecipherable map. We must explore a narrative landscape that is a topographical representation of its own impenetrability.

Detours, dead ends, but mostly spirals, this film acts like a Möbius strip performing a tease.

At last, a character, Motoki, enters this frame, plunging into the space before the lens. His voice on the sound track has prefigured this corporeal intrusion, but now that these two representations (character in close-up, voice on the sound track) coincide, we are granted a point of view on the scene, the beginnings of an imaginary position within the narrative. Our vision is that of the "filmmaker" through camera to character, Motoki. Our first position is on an axis between imaginary filmmaker, camera, and character.

Aspects of this fixity of spectatorial vision, gained through the introduction of a character, remain even after Motoki, following an aggressive gesture of rushing toward the camera, leaves the frame. The image ironically gyrates, a high angle on the ground tracing the motion of the imaginary filmmaker running with the camera, the quick, disturbed, jostled movements of the frame past a row of trees. To those familiar with the handheld cameras of some fifties and sixties avant-garde films, these images would be known. They recall the physical lyricism of Stan Brakhage's camera-eye, going far beyond the cinema verité mobile camera to effect a more emotive and immediate expression of subjectivity. Then a hand covers the lens and the image goes black.

Our second position is developed as the character, Motoki, enters various frames running toward the camera or across the screen. The telephoto lens transforms space. Time and motion are expanded, and all depth is flattened into collagelike representations composed of signs, such as a traffic sign surrounded by tree branches and writing. For a moment this telephoto lens appears to turn representational space into what Lyotard calls "figural" space (1978: 9–23, 271–279), the space of inscription of primary processes. The representational scene flirts with its transformation into a series of figurative tableaus and then stops short, precisely at the moment in which we realize that Motoki has been running toward something. Abstract metallic sounds have punctuated this interval but give way to an apparently offhand comment by an onlooker, who asks as Motoki steps out into traffic against the traffic light, "Are you trying to commit suicide?" Soon we realize that Motoki has been running to the scene of the filmmaker's death, depicted in three shots that define the diagonals of a prism: (1) a low angle long shot of the filmmaker on the top of a building that zooms in at a forward, upward diagonal; (2) a close-up of Motoki looking left, as his eyes first look up, then descend (following an unseen fall), which is submitted to a zoom-out placing Motoki in long shot at the intersection; (3) a zoom-in on the body of the filmmaker on the ground with the camera at his side.

At this instance of the filmmaker's death, the camera's presence in the scene reminds us that the film we are watching is clearly another film, made by another filmmaker. We may have already been aware of this when the camera work switched earlier to angles whose subjectivity was no longer

15. A publicity still that depicts Motoki filming a demonstration offers a shot that never appears in the film. The only demonstration footage pointedly leaves out any representation of a filmmaker. *Tokyo senso sengo hiwa* (The Story of the Young Man Who Left His Will on Film, 1970). Still courtesy of Oshima Productions.

marked. The framing process that investigates the subjectivity of the image is well under way. As has been discussed by Edward Branigan (1984: 147–155), this film challenges the whole conception of point of view in the cinema (though as Branigan notes on page 154, we disagree on the significance of the avant-garde film-within-the-film, a point I will return to shortly).

The interval of shots that follows represents Motoki grabbing the camera and running with it. These shots are similar in framing to the previous running sequence, except that now a montage alternation of shots establishes that Motoki is running from the police. When Motoki meets the police in the frame of a single shot, the police confiscate the camera. Motoki cries out, "It's my camera, give it back." The chase is reversed (Motoki running to catch the police). It ends at the entrance to a dark tunnel.

The enigma set up by this opening sequence will later be partially clarified through the introduction of further narrative complications, some of which annihilate the possibility that this introductory segment could ever have taken place in the manner it is shown. Motoki and the imaginary off-screen filmmaker will later be presented as perhaps two aspects of the same

16. Members of the film collective debate theories of film and political struggle, as well as the reality of events occurring in the film's narrative, as they edit film. *Tokyo senso sengo hiwa* (The Story of the Young Man Who Left His Will on Film, 1970). Still courtesy of Oshima Productions.

person, or as partial, continually displaced representations of a love triangle among members of a filmmaking collective. Motoki, a woman named Yasuko, and another man, Endo, are the "characters" in this love triangle of shifting identities. Character, once again, is the most complex of categories for this film. No stable histories or identities are assigned any one of the three, with Motoki sometimes suggested to be the most split or multiple personality.

THREE GENRES STRUGGLING TO MAP TRUTHS

We will later come to understand a context for Motoki's offscreen comments during the initial segment as he argues with the imaginary filmmaker for possession of the camera. These comments represent the struggle to obtain the camera to film a demonstration, a goal of the radical collective.

The scene that begins to clarify this context is the discussion in the filmmaking collective that occurs as Motoki is lying on a cot, silent. It follows immediately after the dark tunnel that ends the extended first sequence. In the discussion, a documentary film of the demonstration is represented as having been shot and subsequently stolen by the police from Motoki at the demonstration. If this assertion is true, the beginning of the film is false and vice versa.

In the conversation between Motoki and Yasuko what Lyotard has called the "logical incompossibilities"—that is, statements that rule each other out as possibility—are multiplied. Yasuko tells Motoki, whom she believes to be her lover, that Endo, another male member of the collective, fell at the demonstration, whereupon the police stole his camera and the documentary footage. Motoki insists that her lover (Endo) committed suicide. This version coincides with the opening sequence, assuming that Endo is the filmmaker behind the camera. Thus on one hand, Yasuko's lover is the imaginary filmmaker, and, on the other, the surviving, opposing character, Motoki. This might easily be resolved by positing Motoki and Endo as a single character, a schizophrenic personality whose psychic disorder creates the multiple representations within the film. However, no sooner is such resolution offered than it is contradicted, and the figure of displacement continues to operate.

Instead we must assess what we have been shown: an imaginary filmmaker's attempt to shoot an avant-garde film, an interruptive claim of political imperative, a witnessing of a suicide, and several attempts to regain possession of the camera. What sets up the confusion of these events are gaps in this representation. What underlies these gaps is a theoretical inquiry into the meaning of events, which is ultimately where the film is leading.

"Let me go over everything that happened today." As Yasuko narrates, in voice-over, we see the suddenly actualized insert of images of the Okinawa Solidarity Day demonstration, angles on the police, the banners. This is the footage that we could imagine to comprise the collective's documentary, that either was stolen by the police or was never filmed. We are told of a war between factions at the demonstration, resulting from differences concerning protest strategies. Yasuko indicates that Motoki and she were both caught in the war between factions. She wished for a unity of purpose that would defy the police. He left one faction, depressed by its line. Yasuko mentions Motoki's remark that one faction, Kakemaru, claimed that a united front would constitute an "illicit union." From this exchange, we surmise that Yasuko and Motoki were themselves divided, one from another, as Motoki appears to rebuke her desire for a united front. Factional splits take on an emphatic life of their own, invading the film's representation, as if to say all has become fragmented.

It is at this point that Motoki, framed with Yasuko through the barrier of a cyclone fence, is depicted in anger, rejecting what we have just seen and heard. Retaining his story that another has committed suicide and rejecting the incipient interpretation of an imagined suicide as a metaphor for the death of his Marxist self, he asks, "How long are you going to keep up this nonsense, making film into a weapon?"

The validity of the insert of the documentary footage has been doubly questioned. Note that "making film into a weapon" is close to the position of filmmaking as practiced by the American newsreel collective and militant Latin American films, as well as Japanese documentarists on the left. In terming this concept "nonsense," a character casts doubt on its validity. He questions documentary as effective radical practice, but as this is voiced only by one character, this questioning of validity is itself uncertain. Yet neither is his critique merely beside the point, as future turns of the narrative make clear.

For more fundamentally, we, as audience, are still uncertain of the documentary film's existence. Three genres of filmmaking will be juxtaposed in the film, as a short documentary and an avant-garde film will be encased within the film's narrative frame. These three genres pose theoretical questions for each other. Can we believe that the appearance in a fiction film of the footage of the documentary argues for its existence? Can we believe documentary discourse to be the only valid weapon, or tool if you will, even in a political struggle?

To answer these questions we must ask another one: How is the resistance of the avant-garde depicted and used in the film? As a high angle on rooftops takes over the frame, a dialogue (voice-off, a conversation between the members of the filmmaking collective) discusses the images we are seeing as the testament of the suicide victim. An angle on a shopping street is accompanied by their question, "What was he thinking about when he shot that?" A shot taken from a straight-on angle very close to the ground frames car wheels passing in opposite directions. Another image contains a mailbox, a street sign, and a tunnel, to which one member proposes, "Maybe by linking meaningless shots he wanted to make the sense of image sharper." This is denounced: "To create meaning by paradox is morally bankrupt."

This first projection of the testament, the avant-garde film within the film, is paradoxically presented with a negative commentary that ironically points to its interest, points to film as a new kind of effective weapon, one to be used against a moral stance that believes in the religiosity of clear meaning. If it is morally bankrupt to create meaning by paradox, poetics itself is condemned, including Oshima's films whose paradoxical constructions are intricate and profound. The clue to the irony here is that the stern Stalinism of this character's pronouncement is itself framed paradoxically, one in a series of questions and statements displaying a bewilderment concerning signs and the self. Before this projection of the film testament terminates, it continues into the very images that opened the film proper, the images of Motoki confronting the imaginary filmmaker and ending with the hand over the lens causing the image to go black.

Returning to the logic of the opening, the avant-garde film *should* be on the same roll that is in the camera when its maker is confronted by Motoki.

Yet there is little complacency in this "should" in a film that revises and displaces so much. The projection of the film testament begins to indicate a will, a reason, a conception behind the avant-garde film, a legacy of signs worth deciphering. Yet for the collective, it leads only to a discussion of how to recover what for them remains the only significant film, the documentary.

For Motoki it leads elsewhere. He takes off chasing "himself," wondering if "the filmmaker" ever existed. The chase becomes a figure for the text as the landscape of an identity crisis, when, in an angle from behind where he is last seen standing, we now see him in the space of the shopping street. In the narrative he has "entered" his avant-garde film, entered the film within the film. Or more precisely, he is shown standing at the threshold, his entrance withheld while we cut to other variations that do not *yet* accomplish the turning inside out of the film but rather chronicle its twisting along directions and reversals of desire.

WAR OF IMAGES

A second projection of the avant-garde film testament screens the images in the place of sex. Yasuko refuses Motoki's body and has changed her position. She now believes in the suicide of her former lover. The projection of the avant-garde film will be evidence for her of his having existed and having loved her. She will project the images onto her body and masturbate in their light, beneath their motion. Motoki, now also changed, only sees "pieces of film spliced together, junk." He reacts violently, first against the film, as he physically attacks the reel at Yasuko's moment of ecstasy. This symbolic attack is shortly made direct, when he subsequently attacks her outside.

In this second projection of the film testament the images are almost disturbed beyond iconic recognition by their projection onto a body. The image is no longer the realm of semiotic production, but a force that displays its effects, in process, on a body. Yet the image that results from this projection, the molding of signs and architectonic space to the contours of a nude female body, is itself highly resonant with connotations, conflating social space and the body as object of desire.

Something else has passed by on the screen which is quite remarkable, if not remarked on, in the psychodrama between Motoki and Yasuko occurring in front of the screen. Before the avant-garde images appear, we see a fragment of the riot imagery from the documentary film. We can now imagine there to be three short films on this same reel, one documentary, another, the avant-garde film testament, and the third, the chase scene of the initial segment. They are perhaps one film loop, one continuous strip, each fragment always projected in the shadow of the other's passing.

A third projection of the avant-garde film testament repeats aspects of the second, differently. This time Motoki and Yasuko embrace before a screen as the film testament is rear-projected on this screen behind them. A dialogue, supposedly referring to the past interaction of Yasuko and the dead film-maker, annotates the erotic scene being acted out between her and Motoki.

The dialogue takes the form of a poem, initiated as Yasuko's response to Motoki's question, "Didn't he say anything?"

> that morning he embraced me
> without speaking he simply embraced me
> it was like wind blowing
> water flowing
> clouds racing by
> the sun was shining, it was dazzling.

Motoki then looks at the film on the screen behind him and asks, "You were embraced in broad daylight under this window?"

Motoki calls the film testament a window, a poetic image that also will pre-figure our learning that the first rooftop shot is out of the window of his boy-hood bedroom. What does the window mean here if we are to take this metaphorically, in a theoretical sense? Not André Bazin's famous "window on the world," in which film provides a transparent view of the world received as real. In this case transparency is in the other direction (an effect accen-tuated by the perversity of the rear-screen projection). Yasuko says, "Yes, that morning he embraced me in silence. Yes he's there. He's watching us from behind the screen." The imaginary filmmaker again appears on an axis aligned with our position as spectators, as if watching the characters in the foreground, and, by extension, us through a window. No longer behind a camera that is equated with our vision, the imaginary filmmaker rather faces us with a challenging gaze of anteriority.

The poem is turned into its negation by Motoki: "The wind doesn't flow." Then Motoki, supposedly describing the film, is forced to attempt a repre-sentation of the unconscious: "It's a street of broken-down signs, a mailbox, weathered and peeling, just junk and more junk."

A poem initiates a series of images, as a past embrace is juxtaposed to a present embrace. A counterperformance of the poem initiates a negation that spills over as a crescendo of sexuality toward violence. The repetition compulsion here is displayed in its relationship to the figure of *mise-en-abîme*. The intervoluted frame becomes an erotic zone on the contour of the film which cannot be left alone. It is the object of persistent play and fascination.

The intertitles "The War of Landscapes" and "Unilateral Withdrawal" bracket a segment in which Motoki and Yasuko act out, literally, the explo-ration of meaning of the avant-garde film testament. The scene masterfully uses editing to present a progressive sliding of representation from a plane located in the illusion of actual event structures to a far more allegorical plane. This sliding is accomplished by a shift in costuming and mise-en-scène as the images of the main characters consulting a map alternate with them following these written directions into the landscape of Tokyo, which will become, allegorically, the landscape of representation. At first they are simply in their street clothes. Then suddenly, when we cut back to them, they are dressed in the combat gear they would have worn to the riot, until in a later cutback they are carrying weapons. This escalation is fascinating, for not only does it echo the escalation of militancy in student riots, it conflates the fiction film frame with the documentary film-within-the-film in a new and challenging way. It has our characters lend their militant and political aspirations to investigate representation; in so doing, they combat any depoliticalization of semiotics and show that avant-garde landscapes can indeed be construed within their ongoing struggle.

Motoki and Yasuko visit each shot of the film testament, finding only arrows echoing the map they possessed at the start of their attack. Signs point to other signs; signifiers freely circulate. The signs are not game; the film cannot be captured, especially by this strategy. The only option left to militants is a discharge, which will come in the form of repeated scenes of violence, echoing the earlier rape scenes in the film.

Here we should recognize the marvelously conceptual aspect of this sequence and its relationship not only to a reflexive view of semiotics, the processes of signification, but also to the processes of the unconscious. Several intertextual references will help here. Throughout this film, the image emphatically frames the tracing of the stripes of crosswalks, the bold alternation of black and white patterns on street signs and signals. We should recognize the similarity of the framing of these patterns to conceptual art of the sixties and seventies, particularly works of Daniel Buren, who in sculpture and installations foregrounds and displaces the graphic elements regulating cityscapes: the stripes, markings, and sign systems of urban spaces. In both conceptual art and Oshima's framings, the diagonals of a constructivist aesthetic are posed as emphatic, as beyond mere referentiality, as self-conscious and as thought-provoking. Maps are among the documents other conceptual artists have reframed to emphasize their otherwise unseen implications. Let me also suggest another art intertext here, one that derives from the arrows and curved lines that occupy the map the characters draw across the series of alternating images that comprise this segment. Compare their arrows to those found in works of Paul Klee, such as his paintings *Schwankendes Gleichgewicht* (Fluctuating Equilibrium, 1922) and *Eros* (1923); in both cases the arrows mark strategies of desire in a landscape that is emblematically the imaginary, the unconscious. So the graphic components of this sequence, in relationship to the rest of this film, suggest a level of meaning not usually associated with fictional film: a level that is highly conceptual.

This suggestion may seem to push certain graphic similarities of the film into a too close relationship to evocative thought structures in art praxis (and ones thought to be only European rather than Japanese). On the contrary, the cross-fertilization of art, literature, theater, and film, and the international exchanges in all these fields, is vital to understanding what is at stake in Oshima's films. Avant-garde artists in Japan (termed *zen'ei bijutsu* in Japanese) were active even in the late years of Meiji, and certainly have been from Taisho (beginning in 1912) on. Art of the early sixties developed as performance art with conceptual elements, notably the Gutai performance group and the Hi Red Center, a group composed of Takamatsu Jiro, Akasegawa Genpei, and Nakanishi Natsuyuki, who created works that might also be seen as having useful intertextual reverberations here. Consider this description of a Hi Red Center event: "The Ochanomizu Drop [Dropping event] was performed in and around the Ochanomizu section of downtown Tokyo on 10 October 1964. Takamatsu, Akasegawa, Izumi [Tatsu] and Nakanishi dropped old clothes and everyday objects from the roof of Ikenobo Kaikan hall and watched them fall and land on the street below. They then packed the dropped things in a suitcase, placed it in a public locker, and sent the locker key to a name they picked at random from the phone book" (Monroe 1994: 178). This same group made a two-sided poster of their art events, with a map bearing descriptions and labeling sites and photographs from the events in rows filling the other side; many of the photographs bear great resemblance to shots from Oshima's films from this period and after. By 1970, when *The Battle of Tokyo* was made, Oshima might have actually assumed a greater affinity among young Japanese for the works of the Japanese avant-garde than has proven to be the case with some U.S. audiences for this film.

Consider also the use of concrete music by Takemitsu Toru, who was just earning his reputation as one of Japan's most celebrated avant-garde composers. Takemitsu, who is noted for his highly personal musical idiolect, punctuates the silences of these sequences with his abstract music. Takemitsu's abstract sound space places the filmic narrative here at a defamiliarized remove, similar to the function of the film's structured, philosophical dialogues. Takemitsu's music also parallels the avant-garde film-within-the-film, offering us musical imagery that professes signs of an interiority listeners may experience as bold and intriguing but difficult to decipher. In contrast, there is also a playful musical element to Takemitsu's score, a light melody that also recurs, which corresponds to the simpler motor forces of this narrative, the quest for the camera, the quest to resolve the conflict in the couple, the chase scenes themselves, in all their playful iterations. The lightness of certain musical interludes underscores comedic elements; like *Death by Hanging*, this film, for all its seriousness, can be quite funny. In contrast to the more abstract musical interventions, the light musical themes establish a filmic dual tonality, with the lighter musical interludes encouraging the audience's intermittent laughter. Ultimately the indecipherability surrounding the avant-garde gives way to pathways for audiences to enter these more abstract spaces, as the play of visual abstraction in relationship to narrative, and musical abstraction in relationship to lighter interludes, creates an access to the spaces contemporary artists explore.

As the intentional operation of recapturing the meaning of images fails, a series of uncanny occurrences suggests that the sites of the avant-garde film testament are connected to the return of the repressed, Freud's (1900: 5:577) concept that repressed memories will resurface in another form, including dream imagery and symptoms. First, Motoki returns to the house with his name on it, wanders through a bourgeois interior, and opens the window of what used to be his room to expose the rooftop image that began the avant-garde film testament. Setting out to reshoot the film ("I'll take the same landscapes he did, then he'll disappear"), he returns to each site. Each time he sets up the shot, Yasuko interferes, inhabiting the frame, resisting his desire to reconstitute the non-narrative space. Each time that resistance leads to physical aggression victimizing Yasuko. The violent sexual scene is discovered in the space that previously eluded understanding. It emerges in the attempted filming of a mailbox surrounded by signs, as Yasuko stubbornly refuses access to the mail slot, even when the postman appears to withdraw the letters. The postman beats Yasuko into submission. Violence is not discovered as a scene from the past, but emerges in the present without explanation.

These dreamlike acts evoke the disputed terrain of communication and its relationship to the unconscious that can be seen as mapped differentially in the theoretical texts surrounding Poe's "The Purloined Letter" discussed in the chapter 2. Recall that at stake is the symbolic relationship among (1) the "letter" as an individual signifier, as a trace of meaning; (2) letters as documents and enunciations, as encoded language sent and received; (3) large-scale delivery systems of communication such as the postal system and the telephone; (4) letters as philosophy; and (5) the signifier as an operation in the unconscious. The debate that rages among these theorists is how closed the logic of the unconscious can be said to be, what chances there are to be taken, or what may be traced through knowledge of predictable circuits. The open question is the potential for decipherment of the unconscious in the realm of letters and communication. This film renders as visual images elements of this debate, associating the slit of the mailbox with female sexuality; this slit offers resistance, just as the key to identity refuses to be found by simply following the "battle map" of the city.

Motoki is rewinding the camera, preparing to shoot the segment of the imaginary film that will "end" with his plunge into its frame. Yasuko walks through a high angle shot into the flow of traffic. To avoid her, two vehicles swerve from their proper paths and almost collide. A new path for the filmic narrative is the emblematic indication of this sequence. This new path has been produced through overcoming the resistance posed by her body and takes the form of an abduction of Motoki and Yasuko by the passengers of one car.

In the car the shots are fragmented as close-ups of Motoki's face, Yasuko's foot, then a pan to the rapist, followed by a shot of Yasuko's face, impassive. All this is preceded by Motoki's deposit of his camera in a roadside store, which means that witnessing is no longer augmented by mechanisms of recording within the diegesis as the search for recovery of memory through the taking of new images has been suspended. The inversion of narrative space as the culmination of a pattern of convolutions I have been tracing becomes depicted literally through the impossible point of view established by a literally inverted image, a careening turnpike "ceiling."

The film will "end" (though this ending is still problematic). The film's proposed ending offers itself as false, suggesting that perhaps no film-within-the-film has ever been made. Motoki and Yasuko together will film the film testament, as we move toward another attempt at closure with the following series of shots:

1. shot of Yasuko looking over a rail
2. zoom in, high angle on her fallen body strewn on sidewalk
3. close-up of Yasuko, her eyes closed
4. zoom out, high angle on empty sidewalk
5. close-up of Yasuko
6. high angle on a fallen body
7. close-up of Yasuko
8. high angle with no body.

Next Motoki is seen in close-up filming on the same street as the beginning images prior to suicide. This time others enter the subjective frame and demand the camera back. The oscillating images that portray Motoki running give way to a confrontation with Yasuko on the staircase landing. Motoki goes to the railing, then a subjective shot follows his point of view while falling. A close shot of his body shows others entering to grab the camera.

Representation can suffer infinite deaths and still survive: in the end, we are greeted with the circularity of the imagery, and something more. The closing of the image loop brings us back to the figure of mise-en-abîme and the Möbius strip. Motoki, like the time traveler hero of Chris Marker's *La Jetée*, witnesses his own death, but unlike *La Jetée*, no science fiction apparatus assures us in this case that this oxymoronic situation can be deciphered.

Among Oshima's "difficult" films, this one stands out as most puzzling. More than ever Oshima will construct images as sign systems of a dream logic, images deceiving in the concreteness of their representation, as the meanings evoked by them drift far away from their everyday, literal interpretations. Let me return to the question of the avant-garde film-within-the-film.

Sato (1973: 325–327) tells a story concerning the production of this film that is amusing in its offering of a quite simple, even mundane version of its genesis. According to Sato, Oshima wrote a first script treatment based on the idea of a man who leaves his will on film before he commits suicide out of despair with the student movement. Haru Masato, who was a twenty-year-old avant-garde filmmaker whom Oshima met when he judged a young filmmakers contest, became Oshima's prototype of this man. Sato (1973: 325–327) suggests that the avant-garde film-within-the-film simply stems from Haru as model. This explanation, however, looks less at how the avant-garde imagery is mobilized in the film than it should; it some ways it parallels Branigan's (1984: 154) contention, alluded to earlier, "that the testament film is ultimately censured because it blocks a social geste and elides ideological context. When we return to the landscapes of the testament film to watch Motoki refilm them we see considerably more that was evident in the testament film; we are shown what is absent in the testament." Branigan's assumption that the testament film is censured by the narrative discourse, by the authorial voice of Oshima, rather than just critiqued by characters in the film, is unfounded. When the characters return to the scene, they find another context, other images, but what this otherness signifies is not as unilateral as the failure of the testament images to signify ideologically. Certainly this film does not simply ask for images to have clear ideological signification, with no inquiry into truth, into subjectivity, into dream logic. It would be negating itself, which is not what the film does, not even what the circularity of the ending does. This film flirts with nihilism, but tips its final hand-off to the imagination, to renewal, to creative regeneration.

Isn't this what Oshima sees in the Haru-type imagery that so fascinates him? It coincides with his own subjective investment in framing and images that do not "speak" directly but suggest through their composition a complexly subjective space.

Sato's (1973: 326) interpretation also stresses the nihilism and despair at the failure of the student movement in the fall of 1969. Students struggled to stop the prime minister from visiting the United States by staging demonstrations that were called "the Tokyo War," which made the aftermath, the year following the students' defeat, the "postwar" of the Tokyo War (a play on the Japanese word *sengo* as the appellation describing the period after World War II). In this interpretation Oshima is chronicling that despair through fictional means. However, is Oshima only interested in retelling and commenting on the history of those demonstrations, or is he looking at the process of political opposition and the negotiations of alternative collectivities, theoretically? If his engagement is not to be explained through reflection theory, if it is more theoretical, then we need to do more than trace historical references. We need to understand each debate staged in the film in its contribution to political theory.

What I have tried to do here is to see the film as powerfully questioning any such fixing of interpretations, to see it as more interested in contradictions between different modes of representation and their ability to offer us a view of a moment in history, of objective reality *or* of subjectivity. So the two lines of Sato's interpretation, the first that reduces Oshima's investment in portraying avant-garde expression to an anecdote of production and the second that thematically reduces his portrayal of student protest to a chronicle of despair, miss the tension of debate the film engages. This film, like the others in this chapter, loses in reductive readings its very engagement with the apparatus of representation in relationship to history and the unconscious. Such engagement was most successful in Oshima's next film, *Ceremonies* (distributed under the problematic translation *The Ceremony*), which reached Oshima's largest international audience and garnered huge critical acclaim.

RITUALS, DESIRE, AND DEATH IN OSHIMA'S *CEREMONIES*

Funerals, weddings, and gatherings of the *ie,* the family clan, are the obvious ceremonies referred to in the title of Oshima's 1971 film. An ear to the ground, the buried body of the imaginary, a double triangular game of pitches, hits, misses, and losses, eight rituals of death positioning the crucial annihilation of patriarchy are also *Ceremonies,* rituals of acting out that the film ceremoniously performs.

Recall my earlier reference to acting out as a psychoanalytic construct indicating actions taken by a subject in the grip of his or her unconscious wishes and fantasies. The textual analysis of *Ceremonies* will involve portraying the pivoting of the film through the bifurcated trajectory between conscious recall and unconscious acting out, reenactment. It will also involve further exploration of how a text might be seen as a trope for the psyche, for subjectivity, beyond the psychological construction of characters, beyond the representation of fictional psyches.

The attention of the analyst, then, is first offered to the conventional categories of character and narrative structure, the elements of fictional representation that we must work through to move beyond. The main character is Masuo, whose name means "Man of Manchuria." Although Masuo is situated within an ie, a Japanese family structure, a heritage of determining family relations that should provide his only self-definition, his voice-over moves him outside that construct, to allow us to see him as a kind of narrative center of critical importance that cannot be reduced to the term "protagonist." Masuo is a site; he is of Manchuria. He is the representation that recalls the past as an address to four other characters, his cousins Terumichi, Setsuko, and Tadashi, and his aunt, Ritsuko, who also happen to be the players in the imaginary baseball game in its three-strike inscription at the film's beginning, middle, and end.

Opening Masuo and Ritsuko	Telephone at station—zoom in to close-up on Masuo					
1947 1st flashback Voice-over narration addressed to Terumichi	Manchuria	Satsumo estate Ceremony for 1st anniversary of Masuo's father's death	Masuo's bath given by Setsuko	First sake Terumichi with disinfectant	Courtyard, cousins as children, ear-to-ground ritual	Cousins' baseball game
Back to present Masuo and Ritsuko	On train, corridor Masuo asks about baseball memory					
1952 2d flashback Voice-over narration addressed to Setsuko	Masuo's return from baseball tournament for mother's death	Masuo and Setsuko at altar / father's will revealed	Grandfather's seduction of Setsuko	Terumichi replaces Grandfather	Masuo and Ritsuko at altar	Mother's funeral Father's will read Grandfather "rehabilitated"
Back to present Masuo and Ritsuko	Dockside Question: round-trip ticket for Ritsuko? Compare boat trips, Manchuria and present	Masuo and Ritsuko				
1956 3d flashback Voice-over narration addressed to Tadashi	Uncle Isamu's wedding ceremony—songs of each family member	Cousins drink—Masuo gets sword—he, Terumichi, and Ritsuko in bed	Masuo watching Setsuko—gift of sword	Masuo sees Ritsuko with Terumichi	Next morning—Terumichi's death	

Back to present
Masuo and
Ritsuko

Interior of boat
cabin—Ritsuko asleep,
kiss in close-up

On deck—Masuo
proposes
marriage to Ritsuko

1961
4th flashback
Voice-over narration
addressed to
Ritsuko

Masuo's
brideless
wedding—
Tadashi's right-
wing outburst

Tadashi dead,
brideless
honeymoon

Masuo, Ritsuko,
and Terumichi
coffin ritual,
displace
Tadashi's corpse

Back to present

Masuo and
Ritsuko

Back to present
Masuo and Ritsuko on way to
island—announce Terumichi was
Grandfather's *son*

1971
5th flashback
Voice-over narration
addressed to
Ritsuko, again

Grandfather's
funeral—
Masuo head of
ie

Masuo and
Ritsuko
embrace—ritual
burial—telegram
Terumichi dead

Back to present
Voice-over describes
action—no
direct address

Masuo and Ritsuko arrive on
island—find Terumichi dead,
testament, Ritsuko's suicide

Final scene—Masuo alone, beach—
then imaginary reenaction of
childhood baseball game

Fig. 1. Major sequences in *Gishiki* (Ceremonies), displaying flashbacks and
narrative patterns.

Analytical Conventions of the Text

The flashback narrative structure can be understood as an exoskeleton for the film, a formal order of double, linear narrative progressions within two distinct temporalities. I have described this exoskeleton aspect of the film-work using a diagram (fig. 1). As we can see, the "present" sequences narrate the journey of Masuo and Ritsuko by train, ship, and then small boat to Teru-michi's island on the days following their grandfather's death, during which his funeral was to have taken place. Intercut with this voyage are five flash-backs referring to five separate historical moments, 1947, 1952, 1956, 1961, and 1971, which trace the troubled survival and then demise of the Sakurada ie in postwar Japan.

Laid out like this by the analyst, the body of the film rests in a state that makes it appear far more conventional than it did as we were watching its moves. In this funerary pose we might forget that the diagram is only of a shell, a deceiving organizational defense, not the filmwork, the functioning of the text. And we might take Masuo and the Sakurada ie as something other than symbolic fictional constructs, as we try to fit the film far too neatly back into its skeletal frame, claiming that all its difficult disjunctures are a prob-lem or emblem of Masuo's imagination. The text would be conventionalized to represent a character's memory, his psyche. The flashbacks would conform with the Hollywood dream or fantasy sequence, a vision motivated by the ex-planation that they belong to a character in a distorted mental state.

Psychical Excess as a Textual Trope

The film, however, performs specific maneuvers to escape these analytic con-ventions whose function it is to simplify and thus restrict the analysis of a filmic text. If Masuo, Man of Manchuria, the central character, the main ac-tant, seems to be the voice that recalls the images and the diegetic sounds of the past, where is the electronic music coming from? This is not as face-tious a question as it might appear, since the reflexivity of Oshima's *The Bat-tle of Tokyo, or the Story of the Young Man Who Left His Will on Film,* as we just saw, is always asking just such pointed questions about filmic construction to indicate a similar concept of filmic textuality, a film with a will of its own. Its main character, Motoki, like the Boy in *Boy,* or the criminal/victim in *Death by Hanging,* or the couple in *Realm of the Senses,* or Masuo in *Ceremonies,* is not to be taken as an explanation of the text but as a device within it, and not just the device that formalist/structuralist theorists of narrative recognized and defined. It is a device that lends its human, representational form to film to facilitate a sliding between the psychology of character as construct within narrative structure and the sense in which the psychoanalytic processes en-acted in the text exceed the location of any one character's psyche. These texts by Oshima, along with some other modernist works, perform a theory

of subjectivity, the divided psyche, the processes of displacement, condensation, and reversal into the opposite, rather than merely representing a
character as displaying this psychic state. The text itself is constituted as a
trope for the psyche, for subjectivity. Characters and narratives offered up
by such a film are at a certain level elaborate ruses, structures that (falsely)
mirror, motivate, deflect, and activate textual figuration. In its performative
theatricality, the text is always turning in surprise on its own next move, always knowing and forgetting that these surprising sequences were bound to
happen. As we shall see from the detailed analysis of specific sequences, editing patterns, camera angles, and sound montage, it is in the very construction of image and sound composition that the text's processes are presented
as psychic processes. The text seems to be performing mental acts in which
charged energies are the forces that shift the representation into the dynamic, odd forms it manifests. After examining the lines of this force, the
designs it composes throughout the film, I will speculate on how this psychic
force might itself be seen as formed in social history.

Ear to the Ground, Dead Brother

Masuo's dead younger brother is first mentioned by Grandfather as part of
a statement that serves as a sound bridge between the scene in Manchuria
at the beginning of the first flashback (1947) and the segment that follows,
the ceremony at the Sakurada estate commemorating the first anniversary
of Masuo's father's death. "Masuo is irreplaceable," the patriarch says, then
directs a question to Masuo whose suspended answer will resonate throughout the film: "What happened to your younger brother?" Masuo is told he
must "live for his younger brother as well," an admonition made during a
tracking shot from a close-up of Grandfather along a diagonal to frame the
young Masuo in parallel close-up.

   This compositional displacement from elder patriarch to Masuo is a ceremony of visual replacement that indeed marks the character's irreplace-
ability within the *ie* and inscribes a complicated reference to Japanese traditions of inheritance. The scenographic frame found by the camera
movement here delineates the strict rule for replacing patriarchal power
within the ie from generation to generation. The eldest male son assumes
the head of the ie and all property rights without any rivalry, merit system,
or possible division of lands. The other sons split off from the ie (move to
the city or to imperialist territory) to leave the family lands intact. The mys-
tery here is the skipped generation, that of the dead father. Was Masuo's father the legitimate heir, and if so, was the move of his family to Manchuria
only a result of the war? What of Tadashi or Terumichi, and their fathers?
The revelation of the family tree is partial; its forms and branches are withheld by the narrative, although Uncle Isamu, the communist, suggests the

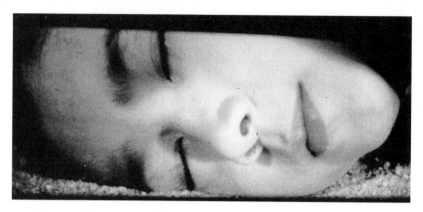

17. Extreme close-up; Masuo's head fills the frame. *Gishiki* (Ceremonies, 1971). Still courtesy of Oshima Productions.

explanation that will finally obtain, when at the beginning of the family dinner segment he charges that Grandfather was the illegitimate father of all the children in the family. A family tree whose latest branches stem from a diseased trunk: we are therefore quite accepting of Terumichi's entrance later in the scene with a horticultural spray gun, to dose the gathered relatives with disinfectant to "purify Japan." It is the first of the "acting out" scenes in which the narrative exposition snags at a moment of partial disclosure, generating a friction that sends the representation off into another register, that of the symbolic gesture.

Masuo passes out at the end of the disinfectant scene, ostensibly inebriated by his first drink of sake. But the elaborate crane-in on his drooping figure is accompanied by a voice-over address to Terumichi, "It was you who intoxicated me," suggesting the overdetermination of this momentary "death" and the homoerotic tie between the two cousins that is based in Masuo's and Terumichi's intuitive understanding of their grandfather's corruption, a knowledge that will be triangulated in their relationship to both Setsuko and Ritsuko. The following scene in the family courtyard returns to the register of acting out, and it is here that the dead brother emerges in absentia as the fixation that encapsulates for the character Masuo the tension of suggested incestuous sexuality and criminal imperialism displaced into another scene. The other scene is a ritual in which Masuo puts his ear to the ground to listen for the cries of his dead brother, supposedly buried alive in Manchuria. Its first inscription is given as a series of shots from widely disjunct and tricky angles, a turning of camera vision in a pattern of irregularity that can only be compared to the bold planar gyrations of constructivist sculpture. The pattern of shots is as follows:

1. Long shot of the courtyard; Masuo bends to put ear to ground
2. 180° shift to a close-up of Masuo listening to ground
3. Long shot from this side; Masuo extremely distant, near altars/monuments.
4. Extreme close-up; Masuo's head fills the frame; flute music begins, then a crane movement from Masuo's postrate body reveals the entrance of the other children into the scene. Ritsuko and Tadashi imitate his listening pose, while Terumichi stands near them (indicated by just his feet in this frame).
5. New angle as Tadashi stands to sing a song, "Under Red Sun of Manchuria," which was a Japanese army song of the Manchurian occupation.
6. Return to the extreme close-up on Masuo
7. End with a shot of the four children standing as Masuo tells of digging the grave of his brother, and hearing the brother still crying after Masuo left to catch up with the other fleeing Japanese. Terumichi makes the group promise not to tell what Masuo has said.

The play between extreme close-up and extreme long shot, as well as the craning camera movement that discloses the entrance of the others into the scene, is certainly an elegant and flashy use of wide-screen technique; but more significant, the scope of the cinema here is extended into a realm of imaginary representation, where elements appear in a space whose scene is not so much ordered as floating, circling, jumping along a sculptural pathway that forms its own dynamic logic. At the base of this construction is an association of the other with the self and the self with the other. A displaced cry of anguish that Masuo associates with the dead younger brother, and with which his young cousins attempt to emphathize, figures as the secret of a childhood among war criminals. The surrealism of the scene, which the mention of frogs, moles, and snakes augments, does not "belong" to Masuo's imaginary alone, an obsessive syndrome that we might understand as his character trait; the children and their reaction to the world they have inherited belong to a larger imaginary of the film, a psychic formation that generates narration of this family as a response to the "real" of postwar Japan, a provocative assertion that I can only "prove" by continuing to trace and retrace the lines of the cinematic imaginary in the film.

The dead brother returns later, after Masuo discovers Ritsuko and Terumichi in bed together, embracing, the very bed he shared with them moments before, until he left to give Setsuko the sword that will be her suicide weapon. Masuo returns alone to the courtyard, accompanied only by the dissonance of the electronic music to reenact, as a young adult, the earlier scene. Then the ritual has a somewhat inverted return after the grandfather's death, when Masuo curls up on the ground in what is more like a fetal position than

18. Rituals include Masuo curling up on the ground in a fetal position as Ritsuko attempts to comfort him with an embrace. *Gishiki* (Ceremonies, 1971). Still courtesy of Oshima Productions.

his earlier ear-to-ground listening, as Ritsuko attempts to comfort him with an embrace. Masuo's monologue, though, draws the connection as he complains of being "suffocated, buried alive," as more dissonant music is heard. When he adds, "Someone is listening to the earth . . . it's my older brother," it becomes clear that the scene is one of projected self/other reversal, with the fetal younger brother also being the aborted self.

At the end of the film, Ritsuko joins her husband, Terumichi, in suicide; the scene takes place in a pink-toned set, a fantasy exterior that Ritsuko and Masuo discover inside Terumichi's island hut, and which appears to be a Bali Hai fantasy borrowed from a Hollywood Orient. Masuo is left alone to return once more to his ear-to-ground listening. This time the ritual frames a return of the baseball game and thus explicitly connects the acting out of listening to the dead brother with the acting out of the familial configuration within the frame of a baseball diamond, which I will discuss next.

Strikes and a Home Run

The family game of baseball that is depicted in the 1947 flashback may never have taken place. That is to say, when the flashback ends, it does so

19. At the end of the film, Ritsuko joins her husband, Terumichi, in suicide in what appears as a Bali Hai fantasy set borrowed from a Hollywood Orient as Masuo watches. *Gishiki* (Ceremonies, 1971). Still courtesy of Oshima Productions.

on a shot of Masuo pitching with the "reverse shot" being a dream screen formed by the glass pane of the train door, which is held in frame until Ritsuko enters to report her own nightmare. She responds to Masuo's question of whether she remembers the game we have just seen with a flat denial that it happened, telling Masuo that he was the only family member ever to play baseball, despite his desperate insistence that she "was the batter and Terumichi was catching."

Did the familial game take place? Of course, if one considers that Masuo's address to Terumichi over the game image is only apparently disjunct in its concern with whom Masuo's father had intended to marry, why Setsuko could not comply with those intentions, and the unknown story of Terumichi's mother. For Setsuko certainly was the referee of the children's attempt to figure out sexuality in the older generation and in themselves. Masuo, as pitcher, throws balls into the strike zone over home plate, enacting a male configuration that can only curve desire along this formation, the show of prowess that he is always losing. Masuo, a virgin at the film's end, surrounded by the dead family, is presented with the reenactment of his blocked desire. It materializes as the youthful family, once again playing baseball with him, Masuo, the lone and abandoned adult, who nonetheless confronts his youthful self pursuing a long fly ball into his own disappearance. No one can hear Masuo's painful narration of the past; Ritsuko was with him in the present even as he, in voice-over, spoke about not being able to speak to her. The others were already the phantoms they appear to be in this final act.

But to hit the ritual of baseball even further, we must follow Masuo as he steals home late for his mother's funeral wearing his player's uniform from the national championship game. Rather than being bawled out by his grandfather for missing the ritual of death of his mother, he is told that "it is not important where women are buried" and that "your mother was a pitiable woman." This denial by the patriarch of the maternal meets with a symbolic rebellion on Masuo's part; as retribution, he attempts to burn his baseball artifacts as sacrifice on her altar, to denounce the only male activity in which he excelled. Stopped by Setsuko who reclaims his glove, he also receives from her, at his mother's funeral, his father's will. Setsuko usurps his dead mother's place and through her connection to his father guides him back to the patriarchal will.

Disclosure here is accomplished with delays and questions ambiguously floating over the scenes. For example, the scene of the sacrifice of baseball begins with a close-up of just the fire and the polysemic, voice-over query addressed to Setsuko, "Did you know what would happen that night?" The film's viewer certainly doesn't, and takes this question to refer to the scene I have just spoken about that follows immediately on the articulation of the question. But the filmwork is directing the voice-over to bluff a bunt when it is preparing to drive hard into right field, and it is here that the baseball game, always an acting out of sexual desire, gives way to the ritual of desire, sex, power, and death.

Desire, Sex, Power, and Death

The manipulation of drives is the way power aligns itself with the symbolic order. Desire, sexuality, and death can become the tools of power, what it needs to exercise control and maintain its hold. This is made clear when, in the scene following the one analyzed above, Grandfather Kuzuomi and Setsuko have their showdown, no duel in the sun, no samurai swords, yet. The conflict is across a sexual boundary marked by a dividing screen in the foreground that slices the room and the frame into equal halves, Setsuko in the light, Kuzuomi contained in darkness. As the camera cranes in a semicircle, violating the screen separation, Kuzuomi crosses the line on the tatami beyond which Setsuko has been kneeling. He places Setsuko's head on the line and his hand on her thigh. The line of the tatami, like the dark screen divider, is a demarcation of space that operates as a territorial indication of ag-

20. Kuzuomi places Setsuko's head on the tatami mat line and assumes a patriarchal control. *Gishiki* (Ceremonies, 1971). Still courtesy of Oshima Productions.

gressive authority. Setsuko is lined up for one more rape, necessitated by her voicing a memory of the past that Kazuomi, as authority, had suppressed. Setsuko recalls an earlier rape by Kazuomi through which he kept her from marrying his son, Masuo's father, Kanichuro.

The centralized symmetry of this high angle on Setsuko pressed against the line of authority is part of a larger system of symmetrical composition operative in the film. All the major family ceremony scenes, the dinners and funerals, contain highly symmetrical establishing and reestablishing shots, in which patriarchal power fills the center of the frame and the family is lined up in two parallel lines symmetrically filling the right and left of the image. Close-ups of Kazuomi display the same absolute formal symmetry and are even lit from both sides to accentuate the symmetrical effect. In the earlier flashbacks, the young Masuo is similarly centered in the symmetrical frame, and Terumichi briefly matches Grandfather's symmetry when Masuo falls from favor, disgraced by his reaction to his "brideless" marriage, a scene we will examine shortly.

Contrasted to the use of symmetry to inscribe authority's power are various asymmetrical compositions that are used to indicate the breakdown of

21. The centralized symmetry of this high angle on Setsuko pressed against the line of authority is part of a larger system of symmetrical composition operative in the film *Gishiki* (Ceremonies, 1971). Still courtesy of Oshima Productions.

authority or defiance of its rule. If we return to the sequence discussed above, where Setsuko has been symmetrically framed, about to be raped, what follows is Kuzuomi's retreat, with Terumichi's entrance revealed by another swooping crane movement. Mysteriously, the line shifts between shots: instead of being underneath Setsuko's head to mark the central symmetry, it suddenly appears as a dynamic angle at Setsuko's side as she initiates Terumichi into a willing and gentle sexuality, consecrating their complicity. She guides his hand into the slit of her robe, given in extreme, metonymic close-up, as she tells him not to hurry.

Thus there is a sexuality that deregulates authority, and it is associated with the feminine, with women as initiator, with Setsuko and her daughter Ritsuko, with Terumichi whose oppositional stance affiliates him with the women, and to some extent with Masuo in his misrecognized sympathy with the knowledge of the other three. Setsuko's final statement is a spectacle made with blood; after a shot of the family ceremoniously grouped in a semicircle at the site of her suicide, a closer shot depicts a sword pulled from her body giving way to a spurt of blood defiantly crossing the image. Like her mother, Ritsuko had movements of compliance: as a youngster, in her sailor middy, and later in her fifties pink crinoline when she stood to sing the song of the faithful Japanese woman at the family gathering. She was presented as contemporary, Americanized, but nonetheless the traditional ideal, centered within the image and the family. Toward the end of the flashbacks, and certainly within the "present" journey to the island, she is portrayed off center, with a gaze that is directed away, and ultimately inward, her defiance taking the form of a removal to the edges, a refusal to participate.

No woman performs more of a decentering act, though, than does the absent bride. Like Ritsuko, she is supposed to represent the ideal of pure Japanese womanhood, but she is absent from her own wedding, no longer existing. Perhaps no such embodiments of the ideal of pure Japanese womanhood have ever existed, as Grandmother hints in her narration of her own honeymoon. At the wedding, amid the Westernized tables of the modern banquet hall, the camera roams, searching for her, returning only to the empty space beside Masuo, never attaining the symmetrical lines of the earlier family gatherings. Authority/power is not the same as it had been: it demonstrates in its most recent ceremony its own new weakness, its desperate attempt at realignment, even as it attempts to hide its own dysfunction; the emperor has new clothes, and for a moment no one says a word of protest. However, the disturbances do continue, in the form of Tadashi's fascist outburst and accidental death. Tadashi disrupts the wedding by reading from a tract called "Project for the Reconstruction of a New Japan," which was a widely circulated right-wing program from the thirties. Though Tadashi represents an extreme right-wing position, the psychic components of his discontent and even some of his political pronouncements are congruent with the reactions his cousins have to the familial industrial order.

The cousins are bound in a knotted tangle of right and left rebellion, although Masuo is sometimes left silent, staring out from the center of the frame, momentarily silenced, as when he alone has no song at Uncle Isamu's wedding, telling us only that had he sung, it would have been a song of the sentimental left, something like "Ban the Bomb." Masuo's voice comes from the unconscious, as contortion. His cries are those of a fragmented logic that can turn an entire scene into a spasm of imagery and sounds that include among their meanings, that this never really took place.

Such a scene is the false honeymoon with the absent bride, in which Masuo first attempts to make love to a pillow substitute and then "rapes" his grandfather whom Terumichi forces to comply with this ceremony of both humiliation and consummation. The scene engages the theatrics of sex and death, the honeymoon and the wake, as each gesture gives way to the image that the film seems to highlight as its decentered fold, Masuo embracing Ritsuko in the coffin, angled in a canted close-up. It is a rebellious image, charged and erotic, full of force, but hopeless. Glances do not meet, and Terumichi slips out of their hands through the door to return only as a telegram, later inscribed over another scene of their embrace, only the words, "Terumichi dead, stop, Terumichi dead." The stop in between the repetition is the signal that counterceremonies of the imaginary are wrought in pain and death; Setsuko, Ritsuko, Terumichi, and Tadashi all represent a certain resistance, a desired rebellion to Kuzuomi's authority, but all of them find their ultimate cry of rebellion in deaths that are accidents, suicides, or possibly murders, deaths that are violent, outside ceremonial mourning, deaths that seem to be the only way out.

The Imaginary and Ideology

The historical references in the film, the flashback periodicity that chronicles postwar Japan, invites an ideological reading that maps the events of the fiction onto events of the "real" of history. One mentions the American Occupation, the U.S.–Japan security treaty of 1951, the growth of Zaibatsu, the big industrial concerns modeled on the family, the sixties demonstrations against the renewal of the U.S.–Japan security treaty, the suicide of Mishima, the bourgeoisification of Japanese values (McCormick 1974). If the discrete references to a political reality punctuate the film, they are also particularly and deliberately vague. For to clarify merely a political reality would withdraw the film from the realm of inquiry through which the narrative and the film-work have been voyaging. For it has been asking the question I framed earlier, how psychical force might itself be formed in history. It is exploring the extraordinarily difficult theoretical problem of the formation of the subject in culture, the question of the affectivity of a political/social order on the psyche.

The film serves to convey the very issues that elude the social psychologist studying Japan in this postwar period. The points of conjunction with these studies will provide the denouement of this textual analysis. Consider a theory of Japanese psychology developed by Doi L. Takeo (1963) based on speculation on the significance of the word *amaeru* (p. 266), whose polysemy allows it to mean for the Japanese all of the following: to depend and presume on another's love, to indulge another, to wish to be taken care of (as with a small child's feelings toward his/her parents), to wish to cling to the love object. Doi takes this linguistic multivalence to indicate certain characteristics of the Japanese as desiring subjects. He claims that the "dependency on parents is fostered and institutionalized into the social structure" and that this is coupled with a "strong psychological importance of dependency on parents and the continuing importance of the originally infantile wish to be loved" (p. 268).

I suppose in some ways *Ceremonies* could be taken to be an illustration of this "finding." But then the film could also be taken as a deconstruction of the simplicity of a formation of a unified social subject who could be encapsulized as desiring love. Certainly there is nothing in the supposedly specifically Japanese social psychology of Doi that is not a description of the Western subject as well. So if the *psyche* of the Japanese is *not* different in kind, what is different are the historical conditions to which this psyche is subject, and it is here that the double temporality of the flashback and the historical references have resonances that are particular for this film as psychic trope.

We see our subject *Masuo* as site, locus of activities suspended between two temporalities, a present that is a journey with a dead end, to the isolated, uninhabited island, Terumichi's island, the island of the dead lost brother (for Terumichi is a double for the lost brother and a past that creeps up on the present, a history that develops, pessimistically, foreclosing any theory for the subject in the imposed doom of capitalist expectation). Masuo reaches the end of the line, the refusal of his generation to continue. It is in this act of violent, total negation that the film's "acting out" becomes a social critique we can remember, but its force of affectivity surges from the unconscious as poetics and theatrics, not to be reduced to discourse.

FIVE FILMS OF A REVOLUTIONARY MOMENT

Taken together, these five films—*Death by Hanging, Diary of a Shinjuku Thief, Boy, The Battle of Tokyo,* and *Ceremonies*—made in under four years, testify to a moment of political upheaval that spurred a theoretical engagement with filmmaking that rarely has been possible in film history. The works, as we have seen, are radical, complex, and yet rewarding in their intensity of vision. They define a new aesthetic for film. I have tried to show how much psychoanalytic structures define the poetics and the politics of these films, how in both form and meaning they are deeply concerned with the poetics of the psyche.

I would like, in summing up this chapter, to emphasize characteristics that make these films a successful theoretical venture into revealing the unconscious of history, the manner in which Brechtian ideas might be mixed with psychoanalytic ones in a cinematic context. I present this linked list of the means by which this group of films accomplishes this:

1. Narrative figuration that foregrounds uncertainties and contradictions. This helps to create:
2. Active sequential fragmentation. These fragments and sometimes highly autonomous segments are tied together by an:
3. Active poetic linkage of elements. Visually, a highly composed image uses:
4. Symmetry and asymmetry in dynamic opposition. In addition to formally foregrounded compositions, the films use:

5. Reflexive narration and theatricalization.
6. Political messages are pointed, yet complexly articulated, more aimed at the consciousness of theoretical issues of self, other, family, history, and the state than at discrete "lessons." This is due to a:
7. Conception of the self as a fragmented psyche that inhabits and acts in a social space where ethics and freedom are constantly at issue.

CHAPTER FOUR

Signs of Sexuality in Oshima's
Tales of Passion

Realms, Empires, the Senses, Passion: these are the *mots clefs* that circulate in the highly significant European and American titles of Oshima's pair of films, *Ai no korida* (Realm of the Senses, 1976) and *Ai no borei* (Empire of Passion, 1980). Behind these keywords lie both the continuing work of Oshima's films on the representation of sexuality, desire, and the imaginary in a contemporary social-historical context and the tale of a Japanese filmmaker whose film production is increasingly that of an exile. Distance comes to Oshima, as critical essayist and film director, through his own displeasure at the traditions of his native country, but his exile is also due to the recent state of the Japanese film industry and the types of films it is willing to finance.

This chapter examines how this pair of films by Oshima signifies a fascinating cross-referencing of the different historical representations of sexuality within Japanese and Western culture: therefore, the title "Signs of Sexuality." I wish to particularly take into account the fact that this pair of films finds Oshima choosing his direction from an imaginary realm of thought that crosses Japanese and Western cultures and their different histories of sexuality, censorship, the subject, and the psyche. In this context, *Realm of the Senses* and *Empire of Passion* are French/Japanese films. They are Japanese in the sense that their director and cast are Japanese, the Japanese language is spoken throughout, and their stories take place in Japan and refer to Japanese history; they are French in that they are produced by Anatole Dauman, with European and American distribution more of a goal, as we shall see, than Japanese distribution. In offering Oshima French money, Dauman also offered him conditions of production that were not possible in Japan and the concomitant ability to make a film that could never have been made in Japan at that time. Dauman supposedly offered Oshima the financing to make a film of hard-core pornography in France, because he was impressed with the success of Oshima's previous films at French film festivals. Oshima writes of the conditions of this agreement, saying that Dauman promised him no other restrictions on the creation of the film.

According to Oshima, the choosing of the title *L'Empire des sens* for the French release of *Ai no korida* and its subsequent translation into English as *In the Realm of the Senses* (the U.S. title *Realm of the Senses* drops the prepositional phrase, which the British use) was the outgrowth of the type of anecdotal occurrence that haunts film history. Apparently, Oshima found his European friends somewhat taken aback by the idea that he was to make a film whose proposed title meant "bullfight of love"; supposedly, he heard one too many times a response signaling a literal interpretation of the title along the lines of "I didn't know you had bullfights in Japan." Oshima claims that in talking this over with his French producer, Dauman suggested a title that would echo the Roland Barthes collection of essays on Japan, *L'Empire des signes,* which had just appeared. Oshima finishes this tale with an ironic smile, "Not such a bad idea, no?" (interview with author, 1984).

This tale of course makes anecdotal shrift of a choice that entails a theoretical *parti pris,* but Oshima's wink should be a clue that whatever marketing boost the film received in its triumphal Paris release by making commerce with this French intellectual reference, there is much more at stake in the transformation of this film's title as well as that of the subsequent film, which also reworks some of the same material under the title *L'Empire de la passion* (Empire of Passion). In this case the original Japanese means "phantom of love," which works better in English than "bullfight of love," but used alone would not make the same connection to the earlier film that *Empire of Passion* makes to *Realm of the Senses,* or *Ai no borei* makes to *Ai no korida.* The pairing of these films, which would have been lost with dissimilar titles, plays significant functions in understanding both. It should come as no surprise that the polysemy introduced by these multiple titles in their various languages corresponds to ambiguities that richly define Oshima's textual practice. As we have seen, his films often mark their plurality of interpretations with signs inviting the spectator to take various entrances into these texts; the title *Tokyo senso sengo hiwa* and the English-language title *The Battle of Tokyo, or the Story of the Young Man Who Left His Will on Film* are other examples of such indications of multivalence. Here the context of international production and distribution serves as a supplementary sign of this multiplicity of meaning.

Let's return to these keywords and the doors they might open. The English words *realm* and *empire* are of course, in a sense, synonyms—the American titles alternate between these synonyms, while in French, for example, a single word, *L'Empire,* occurs in both. *L'Empire,* all by itself, suggests many different meanings, ranging from a political state to "power," or "control" in certain French idioms. *Realm* in English suggests the common phrase "realm of the imagination." In English, its use suggests our sense of fiction, the assigning of a topos to the narration of fantasy. This usage crosses over to an English assimilation of Lacanian psychoanalysis; English speakers have a marvelous tendency to transform Lacan's designation, "the Imaginary order" (meaning the aspect of his psychoanalytic topology devoted to libidinal investment and fantasy) by their more familiar phrase, "the realm of the imaginary." These references to fiction and to the psychoanalytic concept of the Imaginary contained in the word *realm* certainly suggest wonderful ways of viewing Oshima's films; as we shall see, the examination of the topology of fiction and the analysis of psychic forces in eroticism are two very central impulses in these works. *Empire* in English and French signals a historical construct of power and the history of imperialism. This then emphasizes that Oshima's films can be read as metaphorical re-viewings of the Japanese imperial heritage, particularly resonant with the single shot in *Realm of the Senses* where the lead characters cross Japanese troops marching through the streets, which, as Heath (1981: 145) has remarked, serves as a minimalist reminder that this story of sexual obsession occurs as Japan engages in what it terms "the Greater East-Asian War." References that would dominate a more "realistic" film style here become selected gestures toward the real, enough to indicate clearly and forcefully the film's ideological implications, but never compromising its simultaneous investment in fantasy. In *Empire of Passion,* similar ideological signifiers surround the village police. The prepositional phrase, "In the realm," leads us into interiority and inside the boundary of the imaginary, but we are also inside the historical empire of Japan. This double emphasis can be taken as highlighting these topologies and chronologies and as questioning their intersections over the course of the films, as we shall see.

To continue this semantic investigation into the second half of the titles, we encounter the words *senses* and *passion* in English, *sens* and *passion* in French. In French *sens* is ambiguously multiple; Oshima's empire is at once one of "the sensual," "the sensorial" and "meaning," meanings that are not entirely lost in the English *senses,* but that are far less evident. *Passion* in both languages can indicate both desire and pleasure. All of these connotations exist in paradigmatic comparison to Barthes's *signes* (signs, semiotics).

Surrounded by the semantic space of these titles, Oshima's films then can be seen as a specific commentary on Barthes's *L'Empire des signes* (The Empire of Signs) and the manner in which it represents both a romance with and a misunderstanding of Japan, while still presenting incisive analyses of some of what constitutes what we might call the "difference of Japan." To pursue this, let us look briefly at Barthes's volume.

Barthes's vision is of a Japan founded on a ritual exchange of signs whose signifiers take on the minimalist splendor of an aesthetic tradition permeating all aspects of daily life, but whose signifieds remain opaque, if not ab-

sent. The tea ceremony epitomizes a semiotic structure that Barthes finds reiterated even in pachinko, the Japanese electronic game roughly equivalent
to Western pinball. Barthes's essays are the brilliant product of the elegance
of his semiotic project and of a three-week visit to Japan. They are also the
product of a lingering far-Orientalism (the positing of an exotic and romantic difference in Oriental culture) parallel to what Edward Said (1979)
found to be the ideological underpinnings of a Western view of the Middle
East. The essays provide testimony to the dangers inherent in letting history
and anthropology be evacuated from a semiotic study. For as scintillating and
provocative as Barthes's essays are, they remain founded on an ignorance of
Japanese historical explanations and evolution of the phenomena addressed,
assuming an emptiness of signs that are themselves filled with the "invisible"
weight of a cultural investment determined by a specific history.

Oshima highlights this difference in shifting his title as we discussed
above, from "sign" to "meaning," from "sign" to "sensuality," from "sign" to
"passion." To proclaim his notion of sensuality and of interpretation in a
Japanese context, Oshima offers us first a tale of the sexual act itself and then
a ghost story infused with sexuality. Ironically, the tale of the sexual act, *Realm
of the Senses,* was so transgressive of current Japanese laws governing representation of sexuality in the visual image that it has never been shown in
Japan in an uncensored print; the omnipresent visual pornography one
sees on Japanese newsstands and in films is not allowed to show images of
genitals and therefore cannot directly represent copulation. These laws that
governed the film's interdiction in Japan are laws that do not correspond to
Japanese visual traditions of sexual presentation; the *ukiyo-e,* the Japanese
woodblock print, had as one of its most significant subject matters the representation of sexual intercourse in which genitals not only figured but were
exaggerated in size so as to dominate the composition, twisting the surrounding space into a surface designed to glorify their acrobatic feats of penetration. The laws that forbid genital representation are of relatively recent
vintage. These laws were in part products of the Meiji restoration's response
to Western expectations. Japanese traditions of sexuality are different, and
it is on this "forgotten" visual, theatrical, and literary heritage of sexual and
psychoanalytic signification that Oshima draws. Oshima's Japanese precedents are many, including the ukiyo-e, the tales of Saikaku, and parts of
Kabuki plays devoted to erotic themes.

VOYEURISTIC EPISODES AND THE THEATRICALITY OF SEXUALITY

Episodic in its structure, *Realm of the Senses* traces the history of a seduction
of a serving girl, Sada, by her boss and master, Kichi, as it becomes the story
of their mutual sexual obsession. Each of the episodes is centered on a different sexual scene, a different sexual encounter of the lovers, or encounters

that involve them with others. Their rites of sexual pleasure build increasingly toward sadomasochistic behaviors, but the sadomasochism is only indirectly willed here, as we shall see. The driving force of these characters is not to hurt or be hurt, or even a game of mastery, though these do appear as secondary factors accompanying the central desire. Their desire mocks the notion of will and rationality. It is a desire focused finally on a single object, the impossible sustained pleasure of a nearly constant state of ever-increasing orgasm.

Certainly, the film orchestrates voyeurism in relationship to these sexual scenes, as Heath has so deftly demonstrated in his article "The Question Oshima" (1981: 145–164). Desire is shown as first nourished by the look through an opening in the shoji (the sliding screen) as Sada and another servant watch the master making love with his wife. Heath shows how the audience, first placed in the position of identification with this look, thereafter identifies with other servants looking at Sada and Kichi. He suggests that this ritual of voyeurism in Oshima's film, in being so pronounced and explicit in its repetition of a refigured primal scene, asks the question that cinema must pose for its audience, the question that clarifies that all cinema is driven by voyeurism.

Finally, though, Heath wonders if this film doesn't rejoin a more classic ludic structure of posing the game of voyeurism without really calling the question once and for all in a manner that would transform cinema into an object forever engaged in self-deconstruction. As rich as Heath's engagement with voyeurism proves theoretically, it considers only the portrayal of the gaze and not the portrayal of the object of the gaze (the representation of sex itself within Oshima's film), and it considers voyeurism only in the frame of a Western filmmaking tradition. His argument wants to emphasize Oshima films as primarily Brechtian or Godardian, in all aspects. We have already seen the validity of much of this claim, as Oshima consciously aims at discursive reflection on both social issues and theatrical and filmic form. Heath frames the sexuality and violence in *Realm of the Senses* as a discourse on voyeurism. While I agree that this discourse is significant, it seems to me that Oshima's works have a far greater investment in the imaginary of fiction and in the fascination of sexuality and violence than such an exclusively discursive reading would allow. Heath's reading of Oshima parallels Barthes's looking elsewhere than at the sexuality and violence in Japanese gestures, though Heath's selectivity is based on different premises. What question does Oshima raise once we ask questions about his films as allegories of sex and violence in the visual realm?

The sexuality of *Realm of the Senses* is presented in a particularly theatrical context in which sex doubles as performance. The mock marriage of Sado and Kichi that takes place in their room at an inn introduces a dancer whose song and movements are a folk variation of the Bungaku (masked dance) tradition. The geishas who watch the "marriage" and its consummation be-

22. *Realm of the Senses* does not separate sex from music, dance, and theater. This shot shows how hands and eyes explore slits in the Japanese robes, which also act in the film as a theatrical curtain whose drapes can be drawn to reveal the sexual organs as the actors in the spectacle. *Ai no korida* (Realm of the Senses, 1976). Still courtesy of Oshima Productions.

come performers of their own sexual perversions as the marriage finds its extension as an orgy. As in the scene early in the film in which Sada is presented as having sex with Kichi while she plays the samisen, *Realm of the Senses* does not separate sex from music, dance, and theater. It stages the sounds, gestures, and rhythms of sex as the equivalents of these other performances, capable of being blended with them.

This simply extends a visual metaphor present throughout the film in which the kimono acts as a theatrical curtain whose drapes can be drawn to reveal the sexual organs as the actors in the spectacle. This follows a coding in Kabuki, known as the *obi-hiki*, which translates as the pulling off of the obi (Halford and Halford 1956: 448). An obi is the highly decorative midriff tie that holds a kimono closed. In Kabuki the voluntary loosening of the obi indicates willing participation in a love scene or seduction, but if the man pulls at the obi, this can indicate sexual aggression against the woman's will.

Villains of the Kabuki stage enjoy the pursuit of love in this lusty fashion. A conventionalized struggle with the lad will usually end in the unwinding of

her obi; the villain will strike a triumphant pose grasping the end of the obi,
sometimes between his teeth, during which time he will hold the big toe
of his right foot in a transparently erotic gesture. A milder suggestion of
violence is conveyed by pulling at the long sleeve of a woman's kimono, but
this may only indicate a desire to prevent someone leaving. (Halford and
Halford 1956: 448)

Realm of the Senses marks, by its version of the obi-hiki and by other means,
the transformation of the space of the brothel into a theatrical space, a space
of performance. The rooms of the various inns in which the couple take
refuge and the kimono and *yukata* (summer robes) they wear fill the screen
with lush, patterned reds, reds that echo and frame the redness of the sexual
organs and that also prepare for the red sash to serve as strangulation weapon
and the red blood of castration that becomes Sada's means of inscribing in
writing on Kichi's lifeless body their love, in a high angle shot that turns the
lovers' bodies into a Japanese print, where calligraphy joins the image.

Unlike most other pornography, *Realm of the Senses* does not *reproduce* the
taboos as it violates them; it does not present sex as "naughty" or as an escape fantasy. Instead it appeals to aesthetics and to a notion of theatricality
in which the private, the taboo, cannot exist; the Japanese inns become,
metaphorically, a "magic theater," a space separated from the "real" world
and closely linked to the dream. The senses, sight and hearing, become engaged in perception of a ritual that places the subject in a realm of projected
pain and pleasure; the "real play" is staged in the viewer's psyche. The viewer
can only be brought into the theater in this sense by being exposed to sights
and sounds, and the images and sounds have been orchestrated to that psychoanalytic effect. One aspect of the psychoanalytic dimension of theater,
and by extension, film, is that it can create such exposure. *Realm of the Senses*
takes seriously the psychoanalytic jeopardy in which it places its spectators.

However, like other pornography, it reproduces many of the frames surrounding presentation and narrativity in the theater. If Oshima's filmic theatricalization of sexuality and desire take the psychoanalytic apparatus of narrative and pornography into account, it mobilizes in the process a series of
images whose romance is with violence. If interpretation of such a multiple
text depends on where you choose to select, how you divide and combine
the images, there is in any case an undercurrent of violence and the threat
of castration throughout which comes to dominate and conclude the film.
The film has a movement, a narrative trajectory, that passes through the euphoria of desire to end in a sign of death.

A Samisen, an Egg, a Dildo, and a Silk Sash

The sexual activity in *Realm of the Senses* encompasses a series of episodic variations, but it also develops a narrative, a series of role changes. First there is

Sada, the object of the master's attention, his desire, his aggressive sexual gestures, and his power. In the beginning Sada is passive; she backs into Kichi while on her knees mopping floors. Kichi is active; he summons her to his room and takes "liberties." Kichi's aggression, at first resisted, becomes more seductive; as Sada learns her pleasure, Kichi is less aggressive and also less in command. A meeting of the couple in which Sada plays the samisen and sings as she sits on Kichi during a sexual encounter is pivotal. At first Kichi demands she sing to disguise their sexual activity, but as the scene progresses it becomes one of a woman singing her pleasure. The singing joins representations of sexuality, and especially orgasm, throughout the film that are as much auditory as visual.

The rickshaw scene similarly begins with Sada's refusal of Kichi's sexual advances. They are dressed, outside, and, besides, Sada tells Kichi she has her period. Kichi then performs a gesture that transforms the scene: he withdraws his finger from underneath Sada's kimono and licks Sada's blood, displaying his willingness to break the taboos about feminine sexuality and savor sexuality in all its visceral exchanges of fluids.

This scene is all the more intriguing given the traditional Japanese menstrual taboo. A story from *Sado no shima,* "Otawa Pond," has intrigued the folklorist Segawa Kiyoko for its inscription of this taboo, particularly the restriction against "going forth" and "entering water" during menses (Dorson 1962: 236). In the story, the young woman who was a servant at a Buddhist temple violates the taboo by washing her stained undergarments in the pond at the foot of Mount Kinhoku, a mountain that "abominated the presence of women." Despite her Buddhist prayers, she is transformed into the bride of the kami of the pond, a curious nuptial that enables the former male kami to ascend to heaven while she becomes the *kami* in his place. I read the story as indicative of the struggle between Buddhism and Shinto precepts in Japanese folklore. Seen in relationship to *Realm,* we can see that a violation of the menstrual taboo places humans in a nether world, outside prevailing moralities, and into contact with more ancient forces, where precisely the role of women as kami, on one hand (goddess, spiritual force), or abomination, on the other, is the question.

In both the samisen and the rickshaw–menstrual blood scene, female sexuality is affirmed by the film's creation of an aesthetic that can incorporate as desirable and pleasurable that which might be considered crude or bizarre. The aesthetic texture of the film's imagery that combines colors and patterns artfully in the manner of ukiyo-e composition and its careful audial rhythms that borrow from the highly modulated volumes and rhythms of the Japanese flute, samisen, koto, and drum performance traditions give an enveloping sensual support to sexuality's representation.

As in the writing of Georges Bataille, the fluids and tastes of sexuality are not only those produced by the body, but through an extension of the

23. The fluids and tastes of sexuality echo symbolically when Sada lays an egg that Kichi had introduced into her vagina. *Ai no korida* (Realm of the Senses, 1976). Still courtesy of Oshima Productions.

metaphor of appetite, echo symbolically as eating. The sexual play of food recalls the saucer of milk that elicits a bet between the young narrator and Simone at the opening of Bataille's novel, *L'Histoire de l'oeil* (The Story of the Eye). This results in the narrator's description of a nearly inoperable view, all the more erotic as one reads the verbal passage trying to imagine the logistics of seeing such a scene. He tells us he sees "her pink and black flesh bathing in the white milk," and if one wonders how, one retains the graphic image of the color contrast described. The image that follows immediately, however, secures the erotic in a more probable voyeurism, as Simone poses above him, a leg up on a bench, milk dripping down her thighs, as he masturbates on the floor below, culminating in their mutual orgasm, "without ever touching one another" (1967: 4–5). Bataille tells a story of the eye as sexual organ, using food as a supplement to a scenography in which taboos are broken "innocently" as child's play.

In a like manner, Kichi will use his chopsticks to dip food into Sada's vagina as if were a sauce. Then an egg introduced by Kichi into her vagina will be laid by Sada, and she in turn will feed this egg to Kichi. If the metaphor for sexual hunger introduces a number of such substitute objects, the portrayal of female sexuality here is ambiguous. If the vagina is a sauce,

24. Supplemental scenes of violence and role reversals, along with a series of scenes of jealousy and possession, turn the seduction into a *korida,* a bullfight, as when Sada makes love to Kichi with a knife in her mouth. *Ai no korida* (Realm of the Senses, 1976). Still courtesy of Oshima Productions.

the scene of the egg becomes a mockery of female powers of reproduction and humiliates Sada.

This recalls and prefigures variations on sexuality as humiliation and violence that occur elsewhere in the film, including two particularly violent sexual scenes that involve lesbian sexuality and two scenes that concern impotent men. When in the very beginning of the film her female co-worker at the inn makes a sexual advance, Sada responds at first with a refusal and later with a violent fight in the kitchen. Later in the orgies following the mock marriage, a group of geishas rape a young woman with a dildo, a dildo that has the form of an elegantly decorated painted bird. This fantasy of a violent female sexuality is symbolically crucial to the film's realignment of sexual difference and the force of sexual drives within the gendered subject, for if Sada is to become the aggressor and Kichi is to become the willing passive object, this reversal happens in the context of these auxiliary sexual scenes. Lesbian desire or reaction to it seems to operate as a symbolic representation of excess as regards female desire. Women are active agents of sexuality, an agency that includes violent overflows.

The aggressive female is joined as supplement by the passive and even masochistic male. In the beginning this male takes the form of the old man who begs Sada to touch his impotent organ. Later in the film, Sada's former client, to whom she returns to earn money for herself and Kichi, echoes the first man's pathos. This client, whom she calls "Sensei" (teacher), is an impotent masochist who asks Sada to hit him, introducing Sada to the sadomasochism that will spill over into her lovemaking with Kichi.

These supplemental scenes of violence and role reversals, along with a series of scenes of jealousy and possession, turn the seduction into a *korida*, a bullfight. At different moments, Sada threatens Kichi with a scissors, makes love with a knife in her mouth, tells him she would like to cut off his penis to hold it always inside her. The constant demand for sexual arousal has become hers, the woman's, and coupled with images of women's aggression and men's passivity, it becomes the driving force of the narrative.

Biologically, the impossible sustained pleasure of a constant and ever-increasing orgasm is closer to the realm of possibility for the female. The male orgasm is temporally more finite and in need of time for recuperation; the female orgasm, of course, shares this quality of momentary presence and long absence but contains within its potential multiplicity the promise of the infinite. It is for this reason, perhaps, that the fetishism of Sada and Kichi's sexuality shifts from the focus on the phallus itself to the phallus as instrumental in Sada's pleasure. An earlier image of fellatio that frames the fluids dripping from Sada's mouth cedes the way to other sexual acts that place other demands on the male organ.

Both partners give themselves over to an ideal quest for Sada's satiation, never, of course, possible, for that which Sada desires is to be perpetually aroused. Female orgasmic multiplicity, in being extended as perpetual arousal, meets impossibility, not only physiologically (the limits of the body), but logically. Excitation needs both calm and release as defining contrasts.

We can read this impossible ideal quest as metaphor of the centrality of desire to theoretical and fictional strategies of the postwar period. To theorize desire and to inscribe it become goals for societies not at all sure of what the twentieth century is doing to human desire; liberation, celebration, and the knowing of desire that previously had been stimulated by the novel, then by psychoanalysis, then by sex therapies and Hollywood films, are coupled with desire's paradigmatic inversion, feelings of overwhelming powerlessness, futility, and impotence. In Japan this paradox might be seen in the popularity of the writing of Tanazaki juxtaposed to the writhing bodies of Buto, the modern dance form devoted to angst.

The film's depiction of the impossible search for an object of desire that is a state of arousal that never ends, that is indeed "an object" only in the sense of a point that might serve as aim or goal, but not in the sense of part object or love object, evokes comparison with a Lacanian notion of desire. Lacan's seminars of 1956–1959 on desire began to theorize this conflict in light of the resurgent interest in de Sade as well as Lacan's contemporaries, the writers Maurice Blanchot and Pierre Klossowski. Drawing on the Freudian principle of the inherently contradictory pursuits of excitement and stasis in orgasm, the idea of the drive and its aims that culminates in *Beyond the Pleasure Principle*, Lacan posits the subject in just such a state of constant *relation* to the love object. In terming this object "petit objet a," Lacan draws it as an ephemeral end point in a diagrammatic formula of desire. Sada's desire for constant arousal makes clear in extremis a displacement that is always a factor in desire; it is not the lover, the phallus, the vagina, or the fetish object *alone* one desires, but rather these objects as signifiers of desire, as provocative of one's own sexual desires, one's pleasures, and one's satiation. Lacan, following Freud, proposes to explore how the phenomenological world of sensation affects the imaginary. Oshima gives us characters who are ciphers of a similar exploration.

Recall the discussion in chapter 2 of Lacan's treatment of the paradoxes of desire entailed in the problematic assumption by the subject of his or her own desire. Once Kichi and Sada have given themselves over to the unfettered exploration of each other's desire, it is with these paradoxes that they experiment. *Realm of the Senses* is a film so deeply engaged in the exchange of desire that it perhaps proposes a consideration of theories of desire less bound to autonomous subjectivity. Lyotard's *Libidinal Economy* (1993) and Gilles Deleuze and Felix Guattari's desiring machines in *A Thousand Plateaus* (1987) might be seen as such attempts to free the energy of desire. Lyotard emphasizes the flow of desire in all encounters and investments, championing particularly libidinal exchange in aesthetic experiences. In a sense, Lyotard desublimates the Freudian notion of sublimation, releasing libidinal investment in art, music, intellectual life, and so on, into a joyous self-awareness. Deleuze and Guattari use apparatus metaphors to emphasize the automatic and constant flow of desire in humans constructed for just this purpose and to deconstruct any notion of central consciousness or unified subjectivity behind this desire, able simply to channel and control its flow. Their machine metaphor is meant to liberate human desire from Oedipalization and its attendant guilt and renunciation, structures that imprison creative desire through such confinement.

Lyotard's or Deleuze and Guattari's theories might be suggestive for aspects of the film's representation of desire. In particular, Lyotard's theories might illuminate the relationship between sexual representation and sensual presentation, helping our understanding of the force of crescendo that builds in each episode of the film and across the film toward a climax, but which is only betrayed by stopping its invaginations with castration. It perhaps yields to this ending only to acknowledge the political aspects of a libidinal economy, limitations on pleasure imposed from historical and economic forces. The desiring machine metaphor in Deleuze and Guattari might be used to develop the inescapability and the mounting fascination that may begin with Kichi as motor force but flows to Sada. Kichi must go along with her drives not as submission but through an enmeshment that is seen as the fruition of multiplicities. The mechanics of their entwined desire is a machine larger than the simple union of two beings, a process Deleuze terms "destratification." Yet Deleuze and Guattari caution that "every undertaking of destratification (for example, going beyond the organism, plunging into a becoming) must therefore observe concrete rules of extreme caution: a too sudden destratification may be suicidal, or turn cancerous. In other words, it will sometimes end in chaos, the void and destruction, and sometimes lock us back into the strata, which become more rigid still, losing their degrees of diversity, differentiation, and mobility" (1987: 503).

If all these theories can account for the film's need to explore pessimistic turns of desire in addition to celebrating desire's release, it is due to each theorist's confrontation in his own manner with fascism and the excesses of capitalist drives. The film proposes, but does not rest on, a free-floating fantasy of unrestricted desire; the pursuit of desire as an endless end in itself is troubled not just at the film's terminus in castration but throughout. For all its brashness and verve, for all its abstraction of character and crossing of gender identity, Oshima's film always attends to the bleaker registers of desire, remaining far more a cautionary parable of desire, as well as one far more haunted by demonic fears, than an infinite bathing in passionate energies of unmitigated positive pleasure. If the castration conclusion of the scenario suggests a Lacanian investigation of desire more than those theories that might question the psychic reality and resolution of castration, what I find most intriguing is the suggestive ways the film opens to a rethinking of desire theoretically from several perspectives.

It is with this theoretical range of perspectives on desire that we note that Sada, after returning from her client, urges Kichi to pursue the sadomasochistic game of a partial strangulation within their lovemaking, with her as the recipient of Kichi's controlled and timed violence. However, this sadomasochism soon reverses roles, as Sada becomes the active violent partner, using her sash to cut Kichi's breath, sustaining his erection, sustaining her pleasure. Breath, life itself, is cut in the pursuit of pleasure, and it is at this point in the film that Sada in a sense becomes a demon, preparing the way for the shift to the ghost story that will occur in Oshima's next film.

The female seductive demon is a classic figure in the Japanese folktale, refigured in various ways in Nō, Kabuki, literature, and film. Never is she more striking than in a play common to Nō and Kabuki, *Dojoji*, in which the dedication ceremony for a new temple bell awakens the serpent demon of a young woman who had chased her lover into the former temple bell and melted it with her frustrated, jealous fury. Sada, by way of a detour through an image of woman as mistress of her own sexuality, finally returns us to this

25. This sumptuous shot of the couple enjoying their walk under an umbrella hints through Sada's expression at her more demonic aspect, at the obsessive quality of their love and the violence beneath the surface; a moment later, they will turn the umbrella into a weapon, rushing at a passerby. *Ai no korida* (Realm of the Senses, 1976). Still courtesy of Oshima Productions.

figure of the female demon whose violence is latent in her sexuality, and whose romance is ultimately with the death drive.

That foreign audiences might find their own associations with this female demon is apparent in the manner Sada and the geisha of *Realm of the Senses* figure in a special volume of *Cahiers du Cinéma* (1980) entitled *Monstresses,* where they are in the company of stills of Gloria Swanson in *Sunset Boulevard,* Brigitte Helm as the automaton in *Metropolis,* Marlene Dietrich in *Shanghai Express,* Elsa Lancaster in *The Bride of Frankenstein,* and Harriet Andersson in the title role in *Monika,* as well as other Japanese heroines of an alluring danger. While the volume visually builds an argument on the stills alone, this is augmented by a series of short essay speculations and developed through a typology of six species of "monstresses," with the Japanese forming all the examples of "L'Amour cruelle," cruel love. Jean-Louis Schefer (1980: 67) offers a rumination entitled "C'est Polyxène" on the dildo-rape scene of *Realm of the Senses* as seductive sacrifice, a communal initiation into the pleasure and pain of sexuality for which the body becomes the altar. Pascal Bonitzer

(1980: 65) speaks of "le trait"—the trace, the mark—in reference to the writing in blood on the body in *Diary of a Shinjuku Thief,* with phrases that beg comparison to *Realm*'s ending. Both of these short, provocative commentaries bring out the rich conjunction of Oshima's imagery with contemporary theory. These readings see bodies as immaterial and abstract. They potentially embrace violence within representation as simply the force of desire, hyperbolically displayed. We are in the allegorical realm admittedly, but is the allegory of female desire? Or of castration fear? Or both? What aspects do we cite in constructing our allegory?

Except for the *Monstresses* volume, the role of brutal sexuality has been largely ignored in much of the critical discussion of *Realm of the Senses.* This absence may be linked to the way in which the perversions serve as supplemental to female desire and its transformation into a she-monster fantasy. Critics have a tendency to see the film as liberating female desire and appealing to women as it does so, an interpretation that fixes on the middle of the film. This interpretation reads the ending only as an acquiescence to this midsection, as a male affirmation to the point of subservience of this female pleasure. A slightly different reading sees the final act as less one of castration than as an ultimate fetishization of the phallus, in which the man is pleased to be so desired as object. These readings are not wrong—they are undeniably a part of the film—but the film is divided and multiple, and in the form of its supplements and its termination in death it develops another strand in contradistinction to this affirmation of female desire.

If the full impact of the ending of the film escapes those who would read the film as affirming female sexuality, the ending is integral to a Lacanian psychoanalytic reading of the film as an allegory. If we cease to consider Sada and Kichi as separate characters, as mimetic human beings, as entities, but see them rather as interactive elements of the fiction in its correspondence with the psyche, then we might say both come to join forces in seeking an impossible object of desire. When their quest for their object of desire realizes only the impossibility of such attainment, it turns into an affirmation of the function of the death drive within sexuality. This reading may seem to be quite aberrant in that it takes representation into another realm of reference, but Oshima's films have always asked for this shift in register of interpretation, this going beyond the obvious.

Realm does so internally, as it shifts to the empty stadium space for a primal scene depicted quite differently from the "classical" version in which a child observes parental coitus. In this scene, Sada chases children, a young boy and girl, while playing a game in which she tries to catch their sexual organs. Setting such a scene in the empty stadium emphasizes its extranarrative status as an insert that partakes of imaginary, dreamlike imagery. The empty stadium not only recalls the korida of the film's Japanese title, it dramatizes, however unconsciously, Lacan's pun on the word *stade* (stadium as well as stage). The scene of genital tag, cut from some prints of the film, carries the sense of latent violence and violation inherent in this intergenerational primal game. Attention to such undercurrents in this other register of oblique representation of the imaginary do help to explain why this film is at once so terrifying and fascinating.

As an allegory for a Lacanian vision of desire, the film brings us the full image of horror latent in Lacanian propositions; the sexual drive, an instrument of the already-written, inscribes itself finally in letters of death, in the blood of the castration. This red blood of castration becomes Sada's means of inscribing in writing on Kichi's lifeless body the metanarrative of the subject.

On Being No Longer Young: Sex, Life, and Death

An elderly woman, a geisha, whose white makeup and elegant kimono do not completely mask her advanced age, is one of the many observers of sexuality introduced in Oshima's *Realm of the Senses*. In the scene in question, three-quarters of the way through the narrative, she sits just outside the shoji that serves as threshold to the room in which the obsessed lovers embrace. She plays her samisen for the couple. She stops when the young woman, Sada, begins addressing questions to her, while still engaged in sex with her lover Kichi on the left of the image:

> *Sada:* Do you think I'm perverted?
> *Geisha:* Why?
> *Sada:* Because I want to hold him all the time.
> *Geisha:* But that's only natural for a woman.
> *Sada:* How old are you?
> *Geisha:* Sixty-eight.
> *Sada:* Do you find this man attractive?
> *Geisha:* I find him very attractive.
> *Sada:* In that case don't you enjoy watching us?
> *Geisha:* It's a pleasure for the eyes.
> *Sada:* Don't you want to make love with him?

This last question initiates the first change in camera angle in what otherwise is a very studied and fixed tableau of sexual display and voyeurism. We cut to a close-up of the geisha smiling, then a reverse shot from behind her, looking at Kichi's reaction, then to a temporal jump cut of Kichi beginning his seduction of the elderly woman who lies willingly on the ground beside him. It is this scene and its consequences for the film as discourse of sexuality, desire, and death in relationship to the representation of the older woman that I will address here.

Unlike a whole series of servants who are repulsed by the two central characters, Sada and Kichi, whose obsession with sex leads them to abandon any

modicum of cleanliness and the decorous Japanese tendency to keep all sexual activity private, behind closed doors, away from public display, the older
geisha smiles on their exhibitionism. As we have seen, she pronounces it, in
a manner that might reflexively seem to comment on the sexual display of
the beautiful bodies in lavishly composed frames throughout the film, a
"pleasure for the eyes." This affirmation is in sharp contrast to the scene of
her own sexual encounter with Kichi, in which the age of her skin and the
decline of her body become the object of another fascination, not that of
youth and beauty but of the specter of death.

The skin of youth is associated with beauty and pleasure, both visual and
sensorial; early in Sada and Kichi's relationship, their first naked encounter
(also incidentally observed by a servant who watches through the shoji) is
marked by the master (as Kichi is known to Sada at this point) saying, "What
fine skin, like shining satin." When Sada replies that she, too, loves his skin,
he says, "I'm no longer young. How I envy you." She counters with "Your skin
is so smooth, so firm. I feel drawn to it." Paradigmatically, this scene is one
of the textual facets that mirror the encounter with the elderly geisha; if Sada
appears younger and more perfect of body than Kichi, as a source of envy
in his eyes, they propose for each other an encounter with skin as polished
silk, as shining, glistening surface whose attraction lures both sight and
touch. Time is a tarnish to such sheen; each line, fold, and crevice etched
into the skin by the passage of time breaks such surface attraction, shatter-
ing the reflecting surface through which the self can mirror its own desire
for youth. For the geisha, whose subjectivity we grasp only momentarily in
her smiling response to Sada's invitation to sex with her man, Kichi is a reflection of youth and desire, just as Sada is for Kichi.

However, once the sexual encounter between the geisha and Kichi begins,
positioning is all. She initially is prone and passive beside him. He begins by
reaching through her kimono to touch her vagina, then smells his fingers,
remarking ironically on youth. Is this an indication of bodily fluids as a sign
of a lingering vitality and desire, belying advanced age? If so, the next shot,
a close-up of Kichi's face as the geisha's whitened and wrinkled hand reaches
up, places this in the context of a contrast of skins. Old flesh is perhaps not
expected to contain or express desire. Here we are reminded of earlier
scenes as well: of the old man at the beginning of the film who seems to recognize Sada as someone he bought in more prosperous days and who begs
Sada to exhibit her body for him as he strokes his penis, which refuses to respond, and of another older man, a bartender, who rejects Sada's offer to exchange a view of her body for a drink by saying, "Mine is only good for pee-
ing these days." If male sexuality potentially meets old age with flaccidity,
female sexuality knows no such absolute, exteriorized sign of incompetence.
The geisha moves Kichi's body to her breast, reinscribing her body as sexually competent, as voluptuous still, and perhaps even beyond the measure

of the taut, trim skin of the youthful Sada, who now watches, crouched like an animal, arched like a cat, the scene of an encounter that she suggested and orchestrated. Suddenly in retrospect, Sada's sexuality, athletic and active, constantly moving, increasingly initiating, becomes framed by the sexuality of an older woman, who does not so much perform for the man as she actively receives his physical attentions.

Alternating close-ups of Kichi and Sada culminate on a close-up of Sada's lips, as if this scene of the seduction of the elder geisha rejoins the scenes at the beginning of the film in which Sada is the voyeur to Kichi's and his wife's sexuality. Sada's desire recharges by reinscribing the spectacle of her lover with another woman; by selecting a woman who is much older, she avoids the threat of jealousy yet relives the moment of voyeurism. Voyeurism here separates from the jealous rage that led to the fantasy images of her slashing Kichi's wife with a razor. Yet this voyeurism as spur to desire will be vanquished by the very effects of aging that were to guarantee its safety. For in a jump cut to the moments after orgasm, we see a slow horizontal tracking shot down the length of the older woman's still body. Her geisha wig has fallen off, revealing the wrapping covering wisps of white hair. The disguise is undone, her proud appearance gone, and she looks old. The pan continues over her disheveled body, emphasizing with its slow movement her deathly stillness. She has become the image of death.

Sada literally crawls over to this scene. "Look," she says, childlike, indicating to Kichi what we assume to be a puddle of urine unseen in the image. Kichi laughs, then says, "She must have lost control. It's horrible." For all the excess of sexual expenditures, for all the visible flowing of bodily fluids (the come that drips from Sada's mouth after fellatio and Kichi's licking of her menstrual blood from his fingers), incontinence of the aged after sex performs as a separate category, one evoking horror. Earlier Sada begs Kichi to refrain from urinating to increase sexual pleasure, but the mixture and confusion of sex and urinary elimination so common and central to Bataille's *The Story of the Eye,* for example, stands beyond this text as its horror. Sex and death are not mixed in *Realm* as they are in Bataille. Unlike his adolescents who find stimulation in corpses and can murder remorselessly, almost innocently, for sexual gratification, here Sada says of the elderly geisha, "I hope she's not dead."

The line this text is drawing between sex and death is not merely imaginary, or subject to interpenetrations. Unlike Bataille's equally episodic sex narratives, Oshima's film never attains Bataille's level of impossible fictional fantasy. Sight in Bataille is imaginary, not operative; events described as seen (the vagina being enveloped by a saucer of milk, for example) would not be available to anyone's operative vision. Oshima's sexual scenes are all, on the contrary, not only observable but marked by multiple voyeurisms. Perhaps consequentially, perhaps incidentally, the world they construct is only intermittently that of a fantasy register. It is one at other times more linked to the geometries of the real and the symbolic, or at least the referential. Sada and Kichi still need money and they still fear death.

This is one of the reasons for this scene of the seduction of the elderly geisha. When Sada remarks to Kichi after the sexual encounter with the older woman, "You're pale. Like a corpse," he responds, "Don't say that. I had the feeling I was holding my mother's corpse." They, as adults, have realized a necrophilic violation of the incest taboo whose meaning is augmented by their further disclosures (the only direct disclosures of a personal past on their part in the entire narrative) that both of their mothers are dead, Sada's since her childhood, Kichi's recently. They are children whose sexual desire is aimed at least in part at the reconstitution of the dead mother. Sada requests that Kichi enact his repressed symbolic incestuous desires for her voyeuristic pleasure/horror as her means of imagining a primal scene to which she never had access, except through the earlier relay of watching him with his wife when she was a servant (the social inferior, the child) in his household. It is no wonder that the scene ends with an embrace between Sada and Kichi, in which she demands, directly, the impossible: "Don't let our pleasure end." That it will end, with castration, that youth and pleasure are circumscribed temporally, despite her writing in blood "Sada and Kichi forever," is the manner in which this film haunts its erotic/pornographic pleasures with death. The beautiful satin bodies will not be condemned to the decay of the old age that this scene presents as symbolic contagion, but their desire for eternal constant pleasure is a desire that is beyond mortality. It is impossible.

The older woman then figures as a symbol within the framework of the desires of the young. Her desire, her subjectivity, present only momentarily as her smile, vanishes. Intriguingly, there is another older servant woman, earlier, who, during one of Sada's absences, warns Kichi of his impending demise. Maternally, she offers him food and when he refuses to eat, prophesies, "She'll end up killing you." Kichi's response is to rape her. These two older women—the openly maternal one who attempts to save the son but is violated in retaliation for her interference in the execution of his desire and the symbolically maternal one, whose own desire is stated and satiated but whose being is only a staging through which death can threaten the desire of the young for endless desire—embody a troubling negation of female sexuality in a film purportedly celebrating female desire.

A STEP BACKWARD OR A PASSIONATE MOVE: THE GHOST STORY

Certain critics saw *Empire of Passion* as a step backward for Oshima. After the new territory of *Realm*'s serious inscription of pornography, to make a ghost story could seem a regression, especially since the lush mise-en-scène is without the graphic justification of the theatrical metaphor that creates a purpose for the visual beauty of the previous film. *Empire of Passion* could seem to be at once too beautiful, too inconsequential, as in Max Tessier's (1984: 95) assessment that the film suffers "paradoxically from a very studied almost academic style, a too solicited aesthetic beauty, unexpected in Oshima."

However, Oshima himself suggests another view, one in which *Empire of Passion* is an exploration of the "roots" of the flowering of love that was shown in *Realm of the Senses* (Daney 1978: 50). The sense of anteriority implied in the choice of the word *root* might refer to the second film as a movement farther back in historical reference (to 1895). "Root" might also indicate a more generative concept that sees the second film as derived from the Japanese folktale; the ghostly and demonic supernatural explanations within a village setting in *Empire* borrow from folklore traditions. The script was adapted from a story written by a contemporary woman writer, Nakamura Itoko, who proposed her story to Oshima after seeing *Realm*.

We have seen how the "flowering of love" in *Realm* also uncovers the female demon figure in Sada as the underside of a woman free in her sexual desire. This suggests that sexual liberation cannot simply be a matter of breaking taboos, or representing their breakage, but requires an archaeology of the history of sexuality that need be far more psychohistorical. If the story of Sada fails to simply emerge as a liberated desire in a period of repression, it is because the images it engenders embrace a stronger internalized repressive force in the inevitability of the death drive and couples this with a fear associated with the female. To sort through these meshes of desire and history, a movement back to the ghost story, where death and desire comprise the fundamental mythos, might allow something to be learned by means of cultural excavation.

Ghosts, Demons, Spirits, and Transformations

In No theater, ghost plays are those in which the departed spirits of warriors recount their last battle, either to lament or seek revenge. Demon plays are, in contrast, tales of a transformation from human appearance to spirit form, and the spirit, *shirei*, can be either good or evil. The terms for such demons abound; evil demons can be *mamono* (magical spirits) or *onryo* (vengeful spirits).

This variety and categorization parallels the ghosts and demons that appear in the Japanese folktale "Densetsu." Humans can be transformed into animal spirits, serpents, foxes, and badgers, whose attributes include a supernatural cleverness and even wickedness. Or the Japanese folktale's ghosts can be ghosts of desire. They return because they long to finish something left undone, and are often sorrowful. Japanese demons in folktales also return, but they are obsessed with a prior wrong and their attitude is vengeful. These stories reflect ancient religious beliefs in *goryo*, spirits that curse mortals. Goryo must be enshrined and worshiped, precisely because they are angry gods.

In Kabuki, ghost stories dominate the repertoire in the summer, becoming a supernatural source of "chills." Kabuki ghost plays draw from the No repertoire and the Japanese folktale, but the ghosts have become far more self-conscious theatrical devices, more greatly distanced from direct worship and belief. Films, even more so, make their ghost apparitions literary and theatrical, while exploiting the filmic techniques to render ghostliness as image, such as superimposition, transparency, fades, animation of inanimate objects, and effects of montage. The best-known films to explore this rich supernatural tradition are *Ugetsu* by Mizoguchi Kenji, an adaptation of a late eighteenth-century collection of "new and old supernatural stories," *Ugetsu Monogatari* by Akinari Ueda; and *Kwaidan* by Koboyashi Masaki, an adaptation of Lafcadio Hearn's retellings of traditional Japanese folktales, first published in 1894. Also, a ghost makes a striking appearance as one of the narrators in Kurosawa's *Rashomon*, while two films directed by Shindo Kaneto, *Onibaba* (1963) and *Kuroneko* (1968), introduce demonic and ghostly images in the context of jidai-geki that depict peasant suffering. What is unusual about the Oshima project is its rejuvenation of the ghost story, its departure from even these modern film adaptations by virtue of its inventive insistence on sex and fantasy. Drawing on the folktales' traditional elements and structures, *Empire* makes the "dreamwork" of the folktale decidedly contemporary, and parallels *Realm* in its figuration of desire.

To examine this transformation, we must first see how similar narratives and structures appear in the traditional folktale. Consider how vengeance for infidelity and murder is presented in the folktale "The Mirror Given by the Ghost." The excerpt below encapsulates the wrongdoing and vengeance from the point of view of the ghost of the murdered wife who tells her story within the tale so that she can enlist her interlocutor, a mortal, to remove a protective seal from the doorway of her former home where her husband now lives with his second wife. She will then be able to have her vengeance and strangle the woman.

> I am the wife of a merchant in the city of Matsue. But my husband is a loose man and he has indulged in dissipation. He brought his sweetheart home and let her live with us. She was evil-hearted and hated me. One day when I was at the well drawing water, she pushed me down into the well. After she had killed me in this way, she reported to the police that I had committed suicide and soon she became the legal wife of my husband. Oh, please just think of my bitter resentment. Someday I shall possess her and wreak vengeance upon her. (Yanagita 1986: 102)

The ghost recounts being drowned at a well, just as the husband in *Empire* is killed and thrown into a well. Yet despite such similar treatment of motives and symbolic objects, this tale adopts a different perspective on adultery and morality. The mirror of the story's title is a device of the frame story of this folktale, a frame that sanctions the actions of the former wife's ghost as justice and allows the moral reminder "that a person will be rewarded according to the way he treats others."

While many stories teach such lessons, others lack a clear moral and instead rest on ambiguity and undecidability. One of the striking characteristics of such Japanese folktales is the odd occurrence left not only unexplained but also outside a direct causality and closure. "Surprised Twice" is just such an oneiric structure, which like some dreams it resembles leaves one to speculate on possible interpretations while it recounts almost surreal occurrences.

> A night school teacher was walking along a road by the edge of a rice field late one winter night and noticed a beautiful girl standing by the road with her face turned down at the book she was reading. He wondered whether she was a ghost and spoke to her. She did not answer but raised her face. He took one look at her face and his hair stood on end. He threw his coat over his head and ran home. He sat down hurriedly at his kotatsu. His wife seemed to think it strange and asked him over and over what had happened. When he told her about the frightful face of the woman, his wife wanted to know what kind of face it was. He could not explain. She asked, "Was it this kind of face?" At that she turned toward her husband and there she was, the woman with the terrible face. He took one look and gave a shout. Then he fainted as he tried to hide in the kotatsu. When he awoke the next morning, the sun was shining brightly on him as he lay face down by the dam in the middle of his field. (Yanagita 1986: 203)

"Surprised Twice" has echoes in *Empire of Passion* both in its loose, dreamlike imagery and in its emphasis on looking. Opposite characteristics are conjoined as the beautiful girl reveals a terrible face. This act is then doubled by the wife's familiar face becoming equally terrifying. Doubling is coupled with a repetition of a demand for explanation: "What kind of face?" The answer remains withheld, as the story represents the terrible face as both inexplicable and as a signifier "unseen" by the narrator or reader, presented only in its mysterious duplication. If the tale's imagery is analyzed as dreamwork in the psychoanalytic sense, we find a condensation of the girl and wife, as the beautiful and familiar in the female in each instance masks the hideous. Misogyny seems to be the dream thought "disguised" by this tale, but while it illustrates a fear and dread of women, it offers no obvious moral or explanation. As we shall see, *Empire* borrows this undecidability coupled with suggestiveness from this sort of Japanese tale.

Intertextuality in *Empire* is not limited to the ghost story. Consider the relationship of the film to two versions of *Muho matsu no issho*, both directed by Inagaki Hiroshi (the first translated as *The Life of Matsu the Untamed*, was made in 1940, the second, *Rikisha Man*, in 1958). Inagaki's films tell the tale of a servant in love with his dead benefactor's wife, though he never dares tell the widow. Both versions gained fame, the first as a wartime retreat into

26. Gisaburo as a phantom tries only to reclaim his place at the hearth or his occupation, pulling his wife in his rickshaw. *Ai no borei* (Empire of Passion, 1980). Still courtesy of Oshima Productions.

the history genre focusing on the Meiji period, the second as a winner of the Venice Film Festival, one of the first Japanese films to be so honored internationally. As versions of the same story by the same director, they also juxtapose two very famous actors, Bando Tomasaburo and Mifune Toshiro. More than just the rickshaw imagery evokes comparison; Inagaki's films ennoble characters whose passion is contained due to honor, even after the natural death of the husband, while Oshima's celebrates a passion unfurled despite all the ways it violates honor.

Wells, Bridges, and the Gouging of Eyes

In *Empire of Passion* desire is again awakened in the woman, this time in an older married woman, Seki, by a younger man, Toyoji. Age is a preoccupation of the expository dialogue between Gisaburo and Seki. Seki does not appear to be her age, nor does she age as time passes in the film. The villagers come to take this as a sign that she is a demon; there is a telling scene late in the film in which peasants laboring in the foreground as she passes comment on her supernatural hold on youth.

We are also told in the dialogue between Gisaburo and Seki that Toyoji is a former soldier, returning from war. Since the year is 1895, the war in

27. Kichi passes soldiers and patriotic crowds, placing the whole of the fiction in a specific and symbolically loaded historical context of 1936 Japan. *Ai no korida* (Realm of Senses, 1976). Still courtesy of Oshima Productions.

question is the Sino-Japanese War, a major victory for Meiji militarism and one that has been linked to both the beginning of Japanese imperialism in Asia and the war with Russia in 1904–1905. In *Japanese Culture,* H. Paul Varley encapsulizes the imperialism of Japan that emerges in this period while linking the Sino-Japanese and Russo-Japanese wars:

> Japan went to war with China in 1894–5 over the issue, to put it euphemistically, of Korean independence. Korea had traditionally been tributary to China, a relationship that gave the Chinese a kind of protectorate over the foriegn affairs of the peninsular, "hermit" kingdom. Victorious in 1895, Japan received, among other rewards, the colonial posessions of Taiwan and the Pescadore islands. Moreover, by fully exposing the weakness and ineptitude of the Manchu Government, it helped precipitate an odious round of concession grabbing by the powers in China during the late 1890's that had been described as "the carving of the melon." The country that took the largest slice was Russia, whose increasing assertiveness from this time on in Asia led to a serious clash of interests and, finally, war with Japan. In its surprising triumph over Russia in 1904–5 Japan not only extended its empire through acquisition of the Liaotung Peninsula and Korea (formally annexed in 1910) but vaulted into the ranks of world powers. (1984: 238)

In *Empire of Passion* the reference to the Sino-Japanese War parallels the soldiers that pass the couple in *Realm of the Senses,* and that, along with a voice-over tag ending, mark that film as occurring in 1936. Both films metonymically give us a highly significant historical reference, using briefly articulated details to place the whole of the fiction in a specific and symbolically loaded historical context. This process places the sexual interactions that are the focus of these narratives in the context of history, of Japanese militarism and international events, as Heath discusses in the case of *Realm of the Senses* (1976–1977: 158), though the precise relationship between these sexual tales and history is left unspecified in ways that he does not fully consider. Is immersion in sexual desire presented as an alternative to engagement in national political conquest or as a supplement, or by-product, of it? Does Toyoji's seduction of Seki indicate how a war experience has changed him and Japan, making the veteran unable to reintegrate into the village culture without disrupting it? Or is Toyoji's disruptiveness a reaction against authority structures of the military and the village? Significant in beginning to formulate a response to this question is how Oshima's writings point to shifts occuring in Meiji Japan as a central focus of his view of Japan's attitudes toward sexuality historically, when he asks the question, "Does this mean that in pre-Meiji Japan people thought differently about sex and had a different sexual culture?" Disqualifying himself from a direct response to this question as he is not "a researcher," Oshima does assert that the "free sexual culture of the Edo period" and "the culture of communal sex, . . . in the folk customs of the farm villages, . . . were crushed in the process of modernization during the Meiji period and later" (1992: 243).

Vestiges of the communal sex culture of the farm villages find complex representation in the film in an early scene depicting the wedding of the village chief. Seki serves at the wedding, where she exchanges ribald commentary with the guests. Still, the marriage signifies how a power hierarchy reigning in the village has turned away from a culture of communal sex. This "turning away" might be seen as an aspect of what Oshima calls that period's "sexual militarism," in which the sexual is negated in favor of militarist ambitions. The film might be seen as challenging this sexual repression, this channeling of sexuality into hierarchical relationships and militarist conquest. Perhaps it is meant to speak to the audience reacting to a parallel sublimation or subordination, in post–World War II Japan, of the sexual into what Oshima calls "sexual GNPism" or "sexual careerism" (1992: 243).

In the final chapter of this book, we will look at how these assumptions neglect to tell the whole story, neglect considerations of gender; the story of "sexual militarism" will there be analyzed differently, from the standpoint of the women who were forced to serve the Japanese army as "comfort women." What is being staged in this film is sexual liberation. Gender is central to this staging, but somewhat unconscious. Seki represents a female passion, just as

28. The rickshaw phantom has precedents in the Japanese folktale and film, as does the woman-demon who does not age. *Ai no Borei* (Empire of Passion, 1980). Still courtesy of Oshima Productions.

Sada does, but one not yet imagined outside a male perspective. Despite the source of the film in a female author's attempt to respond to the issue of female desire, there are limitations on Seki embedded in the structure of this tale, in the unfolding of its scenes. We can see these limitations on female representation by looking at the Oedipal configurations and guilt that haunt this tale. Though their treatment will be most imaginative and contestatory, though patriarchy will be defied, the defiance will ultimately be circumscribed, as if by forces greater than the will to tell the story of desire.

The lovers in *Empire of Passion* kill early in the film. The murder is provoked by Toyoji's desire to possess Seki completely, a desire that has an intermediary stage, another instance of "writing" on the body, though one less apparent as writing, as no actual lettering takes place. During an encounter of oral sex, Toyoji looks up. He demands to shave Seki's pubic hair, marking her body as his by this act of grooming. The film lingers on the shaving just as it had on the oral sex. Once she becomes marked by this shaving, the murder of Seki's husband, Gisaburo, seems as necessary to Seki as it is to Toyoji. The shaving would announce their affair, which in turn would endanger their lives. Together they strangle Gisaburo, an act that now takes the form of self-defense following the convoluted logic that stems from insatiable desire. If I insist on the shaving as writing, let me also suggest that it takes on the imperative mode. We can see in *Empire* a reworking of many of the elements of *Realm,* though here the writing of desire, the absolute demand for possession, and the recourse to death are constructed more completely within the triangulation of woman, lover, and husband familiar from the Western novel, melodrama, and film noir.

Much of the film is devoted to the repeated return of Gisaburo as ghost. Gisaburo as a phantom tries only to reclaim his place at the hearth or his occupation, pulling his wife in his rickshaw. At first he seeks no overt vengeance on her; he demands nothing more than her return to wifely servitude, wishing to be offered sake at his hearth in the most traditional manner, in the same way she most graciously poured it for him before her sexual encounters with Toyoji began. If Seki desired something else, to be served cakes by her lover rather than to be her husband's servant, she is forced to conform once again to the traditional wifely role in this supernatural rite. Gisaburo is in this sense a *patriarchal* ghost. Much older than Toyoji, he wants a return to the family and the village structure that the affair of Seki and Toyoji has disturbed.

Similarly, Toyoji finds himself a slave to a ritual he does not consciously understand: he must repeatedly throw the leaves he has raked into the well in which he and Seki deposited Gisaburo's body. The well becomes a privileged site within the mise-en-scène; inhabited by Gisaburo's corpse, it becomes an image of the center of the earth. Subjective shots from its interior provide a circular frame looking up at the four seasons that pass above and at the repeated returns of Toyoji to the site of his crime. These shots from the hole in the earth, the phantom's-eye view, are visually magnificent, engaging an optic of obsessional absence. Repetition seems to breed more repetition, as obsession forces more murder. Toyoji repeats his crime when he kills the young master of the village near the well. The murder of the master confirms the couple's defiance of patriarchy, their rebelling indirectly against Seki's subservient role in the initial marriage celebration. Toyoji, the soldier returned from the war, will not be reintegrated into a village culture. The war has shifted that culture and changed its young men; the ghost story narrates this shift indirectly, fantastically.

There are, however, ghosts with which to contend; the Oedipal haunting will not let the two murders go unsolved. Finally the pull of the site of their crime is so strong that Toyoji and Seki enter the well to recover the corpse, at which point the ghost has his revenge: he gouges out Seki's eyes with huge thorns. Like Oedipus, who blinds himself as acknowledgment of the truth and as acknowledgment of divine retribution for his transgressions, Seki is blinded for her transgression, but by the ghost. She only indirectly brings blindness on herself, and the relationship of this blindness to knowing a truth is mitigated by another paradigm.

The blinding is part of a larger paradigm of vision and voyeurism. In an

29. Subjective shots from the interior of the well provide a circular frame looking up at the four seasons that pass above and at the repeated returns of Toyoji to the site of his crime. *Ai no borei* (Empire of Passion, 1980). Still courtesy of Oshima Productions.

early seduction scene, Toyoji exposes himself to Seki, asking her to look at his erection as a sign of his desire. After her blinding, this scene is inverted as she stands naked and asks him to look at her when she is covered with dirt from the well. This rhyme and reversal from beginning to end places sight, blindness, and being the object of the gaze in a paradigmatic relationship of inversion that transforms the blinding into something other than a successful act of retribution or an act of Oedipal insight. For when asked by Seki to look at her, Toyoji tells Seki that she remains beautiful. The gaze here remains a sign of the communication of desire; Toyoji gives his vision to the blind Seki verbally, reaffirming his desire for her. Far from critiquing voyeurism, the film seems to present the gaze as an equivalent with the voice and the embrace as an affirmation of desire and love.

Equally, the film makes no apology for its appeal to the eye, its lush mise-en-scène, its visual pleasure. A crucial turn in the narrative marks an apex of such appeal. At the moment that Seki and Toyoji are arrested, they are seen embracing in a shot of luminous splendor. This image is reinforced by an "epilogue" in which a voice-over narration accompanies images of the couple being tortured until death, never supplying the authorities with a con-

30. The film makes no apology for its appeal to the eye, its lush mise-en-scène, its visual pleasure, as in this shot of the couple embracing. *Ai no borei* (Empire of Passion, 1980). Still courtesy of Oshima Productions.

fession. The film ends with a sense that their transgressive love represents not only a lasting desire but an instance of resistance as well.

Enduring Passion

Empire of Passion is a strange tale, particularly for a Western audience, since it refuses to confirm patriarchal justice. While in an Occidental tradition happy endings show the virtues of conforming to the law, the unhappy endings of bleaker stories teach the ironic but inevitable denial of pleasure as they kill off the "illegitimate" desires with which we have been allowed to identify. (Consider the demise of the lovers in Emile Zola's *Thérèse Raquin* and James Cain's *The Postman Always Rings Twice,* which of course have several film versions.) Oshima's film keeps the bleak ending but transforms its signification. The power of the law to suppress is not denied, but its power to suppress does not interfere with a concomitant affirmation of desire.

It is in light of this affirmation of desire that both *Realm* and *Empire* have been called Nietzschean. It might be wrong to assimilate too quickly this stance into a Western philosophical development, albeit one that confronts its predecessors in the philosophical tradition. In response to suggestions of the film's possible Nietzschean interpretation, Oshima has said, "Life for me is a thing that one endures. In life there are not only the nos [of denunciation] there are also 'yeses.' In that sense, my last two films could recall certain Nietzschean ideas. In fact in Japan philosophers explain the resemblance of Nietzschean ideas and the metaphors of Buddhism. But my two last films could not be contained in these metaphors or they would be completely Buddhist!" (Oshima 1978a). I assume that Oshima here might mean aspects of Zen Buddhism, considering its confrontation with the absences of meaning and of a center. Both philosophies give prevalence to emptiness and nothingness. The liaisons between Nietzschean ideas and Japanese traditions have also been explored by William Haver's (1987, 1996) writing on the theoretical commonality of the Japanese philosopher Nishida and Jacques Lacan; besides, the exchange of ideas in twentieth-century thought and literature belies any singularity of Western influence. Oshima, while claiming the Japanese part of what otherwise might too quickly be seen as wholly Western, nonetheless insists on the function of Western theory in providing leverage to escape the parameters of Buddhism and, by extension, a traditional Japanese perspective.

We can see how *Empire* also flirts with an Oedipal mythology to finally twist its Oedipal elements into a different configuration that attempts to release passion from an Oedipal frame. Toyoji in the beginning substitutes himself for the woman's infant son. He first approaches Seki as she is sleeping next to her infant and expresses verbally his jealousy and desire to replace the child. He then pulls her away from her child and into an adjoining room to rape her. She shuts out the baby's cries, then acquiesces. This mise-en-scène of the substitution of Toyoji for the infant son creates the symbolic situation in which "son" and "mother" kill the "father" when they murder Gisaburo. However, the "son" and "mother" ultimately remain passionate. The blinding is displaced from its Oedipal configuration and finally denied what might be called "full Oedipal significance." The implicit moral of the Oedipal story is sidestepped as the film instead conducts a romance outside moral imperatives. This positioning of desire outside morality is not a simple attack on morality but rather a romance with the force of desire itself that attempts to leave the constraints on desire behind, no matter what the consequences.

The imaginary world of the film is so constructed that consequence itself might be a term of double meaning, a way of seeing the film along two different trajectories, one in which the law and its consequences have domain and the other the trajectory of the supernatural, in which all natural law and the laws of humanity are simply irrelevant. If the ghost of Gisaburo is called in Japanese a "phantom of love," how much does its return constitute a seeking of vengeance against love, a haunting of the conscience of the guilty Seki? In the scene in which the ghost comes to take Seki in his rickshaw, she strikes out, frightened at this face that has become a white, blank mask. Blood streams over the mask in extreme close-up. The imagery here is perhaps one of a dream repetition in which the ghost silently asks Seki to reenact her violence against her husband, to see the blood she has spilled. By the same logic of a dream vision, in blinding Seki, hasn't the ghost freed her from sight? Doesn't his action allow her to return to her lover cleansed of guilt? Or another way to interpret the same events: perhaps the ghost means to take Seki away to his realm of death in his phantom rickshaw, just as he tried to retain her at their hearth. Then her struggle throughout the film would be against a phantom who needs to be killed.

Oshima's thoughts on the supernatural aspect of his film support this.

> If one were to construct a catalogue of Japanese phantoms, there would be on one hand phantoms who haunt places and on the other phantoms who haunt people. The case of the phantom Gisaburo interests me: he should have been a phantom who haunted the place, the home, but because he was killed by his wife he haunts a person, his wife. What I found unique here is that he isn't a phantom of remorse, but stays always a phantom of love. . . . I found in the story a [nonmaleficent] phantom who had never before been written, but only spoken, spoken, spoken, from tradition to tradition. . . . The rickshaw phantom had wanted to take his wife to the world beyond, but as his will wasn't strong enough he frees her and she will wake the next morning in her house. (1978a: 48)

Oshima thus locates his phantom within an oral narrative tradition. He also suggests that the phantom is of limited power, engaged in a struggle of wills, a love competition for which remorse is the wrong term. The phantom is not an avenging demon, not because he doesn't desire justice in his own terms, but because he is too weak, too limited in power to seek vengeance. No metaphysical law of the universe weighs in on his side.

Empire perhaps tries to go even further than *Realm* in seeking an imaginary place in which actions could be autonomous and hermetic. Even though it explores the heart of the Japanese village (the characters are too poor to simply run away), the characters attempt to live outside or beyond rules. To do so *Empire* plunges back into the tales of such villages, their oral traditions, to see what spaces they might have imagined for themselves. Intriguingly, we find again in Seki the vision of the she-demon, in this case marked as the woman who does not age. Seki is not as active a destructive and consuming force as is Sada, nor is her representation as demon by the villagers necessarily our response to her. In fact, it is possible to see Seki as an answer to Sada, her sister in the quest for possession of her own erotic power and sensual pleasure. She is a fantasy not yet liberated from the image of the demoness, an image struggling against the ambiguities of the traditions that give birth to her.

VISUAL SPLENDOR, VISUAL CENSOR

The analysis so far only hints at the tremendous sensuality of these two films. Reds, patterns on patterns, the weaves of light and textures designing the image create spaces for which the term "visual splendor" is appropriate. It is a most intimate visual splendor, laced with flesh visible through the folds of cloth and bare flesh. The scenography strives for the paradoxical mixture of compositional complexity and the suggestive minimalism of rendering characteristic of ukiyo-e prints. Especially significant to consider here is the aesthetics of the erotic prints whose exaggerated genitalia and contorted body positions add a turbulence to the figuration.

In its lush visual articulation, the films raise the question of an aesthetics of pornography, a sensuousness at the heart of a sexual rendering. To evoke sexual arousal within the context of visual splendor and complexly allegorical narrative patterns was part of the strategy of Oshima's redefining pornography, despite his refusal to argue for the aesthetic value of his film when charged with obscenity. Oshima's desire to make a truly pornographic film, in which actual sexual intercourse is viewed, did not allow for arguments that his film was artistic eroticism, rather than pornography; no appeal to aesthetics was intended.

Instead, *Realm*'s battle with censorship exists as a direct, intended confrontation with Japan's obscenity laws and years of prior censorship to which Oshima had bowed, particularly the suppression of certain scenes in *Pleasures of the Flesh* (Oshima 1992: 256). At the same time it was a celebration by the producer, Anatole Dauman, of France's relaxation of its censorship laws. Elsewhere censorship of *Realm* came in many forms: outright prohibition of the film in many countries, "clouding" or masking of the genital scenes in some prints, and in Japan a trial aimed at banning of the book devoted to the scenario, essays, and production stills from the film. At trial, Oshima challenged the court to define precisely what obscenity in representation could be. His most intriguing arguments involved asking to crop stills down to distill the obscene in the image and questioning the legal category of "poses of sexual intercourse" and "poses of sex play" as opposed to simply sexual intercourse. Then he extends this formal semiotic questioning of obscenity to the film's dialogue language, asking if the obscene is in descriptive sentences or in individual words or sounds.

It is finally in respect to these issues of representation that we can understand that *Empire of Passion* is the offshoot of *Realm of the Senses,* in an aesthetic sense and as a further exploration of the ongoing allegorization of desire.

CHAPTER FIVE

Warring Subjects

War films as a genre tend to personalize the history of the conflicts they depict. Often only one army is individuated and granted subjectivity, while its enemy makes shadowy appearances as a monolithic evil force to be eradicated. Yet many war films qualify their partisan ideologies with humanist concerns and even antiwar sentiments; if the enemy is dehumanized and opposing forces do not necessarily meet face-to-face, still the face of the individual in a political and historical context is the focus of these narratives.

For the Japanese in the postwar period films directly representing World War II are few, the most famous being Kobayashi's antiwar trilogy, *The Human Condition,* and Kurosawa's brilliant look at the homefront, *No Regrets for Our Youth.* Part of the reason for this may be Occupation censorship. Even oblique references to the war that might feed militarism were forbidden during the Occupation, as Hirano Kyoko shows in her book, *Mr. Smith Goes to Tokyo* (1992). "The American censors allowed no sympathetic, indeed no noncondemnatory, mention of Japanese militarism," she states, and goes on to examine how instances of censored films indicate that even references that would be interpreted as condemnatory were construed as too dangerous to permit (Hirano 1992: 49–53). Hirano (1992: 87–95) discusses at length the censorship battle Tanigushi Senkichi faced in 1950 over his film, *Akatsuki no dasso* (Desertion at Dawn). It is in the context of these years of carefully monitored discourse that war films after the Occupation may be seen; with the curtain drawn so that the Japanese could stage their own reaction to the war, one question a post-Occupation filmmaker confronts is how to react both to the history of the war and to the history of the Occupation's control over discourse on the war. For those writers and directors wishing to condemn Japanese militarism, but to do so in their own terms, the period following the Occupation was one of opportunity fraught with much historical and ideological resonance.

Oshima made two films, more than twenty years apart, directly set in the war period. Both are adapted from literary works, and both choose to focus on relationships between the Japanese and prisoners of war. The first is his 1961 adaptation of the short story "Shiiku" by the writer Oe Kenzaburo. The second, *Senjô no Merry Christmas* (Merry Christmas, Mr. Lawrence, 1983), is an adaptation of a novel by a South African, Laurens van der Post. Oshima sees in each of his adaptations a potential vehicle for a critique of the Japanese state. This critique needed to be made in such a manner that would avoid what Oshima has termed the postwar "victimization" syndrome, which tended to exonerate individual Japanese and blame only those in command. This syndrome was fed in part by the Occupation, which insisted on military leaders' being clearly blamed for the war, for its atrocities and its cost to the Japanese people. However, while this blame may have served an immediate postwar purpose in breaking traditional obedience to the military, it fed into an absence of individual morality that Japanese thinkers such as Oshima find an equally troubling, if not greater, problem. If the Japanese see themselves as victims of past leaders, now eradicated, they may never ask what role each plays in participating in or even indirectly supporting wars of aggression. For these reasons, each of Oshima's works emphasizes particular aspects of the novels, overturning more humanist readings available in these fictions to insist on their legibility as Brechtian allegories.

READINGS OF OE'S "SHIIKU": RACE AND RECOVERY

Oe's "Shiiku" is probably the most famous story Oshima ever adapted, though more of his films are adaptations than is commonly realized. Published in 1958, the story won the prestigious Akutagawa prize for literature. It appeared in English as "The Catch," first in a volume entitled *The Shadow at Sunrise,* later in a paperback entitled *The Catch and Other War Stories,* and then in retranslation as "The Prize Stock." Translation is problematic, as even the varied title suggests, with the earlier version calling the prisoner the "Negro" in neutral passages and "nigger" in certain of the villager's dialogue references to him. The newer translation uses "black man" throughout. The introduction to the second volume suggests the topical interest of the story in the postwar, post-Occupation context, as it suggests the story traces "the impact of the Pacific War on the Japanese mind." While this is a topic of much concern to Oshima, his film departs in major ways from the Oe story. Taken together, both the story and the film show how in different ways contestatory artists choose to remember and allegorize the war.

Oe and Oshima have much in common. They were both young children when the Pacific War began: Oe was born in 1935, just three years after Oshi-

ma. Oe, like Oshima, is also associated with the left and with European influences. Oe studied French literature at Tokyo University, and his writing
is often linked to Sartre, though equally to Camus and other French writers
of the postwar period. Oe grew up in a rural community in Ehime, on the
island of Shikoku; although he was born in Kyoto, Oshima grew up in Seto-
naikai, a region on the main Japanese island of Honshu, directly across the
sea from Shikoku. Oe sought to write about sexuality in a political framework, often seeking a shock value that was meant to transform conformity,
similar to Oshima's treatment of sex in his films.

These parallels, however, were often overlooked by commentators on
Oshima's adaptation. Certain presuppositions of auteurism that need to
emphasize the filmmaker's uniqueness and his lack of indebtedness to others may be the reason shared aspects are overlooked. Given this auteurist
perspective that seeks to fit the film into the logic of Oshima's career, critics assumed that the commission to make a film adaptation was primarily
a compromise for Oshima dictated by commercial imperatives after leaving Shochiku while he worked to establish his own production company.
Thus the emphasis on Oshima's being approached by a producer who had
bought the screen rights to "Shiiku." While critics classed Oe as either a humanist realist or a romantic for reasons that have largely to do with the history of Japanese literature, film critics saw Oshima as a Brechtian, leading
them to emphasize, either on auteurist or conceptual grounds, the changes
Oshima made in Oe's story. Sometimes, however, auteurist criticism took
another tack, granting even the outline of the story (a downed black pilot
being captured by a small village in rural Japan) to Oshima, without mentioning Oe.

None of these critical approaches examines both texts comparatively in
any detail from a historical, cultural perspective. In attempting this now, the
question becomes how each text is a commentary not only on the war but
also on Japanese attitudes toward difference and the "other" as enemy.
These concerns, as much as the World War II setting, are what links this Oshima film and its written source to another he would make years later, *Furyo*.

Oe's "Shiiku" is narrated by the older of two brothers; the story opens
as the boys are playing in a new makeshift crematorium established in the
village as the traditional one has been made inaccessible through flooding
from torrential rains. At this site they encounter a companion they call
"Harelip" who has just returned from hunting wild dogs, one of which he
has captured. Harelip is proudly showing off his captured dog, and in fact
attempting to demonstrate its almost immediate bonding and loyalty to
him, when an "enemy plane" passes overhead, thus distracting the boys and
allowing the dog's escape. This scene provides an important prelude as it
establishes death, domestication, and captivity in an everyday context,

slightly displaced from the more dramatic events to follow. While the crematorium site as children's playground can be read as local color in a realist fictional mode, it provides the story with a formal circularity, as its closure is a joint cremation as well as an evocation of the European front in World War II in which atrocities are uncovered at sites of corporeal disposal. Here the specifics of language are significant. The story opens with the first-person narrator placing the characters at this site: "My young brother and I were at the temporary crematory at the bottom of the valley, the rudimentary crematory that had been made, quite simply, by cutting a space in the dense shrubs and spading up a shallow layer of earth. We were scratching about with pieces of wood in the soft surface earth that smelled of fat and ashes. . . . [W]e had gone to the crematory to look for any well-shaped bones still remaining that could be used for badges to wear on our chests, but they had all been gathered already by the village children, and we found absolutely nothing." A line such as "soft surface earth that smelled of fat and ashes" demands reading as a poetic metaphor for the war itself, a metaphor that establishes an authorial distance from the narrator's consciousness. The boy's narration displays a competition over bone badges, as when it tells us, "It seemed I would have to beat one of my primary school friends into handing over his [bone badge]." This militarism whose goal is a kind of counterfeit war medal displays the ironic critique of the author; while the scene may have much in common with the neorealism of Italian postwar film in its concentration on young boys' reactions to conditions, these boys are much more complicit in a war mentality and the author implies much more distance from the boy's point of view as narrator than is the case with the young boy in de Sica's *The Bicycle Thief,* or perhaps an even stronger parallel, the sequence in Rossellini's *Paisa* (1946) in which a black GI is befriended by a young boy during the liberation of Italy.

The complex interaction of focalization and ironic, implied authorial voice is key to the functioning of Oe's story. The boy's focalization of his father's return with the lone surviving U.S. pilot allows Oe to underscore the fascination with their elders' prisoner on the part of the young boys of the village. This fascination is reiterated throughout the story and rendered as clearly a sexual fascination with racial difference. Oe emphasizes the excitement the group of boys derives from voyeurism and fetishization of the black man's body in language that highlights both obsessional pleasure and its connection to fear. He locates the erotic in the defamiliarization of ordinary experience, a defamiliarization that occurs because the body is seen as exotic and therefore erotic, as this description of the prisoner's first captive meal shows: "The milk over-flowed the corners of his lips, lips that were almost painfully swollen, like a ripe fruit bound round with a cord. It ran down his bare throat, wetting his open shirt and down his chest, where it formed shivering globules like oil on the tough blackly gleaming skin. With lips dry from excitement, I realized for the first time that goat's milk was an extremely beautiful liquid." The eroticism includes the desire of incorporation displaced onto the food that the black man was offered: "Had there been any fragments of food left in it, I would have seized them with fingers that trembled with secret pleasure and gulped them down." Oe insists on the erotic, underscoring this passage with his character's thought, "with a mixture of shame and irritation, as if I had been indulging in lewd daydreams." This psychological examination has to be seen in the context of the Japanese "I" novel and the force the introduction of character psychology had in the context of Meiji literature. *The Catch* is not literally an "I" novel, as it has a fictive narrator who is not the writer, but the confessional seeking language remains, even as it belongs to a period in which authors are seeking to break the solipsism of the "I" novel and to be responsive to social realities instead of the narrow definition of knowable reality as simply the writer's self. This lingering of the confessional in Oe may be seen in terms of the admiration he has expressed for Henry Miller, a confessional writer of selfhood, and European existentialists for whom fiction is an often autobiographically based support for interior musings.

The black prisoner is kept in the basement of the communal storehouse, the building in which the two brothers live with their father in a second-floor loft that was a former silkworm room. Their father is a trapper of weasels. In these details, the peasantry's historical connection to breeding and hunting animals is repeatedly inscribed while the building's spatial dispensation allows for a proximity to the captive even when the boys are not watching or listening (we are told they can't hear the prisoner but are thrilled by the thought of him, below). The trapdoor above the makeshift prison allows for repeated scenes of voyeurism. The original Japanese title "Shiiku" means "breeding," as in animal husbandry, and this notion of the caged animal to which the prisoner is compared establishes an animal-human paradigm that organizes much of the imagery. Details of an almost entirely male context, with the hunt and the trap dominating, provide Oe with a focus on male identity and group interaction.

The story addresses race in ways similar to fifties and sixties U.S. fiction and films, both in its allegorical dimensions and in the manner in which the association of blackness with primitiveness and animality is actualized in the imagery. This imagery is eventually called into question by a narrative structure that locates the animalistic in white (or in this case, Japanese) treatment of the black person. Also noteworthy is the fictional presentation of a black pilot or crewman during World War II; racist policies in the U.S. military made a black pilot shot down over Japan unlikely, if not impossible. The U.S. Army Air Force trained black pilots beginning in 1942 for segregated units; in 1946 the Eighth Army in the Pacific theater was still racially segregated (Binkin 1982: 19; MacGregor 1981: 178, 214). Oe's creation of such a character raises fascinating historical questions. The confrontation with the black man this story fantasizes perhaps owes much more to the Occupation and the Korean War as social circumstance and U.S. narratives of integration in both fiction and film than it does to actual World War II experience.

The middle of the story is a long suspension, a waiting. The village is waiting for an order from the regional authorities regarding treatment of their prisoner of war. This suspended time depicts the boys' desire to keep the black soldier as a domesticated animal, a pet whose principal function is to amuse them as they take him on walks outside. While this part of the narrative is sometimes read as the "development of a human relationship between the boys and the captive airman," such a reading neglects to consider the racism of this "domestication" implicitly critiqued by many ironic devices of the narration. The boys skin a weasel in front of the black airman, hoping to impress him with their skill; but of course the language in which this scene is presented fully explores the irony of the weasel and the man being parallel captives: "We would hope for the sake of our spectator, the Negro, that the death of the rebellious agile weasel would be satisfactory and its skinning skillful. As it was strangled it would release a fearsome stink, a last gesture of spite out of its death-throes" (1981: 46). The weasel's description parallels earlier descriptions of the black man, said "to have a thick greasy neck" with "tough folds in the skin" (p. 34). In this scene the black man is said to be "gazing at creases in the skin [of the skinned weasel pelt] as Father scraped off the fat" (p. 46).

Oe is insistent on the animal parallels and their implicit psychoanalytical dimensions as he describes a scene in which the boys take their captive swimming in spring. First we are told, "Every time we threw water at him, he would shriek like a strangled hen and thrust his head below the surface" (p. 47). Then in another comparison: "His naked, wet body, reflecting the strong rays of the sun, shone like the body of a black horse; it was perfect, and beautiful. Suddenly we noticed that the Negro had a splendid, a heroic, an unbelievable phallus. We gathered around him, clamoring, bumping our naked bodies against each other, and when he grasped it and taking up a fierce, threatening stance, gave a great bellow, we dashed water on him and laughed till the tears ran down our cheeks" (pp. 47–48). This orgasmic scene of group sexual play, of symbolic bestiality, constitutes a mythic rite as power shifts between the two polarities within the category of domestic animal (chicken/stallion) and the fascination oscillates between awe of the heroic and sadism toward the demeaned. It establishes the terms through which the boys relate to their "catch." If the boy narrator speaks of the epiphany that these mingling bodies represent for him, he introduces it in language that makes it clear how they never see the black man as anything other than beast: "We looked at him as some rare wonderful domestic animal, a genius of an animal" (p. 48).

Many critical interpretations of the story see this scene primarily in its mythic and romantic fulfillment, a straightforward celebration of the primitive. The ending of the novella then becomes a dashing of this paradisiacal fantasy by external forces. While the coming of age structure of the novella is pronounced, this romantic reading is only partial and needs to be seen as troubled by elements of irony and language, levels of complication.

Apocalyptic violence ends the story. The boy tries to warn the captive that he is about to be taken to the military authorities; this act of rebellion by the boy against adult authority is first troubled by an absence of a means of verbal communication. "I who could convey nothing to him, could only gaze at him with a mixture of sadness and frustration" (p. 50), the boy tells us, but the black airman's subjectivity here as throughout is rendered only through the filter of the boy's perception. His act of rebellion, his effort to survive, culminates in the desperate act of taking the narrator hostage. The boy can only understand this act in his terms: "As I looked into his expressionless eyes, the realization swept in on me that the Negro soldier had changed back into the black wild beast that defied understanding, that dangerously poisonous substance that he had been when he was first brought back captive" (p. 50). In one sentence, the man who had been both "almost a man" and "a wonderful domestic animal" degenerates first into a beast then into a "poisonous substance" (p. 50). After a night in the captive's captivity the boy describes himself as broken, abject, in the depths of degradation (p. 53). He imagines himself dangling "like a rabbit" (p. 53) or "strangled to death like my father's weasels" (p. 54), expressing the role reversal through further inscriptions of the animal metaphors. The boy's father smashes the black's skull with a hatchet in an attempt to rescue the boy, but the black man moves the boy's hand to protect his head, so that the boy's hand is smashed in the process (p. 55). Harelip suggests the boy's hand smells just like the black corpse, reinforcing the parallels and reversals between these two characters with another of the dominant motifs: odor.

In this catechresis of imagery, consider the role of a final incident in which the children are sledding on the tail fragment of the airplane. An amputee, who had been close to the boy and who takes a turn at the children's game, gets killed. We are told at the story's end, "the clerk, I imagined would be burned with the wood they had collected to burn the Negro" (p. 60), unifying what now comes to be a cast of grotesques—Harelip, the clerk, the boy, and the captive—in imagery of death and destruction, in an amassing of motifs of lost or disabled body parts. This can be read not simply as an alienated coming of age story steeped in romanticism but also as an allegorical antiwar frieze, beginning and ending on cremation, as well as a psychological investigation and confrontation with Japanese racism as it is linked to militarism.

31. Shots of the villagers present a frightening visual analogy for mass
psychology. *Shiiku* (The Catch, 1961). Still courtesy of Oshima Productions.

STAGING THE ALLEGORY

Oshima's *Shiiku* retains the structure of the pilot's captivity in a small Japanese village and iterates the same sort of attack on Japanese insularity implicit in the reading above, though not necessarily in all readings of the
novella. The film, however, changes characters, scenes, details, and
metaphors to attain this end. The changes can be seen as very possibly mul-
tiply determined, some issuing from translation of the verbal into visual
adaptation, some from Brechtian principles of distanciation, some from
film's culturally imposed taboos at this time against depictions of homosexual desire and homoeroticism, some from a concomitant desire perhaps
responding to market imperatives to introduce female characters and heterosexual lust.

The film is Oshima's first collaboration with Tamura Takeshi as scenarist;
together they introduce patterns of narrative structure here that will later
be used in other Oshima films. A major shift occurs in not using the older
brother's focalization and displacing the sexual elements from the boy's fascination with the soldier to a complex narrative of incestuous abuse of patriarchal power on the part of the village head. Here, Tamura's and Oshima's
portrayal of central patriarchal authority as corrupt, through emphasis on

sexual exploitation, prefigures their collaboration for *Ceremonies* and their emphasis on the village as a *huis clos* theatrical space that will be used a few years later in *Hakuchu no torima* (Violence at Noon, 1966). These moves annihilate the possibility of the more benign, humanist or male-mythic readings that the novella, as I have indicated, was prone to elicit.

Using long, mobile takes similar to the camera work of *Night and Fog in Japan,* the film focuses on the staging of discussions and confrontations. Dialogue develops in relationship to the framing of group interaction in its effect on individuals. The first scene shows the black prisoner (Hugh Hurd) being brought across a bridge into the village. The film wastes no time before introducing strong visual imagery. After a close-up on his shackled foot, we cut to a close-up of a young girl, Mikiko (Oshima Eiko), vomiting. The black man is tied in front of a bonfire, as the villagers debate what to do with him; a woman rushes at him with a sickle but is restrained. This attack is typical of the action invented for the film scenario, as it visually establishes the restraint of the antagonism felt toward the enemy captive as the villagers await the regional authority. The holding pattern is illustrated by action rather than simply revealed by commentary.

The short story's central characters, the two unnamed brothers and the harelip, Jiro, are transformed into a quite different set of brothers, the older one named Jiro, the younger, Hachiro. The film's Jiro is of less-than-normal intelligence, unlike the older brother–narrator of the novel, who is an articulate and thoughtful voice. The anomalous village of the novel, where hunting figures but farming is never mentioned, is replaced by scenes in which the black man works alongside the villagers in the rice paddies. The film insists on the village as typical, which allows it allegorically to more completely stand in for all of Japan.

The film adds a village elder, a landlord, Kazumasa, as central figure. Kazumasa's affairs with his son's bride, Hisako, and with a Tokyo refugee, Hiroko, turn the narrative into one of incestuous desire and perverse patriarchal power. The addition of this refugee from Tokyo introduces the awareness of the war's going badly at this point for the Japanese; through her we learn Tokyo was bombed, and thus get some sense of the relationship of events in this isolated village to the larger war. As this same refugee becomes a victim of the village elder, we get a sense of oppressions that do not simply derive from reactions to the war. Instead, war conditions provide opportunities for sexual oppression to be extended to a newcomer. Yet if the heterosexual lines of desire and power are mapped by the film, homosexuality is not. The sexuality of the Oe story, rich in homoerotic attractions, might have yielded in Oshima's hands a film similar to *Merry Christmas, Mr. Lawrence,* yet in the early sixties it seems even the implicit homoeroticism needed to be transposed into heterosexual terms.

Jiro's simplemindedness blocks identification with him as hero. Instead of being a sensitive, if somewhat misled, intelligence, he is the center of a Brechtian scheme of distanciation that is meant to expose the mechanisms of group psychology, particularly scapegoating as an alibi and as a displacement for guilt. Kazumasa retains his power by blaming the black man for the village's troubles: "Everything has gone badly for us since he came!" Jiro's role as strange witness to the villagers' folly is echoed by the introduction of the madwoman who wanders through scenes.

The film invents incidents for both the captive and Jiro. Jiro is drafted. His response to the draft is to run away temporarily. His reaction on returning is to rape Mikiko, an action that seems to be a mimicking of the sexual oppression practiced by Kazumasa. He is tied to a post in the center of the village. His inappropriate, displaced responses accumulate a guilt that eventually will allow displacement of all guilt onto him.

In a scuffle with the villagers, a young girl is thrown over a cliff. The captive is blamed. Then the captive holds the boy hostage, and the villagers kill him. Jiro becomes another scapegoat, assuming the role the black captive played previously. The villagers conveniently blame Jiro, already accused of rape, for the murder of the black captive. Then he is killed in a climactic struggle with the regional authorities. Hachiro, the younger brother, and even the woman he raped come to Jiro's defense.

The convoluted plot additions meant apparently to render the story more Brechtian borrow heavily from the tropes of melodrama, most obviously the accidental pushing of a young girl over a cliff that sets off the scapegoating mechanism. These are not yet masterful in their formal presentation; we do not yet have here the involutions of later Oshima films, where interwoven presentations of implausible events doubling on each other are offered with dramatic and theoretical ironies (the formal innovations discussed in chapter 3). We do have, though, many of the components, such as the repetition of women fighting off male aggression, denials that events just witnessed ever occurred, and lines spoken which gain an ironic humor from their placement in specific contexts, as when the villager who has just killed the captive proclaims that the prisoner was still in uniform and therefore could be said to have died for his country. We laugh as we know any sense of honoring the rights of a prisoner of war have been absent all along, a reference to the Japanese militarist belief that all captured soldiers were dishonored. The only semblance of generosity toward the enemy comes as an ironic alibi for the villagers' murder. It is through dialogue strategically staged that the film develops the ironic countercurrents of discourses within the allegory; the opinions characters give are situated so that each comments ironically on what was said earlier.

In addition, visual composition so deftly stages the Brechtian allegory that the film achieves considerable power. Circle motifs that show the villagers

32. Circle motifs that show the villagers gathered together, as in this one in which they form a semicircle surrounding their black captive, occur throughout *Shiiku* (The Catch 1961). Still courtesy of Oshima Productions.

gathered together, most particularly the shot that shows them gathered around a document from the regional authorities, as well as shots during the sake party, and a later shot from below that shows them standing over the makeshift dungeon in which they keep their black captive, present a frightening visual analogy for mass psychology. The use of slats to frame close-ups, especially effective in the wide-screen format, has the act of looking placed in systematic juxtaposition to the act of imprisonment.

Black and white contrast throughout, most emphatically in shots where skin colors contrast. One of the most decisive aspects of Oshima's film is to use a situation of racial contrast to graphically juxtapose Japanese characters with a black man; few Japanese films had ever presented a black person on screen. The film contains powerful images of enslavement; it also contains equally powerful images of rebellion.

When the black man's stranglehold on Jiro is framed in extreme close-up it embodies a primal fear of black strength. Subsequent images then recontextualize this image, as we focus not on it but on the hatred that it evokes as the captive is brutally murdered. One possible reading of the film could isolate and emphasize this image, holding that all the film was angling toward this stranglehold as both manifestation and confirmation of Japanese fears of the racial other.

The film ends on burning the body of Jiro and the black man, as Hachiro is seen apart from the group, off by himself. This spatial isolation of Hachiro uses the younger brother, a rather innocent observer in the conflict, to stress alienation from the village and following the allegory, from Japan.

Despite all differences inscribed in the short story and the film, both exude deep alienation from the Japan that perpetrated the war. Now that Oe has won the 1995 Nobel Prize for literature it is more timely than ever to analyze how Oshima's adaptation critiques Oe as a dialogue on the war by their generation. Oshima mitigates Oe's fascination with the primal, instead placing his emphasis on xenophobia and the mass psychology of fascist tendencies in village culture. He hits harder on the abuses of patriarchy within the village hierarchy. He thus attempts to turn Oe's fauvist tendencies toward greater political consciousness; even so, he retains something of Oe's embrace of the odd and the wild, the lore of that which does not quite fit norms and cultural expectations, of the violence that breaks out unexpectedly. It is perhaps this fauvism that Oe and Oshima have in common. It gets translated in the film by the minimalist sets, dark spaces of wood and rock juxtaposed with gleaming muscle and corporeal expressions of anger and fear. Oe and Oshima share a dark, rebellious force that ideological analysis in commentary has often ignored. Oshima, like Oe, can write in blood.

LOOKING THE ENEMY IN THE FACE

It will be many years before Oshima returns to the war as subject and setting; when he does, it is to one of the most controversial aspects of the Japanese war effort—the brutal treatment of enemy prisoners. Seen theoretically, *Merry Christmas, Mr. Lawrence* is a radical and deconstructive incursion into the genre of the war film. It remains concerned with the face of the warrior, in this case the modern soldier who comes to the global conflict of World War II bearing a strong national identity. Yet rather than attempt to concentrate on just one side in the conflict, it examines the cultural and psychoanalytic determinations of actions in a war. Few fictions have pursued so determinedly the exploration of tortures and violence of war on a global scale as an interaction of individuals face-to-face, with so much attention to the philosophical and theoretical issues involved, as does this film. Already, van der Post's novel, *The Sower and the Seed,* posed many of these questions, but the structuration of Oshima's film both amplifies and further problematizes its philosophical implications.

Ironically, this film may appear on the surface to be less serious about its propositions than other of Oshima's films. It seems, at least initially, in its 70-

millimeter, Dolby format both more commercial and more accessible, less marked by the twists of fictional discourse through which many of Oshima's previous projects have challenged the ideological functioning of fictions and myths. In its casting of two superstars, the British David Bowie (as the South African, Maj. Jack Celliers) and the Japanese Sakamoto Riuichi (as Captain Yanoi) opposite each other, it might seem simply to be pandering to the global marketing practices that now dominate the film industry. This appearance is misleading, for as I shall show the film is far less conventional than it might first appear, and this casting, like so much else about the film, is part of a strategy to use a global cultural marketing against the grain of typical patterns of exploitation. The extravagance of image and sound (to which the cropped video version in home distribution does a great injustice) does more than produce mere commercial values; shots are worked with the same artistic care that characterizes Oshima's more intimate films. The framing of each composition and the timing of each utterance or each entrance of musical segments of the magnificent score by Sakamoto Riuichi are incisive. Despite the grandiose scale of the image, there is an understatement, control, and sense of purpose that is so opposite to the kind of extravagant entertainment production represented by David Lean's *The Bridge on the River Kwai,* a film whose narrative addresses certain of the same historical instances and to which journalists tended to compare *Merry Christmas, Mr. Lawrence. River Kwai* is set in a Japanese prisoner-of-war camp in which the Japanese violate the Geneva convention in ordering British prisoners to build a strategic bridge. They at first balk at the order; however, the British head of prisoners takes on the project as a challenge through which he can prove British engineering ingenuity and rally prisoner morale. The officer invests so heavily in his command of the project that he insanely tries to foil the efforts of his own forces to sabotage the bridge. The film is played for entertainment values (identification, suspense, and the whistled theme song) and is mildly antiwar in its absurdist treatment of the commanding officer. The Japanese are simplistic stereotypes and hardly seen.

While *Merry Christmas, Mr. Lawrence* risks a likeness to Lean's film, particularly in its star casting, its focus on the Allied officers' disputes, and its use of motifs within its musical score, these superficial similarities give way before profound differences. Oshima's strategy in composing his film is to cull from literary adaptation a rereading, an imaging, that positions the viewer in a symbolic matrix in which philosophies of self and state are questioned, both historically and as contemporary constructs.

THE BOOK AND THE FILM

Oshima was no stranger to literary adaptations, but in choosing van der Post's *The Sower and the Seed,* originally published in 1963, he has done something quite rare in the history of adaptation and certainly in the history of the war film. He has chosen the story of the other, the former enemy, as his source, leaving the point of view implicitly maintained by the other largely intact. Of course, given this book and this filmmaker, such an adaptation is not the impossibility that telling the story of the other would be in most circumstances. Oshima has long been critical of aspects of Japanese nationalism and cultural identity both in his films and in his writings and interviews, and van der Post's novel is itself an attempt to overcome Western ignorance of and prejudicial assumptions about the Japanese, substituting instead a construct of difference in historical formations. If East does not exactly meet West here, if the Japanese view does not precisely reduplicate a British, Dutch, and U.S. perspective on the Pacific War, an encounter of perspectives takes place in which attitudes toward otherness and rival colonialisms are in dialogue. Perhaps one indication of what it means for a Japanese filmmaker to tell van der Post's story is found in the fact that funding for the production came from Australia and New Zealand, not Japan. In many ways, then, the film is a text for a global *époque,* a 1980s context in which culture has circumvented national boundaries by a system of exchanges taking place in terms of both production and reception. Yet as a story about the past, about personal and political histories, the film retraces the strong implications of cultural difference in determining perception and action.

Oshima's rewriting of van der Post's text transforms the narrative on some structural levels. The novel's use of several embedded narrations, both verbal and written, and its use of temporal ellipses between sections give way to a more direct, condensed, and concise narration. Yet other techniques are substituted which perform similarly to those of the novel; for example, what is in the novel presented as a diary kept in prison by Jack Celliers, the haunted South African who sacrifices himself in an act of resistance to the Japanese camp authorities, is rendered through Celliers's direct first-person narration illustrated by a flashback. Instead of being read by other characters years later, after his death, Celliers's memories are staged as his intimate revelations to John Lawrence while the two share a cell awaiting execution. This flashback restaging is the most delicate and perhaps awkward moment of the film; the scenes are set in South Africa but characterized by their European aspects. The farmhouse and garden and the British boys' school are exported cultural artifacts and presented with a physical exaggeration, a saturated mise-en-scène that distorts mere realism into an unsettling description of events.

Incidents that in the novel occur in two different prisoner-of-war camps in the film are folded into a single site and time. Such changes do collapse events and characters that are temporally and spatially distinct from each other in the novel's narration but do not substantially alter the novel's view of the Japanese characters and of the Japanese national identity in 1942. Van der Post's text is highly critical of the Japanese, but not naively, in contradistinction to the prejudices dominant in wartime thought, prejudices that are given voice in the novel through one of the British characters, the prisoners' official leader, Hicksley. The novel, which articulates its critique of the Japanese in the postwar dialogue of John Lawrence and the narrator, precedes from a knowledge of the culture and its operative assumptions. Oshima (1983b: 20) has said he was drawn to the project of adapting the book after reading its Japanese translation in 1978 and he was "immediately interested in its style, its characters and its philosophy." Despite the fact that Oshima elsewhere (1983c: 8) has said "the author [van der Post] described the Japanese from an Occidental point of view and I had to redefine them from my own point of view," he has in many ways sharpened the sense, already inherent in the novel, that basic traditional philosophies of the Japanese ascendant during the thirties and forties played their part in shaping wartime policies of cruelty and torture.

There is also a compression and elision of some expository material in the film, such as the novel's greater attention to Celliers's South African, Boer heritage. This elision does not change Celliers's character dramatically, for in the novel Celliers hardly typifies his ethnic heritage. We are told he was a lawyer who defended blacks in sympathetic comprehension of how they could not submit to the laws under which they were charged; this background and his identification with the suppressed blacks is retrospectively represented while Celliers is recounting his trial by the Japanese military court. The film does not totally erase Celliers's South African background, but it does make far less of South Africa's history of racism and competing colonialisms in its psychohistorical presentation of this character. The film depicts incidents occurring in South Africa in its flashbacks showing Celliers's betrayals of his brother, a hunchback whose deformity he resented, ashamedly hiding it from his mates at his boys' school and thus leaving his brother vulnerable to their ridicule. Yet it does not bring in South Africa as a factor in constituting Celliers's identity both in relationship to the Dutch colony in which the prison camp is located, Java, and the British soldiers with whom he is grouped at the camp. The effect of this shift of emphasis and elision of certain incidents is to deemphasize some of the historical specificity and detail of van der Post's novel in favor of a concentration on symbolic confrontations. For example, in the novel, we are told that prior to his capture Celliers had parachuted with four others into Bantam, where after rejection by pro-Japanese natives he links up with Ambonese guerrillas who are called the "finest soldiers in the old Netherlands East Indies Army" and are said to be delighted to meet in Celliers "an officer who spoke Dutch even though in British uniform" (van der Post 1963: 140). Celliers is said to admire his "staunch, hymn-singing, yellow soldiers," a phrase that encapsulates colonialism and racism even as it signals Celliers's appreciation of the other (van der Post 1963: 140).

Unfortunately, the film becomes less ironic about the constitution of a national identity than is the novel in these particular passages, but this seems to be the cost paid for a narrative economy that remains in the scene of the camp itself (except for the trial scene, the flashbacks, and the coda). This scenographic restriction keeps history as implicit reference rather than highlighting it explicitly in detail. As we shall see, the film substitutes visual and auditory signifiers to represent some of the same material differently, condensed into scenes staged within the camp.

Similarly, the history of Japanese invasions of Burma, Malaya, Singapore, Java, and Sumatra is even more briefly referenced in the film than it is in the novel; the only trace of the military invasions of the Pacific War comes in Celliers's trial and is stripped down to what is necessary to explain the charges against him. Neither text discusses the motivation of this military action as an oil-seeking move on the part of the Japanese, crucial in their effort to deprive their enemies of oil sources while they assured the fueling of their fleets, nor does either fully depict the extent of the Japanese repression of resistant indigenous populations. These omissions might be seen by some as consonant with recent Japanese revisionist history that denies Japanese imperial intentions and minimizes its war atrocities. There is a danger that the absence of a more detailed historical context does perpetuate revisionist myths. Yet nowhere is it suggested that we take the film to represent the extent of Japanese war activities; rather we are asked to see events in the camp as a means of symbolically presenting the investments and traditions that made cruelty follow as a matter of course. The decision to focus on the *huis clos* drama of a single prison camp for British and Dutch officers and on the cruelties inflicted there is one tied to a register of representation that asks us to fill in the gaps by inference. Our historical knowledge of the battles during the period from December 23, 1941, through March 1942 when the Dutch surrendered Java is the context evoked when immediately preceding the prison camp's introduction in the first scene of the film, the date and place is flashed on the screen: 1942, Java.

FRIENDS AND ENEMIES: MALE TO MALE INTERACTIONS

As Derrida has recently reminded us in his lectures on friendship (1994), the canonical texts on friendship concern male to male relationships. Certainly this philosophical emphasis on male friendship is an outgrowth of patriarchal assumptions and structures. It is for this reason that the context of war as a male enterprise has made the war film a particularly strong narrative support for stories drawing on that canon. Male bonding, the love felt toward friends, is here the alternative to the enmity that is felt toward enemies. Derrida argues that friendships are personal whereas enemy relationships are political, forcibly distinguished from personal interaction. Hatred breeds and implies a certain political distance. It follows that those moments in which the enemy is perceived as potential friend and the friend as potential enemy are the most disconcerting as they trouble the boundaries of the oppositions.

In *Merry Christmas, Mr. Lawrence* the lines of friendship are complex and challenge these boundaries. The two main Japanese characters, Captain Yanoi and Sergeant Hara, are juxtaposed with the British soldiers, Colonel Hicksley, Colonel Lawrence, and Major Celliers, a confrontation of enemies. Yet the lines of friendship cross these groupings and do not necessarily prevail within them. Sexual attraction and political repulsion each in different ways color the formation of friendships.

The Japanese principals, Captain Yanoi and Sergeant Hara, are not friends. They are separated within their culture and within the highly stratified and politically divided Japanese military by differences in class, educational refinement, and outlook. The proud, elegant, and controlled Captain Yanoi reveals to Lawrence his history as a military officer midway through the film while the two are discussing the British prisoners' objections to his loud and incessant martial arts sword practice. Yanoi tells Lawrence that he was a member of the Kodo-ha faction. As Lawrence is familiar with the historical circumstances, they speak in generalities. However, the specific historical reference is of great importance as the Kodo-ha faction was a group of young rebellious officers whose insurrection in the "February 26 incident" of 1936 was violently repressed by the opposing Tosei group (Hayashi 1959: 4–6); by understanding the specifics of this reference we are better able to grasp the construction of Yanoi's psychology, as well as historical divisions within the Japanese military. We learn that he escaped the death meted out to many of his comrades, as he was in Manchuria at the time, but he confesses his regret at missing this confrontation. This history explains (for Lawrence, who is obviously familiar with the history and the hierarchies of the Japanese military, and potentially, for the audience) why someone of Yanoi's training and refinement was in 1942 appointed to head the prison camp, considered a quite lowly post. It also presents the Japanese military not as a monolithic entity but as one racked with its own dissent, while it clarifies that Yanoi's Bushido attributes are those of an ideologically motivated and driven believer on the far right.

Sergeant Hara, by contrast, as was typical of the noncommissioned officer in the Japanese army, is from a rural community. He is loud, demonstrative, and violent, but he also has a sense of humor and imagination. He, too, has his moments of insubordination, as in the opening punishment scene discussed below. Along with other Japanese soldiers in the camp, he is wary of his commander, Yanoi. Like Yanoi, Hara has revealing conversations with

Lawrence, and at moments their relationship to him seems to border on friendship. Yet this friendship is always subject to their power over Lawrence and his status as their enemy, factors that eventually lead to their violent repression of him. Each seems to have a greater affinity for Lawrence than for the other. The two Japanese officers rarely converse with each other, but Hara and Lawrence laugh together and debate philosophies and Yanoi repeatedly confides in Lawrence. Yet despite all that separates Yanoi and Hara, they share military and cultural codes.

On the British side, a similar antagonism reigns between Hicksley and Lawrence. Hicksley is suspicious and jealous of Lawrence's ability to communicate with the Japanese and threatened that he might be replaced in his command of the British prisoners by another officer, Lawrence or Celliers. The true friendship in the film is that between Lawrence and Celliers. Their interaction dates back to the British campaign in Libya (though when asked by Yanoi, Lawrence says that they were "not close friends" then). In the camp they establish an immediate and deep affinity for each other that grows as each in his own way confronts his captors in shared imprisonment.

In contrast to Lawrence's friendship with Celliers is Yanoi's attraction to him. It is not a friendship but a homosexual fascination whose palpable physicality is delineated in Oshima's montage of their interactions. In choosing two stars to play these roles, Oshima chose not only two men of distinct beauty but also two men who exert their presence, their sense of performance, through their glances, their stances, their deliberate gestures. This casting heightens the physical charge of their confrontations on-screen, and because of the intelligence each conveys, this physicality is imbued with intellectual investment. It is an attraction that is steeped in an underlying sense of mirroring, including the reversal characteristic of mirror images. Celliers is the other, who, across non-negotiable differences such as his belief in individual will, is parallel to the self. Or to put it differently, he is the ideal self who has been repressed by the force of Japanese culture.

Celliers and Lawrence are fully aware of Yanoi's attraction to Celliers. Lawrence identifies it as the reason Yanoi becomes so obsessed with practicing his swordplay. Celliers mockingly responds to Lawrence's intimation of Yanoi's sublimated desire that Yanoi should "be more direct about it." The casting of Bowie makes this remark particularly powerful as he represents someone whose stage persona is marked by the direct expression of desire and bisexuality (Hopkins 1985: 63, 76–77). Bowie once defined his Ziggy Stardust and Aladdin Sane stage characters as "Japanese theater meets American science fiction" (Hopkins 1985: 100), a phrase that echoes the annexing of the imaginary and the mélange of influences one finds in Oshima's films. In this scene requesting desublimation of desire, history and fiction are juxtaposed with the popular culture of the present, providing a moment of metacritical irony concerning directness and desire.

The violent condemnation and punishment of homosexuality depicted in the opening scenes of *Merry Christmas, Mr. Lawrence* can be seen as a commentary on this pattern of friendship, antagonism, and animosity. It becomes a kind of matrix for much of what follows. Sergeant Hara forces Lawrence to witness Hara's brutal punishment of a Korean guard charged with sexually molesting a Dutch prisoner. This scene is one of the few additions Oshima made; van der Post makes a point of the Japanese forcing their captives to witness violent ritual punishments, but Oshima adds the dimension of the punishment pertaining to the criminalization of homosexuality. The issue of rape is never directly addressed by the film and it seems to link homosexuality per se with violence. In writing about the film, Oshima has said, "homosexuality is the synthesis of friendship and violence: military men are attracted by their enemies, as men, in compensation for their frustration" (1983c; 21). In the film's terms, the Korean is punished for homosexuality, not for forcing a prisoner to submit sexually, a position that contains its own ideological problems as sexual desire is represented by violent aggression, a problematic representation that indeed runs through other of Oshima's films and will be discussed further in chapter 8. Yet even if we take issue with the implicit equation of all homosexualities with violence, we can grant this film its power to explore the relationship between homosexuality and violence in this context of repression and military rule. We can also see how opening with this scene establishes the law for the exclusion of sexuality in this military context while it simultaneously foregrounds a fascination with homosexual acts, a contradiction that will haunt the narrative.

Hara continues to embody that contradiction as he repeatedly requests that the condemned Korean demonstrate "how he used his thing" on the Dutch prisoner, held nearby. Already in this scene, the logic of the law is called into question, as it will repeatedly throughout the film. Here Hara offers to mitigate the punishment of death for homosexuality if the condemned man performs the act once more in front of witnesses. The mitigated sentence is a voluntary, ritual suicide. Further, Hara later defends this by claiming that it is out of compassion that he is allowing the guard to commit suicide, thus enabling his family to receive a pension that would be denied them if he were executed, a consideration that is itself repeated in another context in the film. Hara's sense of the law seems illogical, convoluted, especially from a European perspective, but its apparent contradictions are presented as a condition of a Japanese sense of power, order, and propriety. Similarly, later in the film Hara will claim one minute that "samurais accept homosexuality" and taunt Lawrence the next with the claim, meant pejoratively, that "all British are homosexuals."

As the narrative to follow centers on the homosexual implications of Captain Yanoi's fascination with Jack Celliers, it is significant that Yanoi is the one to whom the disgusted Lawrence appeals and whose appearance on the scene interrupts and postpones Hara's demonstrations. Yet Yanoi will increasingly displace the force of his own homosexual feelings onto violent punishments that mark his reactions to the immediate political antagonisms that obtain in the camp.

The political antagonism in the largest sense is of course the war between the Axis powers and the Allied powers, but in the camp it narrows to a conflict between Yanoi and Hicksley concerning Yanoi's request for the names of armaments experts among the prisoners. Yanoi insists that Japanese are not bound by the Geneva convention decree against forcing officers to work in a skilled capacity for the enemy. Hicksley, unable to resist Yanoi's commands on principle, does so by maintaining that there are no armament experts in the camp. Yanoi's fascination with Celliers gains new impetus in light of this conflict as Yanoi becomes intent on replacing Hicksley with Celliers, thinking that he can use Celliers to bend the officers to his will. This is, of course, a fantasy on Yanoi's part, for it does not account for Celliers's power to resist. Celliers has power over Yanoi even in a situation in which Yanoi nominally holds all the power.

A GAME OF WIT AND WILL

To understand how this conflict is symbolically shaped, let us return to the moment we first see Yanoi interact with Celliers. It is in the courtroom where Celliers is being tried for *wagamamma* (willfulness), for his persistence in fighting in Java after the British command has surrendered. Though Yanoi is but an auxiliary questioner solicited to reinforce the judges, it is his gaze at Celliers (emphasized by a slow zoom-in on him as he stares) and the effect of Celliers returning this look that is highlighted throughout. The scene is staged with great attention to the wide-screen image's ability to emphasize symmetrical arrangements that enforce power, the way the prisoner's dock faces the center of the judge's platform, with straight-on shots of the main judge, of Celliers, and of the group of judges seen from behind Celliers centering them in the frame. The asymmetrical decentering of that power is represented by the angle conditioned by the exchange between Celliers and Yanoi, at a forty-five-degree angle to the axis of the other more symmetrical shots.

Celliers exerts his strength in resisting their inquiries through verbal bantering and acerbic wit that defies the matter-of-fact expectations of the Japanese investigation. For example, when asked his name he replies, "Jack Celliers, what else would it be?" This elicits a Japanese officer's response that a Japanese soldier would lie about his name if captured but of course would never allow himself to be captured. The contradictory logic here on the part of the Japanese, and Celliers's immediate questioning of the question posed to him, is then amplified by Yanoi beginning his address to Celliers with the flourish of the "To be or not to be, that is the question" quote from Hamlet's soliloquy, a citation that calls forth a European notion of will as opposed to the Japanese construction of the subject.

The question of will and individual subjectivity is present in many Oshima films, most notably, *The Battle of Tokyo, or the Story of the Young Man Who Left His Will on Film*. His protagonists, often antiheroes, distinguish themselves by defying expectations of conformity. Celliers represents the European subject who has a heightened sense of self and the integrity of his actions as a response both to others and to his internal sense of justice. This is the polar opposite of the Japanese code of submission to the group and therefore extremely threatening to it. The wit is an emblem of that sense of self, and the reference to Shakespearean tragedy provides the historical and cultural context for such subjectivity.

Later, when Japanese guards come to his cell to take him to his execution (the first of three attempts to execute Celliers in the film), the wit will be played out in Celliers's pantomime of shaving and having a last cup of tea while he holds an imaginary two-part conversation between himself and a nonexistent cellmate. The Japanese guards are shown watching the performance, dumbfounded, not understanding the role this enemy grants the imaginary in the affirmation of self and in resistance to their imprisoning power over that self. The cellmate will later be embodied by Lawrence when they come to share imprisonment; their conversations substitute for the solitary banter and imaginary life here. Wit is both an emblem and a means of resistance when no other resistance is possible. Oshima extends the representation of the wit beyond the realm of possibility into a fictional exaggeration that will affect representation itself.

SHIFTS IN THE REGISTER OF REPRESENTATION

The resistant power of this wit, the internal strength procured in the imaginary, bursts through the register of representation at the moment of Celliers's execution. Taken before the firing squad despite Yanoi's efforts to argue for the dismissal of charges against him, Celliers is shot at close range by the whole squad. He survives. This implausibility constitutes a complete rupture of realistic narrative logic. It is reminiscent of the moment when the Korean, R, in *Death by Hanging*, is not killed when hanged, thus engendering the legal and logical inquiries that comprise the rest of the film. *Death by Hanging*, however, is more consistently Brechtian, more consistently discursive in its ideological reconstruction of narrative form. *Merry Christmas, Mr. Lawrence* introduces its shift in the register of representation and then treats it for a time as if it were nothing; once Celliers is taken to Yanoi's prison camp, he is presented simply as wounded (as if from a severe beating, as was the case in the novel) and Yanoi is presented as concerned about his recovery. What do we make of this kind of violation of narrative logic, even of alternative narrative logic such as the consistent departure we expect of the Brechtian drama? It is an instance of surrealism thrown in, all the more surreal for seeming random or casual in the context of a representation that was up to this point following realist codes and eschewing the theatricality characteristic of many of Oshima's other works. It is not entirely random, however, and will be taken up again.

Consider, for example, Celliers's manner of opposing the *gyo,* the ritual fast that Yanoi orders to purge the camp of lassitude in the wake of Hicksley's refusal to cooperate and the tragic replay of the Korean's punishment that causes the Dutch soldier to bite his own tongue off and choke to death. Whereas Hicksley fumes at the fast as punishment and Lawrence comprehends it as a Japanese response intended not to isolate and punish the prisoners so much as to assert the group dynamic of the entire camp to which all must submit, Celliers devises a protest ritual in which the prisoners are handed flowers and sing hymns together in the memory of the Dutchman. The scene is a symbolic acting out of will, of a group identity steeped in Christian ritual in opposition to the ritual imposed by the Japanese. Celliers does not create or impose this reaction so much as lead it, for just moments before in Celliers's absence the men responded to the roll call imposed by the Japanese by calling out their orders for their favorite food and drinks, recalling Celliers's earlier pantomimes. Yet Celliers (who sings "Rock of Ages" off-key, a moment that adds reflexive comedy on the casting of Bowie) marks himself as leader assuming full, individual responsibility for the protest when the Japanese seek to punish. The flowers are reminiscent of the U.S. protests against the Vietnam War as well as prefigure recent Chinese protests for democracy, but when Celliers eats one as he about to be arrested they are inscribed as a surreal act of symbolic defiance. Nor is it entirely symbolic, for along with the flowers, Celliers has passed out bean cakes, so the eating of the flowers marks his intention to violate the gyo. Not only does Celliers defy through these acts Yanoi's plans to use him to control his men, he deflects Yanoi's attention to punishing him instead of continuing to assault the morale of the group as a whole.

When a radio is uncovered as well, however, Lawrence is singled out for punishment along with Celliers. The isolation of the two in a cell together provides the film with two extremely important scenes for articulating the difference of the Western subject from that formed in Japanese culture. The first scene that I will look at here is the confrontation between Yanoi, Lawrence, and Hara after Yanoi announces to Lawrence that he has been sentenced to death. The other is the flashback sequence that illustrates Celliers's narration to Lawrence of his thoughts that night in the cell as he awaits his own death sentence, a shift in the representation that is so great that I will discuss it separately in the next section.

The culmination of the strategy of representational shifting comes in the kiss that Celliers plants on either cheek of the astounded Yanoi when the captain calls all the men out into the yard to retaliate for Hicksley's continued defiance of his request to name munitions experts. Yanoi is about to execute Hicksley when Celliers deliberately steps forward and interrupts the ritual beheading. The kiss literally stops the film, as the gesture is rendered in close-up in stunning, pulsating slow motion. The moment is vertiginous. The kiss is transgressive because it undercuts authority with intimacy, states boldly the latent homosexuality and violates Japanese taboos against kissing and other public displays of physical affection. Again, it is a reference to Vietnam protests as it literalizes the "Make Love, Not War" slogan of sixties cultural protests against imperialist incursions. When Yanoi tries to strike Celliers with his sword after this kiss, he falls backward, as if arrested by a supernatural force.

The kiss once again foregrounds the sexual nature of the confrontations between Yanoi and Celliers. Earlier Yanoi asked the question, "Who are you? Are you an evil spirit [kami]?" Celliers responded then that he was an evil spirit: "Yours, I hope." The Japanese are portrayed as investing psychosexual and cultural dynamics with a supernatural value. Yanoi's aide tried to assassinate Celliers, recognizing the threat Celliers posed as a drain on Yanoi's spirit. Lawrence, in turn, knew he must argue against the supernatural interpretation, since superstitious beliefs could motivate his Japanese captors to even more violence. Lawrence increasingly comes to blame Japanese religious and cultural beliefs for the collective Japanese behavior.

When Celliers kisses Yanoi, it is as an assertion of all that Yanoi has repressed to become the controlled and controlling Japanese officer that he is, as he whips out orders and literally whips anyone who defies him. To confront the other is presented as sexually charged. To expose that sexual investment is in this context to unravel the power of the sadistic command.

MEMORY AND IDENTITY

Given this overarching concern with psychosexual investments as underlying political confrontations, it is significant that the narrative of the film grants so privileged a place to the flashback. As I have argued in *Flashbacks in Film* (1989), the flashback is a device film narrative uses to underscore subjective formations of memory and history. Here the flashback is not only to another time but also to a quite different space, that of the South African boyhood of Celliers and his younger, hunchback brother.

The transition to introspection is elaborately indicated. First, Lawrence tells a story from a romantic encounter in his past while the image remains resolutely on him in the present. Then Celliers is seen alone thinking as a track forward on him indicates, in a borrowing from classical flashback rhetoric, a move to interiority. The voice of his brother calls "Jack," followed by Lawrence calling his name in the present, a temporary retreat from the move into interiority. Then Celliers says, "The past, again and again," verbally announcing the haunting quality of the memories, and only then does the image dissolve to the scenes from the past. This elaborate articulation of the transition from present to past, from an exteriorized image to interiority, has a dated quality, coming as it does years after the modernist cinema established the direct cut to the past as de rigueur. It bears the traces of older film styles in which temporal inversions were embellished with explanatory language and filmic punctuation and evokes the same emotional symbolic investment earlier film styles made in the past. Here the effect is to renew the flashback, to make it obvious and pronounced as a trope once again.

The strangeness of this flashback is evidenced in two separate critical reactions to the film when it was first released. One critic saw the flashbacks as "the weakest part of the film, . . . which Oshima should have had the courage to cut because they break the unity of action and atmosphere" (Martin 1983: 20); another saw the flashbacks as the film's greatest strength since "the flashback overturns everything and we find in this moment of greatest disturbance, the greatest Oshima. . . . [W]e know that a flashback, especially a long flashback is dangerous to the unity of a film as it always risks breaking the rhythm. But this break is necessary here; it takes on as its own the troubling of the world" (Bonitzer 1983: 20). Both views indicate how strongly this flashback is reinforced as strange, as it imbues the past with the power to determine the subject. Celliers announces to Lawrence just before the dissolve into the flashback that his "specialty is in the field of betrayal"; the flashback works to provide him with subjective, individual reasons for his resistance to the Japanese. Confronting the meaning of that betrayal motivates his ability to act decisively in the present. As in the hymn "Rock of Ages," that Celliers introduces as part of his protest, his actions in the present are meant to "save him from this guilt."

Two incidents dominate this flashback, each centering on Celliers's attitude toward his brother's deformity in relationship to mockery by their peers; one involves harassment of the younger brother by neighbor children on the way home from church and the other his harassment as part of an initiation ritual at the private school both brothers attend. The first incident establishes Celliers's consciousness of the precarious place of his brother in the world so that his refusal to intervene in the second incident is charged with the weight of that knowledge. Again the register of representation is disturbed in that the younger brother does not age. Further, the brother's singing, presented as central to both scenes, is rendered as an ethereal soprano; the clear, youthful voice of a boy whose prowess in the upper registers is tinged with transsexuality, a voice that the absence of aging further associates with the asexuality of the castrati.

That castration lurks in memory is prefigured by Celliers's earlier comment to Lawrence that Lawrence's groan while dreaming of the past "sounds like she cut it off." Here it is manifested by Celliers's statement as the flashback ends that following the incident of betrayal, the younger brother never sang again. The flashback reveals the guilt Celliers has carried because he betrayed his brother, but it also indicates a deeper guilt that remains unarticulated, the guilt he carries simply because his physical strength and beauty contrasts so with his sibling's deformity. Bonitzer (1983: 21) has argued that the brother constitutes the "angelic and monstrous double," the *"part maudite"* in Georges Bataille's terms, representing an irreducible heterogeneity. There is certainly something to this analogy that cuts to the core of this relationship between brothers, one who looks like an angel but cannot sing on key, the other whose looks are deformed but who has the voice of the angel. Celliers says it clearly: "I couldn't bear the thought that anything related to me was not of the best." For in this myth the brother is the archetypal other through which the self is mirrored. Difference is seen as threatening, even if ultimately the order of mirroring could reveal a certain symmetry through which differences are reconcilable.

When in retaliation for his kiss Celliers is finally tortured to death by being buried alive in sand, an imaginary sequence returns him to the scene of his brother's house where his brother forgives him, begs him not to apologize, and sings once again. This imaginary reconciliation is followed immediately by a visit from Yanoi, now deposed as camp commander, who takes a clipping of the dying Celliers's hair. Later we learn that Yanoi asks Lawrence to take the hair to Yanoi's ancestral village and consecrate it there at the altar of his family.

We can see how the structure of the film takes this personal myth, this developmental incident from the past, as a base on which huge cultural differences are overlaid. One could say that the tendency toward introspection and awareness of the constitution of the self in the past granted the Western characters in this film is presented as their strength in contrast to the adamant assertion of internally contradictory beliefs as universal laws that characterize the Japanese captors. In *The Seed and the Sower,* Jack Celliers's awareness is presented succinctly in the statement, "He felt the first necessity in life was to make the universal specific, the general particular, the collective individual and what was unconscious in us conscious" (van der Post 1963: 150). If this is a credo steeped in Western individualism, it is also one implicitly founded on psychoanalysis. When Celliers asks Lawrence to explain what is wrong with the Japanese, Lawrence says, "They are a nation of anxious people. They found they could do nothing individually so they went mad en masse." Implicit in this aphoristic presentation of the mass psychology of fascism among the Japanese is the sense in which this culture suppressed individual will and created a desire for conformity above all else.

Merry Christmas, Mr. Lawrence can be seen as a serious call for the historical psychoanalysis of the subject. It does not present the Western subject as its ideal or as free from the contradictions that confine Japanese subjectivity, only as slightly more able to look into the mirror of the past. Lawrence repeatedly says, "We are all wrong," recognizing that from a more global perspective the history of the subject leaves no one any simply heroic ground on which to stand. If in van der Post's novel this deconstructive stance is too simply circumscribed by a prevailing Christian theology, the film, despite its borrowing from certain Christian symbols in constructing its imagery, is less intent on a specifically Christian closure. What does emerge at the end, however, is clearly humanist.

The coda to the film has Lawrence visiting Sergeant Hara who has been condemned to death by the Occupation forces, following Yanoi's execution earlier for his war crimes. Lawrence tells Hara that he wishes he had the power to pardon him and equates the postwar executioners in the limits of their vision of the truth with the Japanese war criminals. This ending is cumbersome for a theoretical reading of the film that like this one emphasizes its deconstructive tendencies. For his part, Bonitzer (1983: 19) dismisses this ending, proclaiming, "Oshima is not a humanist filmmaker" and the "true ending of the film" is the "ceremonial and magnificent scene" in which Yanoi cuts the lock of Celliers's hair.

Although this is tempting, the coda is not simply a studio-imposed ending that the viewer can dismiss as outside the auteur's intentions. Lawrence and Hara are as central to the narrative as are Celliers and Yanoi; returning to their relationship is a means of responding theoretically to the questions posed in the earlier confrontation between Lawrence and Yanoi at the Buddhist altar while Hara chants. Yanoi announces to Lawrence that he has been sentenced to death for possessing the radio and Lawrence teases out the illogic of an order predicated on needing to punish someone for the crime whether that person is innocent or guilty. Lawrence first responds by asking if they "are by chance, fans of Gilbert and Sullivan," and then by attacking the altar. At this point his patience with comprehending and explaining Japanese otherness has snapped.

He and Celliers are saved by Hara's illegal intervention. Drunk on sake, the sergeant frees the two condemned men in a gesture that gives the film its English title, *Merry Christmas, Mr. Lawrence,* for this is what the drunken

Hara calls out to his amazed captives. Hara's gesture is like a moment of childlike regression that his inebriation and the mythology of Santa Claus permit, a moment in which he can step outside of the order to which he ascribes, outside of Yanoi's authority, and act. This scene and the coda that takes up the memory of that night and the impossibility for Lawrence of mirroring Hara's action except as enunciated desire together break down what otherwise might be a simple polarity of enemy forces.

While much of Oshima's previous work does present a divided subject beyond the unified idealism of humanist concerns and implicitly critiques various humanisms attached to characters and philosophies in the Japanese film tradition, this aspect of Oshima's work is not simply parallel to the Western writers to whom one might compare it (Bonitzer mentions in this context, along with Bataille, Pierre Klossowski, and Witold Gombrowicz). The interest in humanism in Japan had a radical edge late into the twentieth century because humanism represented a welcoming of Western influences to counter earlier Japanese worldviews (for a discussion of humanism in a Japanese context, see Desser 1988: 21–24, 76–77). If Oshima's first film, *A Town of Love and Hope,* was a reaction against certain humanist assumptions that had sentimentalized socially conscious cinema in Japan, we have seen that Oshima's *Shiiku* used many of the tropes of humanist narrative to present the racism operative in a small Japanese village. One instance in which humanist concerns become central to Oshima is in the critique of collective barbarism. *The Catch* shares with *Merry Christmas, Mr. Lawrence* the insistence on Japanese collective cruelty and insularity.

Similarly, Christianity must be seen in a Japanese context. Because of its history of survival in Japan only among an outlawed resistance group, Christianity had distinctly different meanings in Japanese culture. Oshima attempted to present the politics of Japanese Christian revolts in his 1962 film, *Amakusa Shiro Tokisada* (The Revolt of Shiro Tokisada), and simultaneously to use this failed revolt as a metaphor for the successful repression of student demonstrations. Again, there is a humanist tendency in the way Oshima will present the rebellious, although he will not falsely sweeten the outcome of such rebellion or sentimentalize defeat.

To tell the story of the other, to tell van der Post's story, is to tell a story steeped in Christian humanism. Oshima does not simply eliminate all moments in which the humanism emerges, as it is important to remain in that challenging perspective of the other and because his deconstructive tendencies and his critique of certain humanisms do not foreclose all humanist positions. Fundamental to this is the notion of the subject active in and responsible to history. At the film's end Lawrence may represent a Christian forgiveness and a deep sympathy with his former enemies, humanist ideologies that seem to mitigate the critique and depart from the interpsychic sexuality that is foregrounded earlier in the film. It may even seem as if the end of the film partakes in this Western humanism to exploit the avenue it opens for forgetting Japan's war crimes. Yet this coda also includes Lawrence's remarks on the absence of any singularly true position of authority and celebrates Celliers's resistance; above all else it seems it is this spirit that Oshima is recommending the Japanese learn from the other.

CHAPTER SIX

Popular Song, Fantasies, and Comedies of Iconoclasm

Oshima is not a director that many associate with comedy, though he has made several comedies, ones shaped with a serious political edge. There is a corollary comedic edge to his dramas that is mostly satirical. One senses that for Oshima, comedy is an extension of his self-conscious dramatic mode, an exploration of absurdity and irony. His films tend to embrace certain comedic forms rather than others, notably the extended conceit that he turns into what we might term a "structural comedy" that often has metaphorical and allegorical import. Most of his films have scenes that are funny incongruously juxtaposed to dramatically rendered events, violence and despair. Hyperbole and displacement figure heavily in this humor. Think of the "rape" of the grandfather in *Ceremonies*, the encounter between the brothers and the "spacemen" in *Boy*, or the mailman and postbox skirmishes in *The Battle of Tokyo*. The sense of humor here is Brechtian or Buñuelian, dark or poignant juxtapositions that affront normality or good taste.

Similarly, his comedies strive for the humor associated with an ironic twist that expresses political tensions, along with a less-conscious laughter that emanates from the release of sublimated tension. Laughter as release gains its significance in light of Oshima's beliefs that Japanese culture demands repression of personal feelings. In many instances comedy is linked to song, to that moment of group participation and even drunken showing off. Characters unite in song, a performative vocal enunciation, in quasi-dialogue with one another. The roots of Brechtian theater in the music hall are here twisted to join a Japanese social tradition, singing at bars, inns, and parties—at any gathering that affords the opportunity.

33. The film is set on a specific day, Kenkokubi (Founder's Day), first reinstated on February 11, 1967, after the Occupation had banned it. Anticipating protest demonstrations in Tokyo, Oshima planned ahead to shoot his film to surround and include this demonstration. *Nihon sunka-ko* (A Treatise on Japanese Bawdy Song, 1967). Still courtesy of Oshima Productions.

POPULAR SONGS OF THE IMAGINARY

Not really a comedy but an extended fantasy that has many highly comedic moments, *Nihon sunka-ko* (A Treatise on Japanese Bawdy Song, 1967) displays a cleverness that comes largely from the literal interpretation of figurative language exchanges, particularly the language of sexual come-ons in the bawdy song. These aberrant interpretations do not simply register for characters within the fiction, but "the narrative" itself generates them, as if each subsequent event becomes predicated on taking this figurative representation literally. It is also a film of extreme juxtapositions of an oneiric nature, where death, sexual violence, and mourning do not register with the weight one might expect.

Public, spontaneous, social singing is a custom of modern Japanese life. Certainly the spread worldwide of Japanese karaoke singing (the bar and party amusement of overdubbing or lip-synching to recorded music) makes this comedy of Oshima's more timely than ever. Karaoke seems to garner its new popularity from a desire of the inebriated to participate in the fantasy actions of music videos and from the inexpensive Japanese display systems designed to coax performance out of an audience. Intriguingly, *Japanese Bawdy Song* just predates this phenomenon, giving us more artisanal song-sters; rather than hinge on the mimicking or appropriation of the already-recorded performance, song here is a participatory social event, passed from one generation to the next. The film takes as its basis the Japanese so-cial love of song, a heritage that undoubtedly grew from the agricultural work songs of Japanese villages, but through which the entire history of Japanese culture and its various contacts with the West can be traced (Tsurumi 1987: 79–102). Oshima veers his attention in the film toward the off-color lyric, particularly, but places this tradition in the contrasting context of military songs, on one hand, and leftist protest songs, on the other.

The title of the film derives from a book by Tomomichi Soeda that came out just the year before the film. It studies song as both an expression of dis-content among the Japanese and as their escape into fantasy. Its premise that bawdy songs are expressions of the unconscious of a people shares much with Freud's *Jokes and Their Relationship to the Unconscious*, particularly the sec-tion on "dirty jokes."

The film is set on a specific day, Kenkokubi (Founder's Day holiday), first reinstated on February 11, 1967, after the Occupation had banned it. An-ticipating protest demonstrations in Tokyo, Oshima planned ahead of time to shoot his film to surround and include the demonstrations. Sato (1973: 162–177) takes it as a parallel to *Violence at Noon* as a parable of postwar democracy in which a younger generation dismisses an older one with bawdy song, seeking rebirth. It also parallels *Night and Fog in Japan* and *Cruel Story of Youth* in exploring the generational conflicts between a politically orga-nized older generation and a younger generation more given to personal re-bellion; it repeats *Cruel Story of Youth*'s scene in which the young protagonists come upon a demonstration and recognize a participant.

In a letter he published at the time, "To the Friends and Collaborators on *A Treatise on Japanese Bawdy Song*," Oshima announces to his crew and to a cast not yet complete two weeks before the shooting begins that "this time we are going to being shooting without . . . a script" (Oshima 1992: 123), em-ploying instead a process of extemporaneous collaboration. On completion of the film he published a parallel note, "Today's Youth and *A Treatise on Japa-nese Bawdy Song*," explaining the audition process through which he cast the group of young men and women that, in addition to the well-known pop singer Araki Ichiro and the older, established actors, formed the cast (Oshi-ma 1992: 125). Three of the young cast members had theater experience, two as founders of Joyu gekijo, or Free Theater, an avant-garde troupe. If Oshima stresses this ensemble improvisation and calls Araki the "first New Wave actor" in Japanese film, it is to emphasize how much he wishes to mine the reality of the moment to create film at this juncture. In its exploration of sexual fantasy and its fascination with the self-possession of youth, the film is similar to *Diary of a Shinjuku Thief* but far less orchestrated, seeking to be even closer to the phenomenon it is documenting. What is unusual here is that unlike most cinema verité-inspired films, *Japanese Bawdy Song* seeks also to inscribe fantasy.

The film follows the adventures of four young men, Nakamura, Ueda, Hiroi, and Maruyama, who come to take entrance examinations for Tokyo University after they have just graduated from a rural high school. "Country rubes in the big city" and boys awkwardly coming of age are standard formulas for film comedy, and while the film occasionally exaggerates these students' naïveté, it also assumes the beginnings of a national youth culture. The boys are eager participants in Tokyo scenes, such as the bars of Shinjuku that they discuss from the moment of their first introduction. The young men form a group of four whose school uniforms underscore the conformity of their behavior. In their wanderings through Tokyo, they are stunningly framed against movie posters and their reflections in glass facades, as well as by a giant Coca-Cola billboard. While very boyish, they are not the earnest, feminized heroes, the *nimaime,* that are traditional in Kabuki and reprised in films of Mizoguchi, such as the young law student for whom a woman sacrifices all in *Naniwa ereji* (Osaka Elegy, 1939). Even as Nakamura becomes our central focus, the group and group behavior supersede any individual characterization, especially the sympathy a nimaime would evoke.

Setting the exams on a day of gently falling snow creates an ironic atmosphere, since it turns the university setting into a traditional Japanese landscape in which the snow serves as marker of seasonal beauty. It is precisely the kind of setting in which lovers might meet for the first time, or perhaps more symbolically, for the last time, in traditional Japanese scenography. However, this exterior ironically creates only a setting for comedy as the students gather under an overhang of a modern building to smoke simultaneously two cigarettes each in preparation for the deprivation of the exam. Nakamura finds attractive No. 469, a beautiful young woman taking the same tests. Use of a number to designate Nakamura's illusive object of desire comments on the anonymity of the mass exam, while the film explores an attraction and sexual behaviors that have as background the still-fledgling coeducational transformation of education in Japan. The history of segregated genders in school education gave rise to exaggerated rituals of sexual longing in Japanese culture. This legacy is commemorated in the popular song, "Shichiri ga Hama on Aika" (Elegy of Seven-Mile Beach), written by a schoolteacher for a funeral of middle-school boys who drowned in a boating accident on their way to visit a nearby girls' school. The lingering popularity of this song is analyzed by the cultural historian Tsurumi Shunsuke in the following terms, which have great resonance for *Japanese Bawdy Song.*

In those days of segregated education boys and girls of this age could not mix freely with each other. They had to pass in the street in silence, recognizing each other's presence only with looks, which probably served to create a much stronger mutual fascination than would have existed otherwise. When the schoolboys perished, strong feelings of grief arose among the girls. . . . [The song] was sung at the combined funeral of the boys, amid the tears of all the students, boys and girls. The song later spread far beyond the Zushi area to be widely known throughout Japan, even to the present day. It shows us something of the kind of relationship which existed between teenage boys and girls way back in 1910. And furthermore, [its] taking of a European melody to express one's natural feelings of mourning provides an episode which shows clearly the Japanese music culture of the time, and also the emotions of the Japanese who entrusted their hearts to this music culture. (Tsurumi 1987: 102)

It is as if Oshima has updated this tragedy, recalling the mourning and the song it evoked in a comedic narrative of desire of rural teenagers displaced to Tokyo.

At stake in this updating and displacement is the status of women considered against the backdrop of the confused fantasies spurred by male-defined sexuality. At first, male bawdiness is contrasted with female naïveté or resistance, but by the end of the film this opposition gives way to male violence and impotence contrasted with something like self-aware female desire. The fixing of the paradigm of seduction occurs as the male students head off to the Lawrence bar in Shinjuku on a recommendation. The name makes Nakamura think of D. H. Lawrence's *Lady Chatterley's Lover;* his familiarity with this novel hints at his identification with its motif of male sexual mastery releasing female desire. The visual composition, by isolating the young men against the snow in extreme high angle long shot, prepares us for how ironic this borrowed fantasy will be in light of unfolding events.

Compositional metaphoric expression of the crossroads at which the boys find themselves occurs in a single brilliant shot, as the four boys cross the image horizontally with a group of schoolchildren, while demonstrations cross a traditional curving bridge in the center moving toward the camera from the mid-distance of the shot. Demonstrators carry *hinamaru,* Japanese flags, with the red sun in the center replaced by a black circle. It is in this setting that the boys meet Otake, a former teacher, with his lover, Tanigawa Takako. They call Otake "Sensei," the Japanese honorific for a teacher, but this polite appellation in the context of the discovered beautiful companion of their teacher becomes imbued with the boy's sense that Otake will serve as their initiator, their guide to sexual behaviors.

The chance of big-city encounters leads them to meet three female schoolmates through their wanderings, Sanae, Tomoko, and Kaneda, who had taken entrance exams for the Women's University. Kaneda's Japanese

34. As the students stand up to leave, Otake surprises them by leading them in singing bawdy songs. *Nihon sunka-ko* (A Treatise on Japanese Bawdy Song, 1967). Still courtesy of Oshima Productions.

name transliterates as the Korean name Kim; her Korean identity, perhaps hidden in conformity with the Japanese law that forced Koreans to take Japanese names, perhaps unknown to her, will be significant. Her role will be to raise issues of cultural and gender difference at crucial moments in the film.

All seven go to see Otake at his apartment. He takes them to a restaurant, where they hear military marching songs from a party in another room; these songs are emblematic of another generation's nostalgia for Imperial Japan and World War II. As the students stand up to leave, Otake surprises them by leading them in singing bawdy songs. The songs, incongruously shared by teacher and mixed students, are congruent with adolescent longings. Otake discourses on Japanese bawdy song as belonging to the people. Desire becomes the brunt of the joke, played for comedic excess, as the songs seem to evoke Nakamura's desire for No. 469. It is this figure of the young man filled with fantasy-induced sexual longing, played for bathos, that later plays out as elaborate fantasy scenes in the examination hall toward the end of the film.

Staging Otake's reading from Paul Nizan against an expressionist mural

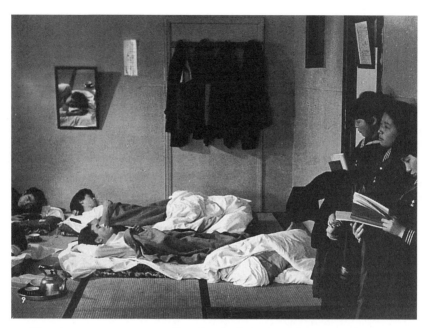

35. The circumstances surrounding the death begin as the group of seven students stays in two rooms of a ryokan, a Japanese inn, on the recommendation of Otake. *Nihon sunka-ko* (A Treatise on Japanese Bawdy Song, 1967). Still courtesy of Oshima Productions.

signals a shift that occurs at this juncture, from a comedy of circumstance that culminates in the performance of bawdy song lyrics to a more philosophical meditation on alienation and despair, in which the songs become a motif of detachment from anything like an "authentic self." Nizan resonates with youthful alienation, with his disgust at the compromises, the death-in-life of bourgeois existence. Nizan's biography, his death at thirty-five and his break with the Communist party over the Hitler-Stalin pact, give this citation of his work additional force. Not only does it implant an explanation of Otake's later death and Nakamura's reaction to that death, it sets the philosophical position of the entire film. We can read this citation in reference to Nizan's posthumous popularity with the emerging new left in France, in which Jean-Paul Sartre's writings on Nizan mark his own ideological conversion to a more engaged literature. A trace such as this evidences the profound exchange occurring between leftist movements in France and Japan leading up to events of 1968 in both countries. Nakamura's quest for No. 469 will motivate the narrative in a manner that recalls Andre Breton's *Nadja,* but the linking of the elusive quest to the daughter of the middle class that No. 469 turns out to be moves the film toward a confrontation with the alienation explored in Nizan's *Antoine Bloyé,* anticipating the numbing effects on the protagonist of a social-climbing marriage even as he still chases his elusive ideal. To explore this alienation the film will take detours into strange realms for what, until now, played as comedy: it will deviate into a confrontation with death and mourning.

The circumstances surrounding the death begin as the group of seven students stays in two rooms of a *ryokan,* a Japanese inn, on the recommendation of Otake. This accommodation is within Japanese tradition; large halls of Japanese temples open as summer camps for boys and girls, side by side, and groups often stay together in large ryokan rooms for economy. The decorum of the mixed-gender Japanese bath is the expectation. But both the mixed bath and the ryokan are also traditional sites for bawdy tales and transgressive ukiyo-e prints, where that very decorum is subject to violation. In the film, the expectations divide by gender, as displayed in Nakamura's knocking outside the girls' room, only to have the shoji, the screen, shut in his face. When he returns to the boys' room, the boys attack him, singing the bawdy song as they strip him. This mock ritual embodies their aggressive sexual desires. Its echo comes the next morning, in a dispute with the girls, in which the boys contend it was Otake who suggested the inn as a setting for sex.

Inserted between the evening misadventures and the morning fight in which the young men vent their frustration at what they take as missed or denied opportunity is the incident that introduces the death. Nakamura returns alone to recover the fountain pen he had forgotten at Otake's. Nakamura finds Otake drunk, passed out, but breathing, framed by stacks of books. Looking around the room, Nakamura sees that Otake kicked over the gas stove, leaving the pipe disconnected and gas leaking. Suicide or accident, Nakamura's only response is to sing a bawdy song Otake had taught them, offering the song as elegy for Otake's generation.

However, the following morning, when the young women go to see Otake to report their fight with the boys, they discover him dead. They return weeping. Police question Nakamura, but he lies and says the stove was burning.

This sets up a wake scene with Otake's friends and the students gathered around his coffin; Takako reappears, weeping. Nakamura sings a bawdy song. Female mourning is juxtaposed to a male reaction removed from and at odds with circumstances. The scene also provides a long and ironic dialogue on the politics of death; the older mourners try to rescue the event by casting it as the meaningful sacrifice of a martyr. Others insist on facing the reality of a senseless death.

The film forces its path back to the narrative strains begun in the comedic vein, despite their unlikeliness after this turn of events. From this point on, however, genre dissolves. One way to understand this is Oshima's tendency for symbolic, ideologically motivated expression that makes comedy virtually impossible to sustain despite ironies and a buoyant sense of humor. As we shall see, all of the comedies strain so hard to raise allegorical issues that the initial lighter gestures, such as witty juxtapositions, sight gags, and even slapstick, become weighted by the film's more serious proposals. The film will become a dreamlike meditation on the violence of (frustrated) male desire, juxtaposed with images protesting the war in Vietnam and the state. Another explanation for this film's floating and shifting modes of expression is Oshima's refusal of genre inherent in his statement that this film is "about the imaginary."

Increasingly the film mixes pure fantasy sequences such as the exam room scenes with scenes of the group interacting realistically on streets and the newly rebuilt Ueno train and subway station. The girls' weeping reinvigorates the boys' search for sex, as they claim that the girls' tears engender desire. Nakamura caps the moment as he again sings bawdy songs. Bawdy songs become the mark of incongruous behavior, such as the violation of the mutual respect that is supposed to govern teacher-student relations in Japan, an incongruous reaction to a respected teacher being near death, an incongruous reaction to mourning. However, this time, Kaneda joins in, stressing that her bawdy lyrics are "women's songs." "On this gloomy, rainy night / A crow looks in the window. / Hey fool of a Manchurian railroad man, in your gold buttons, / It's fifty cents to touch, but looking's free. / If you give me three dollars, / I'll play with you till the cock crows." Though in the sexual genre, depending on puns and innuendo, her song is a lament whose voice is that of Korean prostitutes during the Japanese occupation, the infamous "comfort women" forced by the Japanese imperial army to service Japanese soldiers in occupied countries. The reference to the "Manchurian railroad man" places the provenance of this song in Manchuria, or as the Japanese renamed it, Manchukuo.

Here the film attempts a female appropriation of sexuality and desire, reverberant with anti-imperialism. Still, the appropriation is halting in ways we will discuss further in chapter 8; symptomatically, Oshima, in collaboration with his ensemble cast, imagines female desire primarily as role reversal. Intriguingly, though, this comedic role reversal couples with mourning, and soon it will link to female group identification. The film plays with a romantic notion of the seductive image of a "woman in tears," and begins to create, in a crosscut montage of scenes, Miss Tanigawa, Kaneda, and eventually No. 469 as figures whose interchangeability and identification with one another drives the rest of the film. It will bifurcate into two paths laced together as parallel, crosscut sequences.

On one path, Kaneda urges Nakamura to tell Tanigawa the truth about the suicide. He returns to Otake's apartment, where he finds Tanigawa and tells her, but she doesn't believe him. Meanwhile, in segments crosscut with this, his six friends go to No. 469's house, a contemporary, three-story house surrounded by grounds, indicative of her family's great wealth. She is holding a folk-singing meeting in opposition to the Vietnam War. Songs of the U.S. labor and protest movements, such as "This Land Is Your Land," "Goodnight, Irene," and "We Shall Overcome," temporarily replace the bawdy songs. Fantasy images connect the song "Michael, Row Your Boat Ashore" with images of No. 469 on a raft drifting on a river of blood.

The next intercut segments pair two bawdy songs. Kaneda reintroduces a bawdy song to interrupt the folksingers, challenging their liberal protest politics with her more visceral bawdy song that challenges the Japanese to remember their imperialism; this is intercut with a scene in which Takako asks Nakamura to sing one of the bawdy songs. He does, then tries to have sex with her. Finally Nakamura's fantasies of sexual advances move into actuality, but when he isn't able to perform, bathos reappears.

Strangers carry Kaneda into the house to rape her; ironically, their action is an all-too-literal interpretation of song. Rather than recognize her reference to the "comfort women," they reenact sexual exploitation. Thus in this crosscut segment the film mirrors Nakamura's failed sex, paradoxically, by depicting a fulfillment of the male rape fantasy. This fantasy had been the film's continual allusion through the bawdy song but now collects the clear context of a critique of Japanese imperialism.

The film culminates with an entrance exam fantasy. Its elaborate mise-en-scène begins with students seated in a hall, then introduces a series of shifting occupants of the lecture platform's desk in the depth of the shot, as well as shifts between long shot and close-ups. The desk is first occupied by Nakamura singing bawdy songs, then Takako lecturing on the history of Japan, beginning with a theory of tribal migration from Asia to Japan as the origin of the Japanese people, as the boys strip No. 469 and carry her to the front, where they lay her out on the desk. The shots of No. 469's body laid out on this desk make her appear as a fantasy of a perverse laboratory specimen in a science lecture, an image that we can imagine as one that would not disappear for Nakamura as he took the exams. This male fantasy is crosscut with shots continuing the linkage of No. 469, Takako, and Kaneda in solidarity, including close-ups of Takako's tear-streaked face and Kaneda standing with eyes shut.

The final images are even more enigmatic and disturbing. As No. 469 awakes, Nakamura strangles her, and the film ends on her head against the red of the flag beneath her. Even though the film has shifted from comedy to the grotesque, this is hardly the ending one would expect from the kind of satire the film has generated, but like a final dissonant chord, it closes this meditation on desire with its strangulation.

Finally, the oneiric imagery of a nightmare suppresses and supersedes all else. It is curious that many critics describe this ending as a real occurrence, in contrast to the earlier fantasy image. There is no textual evidence that this is real, as there is no easy way to separate fantasy from narrative reality throughout the film. The film submits the status of the image and the status of genre in film to questioning. Granting reality to this stems from an assumption that the film could not end on a fantasy action as that breaks with expectations of containing and employing fantasy within narrative logic, placing it inside the narrative "real" as motivation and explanation. The point here seems to be the opposite. Fantasy does not so much get the upper hand and take over reality, a conventional narrative trope, as it takes over filmic form, effacing the pure knowledge of narrative reality.

Imagery in montage, then, turns out to be key to this film, disjointed and daring. Tableaus, like the expressionist mural that reminds one of the antiwar movement's use of Goya's *Saturn Devouring His Son,* are more than just background. They upstage the narrative action, mitigating its centrality and its reality. From such an image, we have the sense of a generation devouring and being devoured. This permeates the film, not so much as thematic but as motif. This is the primacy given the visual, the imaginary, the oneiric. It may be hard for spectators accustomed to fantasy being marked and contained to understand Oshima's move in filmmaking at this point as he grants the imaginary more "space" than he does any other representation. It is an imaginary that will not be cordoned off to an internal marginalization. It flows over the edges and spills violently over the end of the film.

This film makes a fascinating comparison to *Kazoku geimu* (The Family Game, 1983) by Morita Yoshimitsu, a comedy examining the pressures on Japanese children to succeed in school and exams, the make-or-break passage that is the lingering trace of the tradition of the Confucian examination system. The tutoring that becomes de rigueur in Japan's upper and middle classes creates so much figurative pressure that it leads to an explosion at end of the film. The difference between explosion and strangulation as comedic endings displays Oshima's difficulty in the genre of comedy. If comedy is one genre that survives the troubles that lead to a virtual collapse of the Japanese studio system, if independents continue to be able to produce films in this genre when all other live-action filmmaking recoils, it was foresight on Oshima's part to move toward this genre. It turns out to be an uneasy solution for him, however. As much as he finds social comedy attractive, he cannot retain the lightness of the comedy of manners. A darker imaginary intrudes, along with a more contestatory politics and a more intellectually demanding comedic subversion of filmic form. Yet Oshima will make several more attempts at comedy, with only a partial success each time.

METACINEMATIC HUMOR

A popular song again resonates throughout *Kaette kita yopparai* (Three Resurrected Drunkards, 1968). Of the song written by the Folk Parody Gang which bears the same name as the film, "Kaette kita yopparai," Tsurumi writes,

> In eight-eight time, it utilizes fully the seven-tone major scale. Appearing in 1967 when economic growth was obvious to everyone, it is a wayward sort of song, its lyrics in bad taste, and it scandalized older people. Children, however, loved it, singing it in buses and so on, while older people hated it. (1987: 98–99)

The lyrics tell of a drunk who in going to heaven has come back home because "sake wa umai shi ne-chan wa kirei da" (the sake is good and the girls are pretty). In the film the song is electronically accelerated, sounding like the U.S. "Chipmunks" recording phenomenon of the early sixties. In using the song as the basis for the film title and certain narrative elements, Oshima again cites postwar popular culture for its rebellious appeal to youth, however slight and indirect that rebellion might be in such manifestations. His film hopes to put pressure behind such incidental naughtiness, connecting it to larger issues.

This film constructs repetitions of events into a comic caper of mistaken identities. Three young Japanese men journey to the beach, have their clothes and identities taken by Koreans, and are therefore mistaken for illegal Korean immigrants by the police. Simultaneously, gangsters responsible for the traffic in immigration hunt for them after a mishap at a bathhouse. Elements of immigration scams that were central to *Burial of the Sun* occur here in a comic context.

My first viewing of this film was in a sense its "ideal projection," one in which the audience was entirely naive concerning its structure of repetitions and completely duped by them due to the site of projection. This screening occurred at the Cinémathèque Française, the famous screening archives in Paris, notorious at that time for its bungled projections, in which sound would be left off, focus ignored, or reels of film projected out of order. The audience clapped their hands to wake up projectionists, shouting "la bobine" only to find as the film continued that the image series shifted slightly and that the film's repetition of an entire segment of images was no mistake but rather a trick narrative device, a joke on audience expectations.

While Oshima's films often foreground repetitions and variations, seldom in the entire history of commercial cinema is exact repetition of a series of shots taken to such extremes. A close look at the sequence submitted to the repetition helps us understand what is at stake in its double inscription in the film.

The opening beach scene mimics silent comedy slapstick, as the three schoolboys clown around. In some clever cutting between extreme long shot and close-up, we see a pretend shooting; in a close-up on this clowning, a hand mimics a revolver held to the head of Chibi, the smallest of the three students. These antics introduce an ongoing visual pun on assassination. Innocent enough in the context of three friends' weekend regression to childhood cops-and-robbers role playing, the assassination image will later accrue, like all the comic gestures in this film, a more serious double meaning.

Our clue to the initial appreciation of this comic assassination routine depends on the Japanese names of these characters, and the joke may be lost somewhat in translation. The names of the boys themselves are comic; in Japanese the three students are O Noppo, Chu Noppo, and Chibi, a comic declension of a hierarchy that is reinforced visually by the differences in height of the three actors, Kato Kazuhiko, Kitayama Osamu, and Handa Norihiko; these names translate roughly as the Big One, the Middle-Sized One, and the Tiny One. The English subtitles attempt to present the same idea but use slang nicknames that in turn recall nicknames in American gangster films, Big Boy, Run of the Mill, and Pipsqueak. We lose the verbal joke that connects the names as a play with diminutives in language, and the awkward "Run of the Mill" is a rather inappropriate choice to indicate the "middle" man. The Japanese names clearly present Chibi as like the Little Bear in "The Three Bears," the brunt of all jokes and odd occurrences, over-determining his role as comic victim in the clowning assassination as well as in later scatological vomiting scenes, in which he complains that a toilet on the train is too foul for even such activity.

In a visual non sequitur that will later likewise accrue meaning, a jet passing overhead interrupts the play. Later, we will understand this plane as part of a series of references to the war in Vietnam and U.S. bases in Japan. Then the boys leave their clothes on the beach and romp in the ocean. A hand appears from under the sand on the beach to steal the clothes, leaving others in their place. Here the live action reminds us of an animated cartoon, where the surreal happens naturally. However, a close-up on a sign reading Danger Underground Cable belies the natural, reminding us that no thief could lie in wait underneath the sand except in a cartoon universe of playful fantasy occurrences. Signs in cartoons may be more functional—a cable labeled to provide shortly thereafter electric, but comically recoverable, shock—but the point of comparison here is to indicate how similarly amusing signs can be in the comic Oshima universe; this one signifies obliquely, reminding us to look at the film as a series of signs borrowed from so many postmodern contexts. What is the underground cable here, the tension and danger underneath the sand? Is the underground cable, like the jet plane that laces the imagery, a sign for modernity itself, or the suggestion of a subversive electronic avant-garde?

36. Extreme long shot of the schoolboys on the beach. *Kaette kita yopparai* (Three Resurrected Drunkards, 1968). Still courtesy of Oshima Productions.

37. Close-up showing mock execution as a hand mimics a revolver held to the head of Chibi, the smallest of the three students. These antics introduce an ongoing visual pun of assassination. *Kaette kita yopparai* (Three Resurrected Drunkards, 1968). Still courtesy of Oshima Productions.

38. Long shot of the school uniforms abandoned on the beach. *Kaette kita yopparai* (Three Resurrected Drunkards, 1968). Still courtesy of Oshima Productions.

39. The students dressed in the Korean military uniforms left in place of their clothes first visit the elderly cigarette vendor who will mistake them for illegal immigrants. *Kaette kita yopparai* (Three Resurrected Drunkards, 1968). Still courtesy of Oshima Productions.

40. The editing pattern illustrated in the next four shots is one often used in Oshima's films; it employs 180° cuts and a jump cut back along the axis of action to emphasize the disjunction of the scene. It begins with this shot of the execution of Dokumushi. *Kaette kita yopparai* (Three Resurrected Drunkards, 1968). Still courtesy of Oshima Productions.

41. A 180° cut to the point of view of those watching the execution. *Kaette kita yopparai* (Three Resurrected Drunkards, 1968). Still courtesy of Oshima Productions.

42. Cut to a long shot on the same axis of action as the previous shot, framing both observers, and execution in the same frame. *Kaette kita yopparai* (Three Resurrected Drunkards, 1968). Still courtesy of Oshima Productions.

43. The triumph of the film, its final Vietnam citation, poses the Koreans and the Japanese coast guard in front of a billboard displaying the famous assassination photo of the South Vietnamese military summarily executing an enemy soldier at point-blank range. *Kaette kita yopparai* (Three Resurrected Drunkards, 1968). Still courtesy of Oshima Productions.

44. The graphic match here, coupled with sublimely abstracted poster-color backgrounds for the closer shots of the official's arm as he aims, gives this final assassination scene a disarming visual power. *Kaette kita yopparai* (Three Resurrected Drunkards, 1968). Still courtesy of Oshima Productions.

Such questions figure again when the three schoolboys, two of whom are now dressed in the Korean uniforms left in place of their own clothes, approach a stand from which an old woman sells sundries and cigarettes. As they attempt to purchase cigarettes, the woman becomes suspicious of their not knowing the new price—a new government cigarette tax has just been added. In her eyes, this ignorance of taxation policy confirms their dangerous foreign identity, and she reports them by telephone to the coast guard they had previously seen patrolling the beach.

These are the sequences that will receive exact repetition later on. In a curious article, "Repetition and Contradiction in the Films of Oshima," Paul Coates faults Oshima for formalism and leaving behind class conflict. While this may seem a mere extension of a tendency to dismiss modernism and modernist texts as apolitical, Coates symptomatically intimates that repetitions cannot account for dialectics, and he charges that Oshima has reached a "dead-end." His article ends on a mention of *Three Resurrected Drunkards* as cementing this fixation on formal repetition. Strange accusation here, for Coates, in focusing on Oshima's repetitions, clearly misses the point of his jokes, which take place in a carefully crafted context, critical of racial discrimination in immigration policy and the role of Pacific nations in Vietnam. Coates's argument appears to be an oblique answer to the widespread championing of Oshima's films in their political engagement with film language (Desser 1988; Polan 1985); his position is similar to an argument that runs through Noel Burch's *To the Distant Observer*, which takes issue with Oshima's critique of Stalinism. In this debate we can see how the anarchist and surrealist strains of Oshima's films, the refusal to simply divulge a singular thematic message, and the simultaneous interest in formal, theoretical, and political issues push filmic expression beyond the reach, ironically, of certain ideological stances and analyses.

This film cannot be understood without giving repetition its theoretical due. The film does pivot on two structural jokes, both involving repetition and both relying on metacinematic awareness for their force. Besides this first structural joke—this series of images from the beginning repeated nearly verbatim midway through the film—the second joke displaces one of the film's initial images, the "assassination image," into various contexts. The jokes coincide with comic treatment and tone throughout the film, but the repetitions develop ideological critique. To assume, as Coates does, that repetition is static is to miss both the variation repetition highlights and what repetition can mobilize in the form of delayed recognition. In fact, what we have in *Three Resurrected Drunkards* is an appeal, through structure and montage, to an intellectual awakening. Comedy, parody, and satire are its means. This is why Dana Polan (1985) turns to Gilles Deleuze's *Repetition and Difference* for a radical rethinking of the function of repetition in Oshima's films.

Because of the cigarette vendor's report, the students are mistaken for Korean illegal immigrants by the coast guard. This opens a reference to immigration restrictions and debates on the racism inherent in controversial policies surrounding Japanese citizenship. In the oneiric structure the film adopts, the boys become enmeshed in struggles that, having placed them in jeopardy, make them doubt their own identities. The film shares with *Death by Hanging* and *The Battle of Tokyo no* an extension of the trope of character self-doubt and confusion translated into oneiric and imaginary narrative turns.

A visit to a bathhouse in which the boys seek refuge (unclothed they can "hide") provides a sequence in which the image is bathed in fluorescent pink. This color is perhaps a suggestion that their place of refuge has tinges of the "pink film" (pornography), which is fulfilled in their meeting there a young woman, Ne-chan (Big Sister, Mako Midori), who is the Korean adopted daughter-cum-mistress of a head gangster, Dokumushi (Poisonous Bug, played by Watanabe Fumio). She urges them to simply steal other clothes on their way out. Despite her affiliations with gangsters, she tries to protect them. Their theft and friendship with her will further endanger them, for though it provides them an escape from their uniforms, they become entangled with gangsters as well as confronted by the two Koreans who stole their clothes at the beach. These men are deserters from Korean forces backing the U.S. troops in Vietnam and are desperately seeking to steal the boys' identities so that they can emigrate to Japan to escape the war. The Koreans are played by actors of Korean ethnicity, I Chong Iru by Sato Kei and Cha Cei Dang by Kim Fhu; their threat to the young Japanese men presents a brutality born of desperation that becomes the film's means of "bringing the war home" to Japan.

So now the young students are chased by three adversaries, the Koreans, the police, and the gangsters. What ensues is a series of chase scenes that take this threesome on all manner of conveyances: boats, trucks, and trains. The object for the students is to get back to Tokyo, away from a coastline of mysterious occurrences and the potential loss of one's identity.

The pink light of the bathhouse returns in a set that is more like a nightclub or a brothel, yet here they encounter a circle of women performing a traditional Korean dance. Later they attempt to execute Dokumushi, but Ne-chan, riding in on a white horse, saves him. The fantasy mise-en-scène here mimics conventions of Korean and Indian films in their mixture of melodrama, fantasy, and comedy. The metacinematic here satirizes Asian commercial traditions of filmic representation.

Then an even more direct insertion of a metacinematic move interrupts the film. Immediately following the rescue, before the repetition will send the film off for a second spin on events, the fiction stops for a poll, in which a reporter interviews subjects on the issues of war and immigration, cinema verité–style. Oshima figures among those questioned, replying, "We are all Koreans." Then the film prefigures the branching narratives of computer interactivity, in which an audience may select from various options at critical plot junctures. So after the trick of restarting the film, frame by frame, sequence by sequence, the narrative the second time through now retells the story with the young Japanese men accepting the Korean identities thrust on them.

The triumph of the film, its final Vietnam citation, poses the Koreans and the Japanese coast guard threatening assassination in front of a billboard dis-

playing the famous photograph of the South Vietnamese military summarily executing an enemy soldier at point-blank range. The graphic match here,
coupled with sublimely abstracted poster-color backgrounds for the closer
shots of the official's arm as he aims, gives this final scene a disarming visual
power.

The publicity sheet Shochiku (reengaged to distribute Oshima's films)
sent out at the time in English makes the film incomprehensible, as it leaves
out all references to Korea and Vietnam, substituting "Young Man" in English for I Chong Iru. Even as it calls the film "Oshima's unconventional mas-
terpiece," clearly the film once again embarrassed the studio politically, and
they did their best to bury it. Oshima's response was a second break with Shochiku, this time annulling his newly signed distribution agreement.

SATIRICAL ALLEGORY OF MISTAKEN IDENTITY:
THE INTERCOURSE OF JAPAN AND OKINAWA

The events that propelled Okinawa into the headlines in the late sixties
were a great spur to Oshima's attention to Okinawa across the seventies. First
he wrote a play, then made a fictional film and a documentary on this island
and its historical relationship to Japan. The events in question center on the
Nixon administration's negotiation with Japan in 1969; to secure renewal of
the security treaty, Nixon agreed to return the Ryukyu islands, of which Okinawa is the largest, to Japan, effective May 15, 1972. Significantly, this "return" meant the first reinstatement of Japanese imperialism. Longed for by
the Japanese, except for those on the left, the "return" was also supported
by many Okinawans for both economic and cultural reasons. However, an
Okinawan nationalist movement was strongly opposed to the island's being
once again under Japanese control, asserting that the cultural differences
outweighed the ancient common heritage reified in myth. For the nationalist movement, the fact that the Okinawan dialect is so different that most
Japanese cannot understand it and the proximity of especially the southernmost Ryukyu island, Sakishima, to Taiwan recall a painful history of political domination by Japan.

In November 1971 the Hakucho-kao dance company put on a drama with
a script by Oshima (Sato 1973: 353). Set in the early Meiji era, the dance tells
of Shaka Noboru, the leader of the Okinawan nationalist movement. He is
introduced as a fallen man who has supposedly lost his mind after the defeat of the nationalists. Okinawan dialect was used for the narration, so that
dance pantomime was the only means the Japanese audience would have of
understanding the action except for the Japanese spoken by the provincial
governor.

Oshima followed this with a film, another comedy of mistaken identities,
Natsu no imoto (Dear Summer Sister, 1972). This humorous allegory is the

next means by which Oshima pursues this most serious of political questions. The strategy here focuses on young teenagers learning about national identity as a by-product of their own identity crises; Oshima highlights a postwar generation too young to react nostalgically. He chooses young bourgeois teens, potentially unaware of imperialism or cultural difference. Shot in 16-millimeter, blown up to 35-millimeter for distribution, the film has an unstudied quality of simply following a meandering exploration of the island, but it strives for the situational kind of surrealism that might be inspired by indigenous Japanese, and in this case Okinawan, folklore rather than a surrealism merely borrowed from the West.

The film begins as a young woman and her slightly older female traveling companion debark in Naha, Okinawa, for their summer vacation. They are drawn to the island by a letter from a young man, Omura Tsuruo, to the younger of the two, Kikuchi Sunako. In the letter, about which we learn more, progressively, as they explore the island, Omura claims he is possibly the illegitimate son of her father, Kikuchi Koseke, an important judge in Tokyo. This parentage is somewhat hypothetical, as his mother also told him he could be the son of the Okinawan police chief Kuniyoshi Shinko (Sato Kei). The question of paternity stems from both men having been lovers of the same woman at Kyoto University during the war. The conflict between a future Okinawan official and a future Japanese official over the same Okinawan woman establishes the opposition of Okinawa and Japan in allegorical terms, just as it will be refigured in the younger half-sister and older half-brother of the next generation. On debarking Sunako and Momoko pass right by Omura, whom they do not recognize, never having met him before or seen a photograph. He catches their attention, however, as he wears a sign, "I teach Okinawan." This leads to a series of jokes on paying for Okinawan words and serious attention to the language difference.

The familial history that marks the situation is complicated by the fact that Sunako is on vacation with Momoko, who is engaged to marry her father, but whom Omura previously has mistaken for Sunako when he spied on their Tokyo household. So as he sees them debark he recognizes Momoko, beginning a game of cat-and-mouse pursuit with them that will last well into the film. Omura is a folksinger, who carries a guitar and sings at nightclubs; as in *Diary of a Shinjuku Thief* Oshima uses two folksingers, Omura and another introduced shortly, to insert songs into the diegesis. On debarking the girls meet Sakurada Takuzo, a former Japanese military officer suffering from guilt and paranoia. He has made the trip to Okinawa to seek his potential assassin. His quest becomes interlaced with theirs, as his guilt accompanies their innocence.

As these characters tour the island, the film documents in passing the southern battlefields so vital to the outcome of World War II, the fishing villages and family tombs that reveal Okinawan culture and the site where young nurses committed mass suicide on June 18, 1945, the day before the evacuation that immediately followed Japan's defeat by U.S. forces. While Momoko secretly meets Sunako's half-brother for dates, Sunako meets Teruya Rintoku, an Okinawan singer and nationalist (Toura Rokko). He provides a means of introducing Okinawan folksongs and of articulating the political anger of many Okinawans. He is also the perfect, overdetermined match with Sakurada Takuzo as he desires "to kill a Japanese worthy of being killed," that is, one politically guilty of crimes against the Okinawans. Sakurada and Rintoku are bound as master and slave in a political and psychoanalytic relationship of mutual dependency and fulfillment, one representing the necessity of guilt to be punished and the other, the necessity of revenge.

When Sunako's father, Koseke Kikuchi, arrives by plane, a beach restaurant encounter with Tsuruo's mother, Tsuru (Koyama Akiko), and the police chief, Kunoyoshi, takes place. Here more of the past is unearthed, emphasizing how all three are far from their student-romance days. Kunoyoshi is revealed to have been arrested for political sedition, leaving Kikuchi a chance to romance Tsuru; yet this is less a willful betrayal than might be imagined since Kunoyoshi had introduced Tsuru as a sister. We have mistaken identities in both the past and the present. The allegory is one not only of political opposites but also of fundamental misrecognition coupled with a playful deceit that turns ironically bitter. On the beach all characters are reunited as a pseudofamilial group; the vacation has led to a confrontation with the past and its residue in the present.

Momoko, engaged to Sunako's father, has been having an affair with Sunako's half-brother; here "incest" is treated lightly, if perversely, unlike its serious and deadly treatment in *Ceremonies*. Sunako, Momoko, and Tsuruo form one jealous triangle; the elder Kikuchi, Momoko, and Tsuruo form another. Both of these triangles parallel the older generation's triangle. Jealousy leads to the angry statement on Sunako's part, "Damn! Okinawa should never have been returned to Japan!" Uttered out of a sheerly personal frustration, the line is ironically comic in this context but is of course where all the triangles and misapprehensions have been leading.

The film culminates in a scene that unites Sakurada and Rintoku in a small boat, watched by those on shore. A pushing match ensues, and the Japanese pushes the Okinawan out; the allegorical parry now becomes a pointed attack on Japan's domination of Okinawa. This image of an Okinawan tossed into the sea resonates with a historical incident, the group of civilians killed in a torpedo attack in World War II following Japanese orders to evacuate Okinawa, a large number of whom were Okinawan children. This historical incident first provoked Oshima's interest in Okinawa, and became the basis of his documentary *Shisha wa itsumademo wakai* (The Dead Remain Young, 1977), which will be discussed in the next chapter.

45. Youthful exuberance is featured in Oshima's attempt to be meaningful for a new generation of youth while creating political debate about the heritage of World War II for Japan and Okinawa. *Natsu no imoto* (Dear Summer Sister, 1972). Still courtesy of Oshima Productions.

In Japan *Dear Summer Sister* became known as a *seishun eiga*, literally, a "film for youth," but here in contrast to the sun tribe films of two decades earlier, these seventies youth films were lighter and perhaps more aimed at attracting a female audience. One senses Oshima's comedies aim at attracting a youth audience in Japan as the question Oshima has been posing throughout his films—"What is Japan, and what does it mean to be Japanese?"—can be meaningful for a new generation of youth facing the future now as children of renewed national economic power. To tie the questions of imperialism and the legacy of the war to questions of adolescent identity, youthful romance, and flirtation seems as much the goal of the film as specific comment on Okinawa. Thus the film ironically offers its most direct articulation of political resistance—"Damn! Okinawa should never have been returned to Japan!"—as displaced, voiced only in the context of a young girl's romantic disappointment: Sunako utters this exclamation in jealousy on seeing the embrace of Momoko and Teruo. Reading this displacement as mere trivialization seems too literal. Synoeciosis throughout the film begs for such lines to be taken ironically.

The film received little overseas distribution. Its screening at the Edinburgh film festival was heralded by Stephen Heath in program notes as a breakthrough in political filmmaking form, though many other film critics appeared to be puzzled by the film, especially those unfamiliar with Oshima's earlier comedies. Clearly, it extends his comedic and detailed descriptions of imaginary characters, creating an argument through fantasy.

This play with fantasy in relationship to ideological arguments creates the excitement, theoretically, in the comedies. Perhaps influenced by the Japanese tradition of Kyogen (the comedic plays satirizing power relationships traditionally presented as entr'actes in No performances), Oshima has attempted to redefine the absurd comedy as one bearing an allegorical rhetoric aimed ideologically, but without a singular thematic message. He has sought to involve comedy in the unconscious to the greatest extent possible. These comedies unleash the relationship of puns, ironies, and exaggeration to the unconscious in its formation of identity and identification. In so doing they ask us to see psychoanalysis, particularly the writings of Lacan, not as guides to rein in the imaginary in favor of the symbolic as some uses of psychoanalysis have tended to do as a means to laudable ideological ends. Instead, they ask us to explore the imaginary in all its dimensions, including the way it interacts with the symbolic in the formation of ideologies.

SURREALISM IN THE BOUDOIR: *MAX, MON AMOUR*

Bestiality in the form of a sexual and romantic relationship between an elegant upper-class Parisienne and a chimpanzee is the extended joke underlying French screenwriter Jean-Claude Carrière and director Oshima's *Max, Mon Amour* (1987). The collaboration with Carrière is a way for Oshima to press his liaison to Luis Buñuel, especially as regards the type of comedy toward which he strives. Carrière was screenwriter on all Buñuel's French collaborations and had a recent history of working with other foreign directors. Adapting to the age of international coproduction, Oshima met Serge Silberman, a major French producer, when Silberman was in Tokyo for the production of Kurosawa's *Ran*. Silberman offered Oshima the Carrière script and the chance to produce his first, and to this date his only film made entirely outside Japan and in languages other than Japanese, in this case English and French.

A sector of the Parisian and British upper classes whose attitudes toward sexuality are so sophisticated and so highly "civilized" that affairs may be taken in stride and treated diplomatically is the context in which Carrière introduces bestiality as a challenge to traditions of sangfroid and the "stiff upper lip." The film opens with scenes establishing a typical infidelity drama, a French film staple, which can be played traditionally in a variety of modes, for comedy, pathos, suspense, or social commentary. From the very beginning, the film strikes an unusual tone. While initially understatement seems to be leading toward dramatic confrontation, instead the understated tone will in fact be sustained. An unlikely coolness rules throughout, supplying a bemused background for social satire with surreal flourishes, images meant to unsettle in their contrast of unlikely copresences.

A British diplomat attached to the British embassy in Paris is at home with his young son, cleaning his hunting rifle, when a phone call from his wife's best friend, Hélène, exposes the fact that his French wife's excuse for her absence as visiting this friend is potentially a lie. The wife (Charlotte Rampling) returns a second later and in front of her son immediately and unhesitatingly replies on questioning that she was at Hélène's. Cutting away from any dramatic confrontation whatsoever, the narrative skips from here to a report from a private detective delivered to the diplomat in his embassy telling of his wife's daily encounters in an apartment she has rented in a lower-class section of Paris.

Having discovered where she meets her lover, the next scene shows the diplomat arriving at the apartment, as his gestures convey his attempt to retain his dignity and avoid melodrama. This absolutely standard scene only becomes undone when the door to the trysting bedroom of the apartment is opened. The film holds first on the close-up reaction of the husband, then a shot of the interior revealing the wife, nude under draped sheets, sitting up in bed next to someone hidden under the covers. Only when she pulls back the sheet do we hold on an image of the chimpanzee embracing her, yet posed with such discretion that it undercuts the disruption such a liaison should pose to otherwise highly organized lives. The joke here is an extended one, dependent on sustaining interest in the quotidian accommodation attempted by these characters to this disruptive obsession and their willingness to pursue it inside the bourgeois frame of their lives. Bestiality in *Max, Mon Amour* seeks the status of true love, cross-species empathy, in otherwise sterile human relationships. While not played directly for the perverse pleasure of violating a sexual taboo, the film focuses obliquely, satirically, and intellectually on voyeurism and taboo violation.

We have here an extended metaphor turned into a joke, a form of comedy in which irony joins the trope that can sometimes seem to be virtually its opposite, allegory. By this I mean that allegory relies on a serious pursuit of a double meaning, while irony gains its strength in a complicity between film and spectator to read one meaning against another, deriving satirical humor from doing so. The mixed form of satirical allegory, relying heavily on catachresis, appears in its most hyperbolic form in the work of the Italian director Marco Ferreri, in such French-Italian coproductions as *Ne touchez pas aux femmes blanches* (Don't Touch the White Woman, 1974), his satire on the western shot in the cavern dug when the traditional market Les Halles in Paris was replaced by the shopping center of the same name.

The link between Ferreri's and Oshima's approaches to comedy was made apparent when Oshima's *Max, Mon Amour* and Ferreri's *Je t'aime* (I Love You) shared the stage at Cannes in 1986, with back-to-back competition screenings of these films using obsessional love as comic conceit. In Ferreri's comedy, a key chain in the form of a woman's body that says "I love you" becomes the obsession of a man played by Christopher Lambert. Of course, the danger in such use of catachresis is that the figuration becomes overextended, pulled so far into a life of its own as conceit that it fails to maintain significance and interest; the pairing at Cannes of these two films perhaps undercut both, though *Max, Mon Amour* fared better than *Je t'aime*, which received particularly unfavorable reception and reviews. This Cannes meeting of the two directors was a replay of the pairing of their castration scenes in 1976, when Oshima's *Realm of the Senses* was shown in competition with Ferreri's *L'Ultima donna* (The Last Woman, 1976), in which Gerard Depardieu plays a man whose despondency over his breakup with his wife leads him to castrate himself with an electric knife. The pairing of the two films ten years later also suffered from the more noteworthy films' being coupled earlier, offering an image of filmmakers in decline. In Oshima's case the stakes were high as he seemed to be attempting to escape Japan and the Japanese film industry context; *Max, Mon Amour* would not prove to be successful enough with critics or at the box office to elicit much demand for Oshima as a virtual expatriate.

The comparison to Ferreri is useful in other respects, for his anarchic, antibourgeois, and surrealistic approach parallels that of Oshima's comedies. Ferreri was himself obsessed with monkey imagery, particularly in the wake of the remake in 1976 by John Guillermin of Ernest Schoedsack and Merian C. Cooper's 1933 *King Kong*, a remake that, while campy, was in other ways an attempt simply to replay the horror and special effects aspects of the earlier film, sacrificing its poetics in the process. Ferreri's responses to the *King Kong* revival were *The Ape Woman*, in which the husband of a hairy woman played by Annie Girardot has her stuffed and exhibits her after she dies, and *Bye-Bye, Monkey* (1978), in which Gerard Depardieu is Lafayette, an immigrant to New York who befriends a baby chimp he finds near the Hudson River.

Similarly Carrière's script for *Max, Mon Amour* tries to answer to resurgent ape fascination and myth in film. Costuming and makeup that permit Max to be acted by a human, as well as evolutionary-anthropological overtones suggested by the film's dialogue, are indebted to Franklin Schaffner's *Planet of the Apes* (1968), based on the Pierre Boulle novel in which astronauts land on a planet where apes rule men, and the 1981 French-Canadian coproduction, Jean-Jacques Arnaud's *Quest for Fire*. These films won a special Oscar for makeup and an Oscar for costuming, respectively, and set new standards for the anthropomorphic rendering of apes in costumes and makeup that rendered not only verisimilitude to the bodies of the animals but also subtle expressions of thought and emotion to the faces. Both of these films in turn borrow from ideas put forth in Desmond Morris's *The Naked Ape* concerning the affinities between human behavior and that of humanity's most closely related counterparts.

If the 1933 *King Kong* started the explosion of ape figuration in popular culture by slyly embedding the lust and fascination of a huge ape for an attractive woman in its spectacular scenes, and converting the woman's initial fear of the "monster" to a stage performance with the ape and sympathetic understandings between them once the narrative moves to New York, it is *Mighty Joe Young* (1949), Schoedsack's return to the ape motif, that bears a closer resemblance to *Max, Mon Amour.* In this film a gentle gorilla befriends a young woman performer, though his presence frightens others. The film culminates in a scene in which he saves children from a burning orphanage, sacrificing himself in this act. While *Mighty Joe Young* clearly has affinities with cycles of sentimental animal films popular in both the United States and Japan, it goes far beyond the genre in its strange fascination with the empathy between gorilla and young woman; it is this bizarrely "naturalized" view of an extraordinary interspecies affinity that has made it, too, a cult classic. *Max, Mon Amour* takes as its point of departure a self-conscious intervention in the history of the ape in popular culture.

The film is most clever when sending up the civilized response of the bourgeois milieu to the chimpanzee lover. At a dinner in a fancy restaurant at which husband and wife meet to discuss their situation, he delivers the line "Have you gone completely insane?" with such understatement, and she responds with such coolness and composure—"I'm tired, let's go home to bed"—that the question of insanity appears an irrelevant query. When her former lover Archibald attempts to have a neuropsychologist intervene, the civilized distinction between sane and insane, normal and abnormal, is once again treated as a comical defensive reaction on the part of bourgeois males to a competition they do not understand.

If she prefers the chimpanzee to her husband and former lover, the suggestion is that the British and French males, in their overcivilized attitudes and their claims on chauvinist prerogatives, have simply lost erotic and emotional interest. Intellectualization comes under repeated satirical attack. One of the most humorous moments is a high angle on the husband's desk as he peruses newly acquired volumes on apes, a spoof at the attempt of a bibliophilic French culture to cope through intellectual expertise. This shot of books recalls some of the montage in *Diary of a Shinjuku Thief* and that film's bibliophilia. A zoologist brought in by the husband's lover, Camille, continues this send-up of intellectual response at the same time that his discourse is used like the sexologist in *Diary of a Shinjuku Thief* to provide ironic theoretical commentary on sexual behavior. The zoologist gives a thumbnail history of bestiality, including a "beautiful Japanese story of a woman who had a love affair with a horse," the film's only reference to Japan. While he asserts that affairs with dogs are considered too commonplace to evoke much interest, increasingly the zoologist reveals himself less scientist than voyeur-fetishist and opportunist as he proposes monitoring the romance in his laboratory to produce a best-seller.

The film gains much from the juxtaposition of the decors of upper-class culture with the chimpanzee problem, especially in the apartment. Both the refurbishing of a side room to be Max's cage only through the addition of a barred gate inside the classic door and the invitation extended to Max to dine with the family amid antiques elegantly and tastefully arranged allow for visual contrasts. The embassy office with its gilt ornamentation allows the competition for the husband's attention between the impending visit of the queen and his preoccupation with his animal rival to be set in a visual land-scape of high contrast, just as an opera gala contrasts later with Max's com-mand over the husband once he has promised to care for the chimp in his wife's absence. Sophisticated high fashion, including the Guy Laroche asym-metrically designed dress and flowing monochrome crepe pants outfits, also contrasts with chimpanzee fur to create visual humor. Yet these are among the few traces of Oshima's and cameraman Raoul Coutard's visual talents; this film is less visually inventive than Oshima's other work.

Moreover, the film depends on comedic bits like the return of the rifle in the opening scene; first used when the husband tries to shoot the ape, the ape later steals the gun to return the fire. The maid's struggle with eczema is later revealed to be apparently induced by an ape allergy. These are the jokes of the French boulevard comedy tradition, not metacritical jokes on that tradition that one might expect paralleling Oshima's metacritical treat-ment of Asian comedy in *Three Resurrected Drunkards.* Actors and acresses in that French comedy tradition become a film's centerpiece, and here Ram-pling's performance gains such centrality.

As to the erotic expectations of an audience expecting bestiality to be graphically represented as Oshima's follow-up to the graphic eroticism of *Realm* and *Empire,* the film offers only the image of woman and chimpanzee hugging on initial discovery and another showing Max caressing and play-fully nibbling on her neck. This occurs after her husband's insistence on in-troducing the chimpanzee at a formal dinner party celebrating her birthday, giving it a contextual humor but not much serious pursuit of kinky visual play. However, verbal references to eroticism sometimes ironically function as both stimulant and metacommentary, as in the conversation between Paul and Camille at the zoo that consigns suggestive sexuality entirely to di-alogue. They discuss watching monkeys engage in sex and the affair of an acquaintance with a large dog. Throughout, the focus is less on the erotics of bestiality than on the social implications of bestial-human romance as commentary on human mores.

Bestiality is structurally presented in this metacommentary as a further extreme of homosexuality, insofar as it presents another "perversion," another crossing of a boundary that upsets repressive bourgeois decorum. This homophobia ironically presents itself in the double entendre of a woman guest at the dinner party on witnessing the foreplay, "I assume, at the very least, that he's a male," and in the phrasing of the husband's question, "Well, how is it with a monkey?" that parallels a question he might ask if he just found out his wife came out as a lesbian, "Well, how is it with another woman?" As the monkey-pleasure question is followed by a close-up in which she does not answer, we sense her positioning herself outside such inquiries, not deigning to reply; the film's focus on the strength of her self-possession as a woman who lives her own desire ties her to earlier Oshima heroines. She is the least compromised version of such a heroine, reflected in the acclaim Charlotte Rampling earned in this role, a portion of which seems to be for a "strength" that belongs to the character. It is intriguing to speculate how the film might have worked had the same portrayal been used in a dramatic context for homosexuality as desire, rather than the comic allegory of bestiality of the film as it is, but it is surely this echo of homophobia that gives the film's argument for bestiality its sharpest political edge. In a context in which right-wing advocates of repression link homosexuality to bestiality to condemn both, this film makes the daring move of humorously defending bestiality, using this defense to satirize, between the lines, homophobia.

Feeding and caring for Max is also presented as having a second child, and if the son is at first a suspicious rival, he becomes a loyal sibling to Max. Finally, Max is integrated into the family, sharing, most symbolically in the French context, their dining room. Here again, the film gains its satirical edge through Max's species, exaggerating the fixation on pets as family members, substitute children, as well as replacements for extramarital lovers by married individuals. The familial aspect of the farce comes by the film's end to a shift in mood, when the wife retells a dream in which she kills Max after neighbors' complaints threaten his remaining with them. This last twist, made more palpable as premonition by the barking of dogs offscreen in the closing shot, perhaps unsettles the potential familial equilibrium that the ending might otherwise have.

Animal rights groups' recent discussion of "species bias" presents an ironic backdrop for a comedy like *Max, Mon Amour,* as premises of respect for animals are extended as a discourse of political and social "rights." A comedy in which animals fill a gap left in human-to-human relationships can be seen as a cultural parallel to the displacements of political activity from the rights of humans to the rights of animals.

A telling commentary on the film was revealed when the archives of Paul Touvier, a French fascist collaborator and the first Frenchman convicted of war crimes, were exposed in the course of his trial to contradict his denial of being anti-Semitic. Touvier's annotated newspaper clippings revealed a continuing virulent anti-Semitism, an example of which was his labeling *Max, Mon Amour* "cinéma juif," apparently blaming Serge Silberman, the producer, for a degeneracy that could only indicate a most literal reading of the film as a paean to bestiality. Such racist reaction to Jewish participation in the French film industry recalls the diatribes of Maurice Bardeche and Robert Brasillach in the thirties and forties against the Prévert brothers and Marcel Carné and charges of "degenerate" Jewish influence through film. It shows that the ideological issues in comedy are never far from the surface, and is in itself almost surreal evidence of Oshima and Carrière's film successfully bothering precisely the sector of the public it was meant to call into question.

If Oshima turns to comedy, it is surely to reach audiences beyond those of his directly political films. In fact, the late work, starting with the eroticism of *Realm* through *Merry Christmas, Mr. Lawrence*'s casting of rock stars to *Max, Mon Amour*'s European setting and humor, all self-consciously seeks a wider audience, particularly an audience outside of Japan. Ironically, though, Oshima's funniest comedies are the ones most difficult to export beyond Japan, as the humor is so tied to Japanese situations and language. Humor, especially irony and social satire, is not as universal as is sometimes imagined.

CHAPTER SEVEN

Documents of Guilt and Empire

Oshima's documentaries may seem to begin as the products of near-necessity, to fill a hiatus from feature production forced on him by censorship and financing problems. His incursion into this genre was facilitated by Ushiyama Junichi, a producer of documentaries for television. In some ways, documentary in Japan had been a haven and a province of the left. This postwar leftist tendency may have been a result in part of some general attributes of the documentary genre. Stakes of documentary filmmaking are different; documentary budgets are smaller, and filmmakers are less constrained by financially motivated censorship and self-censorship. Documentaries can provide another means of addressing significant political issues without the commercial imperatives of feature production. The effect multiplies over time as genre expectations permit documentary to offer a more direct expression of political issues. While at the scale of national broadcast television such freedoms might be expected to evaporate, both of Ushiyama's documentary television series were known for innovation and freedom of expression. Ushiyama sought out Oshima and other well-known filmmakers to lend further clout to his documentary series (Sato 1973).

Oshima himself once referred to his hiatus from commercial fictional filmmaking when recounting his career by wryly saying, "After that [the making of *Amakasu Shiro Tokisada* (Shiro Tokisada from Amakasu, 1962)], there was a three-year period during which I wasn't able to make a film, but even so I didn't die" (1992: 256). The irony here is that during the hiatus in question, Oshima made documentaries for the first time. As this quote comes in a context in which Oshima discusses his whole feature career but omits the documentaries entirely, his comment that he "wasn't able to make a film" seems dismissive of their value but is perhaps only a reflection of the popular and critical primacy of the fictional commercial feature film, even in terms of art and politics. His "I didn't die" indicates that these years, while a struggle for survival, were very productive.

In fact, his documentaries also date from two other periods; two significant ones were made during 1968–1969, when he was in the midst of one of his most active periods of feature production, and then several were made in the years 1975–1979, the period that also includes the making of *Realm of the Senses* (1976) and *Empire of Passion* (1978). Oshima's trips to Korea (1964), Vietnam (1965), Bangladesh (1971), and Okinawa (1977) are outgrowths and stimuli of his documentary work. The "otherness" of non-Japanese East Asia and the "others" who live in Japan are central issues examined sympathetically and politically across the documentaries.

Although the documentaries play a decidedly secondary role in Oshima's recognition as a filmmaker outside Japan, we should appreciate how great a factor they are in the Japanese documentary context. Japan was slower to develop documentary as a form than other countries. The documentary genre became closely associated with the Pacific War in Japan in the thirties, notably with documentaries on China in 1934 and 1936 (Anderson 1982: 147). Increasingly the Japanese government used filmic documentation of its war effort as a major propaganda device, a process Oshima investigates in a film I will discuss in detail later in this chapter, *The Pacific War.* The wartime documentaries introduced Japan to the full power of filmic propaganda, as images were selected and shaped into a one-sided discourse with great emotional appeal.

For postwar contestatory artists who wished to transform documentary into a vehicle for raising consciousness and influencing public policy, it was tempting to use this power for their own ends. Japan's postwar documentary production over the course of the sixties become lively and politically engaged, ranging from films that were just as didactic, slanted, and emotional in their discourse, but from liberal or leftist perspectives, to films that were more exploratory or observational in their practice. The best known of the sixties documentary figures are Ogawa Shinsuke, who began a most active career with *Seinen no umi* (Sea of Youth, 1966), and Tsuchimoto Noriaki, whose first film, *Prehistory of the Partisan Party* (1969), looks at everyday life of the Zengakuren, the student radicals. Tsuchimoto's subsequent films were responsible for raising the issue of "Minamata disease," a term applied to the birth defects and deaths among children of a village contaminated by mercury through fish they ate. Specific corporate heads are charged with the industrial pollution of Japan's seas, a demand of accountability that is rare and progressive in Japan. Ogawa is best known for his series on farmer displacement and the protests that ensued when the Japanese government appropriated land to build Narita airport. A group of six films made between 1968 and 1973 chronicles various aspects of the struggle (see Burch 1979: 360–363; Desser 1988: 158–170; Mellen 1976: 427–449). Oshima, let me suggest, is another major figure in sixties documentary, with his specialties being otherness, exclusion, the aftermath of war, and imperialism. Radical expression gained currency in documentary across the sixties, so much so that many on the left in Japan came to feel that commercial, fictional production was a poor second to the more direct political intervention of documentary expression. As documentaries such as Ogawa's and Tsuchimoto's were shown by organizers to build support for the protests they documented, this belief in their impact is understandable; they were not making them for television or other mass distribution but as "tools in a struggle." This stance recalls the debate among the characters in Oshima's *The Battle of Tokyo, or the Story of the Young Man Who Left His Will on Film,* discussed in chapter 3, where the phrase "turning film into tools in the struggle" is used as an accusation that such a goal risks reducing film to an illustration of a party line. The arguments raised when Oshima's fictional characters theoretically debate documentary efficacy are one measure of how the genre presents a viable alternative for him, but one whose discourse will be ultimately subject to self-conscious scrutiny of its limitations.

DOCUMENTARY DISCOURSE AND THE EMBEDDED SURPRISE

Given the legacy of his inventive feature film work and the sorts of documentary innovations that would come later, Oshima's first documentaries might be initially surprising to viewers whose expectations are shaped by his fiction work. In their use of many quite standard codes of documentary, including a voice-over narration whose discourse is straightforward and sometimes even quite pedantic, the films do not shift documentary practice into the more self-conscious, poetic, or experimental modes that were occurring in Europe and the United States by the sixties. Nor do they recall earlier documentary experiments with montage such as those that characterized Soviet documentary of the twenties, or conversely, the experiments with minimal use of voice-over that Robert Flaherty used. Instead, in the tradition of much documentary historically, a voice situates imagery, or in even more emphasis on voice, the film culls images into the service of illustrating a spoken discourse.

So shaped by verbal discourse is this type of documentary form that U.S. critics and theorists of documentary were critical of its formal assumptions even quite early in the history of documentary criticism. In his essay "The Voice of Documentary," Bill Nichols summarizes the Anglo-American tradition of direct address in emphasizing its shortcomings and outdated quality.

> The direct address of the Griersonian tradition (or, in its most excessive form the March of Time's "voice of God") was the first thoroughly worked out mode of documentary. As befitted a school whose purposes were

overwhelmingly didactic, it employed a supposedly authoritative yet often presumptuous off-screen narration. In many cases this narration effectively dominated the visuals, though it could be, in films like *Night Mail* or *Listen to Britain,* poetic and evocative. After World War II, the Griersonian mode fell into disfavor . . . and has little contemporary currency—except for television news, game and talk shows, ads and documentary specials. (Nichols 1988: 48)

If the cinema verité and reflexive documentary modes that superseded such direct address helped create disfavor for such a guiding, didactic voice in a Western context, we must note that Oshima's context is different: he engages in actively distinguishing his direct address from the overt propaganda voices of Japanese wartime documentary. Initially, this will not be a distinction of mode but rather of what gets said by the voice. The voice remains direct, even didactic, but the points of emphasis and the relationship of speaker to interlocutor change, especially noticeable when one contrasts it with Japanese documentaries from the early forties. The film's narration speaks to its audience as citizens, appealing to their conscience and asking them to consider the lives of others; it does not speak to them as imperial subjects, assigning them a position of subservient obeisance to state policy. Brian Winston, in his "The Tradition of the Victim in Griersonian Documentary," charges that such discourses of liberal reform create a continual illusion of awareness of mistreatment that never ameliorates the situation (1988: 270–287). However, this charge, made in retrospect, thinking over thirty years of documentary practice that has not substantially changed Britain, may ignore more indirect effects of informing and muckraking, what Oshima will call, in an instance we will look at shortly, creating a break between the Japanese and their emperor. I argue that both the mode of address and the recognition of the human impact of policy have a specific valence in sixties Japan. It is speaking to the creation of a questioning subject. It is for this reason that Oshima's documentaries will themselves evolve toward a voice that questions more than it dictates, and questions increasingly poetically.

Oshima's documentaries make use of the customary semiotic components of documentary: maps and charts, interviews, and stock footage. There is little completely staged footage, however. Oshima instead employs direct cinema techniques, in which the camera directly captures unstaged events, mostly seeking unobtrusiveness of crew and director, though occasionally his direct cinematic sequences acknowledge the camera's impact on the scene.

Some of the reasons for Oshima's apparent willingness to begin with a more traditional documentary form may stem from his television producer's assignments. Japan's separate history of nonfiction filmic expression may also be a factor. As I indicated, wartime propaganda played a key role in the developmental history of Japanese documentary; less of an indigenous development of a poetics of documentary preceded or followed the war, leaving the sixties filmmakers to reinvent the Japanese documentary genre but less able to radically depart from the more accessible features of direct address, particularly for a broad television audience.

Yet even from the beginning, some of what I have been calling typical or standard voice-over or editing patterns function less traditionally than first impressions might indicate. When one takes into account the entirety of a given film's unfolding, there is a willingness to violate form and the expectations set up internally by these devices.

One of the most interesting films from this early period is *Wasurerareta kogun* (Forgotten Soldiers, 1963), shot in 16-millimeter, black and white, and just twenty-five minutes long. It traces the protests of Korean nationals who had been recruited during the war to fight for Japan and have since been neglected. The men still live in Japan but are denied both Japanese citizenship and the veterans' benefits reinstituted for Japanese soldiers in the years just before the film's making (after years during which Occupation and postwar governments denied pensions to the Imperial Army as well). The prior service to the Japanese war effort by this segment of the Korean immigrant population, thought by many Japanese to be simply homeless beggars, made them an unlikely cause for leftists as well. Of all who might be seen in some manner as victims of the Japanese war effort, Korean immigrants as a group were among the most tainted by collaboration with the militarists. Outcasts, Oshima looks to them with a sharp eye, ideologically attuned to all the contradictions not only in their situation, but of a postwar Japan that returns compensation to its own soldiers while still denying much of its imperial exploitation of other East Asians.

The film wants to force us to look at these men. An opening montage links a close-up of a man with a damaged face to a close-up on an amputee's stump (before the freeze-frame that gives us the film's title), introducing the brutal confrontational strategy of the film. Rather than simply take in the handicaps in his framing, which would minimize their shock value and avoid exploitation of audience reactions, Oshima foregrounds at all stages the physical evidence of suffering.

The voice-over that begins the documentary sets the scene, while simultaneously marking its staging of events in the manner of voice-over narration typical of feature reporting: "Eighteen years have passed since the ending of the Second World War. After the armistice, wounded soldiers were a familiar sight in every town and village in Japan. Most of them have long since returned to normal life. But here on a train running through the outskirts of Tokyo you notice a man, clad in a white hospital gown, asking for charity." Rhetorically, the phrase "but here on a train . . . you notice a man" didactically points out what in the "real" is the focus, as if the veteran were just happened upon rather than selected through research. This rhetoric is

46. Korean immigrants, who served the Japanese military effort in World War
II but who are denied benefits as they are not Japanese citizens, protest their
treatment. *Wasurerareta kogun* (Forgotten Soldiers, 1963). Still courtesy of
Oshima Productions.

at once didactic explanation and a cover of the process of making and framing a documentary film; it is precisely the sort of discursive directing of interpretation of the image that Chris Marker satirizes in his *Letters from Siberia*.
It may seem astonishing to find Oshima employing it apparently unselfcon-
sciously, but Oshima courts a straightforwardness of form here, placing the
tensions elsewhere. He focuses instead on political marginalization and that
which must be repressed by political discourse as they might be understood
by looking at those people left out, forgotten.

A parade of these former soldiers to the prime minister's residence continues to be descriptively marked by the same emphatic voice: "Disabled, they
can't march as they once did, yet they still feel something of their past
glory . . . and their eyes light up when they hear the songs of the Imperial
Army." Narration here begins to court irony when it describes eyes lighting
up on hearing the songs of the Imperial Army. The phrase risks left-wing antipathy while seemingly seeking right-wing identification; instead, ultimately,
it frames the contradiction and irony of the displaced, nostalgic loyalty of
these men. In so doing, it foreshadows the end of the film when we will hear

the songs sung in a drunken state that forcibly revises whatever associations the songs' mention assumes here.

The spectator's shame is directly demanded by an image that frames a list of demands held in a hook. Even more insistent is a bomber's noise that is added to a shot that zooms in on the scarred face of a soldier whose face exploded. This editing is not subtle or delicate but echoes the placards held by these men: "No eye, no jobs, no pensions."

Scenes of the men demonstrating at the Diet building and at the Gaimusho (foreign ministry) as well as lunching together in a park next to the South Korean embassy alternate with flashbacks to Japanese military activity in Korea and Korean populations in Japan, beginning with the 1910 colonization of Korea. With the second of these flashbacks, the film begins to focus on one man, Ong Sho Rakku, both armless and eyeless as result of U.S. bombardment of the Truk Islands; Ong, the central character, serves as a device to personalize the issue. Later a poetic lament by the narrator repeatedly evokes his name, followed by reiterated questioning of his situation. The film points out that Ong, though born in northern Korea, became a colonial Japanese subject attached to the Japanese Imperial Navy in 1943. In the third flashback we move to the Korean War, a narration that fills in the explanation of Ong's 1962 decision to change his citizenship to South Korean, to appeal to the South Korean government for compensation. This section of the film places the individual in a shifting of nationalities in the aftermath of two wars; implied in the montage is a foot soldier caught in shifting international politics, who has essentially lost any meaningful nationality and along with it any rights whatsoever. At the South Korean embassy, officials tell the soldiers, "You fought and were wounded for Japan, not for our country. You should make your demands to the Japanese government. We are not responsible!" As we have previously learned, the Japanese government has already told the soldiers that they should make their demands to the South Korean government as compensation will be made in a lump sum, government to government. By following the former soldiers' march from governmental office to another government's embassy, the film gives a physical dimension to the point it is making about this group being buffeted back and forth by each government's unwillingness to recognize them or to negotiate. The focus on Ong in montage with the war histories serves to point out all the ironies of the postwar period.

Two key scenes finish this chronicle of a day of protest. The first shows the group on the street, appealing to the passersby for aid and sympathy, having exhausted their governmental appeals. It introduces a moment of cinema verité, as the narrator asks, "How do the people react?" Panning their faces, naming their reactions, the film embeds an internal mirror in which the film asks the Japanese audience to look itself in the face, a goal of Oshima's filmmaking that I discussed in chapter 1. Then, just before the end, a second key scene shows all the Koreans gathering in a restaurant to begin drinking and singing. The narrator speaks: "But as feared, a quarrel breaks out. It is like this whenever they drink together. Futile arguments, expressing their anger and frustration at the misery of their lives. But who will listen?"

Other filmmakers would not have shot this scene, or if they had, they would have excised it from the finished film; it raises too many problems, clouding the political issues with "embarrassing" information. It depicts the protesters as angry, even antipathetic toward each other. The voice-over casts the argument as evidence of "anger and frustration," as a symptom of their misery and further evidence of their mistreatment. It may be this, but it is clearly something more in the context Oshima has provided for this scene, something more in the commentary Oshima (1992: 80–83) offered at the time, in an essay devoted to the making of the film. This antipathetic behavior is an uncomfortable residue, an excess, that also spills out in Oshima's fiction films during drunken gatherings; the harm done to people by history, the personal cost, the psychological cost, is not glossed over, as it is precisely evidence of the sort of contradiction on which Oshima will insist. It is what saves this otherwise highly didactic film from the social-realist premise of controlled argumentation, which has been so subject to patterns of lies. The film refuses to sacrifice the willingness to look critically to achieve the creation of more likable heroes or victims.

A poetic, personal ending follows, repeating the Korean's name, as Ong first stands in front of tombs in a graveyard, then lies in bed listening to the radio. The film ends with the image of him walking the seashore, through a crowd of people, as the narrator directly chastises the audience: "Are we Japanese really so inhuman? Can such ingratitude be tolerated?"

The situation Oshima is documenting echoes in intriguing ways the recent protests of former karayuki-san, also known as "comfort women," Korean and other East Asian women forced into prostitution by the Japanese military during the Pacific War. A documentary film by Imamura Shohei, *Karayuki-san: The Making of a Prostitute* (1975), did much to publicize a similar situation, the historical exploitation of Japanese women sold and coerced into prostitution. So does *Sandakin No 8* (1974), directed by Kei Kumio, a fictional adaptation of the report of anthropologist Yamazaki Hiromi on her fieldwork in Borneo and one of the most directly feminist and anti-imperialist films ever produced in Japan. It traces the efforts of a female journalist to uncover the history of the Karayuki-san (see Turim 1993). In the case of the comfort women as with the Korean soldiers, the Japanese government initially denied its role and responsibility. Finally, enough evidence of the forced prostitution emerged in the case of the comfort women, including, toward the end, a confession of a former military procurer of the women, that the government formally apologized, though it only offered compensation in the form of a lump-sum payment sent through governments rather than specific, individual compensation. We can see from this comparison, then, that Oshima's focus on the individual has a specific political charge in the Japanese context. In defiance of an ideology theory that might focus on systemic factors, this film wishes to highlight individual subjects as that which Japan is most unwilling to acknowledge, given the cultural emphasis on participation in and sacrifice to the communal that sometimes issues as conformity. Risking humanist appeals, risking what Western documentary theories might critique as old-fashioned discursive appeals, the film insists that individual suffering be understood in a manner that would characterize the later Japanese documentaries of Ogawa and Tsushimoto.

Oshima's 1964 *Seishun no ni* (A Monument to Youth) also is about Koreans, this time shot in Korea. A Korean student radical, Park Ok He, who lost her arm in the uprising that overthrew Syngman Rhee, subsequently becomes a prostitute to support her family as the traditional dutiful elder daughter in rural Korea should. The film tells the story of this woman as a man, Ban Ho Chin, tries to free her from prostitution by enlisting her help with an orphanage he runs. Again the personal chronicle is interspersed with footage documenting the history of Korea since the end of World War II. The title refers to a monument constructed to the students who died in the 1960 uprising, visited in the footage toward the end of the film. Like *Forgotten Soldiers*, it has surprisingly revealing scenes of interaction between the individuals as it chronicles the tensions of Park's departure from the orphanage, disappointing Ban's missionary attempts at substituting charity work for her filial commitment to wage-earning prostitution. The ironies of a woman displaced by history are quite similar to her counterpart in *Forgotten Soldiers*, and both documentary protagonists have missing limbs that Oshima uses visually to symbolize their suffering. In addition, *A Monument to Youth*, by virtue of centering on a young woman who once was a student active in political protests but is now forced back into traditional female roles, introduces the female subject.

It is Oshima's next documentary, *Yunbogi no nikki* (Diary of Yunbogi, 1965), that best indicates what is still inadequate in the previous works. Made from stills of street kids in Seoul that Oshima shot while making *A Monument to Youth*, to chronicle the lives of orphans, the images remain disjunct from the narration, though joined conceptually. There are two elements of the narration: (1) passages from Yunbogi's diary as voice-over (a diary that had been published in Korea), and (2) Oshima's voice poetically making links between the lives of the street kids and Korean history, as well as directly questioning Yunbogi. This film, unlike all of Oshima's other documentaries, has received wide distribution, and the comparison to Marker's use of documentary voice-over, poetic and disjunct, essayist, self-conscious and ironic, is apt.

47. This documentary image of young Korean street vendors recalls the boy selling his pigeons on the street in Oshima's first feature film, *Ai to kibo no machi* (A Town of Love and Hope, 1959). *Yunbogi no nikki* (Yunbogi's Diary, 1965). Still courtesy of Oshima Productions.

Radical treatment of documentary form here includes poetic, questioning discourse toward the end, when after describing how students were joined by others in their confrontations with police in the uprising against Syngman Rhee, Oshima asks,

> Yunbogi, will you too throw stones someday?
> Yunbogi, will you too throw stones someday?
> Yunbogi, you are a ten-year-old boy.
> Yunbogi, you are ten-year-old Korean boy.

The weight of ending on this repetition emphasizing both the revolutionary potential of Korean disenfranchisement and the youthful national identity of his imaginary interlocutor needs to be seen in the context of Korean government censorship and Korean sensitivity to foreign criticism, especially Japanese criticism, of poverty in their country. Oshima speaks of both in his "With Heavy Heart, I Speak of Korea," knowing that these issues are complicated by Japanese historical oppression of Korea. In this essay, originally written in 1964 on his return from making the two documentaries I

48. Images of young Korean students running accompany Oshima's evocation of Yunbogi's future protests against his government. *Yunbogi no nikki* (Yunbogi's Diary, 1965). Still courtesy of Oshima Productions.

have been discussing, Oshima says, "The Koreans cannot feel other than ambivalently toward Japan, the neighbor who, after thirty years of domination, is now rich" (1992: 95). Oshima's narration is self-conscious in awareness of his role as Japanese observer. If the Korean boy is a potential revolutionary and as the Korean left earned the admiration of the Japanese left for the intensity of its resistance, Oshima turns both word and future action over to him.

THE PACIFIC WAR

Oshima's documentary form increasingly presents ironies, develops contradictions, and proceeds by indirect telling. The epitome of this strategy is his *Daitoa senso* (The Pacific War, 1968), which Oshima composed from reedited found footage, Japanese government propaganda from the war, served up straight, without contemporary voice-over commentary. The idea was to avoid the strategies of standard Occupation counterpropaganda, on the one hand, and leftist and particularly communist propaganda, on the other, which typically offered didactic explications of Japanese militarism underscoring lies and deceptions.

The strategy of *The Pacific War* instead is one full of risks. The full weight of what the Japanese government had told its people originally was replayed for them and their children, allowing the contemporary audience to hear once again how the announcements of their military convincingly built a war consensus, if one heard these in the absence of other information. In the context of powerful right-wing revisionism that seeks to excuse the Japanese war effort, such a strategy could simply feed latent militarist nostalgia. It is easy to imagine that an audience could be newly inspired by the war propaganda, just as neo-Nazi groups relish Nazi hate literature and film propaganda. If Oshima runs this risk, it is to provoke in his audiences the same sensations he had uncovering the footage in the archives and to move them through the propaganda in its own sequence, following its own logic.

The film begins with titles that announce its strategy but without much of a didactic warning. The titles simply read,

> All parts of this motion picture were filmed during the Pacific War. All narration, sound and music were recorded by the Japanese at that time. Films purchased from abroad are presented as dubbed by the Japanese at that time. This is a record of the Pacific War as we the Japanese people experienced it.

Then the date, December 8, 1941, is followed by two announcements from the Departments of Army and Navy at the Imperial Headquarters. The first reports the upcoming bombing of Pearl Harbor:

> The Imperial Navy has finally risen to action and its battleships sail in the surging billows of the Pacific Ocean with great dignity. Heading for the naval port at Pearl Harbor of Hawaii, the biggest American Naval base in the Pacific—biding their time for the last thirty years—now they challenge the enemy, to ensure the prosperity of the Empire. Prepared for death, they take off to serve the Empire. Those who stay aboard, as well as those who depart, strain their eyes to the distant enemy base, and with the oath of patriotism, wish the eagles good luck. In this way the decisive heroic battle was opened at Pearl Harbor with unprecedented victorious results.

The second announcement celebrates the bombing's success:

> We announce the final results confirmed by the air bombers and photographic reconnoitering party. It is confirmed that the American Pacific Fleet and Air Force in Hawaii were annihilated. Just last spring, the U.S. commissioned new 35,000-ton battleships, the *North Carolina* and the *Washington*, which gave them 18 major ships designed to gain world mastery. However, 9 of these 18 major ships were put to death at this one battle. Not only have U.S. ambitions collapsed, but they have been downgraded to a second- or third-class naval nation.

So far, the military, by omitting any context that establishes its own aggression, has simply claimed it is making a preemptive strike. By emphasizing the U.S. naval buildup, it establishes the United States as potential aggressor, therefore positioning the surprise attack as justified preservation of the empire. But the phrase "prosperity of the Empire" in this historical context means "empire," not just the Japanese government or nation. Imperialism is precisely the question, as becomes clearer in the next segment, Tojo's well-known speech on the declaration of war. Presumably most viewers would know this speech, with its claims that "the government did its best to reach a diplomatic settlement with America, but America did not only not yield an inch, along with Britain and the Netherlands, they demanded our Army and Navy's unconditional complete withdrawal from China, dissolution of the Nanking regime and cancellation of the Japanese-German-Italian Treaty," and its justification that "if the Empire submits to their demands, we will not only lose the prestige of the Empire and completion of the China initiative, but also the existence of the Empire will be endangered."

In bulletins about Tojo's December 13 Tokyo speech which follow in Oshima's montage, we are told that the public, "having remained prudent for the last eight months, but who have been expecting this moment for a long time, now unite for the sacred war to release East Asia and rise to action promising to serve the Country." The astute viewer would already notice the contradiction between Tojo on December 8 and Tojo on December 13; claims of peaceful intentions have disappeared, replaced by claims of fulfilling, in the words of the newsreel's voice-over commentary, the "aspiration of the East Asian people" and what it calls "devout war cries of the public solidified."

What follows are a series of newsreels originally meant to bolster Japanese domestic support for the war. A sequence shows individuals praying at the Shimokawa shrine in Miyagi Prefecture, then another lauds the "young industrial soldiers" of Osaka. Then a series of newsreels shows Japanese penetration of the British Malay Peninsula, Songkhla, Pattani, Thailand, British Kota Bharu, and then Singapore. A break from military victories shows celebrations at the imperial palace and at Hibiya Park, attended by Ambassadors Ott of Germany and Indiri of Italy. Then the newsreels recount more victories, Menado in Celebes, the Dutch East Indies, Rangoon, American Philippines, Manila.

Scott Nygren (1987: 64) makes several useful points in discussing this film in relationship to the animated propaganda feature film, *Momotaro umi no shimpai,* which appropriates a Japanese folktale hero to explain Japanese imperial conquest as motivated by benevolent, anticolonialist sentiment. Nygren notes that after footage of "the surrender of the British flag by troops at Singapore," the documentary cuts to "close-ups of shots of British and Japanese leaders engaged in talks." He goes on to remark that in the original

49. Early Japanese celebrations of the war effort portrayed by a Western-style marching band. *Daitoa senso* (The Pacific War, 1968). Still courtesy of Oshima Productions.

50. Japanese military victories are announced accompanied by a series of newsreel images showing Japanese military occupation of other countries. *Daitoa senso* (The Pacific War, 1968). Still courtesy of Oshima Productions.

newsreels, "the eyelids of the British appear to flicker abnormally quickly, through a shift of camera speed that suggestively recapitulates in a newsreel context *Momotaro*'s image of the British as weak and surprised." That the animated film and the newsreels both use visual devices to depict the colonial powers as weak illustrates for Nygren the political and psychological argument that the films are making to an Asian audience, attempting not only to adopt a feigned anticolonialism but also to undercut what Iriye Akira (as quoted by Nygren) has called Western "pretensions as masters over Asian races." Nygren goes on to note that the contradiction between Japanese domination and supposed aspirations of anticolonialist liberation are embedded in the original newsreels, just as they are in *Momotaro*, but that in Oshima's montage they are juxtaposed with "the vivid addition of mass devotion to the imperial ideal undeniably present in the shots of Japanese crowds."

Ideally, a present-day audience for both films would read the contradiction for what it is, and the mass approval depicted would be a sobering experience, a confrontation with the widely based popular support of militarist imperial policies. At this point, however, it is possible to imagine whole sections of the late seventies audiences still feeling that the professed "noble" purposes and motivations originally given for the war were reasonable. In other words, to a revisionist and lingering right-wing nationalist sentiment, the film thus far might revive Japanese justification.

Beginning with the newsreel of April 18, 1942, announcing the Doolittle Bombers' first attack on Tokyo, the Japanese narration of continuous victories must account for the real threat of defeat. The voice-over minimizes the threat but warns the public "to prepare physically and spiritually to confront calmly whatever may happen in the future." The general election of April 30, 1942, presents a chance for the newsreel to show events seeming to continue with relative normality.

A newsreel of the June 5, 1942, battle of Midway attacks U.S. propaganda as false and claims, "We let them have our flesh, and we get their backbone." Cultural juxtaposition continues as newsreels cover rituals at the Meiji shrine on October 29 and promote the myth of Greater East Asia by covering a "literary meeting with representatives of China and Manchuria" on November 5.

As the film continues, however, the lies and desperate, twisted appeals to patriotism become increasingly internally apparent once the war turns against the Japanese. This shift begins with the penultimate sequences of part one, bulletins from two battles that the Japanese forces lose: August 9, 1942, the battle of Solomon, and February 7, 1943, the battle of Guadalcanal. Just as earlier victory was piled on victory, now these two sequences signal the beginning of a series of defeats and retreats from one occupied country after another. As part one closes the burden of saving face and appearing resolute in the face of an enemy falls on the commentary.

A ceremonial funeral for a fallen military hero is the final sequence of part

51. Traditional martial arts training is presented in a newsreel as central to the modern war effort. *Daitoa senso* (The Pacific War, 1968). Still courtesy of Oshima Productions.

52. Images of corpses create a counterpoint that a present-day audience may read for its contradictions within the newsreels promoting the war. *Daitoa senso* (The Pacific War, 1968). Still courtesy of Oshima Productions.

one. The April 18 entombment of the commander of the combined fleet, Admiral Yamamoto Isoroku, functions in this film similarly to the ceremonies depicted in Oshima's *Ceremonies;* the ritual of homage becomes a site exposing contradictions in a discourse that attempts to cover them. Yamomoto, Harvard-educated and famous for his initial opposition to Japan's military buildup, became, once he embraced the war, the single most important figure in Japan next to Tojo and the emperor. His death was more than the loss of a leader for the Japanese; it was symbolically the precursor of the defeat, coming just before the shift toward defeat of the Japanese war effort. The commentary in the newsreel tries to turn his death into a rededication to the war, but the images of death and mourning, especially placed at the end of part one of Oshima's documentary, bear the traces of the unraveling of the Japanese army and navy and Japan's impending loss of its imperialist conquests.

Part two concentrates increasingly on Japan's adjustments of policy as its war machine falters, then its desperate attempts to keep the war effort alive, and finally its refusal to surrender no matter what the cost. Known as the "readjustment policy," Japan began granting "independence" to its conquered territories. Three segments, set in a pagoda in Burma on August 1, 1943, in Thailand, and in the Philippines, trace this strategic retreat by rendering it as noble.

A sequence of university students going to the front is separated from another that echoes it, "Boy soldiers going off to war," then by two more segments continuing the readjustment policy, showing the March 8, 1944, loss of the Imphal Plain in Burma and the early August rearrangement of the line of Japanese troops. The drafting of increasingly younger men and boys is echoed by a segment on the Women's Labor Service Corps, fifteen-year-olds enlisted as factory workers. The emphasis on the child soldier and child laborers clearly indicates the desperate straits the Japanese nation was in at this point in the war. Selection and juxtaposition attempt to show how decisively the war turned in 1943–1944 for the Japanese merely by a montage of their own propaganda. Montage here is everything as the readjustment sequences clearly express desperation in a context of juxtaposition to other desperate moves.

Oshima's documentary continually highlights the propaganda use the original newsreels make of even disastrous events for the Japanese. In speaking of Saipan, the newsreel proclaims, "All died for honor." Growing pumpkins is shown, which is similar to U.S. newsreels promoting "Victory Gardens," except that by this point in the war, such efforts come as an implied admission that there is no more food.

Inclusion of appeals to the young can be read as a biographical trace on Oshima's part, a reference to his boyhood during the war. A teacher leads schoolchildren in prayers for victory, only weeks before the events the next sequence depicts, the July 18, 1944, resignation of the wartime cabinet. In

53. Japanese troop images may be read with increasing irony as the film progresses. As defeat becomes a greater probability, loyalty, perhaps, takes on other meanings. *Daitoa senso* (The Pacific War, 1968). Still courtesy of Oshima Productions.

54. Oshima's selection and juxtaposition of such images as this "Boy soldiers going off to war" shows the desperate straits of the Japanese nation at this point in the war. *Daitoa senso* (The Pacific War, 1968). Still courtesy of Oshima Productions.

another newsreel from Leyte, the Philippines, kamikaze attacks are presented as a measure of their combatants' devotion for which the Japanese should be proud, but in the montage context of Oshima's film, the kamikaze strategy seems another measure of hopelessness. The air raid on Tokyo and General Tojo's telegram of apology for failing to shield Japan's capital further the air of defeat, yet this is still interlaced with a new segment on boy workers. Finally the evacuation of schoolchildren brings even the theme of youthful hope and regeneration into retreat.

Then comes news of the bombing of the imperial palace and the Meiji shrine and the U.S. taking of Okinawa. Following are reports of the July 26, 1945, Potsdam declaration, the August 6, 1945, bombing of Hiroshima, and the bombing of Nagasaki on August 9. These reports, while mentioning a new type of bomb, claim that the losses seem light. The newsreel, in what is surely the oddest attempt to put a positive spin on events, emphasizes how only a few U.S. planes and single bombs were involved in each instance. The Soviet attack on Manchuria is reported in the interim that comes between the atomic devastation of the two Japanese cities and the August 15, 1945, narration by the emperor of his surrender. Implicit in this series is an exposition of how even at the end the Japanese government withheld information such as the extent of the devastation at Hiroshima and Nagasaki. The propaganda machine was intact until the end, coloring events so as to control the populace. There is little indication that film producers ever wanted to break with the official line or surreptitiously work to stop the war once defeat seemed likely.

The end of the film is simply the Japanese death toll:

2,533,425 soldiers
2,517,406 civilians

Oshima's documentary is not a history of the war, but a document of documents. It covers only what was reported to the Japanese, and covers that only selectively. One could argue that in its self-imposed restrictions, it does not adequately place these propaganda pieces in a broader context that would reveal their full horror. If one does not know about the rape of Nanking, or denies it, as do some Japanese, if one does not understand the oil and resource quest that spurred the Japanese imperialist expansion, if one does not know of the suppression of all domestic dissent and the murder of countless Japanese and peoples of the various occupied lands, the historical implications of these propaganda artifacts are not fully clear. Yet Oshima seems to accept that not all viewers will learn all they need to know about the war from his film. It aims instead at an internal realization of the contradiction and the collapse of a discourse. It inevitably presents this in a perspective not only directed at the Japanese, but with the Japanese themselves at the center, and in that sense even the contradictions it shows could be seen as largely narcissistic and woefully inadequate to the lessons that one might hope that Japanese should learn from the war. If it is easy to point out the gaps, the unsaid in such a documentary, and if these gaps are similar to those left by *Merry Christmas, Mr. Lawrence,* Oshima's fictional film set in wartime, this documentary sets its sights elsewhere.

One topic that is evoked without direct mention is the U.S. war in Vietnam. Perhaps the parallel is suggested through the numerical names of Doolittle's B-29s and the B-52s used in bombing raids over North Vietnam; such links between World War II and Vietnam are more clearly at work in a later documentary of Oshima's, *Human Drama: 28 Years of Hiding in the Jungle,* to be discussed later in this chapter. Questions of the U.S.–Japanese competition for imperial influence in the Pacific that precedes World War II and continues in various late manifestations through this day certainly resonate throughout the propaganda as it is revisited, especially for a leftist audience. So if Oshima is aiming a very critical regard at his nation's imperialist adventure, the resonance of this toward the war going on at the time his film is made should not be overlooked.

RETURNING TO THE WARRIOR

When Oshima scrutinizes the warrior as documentary subject again in *Ikiteiru nihonkai kaisen* (The Battle of Tsushima, 1975), it is the survivors of the Russo-Japanese War, men in their nineties at the time, that receive his interrogation. It is, however, the most gentle of questions he poses, and he will end the film with the equally gentle "as these men of the sea talked, they deeply impressed me." As we shall see, this respect for the subjective memories and positions of these soldiers is constructed by Oshima to provide the backdrop for an entirely different point about Japanese history, one that needs to establish the respect due these individuals to show how the Japanese government used and betrayed them in a manner parallel to the Korean soldiers of the earlier documentary.

The former sailors recall their experiences in great and vivid detail while Oshima narrates in alternation. These monologues and narrative passages are illustrated with wood-block prints and photographs.

Oshima's questions address how they decided when to shoot, why they won this war against the Russians, and what might constitute a just versus unjust war. This last question wants to differentiate Japan's defensive position in this war versus its aggression in all the later battles and wars of the twentieth century.

The most critical point Oshima wants to make is what happened after this war, when, despite the victory and despite the action of these men in defense of Japan, the war treaty provided no reparations from the Russians to the

Japanese. The protests against their government's failure to negotiate in their interest that ensued are seen by Oshima's commentary as the "first split between the State and people."

Oshima's next documentary, *The Dead Remain Young* (1977), chronicles a memorial service for a group of civilian victims of a torpedo attack in World War II, a large number of whom were Okinawan children. The boat, the *Tsushima-maru,* was sunk by a U.S. torpedo while traveling from Okinawa to the mainland in 1944. The name of the boat links this documentary to *The Battle of Tsushima,* for the boat is named after the strait in which the navy met success in that famous battle. The name ties the events of one war to the events of another in a purely dreamworklike associative manner.

The battle that forced the Japanese surrender of Saipan on July 7 resulted in the death of great many civilians, 80 percent of whom were Okinawan. The fall of the Japanese occupation in Saipan placed Okinawa at the southernmost point of Japan's defense. Fearing another slaughter, the Japanese ordered the evacuation of old people, women, and children. Schoolchildren were sent to study on the main Japanese islands. Of the 1,661 people who left, 1,484 died. Only 59 of the children survived; 736 died.

Oshima's interviews are aimed at allowing the Okinawans to express their feelings. Japanese restraint in expressing feelings is often contrasted to both Korean and Okinawan openness. Over the course of these interviews the feelings range from survivor's guilt to an admission of earlier denial—refusal to believe the children were gone—and intense mourning.

The role of this documentary is directly linked to Oshima's *Dear Summer Sister* in its focus on Okinawa, particularly on the children of Okinawa. They stand as a kind of double innocence in relation to the Japanese war effort, first as children but also as a conquered people with a different culture and language from the alleged homogeneity of the other Japanese islands.That homogeneity breaks down with any closer look at regional, ethnic, and class differences, especially those conditioned by the separateness of an island identity.

Guam is the setting of the last of Oshima's documentaries to focus on the soldier and on World War II, *Yokoi Shoichi: Guam to 28 nen no nazo o on* (Human Drama: 28 Years of Hiding in the Jungle, 1977). Yokoi Shoichi is the famous survivor of the war who lived in isolation in Guam, fearing surrender and retaliation for the entire postwar period. To tell his story, Oshima alternates a pictorial and narrated representation of postwar developments, a time line of the postwar years, with the recovery of Yokoi's personal narrative, his Robinson Crusoe–like survival story in which he lived oblivious to these events. A trip with Yokoi back to his hideout on Okinawa is the visual narrative means for the documentary exploration of how he held onto the war while Japan changed. Once again, Oshima's strategy

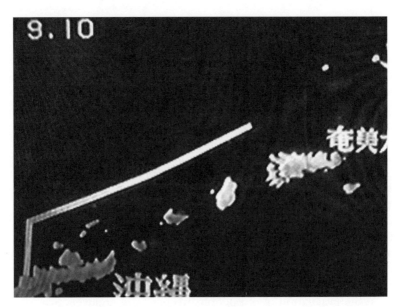

55. A map insert indicates the trajectory of the ship, *Tsushima-maru*, as it sailed into waters where U.S. torpedo ships were seeking naval targets in the final stages of World War II. *Shisha wa itsuma demo wakai—Okinawa gakudo sokai-sen no higeki* (The Dead Remain Young, 1977). Still courtesy of Oshima Productions.

56. A shot of the memorial service for the civilian victims of a torpedo attack in World War II, a large number of whom were Okinawan children. *Shisha wa itsuma demo wakai—Okinawa gakudo sokai-sen no higeki* (The Dead Remain Young, 1977). Still courtesy of Oshima Productions.

57. Portrait of an Okinawan child who was a victim of a torpedo attack
after the Japanese ordered evacuation. *Shisha wa itsuma demo wakai—
Okinawa gakudo sokai-sen no higeki* (The Dead Remain Young, 1977).
Still courtesy of Oshima Productions.

highlights the individual's response while it places the shifts in postwar
Japan in sharp relief.

Of the 21,000 Japanese on Guam, 20,000 were killed and the Japanese
commander responded by committing suicide, the film's narration tells us.
Before turning to Yokoi's story, Oshima prefaces his decision to hide out with
interviews with other Japanese soldiers who either surrendered or escaped
by sea. The interviews with Minigawa and Nihei tell of how hard and dangerous the sea route was; those who surrendered are represented by Yoshida
Yajimi. Some surrendered in April 1945, the rest on September 4, and this
only after the August 15 surrender of the emperor. From these other interviews, Yokoi's actions are made more understandable, given that they establish the fear driving the Japanese soldiers, much of it instilled by their officers, who warned them falsely of torture. While a more traditional taboo
against surrender as cowardly according to the Bushido, the code of the
samurai, may have played a part, Oshima's documentary argues instead that
more immediate misinformation from superiors motivated the Japanese soldier to such harsh alternatives to surrender.

Of the seven holdouts, only three survived for any length of time. Koichi

58. Oshima interviewing Yokoi Shoichi, the famous survivor of the war who lived in isolation in Guam fearing surrender and retaliation for the entire postwar period. *Yokoi Shoichi: Guam to 28 nen no nazo o on* (Human Drama: 28 Years of Hiding in the Jungle, 1977). Still courtesy of Oshima Productions.

speaks of the two other long-term survivors, Shichi and Nakahata, from whom he separated after finding communal survival impossible. Poignantly, he tells of periodic reunions on holidays after he decamped from the others and of the missed reunions as being his evidence of their deaths.

Yokoi also tells of seeing U.S. planes going to Vietnam, providing one of the most significant points the film makes. As the phrasing of Oshima's questions about the planes makes clear, Oshima knew of this passage in Yokoi's previously published memoirs. The sighting of the planes then can be seen as one of Oshima's motivations for making the film, as it works, like his revelations of critical information late in the other documentaries, to cast the film into another more captious light. It provides a sidelong glance at the historical ironies of the repetition of imperialist ventures in Southeast Asia.

One might suppose Yokoi thought, on seeing the U.S. planes, that the war was still continuing. Instead, he tells us the reasons he thought the planes were evidence to the contrary, a sign of a peace treaty:

> The American planes became very pretty. . . . I could see them but they never flew north, always southwards, southwards. I thought they were going

59. The return visit to the island and the representation of recording the interview infuse Oshima's film retelling the story of Yokoi Shoichi with a self-conscious examination of one individual's experience. *Yokoi Shoichi: Guam to 28 nen no nazo o on* (Human Drama: 28 Years of Hiding in the Jungle, 1977). Still courtesy of Oshima Productions.

for practice. They also looked prettier too. Planes during the war were much dirtier and there were more of them together.

Only when he returned to Japan, in retrospect, did he realize that these planes where headed for Vietnam. Again Oshima has linked one war to the next in the most uncanny of ways. Further, he leaves it to the viewer to draw political conclusions from this symbolic anecdote.

Yokoi's is presented as a "human drama," which Oshima constructs both from retelling Yokoi's ingenious efforts at survival and from subjective passages, such as Yokoi's survivor's guilt, much like that of the Okinawan children who survived the sinking of the *Tsushima-maru*. Yokoi wrote in his memoir, and repeats at Oshima's prompting, of seeing the ghosts of friends after returning to Japan:

> When the date of my return to Japan was set, the curtain rail of my room would turn into huge written characters. I would only see it when I was alone. I don't know whether this was because I may have become neurotic and the neurosis was the problem. I would also hear the voices of my friends accusing me of returning to Japan by myself and leaving them behind, and these sounds too would disappear if some person came into my room. I

thought that this had to stop so I got some paper from Mr. Stustsui, and on it I wrote to the spirits of Nakahata and Shichi and to the souls of the Imperial war dead, and kept it by my pillow. I don't know if the reason is that I became more rested, or whether what I wrote really had some effect, but I wasn't troubled after that.

In many ways, this passage serves as an apt metacommentary for Oshima's documentary projects of 1976–1977. They can be seen as efforts by Oshima to exorcise the ghosts of Japanese wars.

AN EARLY CRITIQUE OF CHINA'S CULTURAL REVOLUTION

Moutakuto to Bunka Daikakumei (Mao and the Cultural Revolution, 1969) is a document of great historical significance, as it was made at the moment when parts of the international left were embracing Maoism as an alternative ideal model. Oshima creates a document that honors and explains Mao and is especially laudatory about the early stages of Mao's life and revolutionary leadership, even as it does so in the shadow of questions about the cultural revolution. As the film progresses, it presses these questions concerning the cultural revolution, which many on the left were not yet raising; it begins to explore the contradictions in Mao's mid-sixties leadership.

The film begins with Mao in close-up on October 1, 1966, his face serious even as he listens to cheers of a large crowd. "Why did you start this great cultural revolution?" Oshima's voice asks. Throughout the film Mao will be questioned by Oshima's voice, as images of historical occurrences and quotes from Mao's writings "respond."

Texts that appear on-screen in poetic graphic layout are read aloud. The film introduces famous quotes from the *Quotations of Chairman Mao,* the red book, for example, "A revolution is not a dinner party, writing an essay or making embroidery; it is an insurrection, an act of violence in which one class overthrows another." These citations are initiated by images of loyal red guards, marching in identical uniforms waving their books, and they will continue to punctuate the documentary, though in an increasingly ironic manner.

Historical footage of the May Fourth movement of 1919 against the unequal treaties introduces the retrospective view of history offered to situate Mao. Instead of emphasizing Japan here, the film makes the valid link to earlier signing of the unequal treaties with Britain and Germany. The film neglects to explore Japan's own imperialist role in China at this stage of history, however; in treaty negotiation at Versailles, Japan claimed German possessions in Shandong as its reward for its naval support of the Allies in World War I. Historians now see the granting of Japan's claim as crucial in explaining the eruption of the May Fourth protest, and as prefiguring Japan's invasion of China later in the century (Spence 1990:293–294).

Instead, the film shows images of the Ch'ing dynasty, complete with close-ups on long fingernails, as a sort of historical flashback. The film tells us Mao was born "in these miserable times," a vague manner of establishing his 1893 birthdate, as the Ch'ing dynasty moves toward its collapse of 1912. His natal house, a painting of a student organization, and a close-up of his journal illustrate his youth. While certainly not a detailed analysis of his entrance into revolutionary activity, the film seeks to establish the prevailing conflicts over leadership and politics of his youth. "Sun Yat-sen had become a powerful leader among the warlords in the north, Chiang Kai-shek his apparent heir," is the film's encapsulation of the early development of the Guomindang. Mao, in contrast, "argues for peasant revolution." We are shown how his collaboration with the Guomindang ends with the red purge, and the Long March establishes Mao's leadership. If the history here is sketchy and rushed, it is illustrated by maps that help explain the movements of the opposing parties and with images from the Long March.

More citations from Mao intervene, such as, "Every communist must grasp this truth: political power grows out of the barrel of a gun." The citations surround a poem by Mao, a poem that gives us a softer side, linking him to Chinese cultural resistance and its tradition of leftist poets and essayists. Although not named as such, this montage introduces the notion of unresolved contradiction with which the film will end. It emphasizes that these contradictions were already a factor during the Long March and asks us to consider what historical circumstances, such as betrayals, force such contradictions.

The Japanese invasion of Manchuria is presented as a key moment. "Mao, you suggest an anti-Japanese collaboration with Chiang Kai-shek to form a united front," the narration tells us in its game of direct address to the Chairman. An insert of a fragment of Edgar Snow's famous interview with Mao offers Snow's speculation that Mao could become a very great man. In the mountains, Mao prepares for war against Japan. "You rely on masses," the voice says simply. Japan attacks and captures Beijing, Shanghai, and Nanking; the documentary shows this and the mass slaughter that follows the occupation of Nanking from the Chinese perspective. "You wrote on protracted war, believing China would win in the end," the commentary says, confronting the Japanese audience with the Chinese perspective on Japanese aggression and atrocities. In a context in which Japanese denial of the Nanking massacre is still a burning issue, Oshima's method is to express its impact on China and imply how exposure to such brutality would strengthen Mao's resolve. Although Oshima missed his chance to make the historical connection to Japan's role in 1919, in treating Manchuria he makes the case for identification with Mao and the Chinese against Japan.

In contrast, the film shows the Guomindang reestablishing its government in Chungking, receiving arms from the United States, as China enters the second stage of its war against Japan. It tells us "as World War II breaks out in Europe, China gains new allies." The documentary presents the 7th National Congress of the Communist party, then shows that Mao controls the third stage of the war. Japan is in retreat, as the United States helps the Guomindang to disarm Japanese troops.

The next segment, on the civil war of 1946–1949, begins and ends with more quotes on armed struggle. It begins with "Weapons are important, but they are not decisive. It is people, not things, that are decisive." Then the direct address follows: "Mao, you visited Chunking for the first time in your life; the talks go nowhere. Mao, you sign a meaningless agreement and return to Yenan." From here the film chronicles the Guomindang's all-out attack on the People's Liberation Army (PLA) in 1946 and the counterattack that began as the Guomindang had become scattered and its supply lines thin. Noting that the Guomindang's losses and desertions were high, the film celebrates the October 1947 winter offensive by the PLA and its pursuit of land reform. In the context of the U.S. support of the Guomindang, the voice says of Mao, "You felt that weapons, even atomic bombs, were not decisive." Here military force is contextualized in relation to U.S. domination.

Efforts to put Mao in the most positive light continue, as the film shows the 1949 PLA capture of Beijing, then Nanking, then the expulsion of foreigners from Shanghai. It includes the closing of a Ford showroom. The film then returns us once again to the past of colonialism to fully justify this expulsion, saying that previously Shanghai was a paradise for foreigners and displaying a sign in old Shanghai, "Chinese and dogs not permitted in the park." Noting that on October 1, 1949, the central Communist party government rallied in the same Beijing square that saw the May Fourth demonstration, the film makes the 1949 revolution the completion of the promise of China's revolutionary protesters thirty years earlier.

So far this film is quite pro-Maoist. However, with the positioning of the quote "All reactionaries are paper tigers" at this point between the communist revolution and the internal strife of the 1960s, the film purposefully lets the quote aim for several different political and military targets. The shift from celebration to the renewed questioning begins to emerge, as we are told that Lin Shaoqui was purged (in 1968) because he believed class struggle had come to an end, "but you, Mao, believed that class struggle continued, even in socialist countries." This might still seem to support Mao, and it handles the purge rather vaguely, but given what follows, it can be seen as an indication that Oshima is not taking the pure Maoist line on Lin Shaoqui, seeing his demise rather as a marker of the type of disaffection with both central party rule and the cultural revolution offered in this statement by a student sent to a rural village, after Lin Biao was stripped of power (in 1971, after Oshima's film was made):

> When Lin Shaoqui was dragged down we'd been very supportive. At the time Mao Zedong was raised very high. . . . But the Biao affair provided us with a major lesson. We came to see that the leaders up there could say today that something is round; tomorrow that it's flat. We lost faith in the system. (Spence 1990: 617)

The film then backtracks historically, as if to look for another explanation, a counterhistory to its previous treatment of Mao. It looks back to the years between 1945 and 1950, when Mao meets with Stalin and then Khrushchev. And it shows the withdrawal of Soviet engineers from China in 1960.

A montage of images of Korea accompanies this personal address: "Chairman Mao, you lost your son in the Korean war, fighting against UN forces, primarily the U.S." Then a parallel montage of Third World countries is joined by the pointed question, "I wonder about the strength and depth of your leadership of underdeveloped countries—you know China, but do you know Third World circumstances?" This question is direct and critical and seems greatly suspicious of the manner in which Maoism was theoretically perceived among leftists in Japan, France, and the United States, how China was taken as the theoretical model of peasant rebellion for Third World revolutionary movements. It bears the implied weight of what might be called Oshima's critique of China's late sixties foreign policy. Oshima's concern with Korea and Vietnam, countries that intensely fear China for historical reasons, seems to lie behind this sort of questioning; it is prophetic of the later antagonisms between postwar Vietnam and the People's Republic of China.

At this point in the film it seems clear that Oshima is willing to critique Mao and the Chinese Communist party in the same way that he might the USSR and the Japanese Communist party. The film ends with these scathing questions:

> Haven't you destroyed the myth of central leadership to create the myth of the people's trust in Chairman Mao? Are you teaching revolution? Or is the cultural revolution suppressing revolution? Once you said, as the people learned, even Marx and Lenin may come to appear foolish. You are still trying to express the future of China all by yourself. Isn't this a great contradiction? The great contradiction of a great leader of the twentieth century?

Among Sinologists and certainly among Maoist leftists, the critical view inherent in these questions was rare in 1969 and would only be adopted years later, after verification of the atrocities, excesses, and abuses of power of the cultural revolution forced acknowledgment that it was not simply a period of noble renewal of socialist practice corresponding to revolutionary theory. The accounts of atrocities would take years to be seen by leftists outside China as something more than right-wing propaganda aimed at discrediting Mao Zedong. Oshima's documentary is therefore historically important as an early attempt by an intellectual associated with the left, but taking an East Asian historical perspective, to be critical of the Chinese Communist party in a manner that has become commonplace since the recent repression of the democracy movement.

SUBJECTS AND KNOWLEDGE

I have looked at Oshima's documentary career independently from his feature work to stress its historical and theoretical contribution in a Japanese context. Here Oshima tries to address and increase consciousness in the direct manner he adopts. His means here will often still depend on an ironic voice, even as this voice pursues a discourse directly addressing the viewer. These documentaries struggle with the questions Oshima has his radical filmmaking collective pose in *The Battle of Tokyo, or the Story of the Young Man Who Left His Will on Film:* how to turn film into a weapon in a struggle that simultaneously needs to define itself in relation to larger questions of knowledge, history, and the subject. Sometimes it means shutting down his external voice, allowing documents to speak for themselves, as in *The Pacific War.* Sometimes it means focusing on individuals, the costs and frustrations for people who are introduced as representative of disenfranchised groups. Knowing a political struggle means more than just presenting an analysis of history and social inequities. It means also asking hard questions about investments of desire: why people feel as they do, and why others have not paid attention to their situation. What causes and constitutes "not knowing," even when one knows the information that should make one conscious of a problem?

In closing I would like to make a brief mention of Oshima's documentaries that are less directly political, for in not directly addressing inequities, forgotten histories, and the structure of Japanese nationhood, they still speak to the structuration of subjectivity. *Kyojin-gur* (Giants, 1972), composed of a series of interviews with baseball players from Tokyo's team, looks at how individuals see themselves in relation to this game that has so much historical significance for Japan. *Kori no naka no seishun* (Youth on the Ice, 1962) provides views of ice fishing and of children born into a geographic setting, a village on Lake Hachiro in Akita Prefecture, that imposes its own economic and social imperatives on their lives. *Hahinosu-jo no kiroku* (Hidden Fortress, 1964) portrays a hermit whose desire to live apart from others and shield himself from a modern world takes the form of building a "castle" on a site the government had claimed for a dam. His very individualized rebellion against the Japanese postwar state combines elements of right-wing and left-wing resistance, the polarity that becomes in a certain sense "common ground" for the cousins in *Ceremonies.* It is possible to see each of these films in its own way determinedly asking, What does it mean to participate in the social? How is the subject formed?

So even when Oshima is more directly exploring a political issue such as the formation of a new Asian nation, Bangladesh, in *Joi Bengla!* (1972) and *Ougon no daichi Bengal* (The Golden Land of Bengal, 1976) his focus is on celebration and examination of a nation as a promise to its people, a promise known best by looking at the people and their desires. Alone in his look at nations and peoples, Bangladesh at this historical juncture seems cause for celebration; it is perhaps its hope at this moment, in contrast to Vietnam, Korea, China, and Japan, that so strikes Oshima. Here is where we see something of Oshima's investment in the subject of desire, an investment so strong that it may sometimes overwhelm other ideological analyses he might make. Oshima's political voice, most direct in the documentaries, still carries with it the impulses of desire foregrounded in the fiction films even when they are "coming from the wrong place." Perhaps this is what the documentarist learns in the field, that the desire to make images and to show images may contradict a predetermined devotion to a certain political perspective. One senses that Oshima's documents are fieldwork of this sort, a process open to discovery. The debate over filmic modes in *The Battle of Tokyo* then gives us a window on this process, not as already resolved but as an open question posed by the filmmaker to himself and to us.

CHAPTER EIGHT

Feminist Troubles on a Map
of Split Subjectivities

"A woman whose whole sensual being is as wild and natural as the flaming rays of the Sun!" These are the words used in an English-language publicity brochure to describe Hanako, the heroine of Oshima's *Burial of the Sun* in 1960. Though Oshima may have had nothing to do with this exploitation strategy (indeed, he said years later that he never saw this brochure when it was issued at the time of the film's release), Shochiku's publicity tactics indicate how the heroine of this film could be appropriated for such sideshow barker salesmanship. For in the historical context of 1960s Japan, the depiction of Hanako's physical appearance and comportment in the film, coupled with this publicity promise of wild female sensuality, announces a modern, Westernized woman whose figure, clothing, demeanor, and attitude break with the traditional Japanese ideal of demure, self-sacrificing, and self-effacing purity.

Hanako becomes an image available for sexual exploitation, used to sell the film, with all the misogyny and objectification this implies. The fantasy of a sexually free and wild creature, displaying pointed breasts in tight sweaters and a curvaceous body in tight slacks or short skirts, is part of an appeal to a "pink film" (pornography) market, already lucrative at this juncture and steadily growing within the Japanese industry.

The publicity's comparison of Hanako to the sun also presents this heroine by evoking the sun tribe film genre to which, as we have seen in chapter 2, the title *Burial of the Sun* refers. In 1960 it is unclear what valence the "sun tribe" reference would have outside Japan. Nor would the sun imagery necessarily suggest a subversion of the Shinto sun goddess that it might to a Japanese audience. Even so, the sun metaphors of the brochure evoke flaming female passion, the promise of witnessing the display of nymphomania. It is

Shochiku GrandScope In Eastman Color

THE SUN'S
BURIAL
(TAIYO NO HAKABA)

A SHOCHIKU FILM

60. Cover of a press book used to publicize Oshima's film *Taiyo no hakaba*
(Burial of the Sun, 1960) in Asian
markets outside Japan, emphasizing
in image and in copy the heroine's
seductiveness. Still courtesy of Oshima
Productions.

possible that Oshima did not share his studio's willingness to market his film
and exploit his heroine in such a manner, but one can still question how his
film might unconsciously serve the same ends. The publicity brochure becomes an indication of aspects of the film's presentation and use of woman
as figure. Her superficially free and wild characteristics lend themselves to
imagery of a larger exploitation scheme.

Earlier I suggested that the film's title speaks to the demise of hope in
Japan, as symbolized not just by the slum setting but also as burial of the rising sun, indicating a film that is far more critical, political, and cynical in its
references to the sun tribe genre than the publicity that tries to place the film
squarely within that genre. These dual aspects cohabit the film; while it critiques a potentially exploitative entertainment genre, it simultaneously seeks
to appeal to the audience of this genre.

The heroine serves this dual purpose, for Hanako also offers an eloquent image of the contemporary antiheroine that Oshima draws so remarkably throughout his films. She is depicted as a woman whose repudiation of the traditional Japanese feminine role takes the form of social deviance and defiance. Not simply an emblem of sexism and exploitation, she becomes part of a symbolic reconfiguration of class, gender, and identification. She thus serves as an element in a strategic engagement with the politics of narrative. Her actions unravel commonly held notions of the function of a heroine; she cannot be viewed as an image apart from the text, for she is an agent of its process of posing precisely the kinds of questions about womanhood and society an external critique of her as image would address.

Are these two views of Hanako and the film just a difference of readings? The reading of Hanako as an antiheroine appears closer to the text, while the reading of Hanako as a sexually exploited element appears more sociohistorical in that it considers audience and the system of production, distribution, and exhibition. Oshima's status as an auteur and intellectual filmmaker has obviated concern with the sexual representation and spectator reception of his films; there has been a tendency to assume from the outset a textual system that is so challenging and progressive that such questions fall below the level of discourse adopted by the films. In positing Oshima's metatheoretical discourse on voyeurism in the cinema, Heath (1981: 145–164), for example, did not focus on how women accrue restricted representations within such a discourse, even though his theories that focus comparatively on classical cinema consider just such issues.

In examining the representation of women in Oshima's films, we must consider both kinds of readings, not in isolation, but in interaction. Neither reading stands alone, as "correct"; each needs to take the other into account rather than insist unilaterally on its dominance. It will not do to resolve this tension by declaring that the films display considerable ambiguity as regards the contemporary Japanese woman. Ambiguity, as symptomatic as it might be, is an insufficient label that closes, rather than opens, the analysis before us. Instead, let us consider how this struggle of filmic textuality engaged in by Oshima's films raises crucial questions concerning women's relationship to power, sexuality, and their own female identities.

First we must confront the referential and contextual aspects of this representation, the problem of cultural and historical specificity. This problem takes several forms, many of which are common to other Japanese films and involve the background set for interpretation. Questions need to be posed. What is the history of Japanese womanhood? What is the history of feminism in Japan? Of social classes? What is the history of sexuality there—discourse and social practice? How have women been represented in Japanese literature, art, and theater? How has this changed since World War II? How do all these questions differ when asked in relation to Tokyo, to other Japanese cities, or to rural life?

Much of the writing on Japanese film ignores or vaguely touches on these historical questions, supposing that the films themselves are all we need to consider as evidence. There are three reasons for this vagueness, the first of which is an assumption of a universality that denies cultural and historical specificity. Another is that a portion of the writing on Japanese films remains exclusively formalist or auteurist in approach. Third, writing on Japanese film remains vague historically because it is steeped in the weakest version of reflection theory, analyzing the films to learn about the culture.

For Oshima's films, the issues are even more complicated because of the frame his textual strategies build for sociohistorical references, the very processes we have been examining throughout this book. The means by which his fictions can be understood as discourse are different, just as their processes of textuality are different.

We arrive at a basic question of the ideologies of representation within modernism and by extension, postmodernism: How does one analyze the ideologies of representations within narratives that are nonrealistic? Readings based on psychology of character or psychoanalytic schemas of character relations that form the basis of much current feminist criticism neglect to consider how modernist texts may already deconstruct such categories in their textual strategies. Yet for their part, modernist texts may not take into account certain meanings inherent in some of the images they mobilize as elements of their strategies. I will call these meanings "residual restrictive signifiers," clusters of connotations that surround womanhood and retain key elements of a sexist ideology. Woman (as concept) can be caught up and used by this process in a manner that is irreconcilable with feminism. Yet I want to suggest that some of the means through which women are mobilized within Oshima's symbolic structures do not simply reproduce and exploit sexist attitudes toward women, but rather open up an investigation of women as subjects within contemporary Japanese culture. This is not to say that the films are consistently feminist, but rather that within the exploration of desire that has a certain sexism to it, women as category call the question, or at least can be made to call the question, by readings that force these issues to the foreground. Women in these films complicate the male notions of sexual liberation of desire that are assigned an energetic function of releasing the Japanese subject from the oppression of a group identity.

WOMEN IN DIALOGUE

Let us look further at the example of Hanako in *Burial of the Sun*. Hanako is depicted as the apparently motherless daughter of a lower-class Japanese man living in a slum in Osaka, a city characterized by industrial urban sprawl. The father-daughter relationship is accentuated symbolically; her father is a leader of a right-wing black market gang, which makes her the symbolic

female progeny of a nostalgic criminal militarism. She dresses in flamboyant and sexy fifties Western fashions ranging from sweetheart party dresses
to bobby-soxer jeans and loose shirts (fashions that made her accessible as
a contemporary punk to the audience the film attracted in its 1985 rere-
lease). This assimilation of Hanako to the present is a very specific and fascinating audience appropriation of a filmic text, but it masks the harder
problem of what Hanako represents within the context of Japan historically.
What is the status of Hanako as referential object? This opens up to a larger
question: What is the status of cultural/historical references in general in
Oshima's films?

Hanako is a figure of condensation, several stereotypes drawn to an extreme and then superimposed on each other. Like so many characters in
Oshima, she is obsessed with scams, or illegal commerce. As the lowest class
of prostitute, she represents in extreme form the same strategies of economy
and survival that characterize Japanese bar hostesses.

Constrained by employment practices that relegate women to the lowest
salaries and least secure positions, the urban working-class woman often
chooses the less-than-respectable but more highly lucrative bar hostessing
over the grueling and demeaning corporate "office lady" jobs (Carter and
Dilatush 1976; Matsumoto 1976). Hanako is an exaggeration of this scrap-
ping of the ideals surrounding Japanese woman in favor of a career as cal-
culating sex entrepreneur. Yet despite exaggeration, the image gains force
when we recognize that phenomenon has been the subject of many sociological studies (e.g., Jackson 1976). Women adopt this self-exploitation in a
culture that offers them few alternatives. Rather than vilify or pity Hanako,
the film simply asserts her. She becomes a statement of a rude force of survival that takes its context to task without apology.

Hanako also might seem to be the personification of Western influence.
In one sense, she appears as a residual artifact of the Occupation. She might
also be seen as an echo in the present of the precedent set by the Moga, the
"Modern Girl" of the Taisho period (Silverberg 1991). A number of factors,
including the despair and cynicism that accompanied defeat, economic de-
pression, and a demand for prostitutes and female entertainers by the occupying force, encouraged the growth of illegitimate, parallel economies.
Hanako's dress in American fashions is as symptomatic as is her will to survive through the black market of a particular response to the historical conditions of the years 1946–1952. Such a climate lingered on well past the Occupation itself, which the film portrays through the links it suggests between
two generations of hoodlums; the right-wing elements of the parental generation, nostalgically tied to the militarist ideologies of the thirties, actually
compete with their children, born of the cynical survival tactics that characterized a sector of postwar Japan. The film never suggests, however, that
conditions of life in the Kama-ga-saki slum can be seen as simply caused by

the Occupation or even by foreign influences that predate World War II, a hypothesis that would only support a corruption-from-the-outside mystique serving the nativist myth of Japanese purity. Corruption is instead posited at the heart of the culture; Hanako does not partake in the hypocrisy that covers that corruption with ideologies of communal identities. Utter and desperate selfishness rules her behavior and all those around her. Yet even when Hanako is portrayed as most ruthless and unfeeling, she simultaneously appears logical, entrepreneurial, and savvy. Like Mack in Brecht's *Threepenny Opera,* Hanako is a figure whose cynical rules are meant to point out injustices inherent in justice, the other face of humanist ideals. It is intriguing to cast such a character not as a male seducer and rapist but as a woman who violates the womanhood in her own being: intriguing, but not unproblematic.

In addition, Hanako, like her male counterparts in the street gang, is to be understood as the political opposite of the active leftist students dominating the headlines at the time this film was made. It is as if Oshima, former student leftist himself, looked to the opposite of the educated radical to display, rather than voice, his critique of society. So Hanako is charged with an alienation and rebellion that explode as anger and retaliation, though at the end she simply vows to continue her life with the phrase "We have work to do." The explosion that burns down her father's ghetto comes less from her than from the condensed forces that brought her into this allegorical fictional existence.

A young Japanese woman, even a street prostitute who might be thought by certain audiences to be capable of any behavior, would probably not behave as Hanako does. This implausibility of motivation both indicates the nonrealistic mode of the film's fiction and forces us to ask why a woman was chosen to take this central role in the film. What does sexual difference mean in the allegorical fantasy?

Gender expectations lead us to anticipate that Hanako will be the feminine, humanist center of the film, the woman-reformer. Not only is she not assigned this role from the outset, she resists it at every turn. Her relationship with the youngest gang member, Takeshi, sets up the possibility of tenderness and reform, but their dialogues, typical of the philosophical debates assigned characters in Oshima's films, instead cast Hanako in the role of logically denying empathy and compassion. "Why worry if no one saw—the dead are dead," Hanako comments when Takeshi feels guilty that as a consequence of his raping a stranger, this victim's boyfriend committed suicide. When Takeshi feels queasy about this philosophy, Hanako responds, "At least I'm alive." What makes Hanako intriguing, if absolutely brutal, is precisely her status as woman, as lover of Takeshi. Her response is so unexpected, so outside of her gender boundaries, and the identification she "should" have with other women.

Antiheroines such as Hanako in *Burial of the Sun* become emblems of how the feminine is a site of a historically defined difference in Japan. Oshima's allegories depend on sexual difference as central to portraying the tensions that exist between forces of repression and counterrepression, oppression and counteroppression, within the political unconscious. They are never about women or about feminist issues directly, but instead construe women as an element within configurations of power and desire. Hanako's only route to power is to participate in burials of the sun, repeatedly; she is not a tragic or a sympathetic heroine but an emblem of all that has gone wrong. With no simple humanist response available, we instead get a narrative in which a woman is the emblem of a certain desperation.

Hanako is unique among heroines in Oshima's films only for the degree to which she embodies this. Most of Oshima's women share some of her qualities of witnessing and understanding more than the men around them. Others are intermittently charged with rebellion or corrective action. Feminization of rebellion occurs often in Oshima's films, and it occurs alongside female characters, who, while not rebellious, possess a critical knowledge of Japanese culture that places them at silent or even suicidal odds with it. The Japanese conventions of feminine polite and subservient behavior are here mobilized as the locus of an ideal and of untenable difference, one that is in absolute contradiction with the desiring subject.

Again, feminist sociology has found a similar quiet or desperate antipathy in many Japanese women (Cecchini 1976). Yet the entrance of the feminist critic into the theories of the political unconscious displayed by these texts is not easy. In these allegories the female characters are never placed in the context of Japan's "bluestockings," as the early feminist movement in Japan was called, and the later female role in leftist politics is indicated only enigmatically. Contrast the feminist use of sun imagery in the dedication by Haratsuka Raicho of the feminist journal she began in September 1911 to that surrounding Hanako in *Burial of the Sun* with which I began this chapter: "In the beginning, woman was the sun / An authentic person / Today, she is the moon. / Living through others. / Reflecting the brilliance of others. . . . And now, Bluestocking, a journal created for the first time with the brains and hands of today's Japanese women, raises its voice" (Sievers 1982: 29). Such images of female self-realization are virtually absent from this corpus of films. Still, the role of the antiheroines in Oshima's tales can indicate the female stake in a rebellion against Japanese society, if we extend the process of allegorical readings in our play with these texts.

To see how this works let us look closely at some other female characters in Oshima's films: Makoto and her older sister, Yuki, in *Cruel Story of Youth;* Setsuko and her mother, Ritsuko, in *Ceremonies;* Yasuko in *The Battle of Tokyo;* and the former student Shino and teacher Matsuko in *Violence at Noon.* Women are often paired in these films, their identities defined in relation to one another. Even when a heroine is singular, as, for example, Yasuko, she is presented as a multiple character in which competing and relational identities inhabit the same name and bodily representation. This doubling is a means of problematizing the formation of female identity in a historical context in which it is undergoing transformation.

Take, for example, the pair Makoto and Yuki in *Cruel Story of Youth*. Makoto is the rebellious youth, whom we first meet when she is sneaking back home after a night out with her boyfriend. Yuki is the older sister charged with a maternal role in the absence of their mother, who is deceased. A virtual generational difference is pronounced between them, played out when the two meet together with a teacher at Makoto's private, religious school to discuss Makoto's truancy. However, Yuki is not simply the ideal virtuous Japanese woman, the mother. Whereas Yuki might at first seem to represent all that is traditional and steadfast about Japanese womanhood, we gradually understand that her past was not unlike Makoto's. Her rebellion and love affair took place in the context of the student movement, rather than youth gangs. The fact that she remains a single, working woman is by itself to be taken as some indication of her departure from expectations and norms. Still, she is cast in the role of disciplinarian. In the crisscrossings of the narrative that follows, the two sisters again meet, this time at an abortion clinic; Yuki has come to visit her former lover, the doctor who runs the clinic, while Makoto is there with her lover to have an abortion.

In the reconfiguration of the two couples, Yuki voices her admiration for her sister's ability to act on her desires, in a manner that links political activity and personal rebellion. This scene, praiseworthy for its inventive formal use of voice-over, is also a remarkable narrative conjuncture. The abortion clinic, as site of this revelation, is ironic. For the doctor and Yuki it represents the failure of their aspirations, as community medical care has devolved into the highly commercialized private practice of abortions; in the Japanese health care system abortions are legal, but outside state-funded medical facilities and many abortion clinics are subject to corruption. However, for Makoto, the abortion is the tenderest moment of her relationship; it is represented without guilt as an acknowledgment of selfhood, sexuality, and a defiance of prescribed roles. Visually a shot of Kiyoshi, Makoto's lover, tenderly watching over her recovery as he holds, then eats an apple, registers this affirmation of the moment.

Both sisters, though shrouded with failure and finally death, are seen, like Hanako in her energetic will to survive, as all that is alive in a bleak world. Focusing on the pair of sisters and on women and women's issues in Japan, such as the tradition of religious sex-segregated education and abortion, gives us a different perspective on the film. It becomes more clearly a response to the filmic versions of Shimpa (modern drama) found in films by an earlier generation of filmmakers including Ozu Yasujiru, Naruse Mikio,

254 FEMINIST TROUBLES ON A MAP OF SPLIT SUBJECTIVITIES

and Misoguchi Kenji. It is possible to see *Cruel Story of Youth* as a revision of Misoguchi's *Gion no shimai* (Sisters of the Gion, 1936) or Naruse's *Otome-gokoro sannin shimai* (Three Sisters with Virgin Hearts, 1935) that substitutes distanciation, complication, and a multiedged critique for the more direct pathos attending heroines forced by circumstance to abandon respected Japanese womanhood.

If sisters have been melodramatic figures used to gauge the ravages of modernity in Japanese film, so have mothers and daughters. In *Ceremonies* Oshima embeds a mother-daughter conflict within a larger familial frame generating a critique of patriarchy, as we saw in chapter 3. Here let me emphasize that while Ritsuko and her mother, Setsuko, in *Ceremonies* are both represented as lost objects of desire within the memory of a male character, Masuo, these "objects," as a pair, are granted a subjectivity that undermines and critiques Masuo and his patriarchal grandfather.

The mother-daughter couple share an abiding alienation from the *ie*, the family group, in this case a wealthy industrial family headed by the grandfather. Recall that Ritsuko and her cousin Masuo are incestuously linked through the affair that Masuo's father had with Setsuko, and may in fact be half-siblings. This secret incestuous link was the residue of a grandfather who determined marriages that denied his children's desires. It is in this context that the grandfather further exerts his patriarchal power in the form of rape of Ritsuko.

Knowing alienation characterizes the mother, which eventually the grown daughter comes to share. This alienated disaffection attracts the more naive male hero, but eludes him. He admires these women but remains unable to assume their position and share fully in their alienated consciousness. The film's complex play with voice and modes of internal address that I discussed in chapter 3 sets up this crucial difference in subjectivity, a difference that is a potential of sexual difference itself. Exploitation builds tensions that can initiate a coming to such consciousness within patriarchy.

Setsuko is found stabbed; she either committed suicide or was killed by the grandfather. It is her corpse, dressed in a kimono in the garden, that gives voice to a most directly feminist moment. As the sword is removed, blood gushes forth across the screen, implicating all who stand there watching. Later, the daughter, Ritsuko, who ironically sings the song of the ideal Japanese woman at a family gathering in which each character sings his or her identity, commits suicide, joining her husband, Terumichi, who is also a cousin. She does so as an act of solidarity with his leftist refusal of the family's political meaning. These women who know and who mark their knowledge in their own blood are key in this film's direct and lucid critique of the patriarchal commercial state.

Perhaps Oshima's most complex pair of female protagonists, Shino and Matsuko, however, are found in *Hakuchu no torima* (*Violence at Noon*, 1966,

61. Setsuko is found stabbed; she either
committed suicide or was killed by the
grandfather. It is her corpse, dressed in
a kimono, in the garden that gives voice
to a most directly feminist moment. *Gishiki*
(Ceremonies, 1971). Still courtesy of
Oshima Productions.

though the title literally is closer to "Ghost at Midnight"), a film that I have
not yet discussed in this book but that will serve to consolidate much of what
I want to say about pairs of females represented in Oshima's films. Matsuko
(Koyama Akiko), a high school teacher, is married to Eisuke (Sato Kei), a
man who was formerly the lover of her former student, Shino (Kawaguchi
Saeda). Eisuke has become a "phantom murderer," a serial rapist and killer
of women. He adds to his list of victims, in the film's first scene, the woman
who currently employs Shino as a maid. This highly staccato and synco-
pated film, composed of numerous metonymic shots of short duration, is
bound together by Shino's efforts at intervals, first in correspondence and
later in person, to convince Matsuko of Eisuke's guilt. Shino chooses to contact Matsuko directly rather than aid the police who seek her help in solv-
ing the murders, for she has questions of her own to resolve. Foremost is

62. Women are captives of an abusive killer they both love, and symbolically captives of their own situation in contemporary Japan. *Hakuchu no torima* (*Violence at Noon,* 1966). Still courtesy of Oshima Productions.

Shino's attempt to understand what causes a man to become such a criminal, and it is to her former teacher, an advocate of democracy and of ideal love, to whom she appeals.

Evil and murderous desire composes the philosophical ground from which this bizarre tale is told. Shino and Matsuko participate in a dialogue in which females investigate and question the force of destructive sexuality, a compulsive violence presented as male, as well as their own fascination with and love/hate of the perpetrator of this violence. If Matsuko is at first reluctant to face Shino's accusations and seeks to deny them, it is a contradiction imposed by her own desire for her husband. Yet in the final third of the film, beginning with a scene outside Osaka's castle and continuing through several scenes on a train to Tokyo, the two women begin to share their knowledge.

The camera work of the train sequence is dominated by ingenious alternating angles on the two women and pans on each of them; variation in scale and framing means that no two shots simply repeat or mirror each other and yet, paradoxically, they all do. They systematically link the two women and set up a dialogic tension between the commonality and the oppositionality of their experience, a tension complicated by the way each woman herself embodies a dual identity and switches positions over the course of the exchange.

A remembering of the past complicates this scenario of murder witnessed and guilt investigated; all of these characters once participated in a collective farming venture in a small Japanese village. The film is punctuated by fragmented flashbacks to a suicide that was the demise of this venture; they are inserted abruptly without clear indication of their subjective focalization. The fragmentary images of the flashbacks are at first quite difficult to decipher, but progressively they chronicle disagreements between Eisuke and the son of the village leader, Genji (Toura Mutsuhiro), who had been in love with both Matsuko and Shino. Peasant village culture is thus juxtaposed with contemporary political aspirations for collectives. Obsessions interfere with these aspirations, and politics are contaminated with male compulsions in this allegory of the failure of democratic ideals associated with women. Male drives constitute a refusal of a female leadership alternative. Eisuke rebels unconsciously against Matsuko, his wife.

Genji seems the polar opposite of Eisuke, responsible and honest in contrast to Eisuke's trickery and self-centeredness. However, we first see Genji after his feelings of betrayal by Eisuke have led him to suicide, a suicide that he insists be a double one with Shino. It is Eisuke who saves Shino from hanging but then rapes her. It is only with the culmination of the flashback series toward the end of the film that this event, whose depiction began in the first of the flashbacks, is explained. The explanation is multiple, however. Eisuke first contends that his violence began with violence against a (virtual) corpse (for the film plays with the notion that perhaps Shino was actually killed and then reanimated).

"A corpse is a thing," Eisuke says, yet he contradicts this immediately. Eisuke is, above all, the embodiment of the repetition compulsion, one who acts obsessively, repeatedly, in the same perverse fashion. Yet this repetition compulsion does not rest with him alone; it pervades the entire narrative, governing its structure and affecting the women. Matsuko, the teacher, is unable to bear seeing her humanist principles overturned in her most intimate relationship and unwilling to confront her own dual nature as fascinated woman and principled moralist. This inability apparently forces her suicide. In a repetitive gesture, she enlists Shino to commit double suicide with her, as Genji had done. As with Genji, Shino again survives, and it is that survival that ends the film on a note of utter hopelessness, as Shino carries the corpse of her teacher into the village.

The failure of political idealism, the splitting of the subject that forecloses all nonhypocritical, all positively motivated, action, and the captivation of the subject by forces beyond conscious control are a few of the highly charged pessimistic concepts circulating through this parable. That two women as a pair drive this philosophical inquiry is extraordinary. Their inquiry investigates their relationship to two men, one already a ghost and a martyr and the other a phantom killer and victimizer. Seen as things, to be raped, possessed, betrayed, the women together ask "Why?"

We might ask, in addition, what annihilates their subjectivity, what keeps them from acting as political subjects with a common cause? Sometimes it seems to be an identification with their oppressor (Shino's statement that she is just like Eisuke, and if she had been a man she might have behaved exactly like him). Sometimes it seems to be guilt (Matsuko's maternal, pedagogical hope that she could transform Eisuke through her unconditional love).

Another premise might be precisely the absence of a feminist analysis of power. These women characters, conceived and defined in a challenge to the limitations of sexual difference, are never empowered with the consciousness to effect a transformation of themselves. They may not be the things their rapist insists they are, but equally they cannot be conceived (by themselves or by the film) as autonomous subjects. Feminism is beyond this picture, though constantly evoked by it in absentia.

In a sense that is the condition of virtually all Oshima's films. Never able to imagine or suggest a feminist theoretical reformulation to the philosophical queries his narratives pose, still his filmic parables accentuate the problems incisively. Of course, this is close to some of what Simone de Beauvoir suggests about the writings of the Marquis de Sade, as regards politics, class, power, and sexual difference in her famous essay "Faut-il-brûler Sade?" Yet despite certain overlapping concerns with the power of violence, Oshima is quite unlike de Sade, both because of the changed historical context and because his films are more self-consciously critical of their own suppositions, more willing to tropologically pose questions than simply supply performative answers.

RAPE FANTASIES

It is in light of this proposition that I would like to turn next to just one of those recurring tropes, rape, to investigate the questions and problems its use proposes. *Violence at Noon,* as is true of all the films discussed so far and several other Oshima films, concerns the representation of sexual violence; if I have addressed the representation of women thus far without focusing directly on this aspect of those films, it was to reserve for separate attention what I take to be a major issue in these allegories of subjectivity and power. Rape is pivotal to many of Oshima's narratives. Feminism views rape as a basic violation of the woman's physical and psychological integrity as subject, and no event within a narrative is more highly ideologically charged than the depiction of rape. Most films that depict rape operate within the frame of realism that either creates audience identification with the urges of the rapist or represents the rape in a way that evokes sympathy for the woman as victim. Some even try to present a combination of these two antithetical possibilities.

Oshima's narrative strategies are different. Rape as a narrative event is subject to the same interrogation of the status of an event per se as are all other events in the narrative. Is it to be taken literally or metaphorically? Is the event "real" within the fiction, or "imaginary"? All events in Oshima's films are, in a sense, narrative tropes that one might compare to figures of speech within an elaborate discourse.

Rape as a trope in Oshima's films therefore needs to be analyzed in a manner quite different from the depiction of rape in films whose structure of references is based in a realist tradition. The films avoid eliciting the kind of empathy with character that one might associate with realism, examples of which are plentiful in earlier Japanese filmmakers such as Mizoguchi or Kurosawa. The antisentimental approach Oshima adopts is a reaction to what he has called "mainstream" Japanese cinema, including the "tendency" of leftist cinema in Japan. The questions we need to ask are, What are the sexual politics of the film as it is structured, and what is the ideology of using rape as a trope within the figuration of desire? These are feminist questions drawn not in relation to a "reality" the film is assumed to depict but rather in relation to its use of tropes in a narrative understood as a political and psychoanalytic allegory. Ancillary question then become, Do sentimental traces remain in Oshima's films, and do reference and identification in these films remain despite the textual work of redefinition?

Both *Realm of the Senses* and *Empire of Passion* introduce through rapes an interaction between characters who later become lovers. In *Cruel Story of Youth,* there is an opening rape and a reiteration of rape midway through. In *The Battle of Tokyo, or the Story of the Young Man Who Left His Will on Film,* rape is a figure of repetition, occurring almost periodically, perpetrated not only by the lead character Motoki, who actually has three separate identities, but by other men as well. His sexual violence, once subsided, is displaced onto other characters who also attack his girlfriend. In *Death by Hanging,* the crime the Korean R is accused of is rape, and in the second half of the film, R tries to sort out the difference between his rape fantasies and the rape for which he is condemned but which he does not believe he has committed. These violent beginnings and repetitions become part of a sexual paradigm in which the sexual act shifts meanings. The trope of rape operates rhetorically to literalize what we mean by the "force of desire." It is misleading to extract it from the paradigm, since other sexual scenes interact with and comment on the trope of rape. One of the effects of these shifting representations is to critique the male need to initiate sex violently. This critique of the male is sometimes directly voiced by the female characters, who ask their lovers why they felt they had to behave violently to enact their passion.

One can, however, direct the same critique at the films themselves, which, like their male protagonists, need to begin with and reiterate the violence of desire. Yet we must also see that they do so self-critically as they direct attention at this very question. It is necessary to analyze these narratives as paradigmatic structures rather than linear tales whose ideology is the sum of the interpretation of their individual parts. The issue paradigmatically is the function of desire, within the unconscious and within the social sphere. Some of the exploration is dark and tangled; even in the films that have been read as Brechtian learning plays, the recesses of the unconscious are perhaps less available than is a concept like class relations.

An example of this is *Ceremonies,* which also uses rape as central to its structure. In this film the rape of Setsuko by the grandfather is clearly defined in the film as one of the means by which the patriarch of the clan asserts power. Later in the film Masuo, the weak hero-narrator, asserts his rebellion against this patriarch by seizing the grandfather as his rape victim, though in his "delirium" he calls the grandfather the ideal Japanese woman. The complexities of this pair of rapes are often seen as reducible to a statement such as the one Joan Mellen (1976: 359) makes about the film when she says it exposes "the hypocrisy lying behind the pretensions to dignity of the Japanese family as social institution." If the rapes can be read as a critique of the family and patriarchy, the problems raised by the use of rape as trope are immediately resolved. However, *Ceremonies* is the only film that provides this particular resolution, and even in it we are still confronted with the imaginary rape by Masuo of the pure Japanese woman as his hysterical means of symbolically protesting the rule of the patriarch. Something much more knotted is occurring in these spinning webs of desire and sexual violence than a symbolism of a correct political statement. It is little wonder that Oshima pointedly evades Mellen's implied interpretations in her interview with him:

> Mellen: What is the director's viewpoint toward the people and their relationships, as a family or semifamily?
> Oshima: Both love and hate. I have all human emotions for the family.
> Mellen: Would you say that the film is a representation of your sense of ambivalence toward the family and family relationships?
> Oshima: I am interested in this aspect, but I wouldn't call this my message or the central idea of my film. I don't make films in which I want to send out messages to say something. . . . I don't start out with the assumption that here we have a certain ideology and construct the story of the film accordingly. (1975: 268)

Oshima may end up sounding a bit like an apolitical humanist in this exchange (a stance of which he is not often accused), but his point seems to be that the sexuality and familial relations that structure his films are not available to the type of singular political readings of conscious intention that Mellen regularly seeks in her film criticism. Audie Bock recognizes this, but only in terms of an auteurist anecdote in her book, *Japanese Film Directors*.

> Indeed, in every Oshima film at least one murder, rape, theft or blackmail incident can be found, and often the whole of the film is constructed around the chronic repetition of such a crime. Worse yet, Oshima realized that as the crime in his films escalated, he had more frightening nightmares about himself committing crimes. He would invariably commit rape and mass murder, be caught and then escape to live an ordinary life for some time, only to be caught in his peaceful disguise. (1978: 319)

Auteurism, as I argued in chapter 1, will only succeed in urging us to collapse all the meanings of the films as manifestations of Oshima's own unconscious. My point is rather to show how the trope of rape becomes tied to a narrative working out of the functioning of the unconscious, perhaps specifically a male unconscious at some points in Oshima's films, perhaps sometimes a specifically Japanese unconscious.

Feminist theory can be a major tool in the analysis of this narrative structuration of the unconscious, but it must be directed at the structure and not remain on the surface of representation. It must not see events and their political meanings as the master signifieds of a film, in a form of content analysis that does not consider allegory and filmic expression.

Conversely, while some might hold that to look at Oshima's characters as representations of women is quite beside the point of what they take to be political allegories, I am arguing that these allegories are not simple but already multiple and internally contradictory. The multifaceted feminist questioning of these texts that I have proposed is aimed at revealing and interrogating just this multiplicity.

Let us return to a look at the staccato shots of the opening rapes and murder in *Violence at Noon*. This opening offers such a tour de force of film montage, image, and sound that one is tempted to consider how Oshima might be paying homage to Alfred Hitchcock, rewriting with greater modernist metonymy and abstraction the murder and investigation sequences of the master of the suspense thriller. Certainly the staircase and its wooden banister featured in this sequence (and extremely rare in Japanese domestic architecture) recall Hitchcock, as does the motif of the search for serial rapist/killer, beginning with Hitchcock's breakthrough British film, *The Lodger* (1926). Let us look at some of these remarkable shots to see how the sequence is constructed as one whose sexual violence and formal elegance play at odds with each other.

The first images of the film present a series of shots of Eisuke as voyeur crosscut with extreme close-ups of fragments of Shino's body as she washes the floor, then sings. The voyeurism here is similar to the *Realm of the Senses* scene in which Kichi watches Sada when she is still his maid. Though the fragmentation here is far more extreme, the articulation of voyeurism within a relationship of unequal power is strikingly parallel.

The montage concentrates on fragmented visual abstraction as Eisuke carries Shino up the stairway in bondage. The only dialogue is the ominous line that Eisuke says as they pass an elaborate mirror on a staircase landing: "This is the last time we will be reflected together in a mirror." This prediction carries a theoretical charge within the psychoanalytic frame of Eisuke's acting out of aggression against women, for in terms of Lacan's mirror stage his reference to the mirror is significant. He is "promising" to eradicate the other, Shino, from a shared mirror reflection and thus from the realm of his identity. He will violently remove her from any proximity with his symbolic self-image.

A cut that takes us to a series of shots held as "still-life" images continues to offer mise-en-scène and editing as elements within a psychoanalytic "scrapbook": a rattan mannequin framed against translucent patterned curtain, a corner of the curtain blowing, a high angle on the bottom of the mannequin with a fragment of the curtain behind it, images of flowers strewn haphazardly on the ground, then finally three fragmented images of a woman's corpse. The corpse is offered as another still-life image, in a formal aesthetic that has much in common with the avant-garde film within the film in *The Battle of Tokyo*. The last shot in this subsegment introduces detectives and reintroduces dialogue, resubmerging the spectator in the plenitude of filmic fiction after this formally marked departure into space fragmented and framed as clues to the unconscious.

It should be clear from the above analysis how perversely unlike any pornographic or even realistic depiction of rape and murder this sequence is. The violent action is nearly all offscreen. Violence manifests itself instead only through visual fragmentation and jarring angles in montage, or else becomes displaced entirely by shots that are calm, tableaulike still-lives. Only later, in retrospect, is the titillation of rape as fantasy brought forward, and this only verbally, in a dialogue between the murdered woman's husband and Shino. He asks Shino if the rapist came inside her. When she says no, he speculates that this failure to ejaculate somehow explains the murder of his wife. Here in dialogue we are retrospectively asked to imagine rape in its physical violence, its mixture of sex, anger, and hatred, in its manifestation of a body obsessively out of control.

Let me suggest that the still-life images of the mannequin, curtain, and strewn flowers juxtapose a female world and a gentle aesthetic with a male violence that disrupts this space, just as Eisuke's entrance disrupts Shino's solitary song while she works. On another level, the still-life images fix a context for the corpse as aesthetic object. Not seeing a murder, we have a corpse, elegantly displayed. Given the line that Eisuke gets later, "A corpse is a thing," which I discussed above, the line he uses to justify his first rape of the perhaps already-dead Shino, the ghost story aspect of this allegory becomes clearer. Like Bataille's novel, *La Mort* (The Dead Man), this film can be seen as a meditation on sexuality surrounding a corpse, on the erotics of death, on the ghosts that haunt sexuality. The metacinematic joke in this meditation is the perhaps already-dead filmic character, Shino, who is nonetheless imaged as life and vitality itself.

Already in the sixties Japanese pornography was taking the direction of emphasizing narratives and scenes of brutality, rape, and bondage. This film must also be seen in that context. We can recall how Wakamatsu was celebrated by Noël Burch (1979: 351) as a "primitive" and as an auteur of pornography primarily for his *Taiiji ga mitsuryo suru toki* (The Embryo Hunts in Secret, 1966). The film is a *huis clos* examination of a sadist submitting a female captive to increasingly escalating violence while keeping her locked within his apartment. Wakamatsu's is a disturbingly intense film that through its unrelenting repetitious fixation on attacks and forced submissions sustains a compulsion that does not allow the viewer a comedic response to its excesses, except as rejection of its premises. In other words, its aesthetic impulses force a complicity with its lust for violence, which is precisely what makes it such an extreme and unsettling example of the way pornography became an outlet for desires for overpowering the other, rather than other forms of sexuality. If in the end the victim escapes and then returns to kill her torturer, this ending does not necessarily make her triumphant or the film less exploitive of women. This ending can be read as a weak but intriguing guilt reaction to the pleasure the film has suggested can be found in a fantasy of unrestrained violent negation of the will of the other. As a gesture of repressive retribution of a desire relentlessly evoked and celebrated, it hovers over the closure of the film as an ironic justification of all that came before, permitting the fantasy in a way that a simple ending with the woman's corpse would not.

Oshima's ghost begs comparison to Wakamatsu's phantom embryo. Both embody the haunting of a male psyche fixated on violence, a male psyche whose fragmented identity is filmically manifest by editing that fragments the worlds the films explore. The difference is that Wakamatsu's embryo remains at the narrative center of his film, whereas focus on the pair of women actively decenters the male ghost in Oshima's.

SEX INDUSTRIES

What ghostly traces of *women* haunt this film and others like it? What memories evoke a guilt that solicits this pleasure in violence toward women? One way to answer this question is to extend the obvious psychological cue offered by Wakamatsu's film itself, which locates the violence in the Oedipal fascination with the mother of the film's embryonic hunter, as depicted in the flashback sequences to the sadist's childhood, his primal scenes of paternal violence, and his desire to be once again inside his mother as adored and peaceful fetus. We might simply extend this psychology of character to a psychoanalytic reading of male Japanese lust and ambivalence toward the maternal, but I think it is also necessary to seek additional historical answers by looking at past events in Japanese history. For example, the forcible establishment of brothels by the imperialist Japanese military during the Pacific War, finally acknowledged by the Japanese government in its recent apology to Korea, reveals a link among nationalist conquest, violence, and assumptions of the sexual servitude of others to the Japanese male population. In the postwar period such events were mostly denied. With the general denial and refusal to investigate this past comes the desire to repeat this experience (Japanese businessmen make up a substantial part of the sexual tourism to brothels in Singapore, the Philippines, Thailand, and elsewhere) and to give it renewed but indirect and imaginary life in pornographic fantasy representations. If the pornographic scene is the site of a displaced lust and a nostalgia for power over the other, its appropriation to an expression of rebellion against the state seems more problematic than ever.

It is for this reason that I would like to put these representations of women in still another context, that of the sex industries of Japan and other East Asian countries historically. Given Oshima's involvement in issues of Asian identity relative to Japanese imperialism, the films are especially intriguing to view as paralleling an industry that brought these issues together in violent and direct ways. We might look at the relationship of a film industry both selling images of sexuality and critiquing ideologies of sexuality and that of a sexual service industry selling prostitutes and bar hostesses as well as the "comfort women" of World War II. Even as I draw on the sex industries here as a point of comparison, I want to emphasize the differences between a representational medium such as film and the physical servicing of sexual desire; while both rely on sexual fantasy and desire, the sex industry, in providing bodies performing sexual acts, poses some entirely different issues. Sex acts turned into industry demand physical risks to workers and social consequences for those workers that images do not. Films, once they are made, *only* present fantasies through images; they have the remove of representation, of performance, of art, as well as the critical expressive function of a speech act. As discourses, films can vary in the way they address the conjunctions of violence, power, and sexuality, which is the reason any critique of exploitation and oppression needs to be made textually and contextually, not just in reference to the "content" of isolated images.

Violence at Noon follows a film, *Etsuraku* (Pleasures of the Flesh, 1965), that to date has had no distribution in the United States; thinking of these two films together allows us to see that by the mid-sixties, after Oshima returned

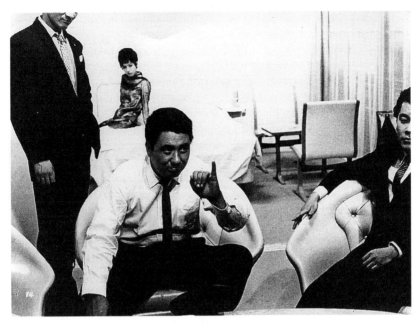

63. The gleaming modernist bedroom of a "love hotel" serves as backdrop
for a male character whose pursuit of pleasure is framed and ultimately
annihilated by his connections and debts to the illegal and violent capitalism
of the yakuza and its penetration into government in the form of graft.
Etsuraku (Pleasures of the Flesh, 1965). Still courtesy of Oshima Productions.

to feature production following a three-year hiatus, his films are studies in
sadism, obsession, and torture, embracing the themes and visual motifs fa-
vored by the hardest core of the pornographic genre. Significantly, each of
these films juxtaposes erotic violence with its consequences; each is ultimately involved in ethics and political critique, even if identification with
male protagonists indulges a sexual freedom anarchistically devoid of responsibility. Each avoids the psychology of character, but instead suggests a
psychoanalytic framework, a theoretical context. *Etsuraku,* adapted from a
Yamada Futaro novel, *Pleasure Inside the Coffin,* chronicles the dissolution of
a murderer, once his crime is witnessed by an official who has absconded with
government funds. They strike a bargain in which the murderer will guard
the funds for the length of the official's three-year prison term; the film turns
on blackmail, as trust is bought under the risk of exposure of the original
murder.

When the woman for whom he murdered marries someone else, the
murderer decides to spend the money pursuing pleasure, buying women.
We return in this film to a "love hotel," the prostitution sites depicted in

Cruel Story of Youth, but this time we see the love hotel from the interior, its gleaming modernist bedroom as backdrop for a male character whose pursuit of pleasure is framed and ultimately annihilated by his connections and debts to the illegal and violent capitalism of Japan's Mafia and its penetration into government in the form of graft. One intriguing way to read *Etsuraku* is to foreground the links it suggests among the yakuza, pornography, and prostitution.

As I have indicated, prostitution and pornography have different statuses, one a service industry in which individuals perform acts, the other a culture industry of representation and artistic expression. Yet from another perspective, the obvious differences blur when both are considered within a sector of the entertainment industry in world commerce that we might call sexual entertainment. In East Asia in the nineteenth and twentieth centuries, the historical fluctuation of patterns of supply and consumption of both are linked to larger patterns of East Asian trade and the ascendancy of given nations as economic and political powers. Further, since both institutions are marginal and in disrepute, though sometimes sanctioned and exploited by governments, they are subject to the domination of the most criminal and corrupt of capitalists. When Yamizaki, the anthropologist who first disclosed the significance of Karayuki-san, points out the role of these industries in government policy planning, she is speaking to the willingness of the Japanese government to embrace its illegal sectors.

It is in this context that we should view *Etsuraku*'s antihero. Though he attempts to act on desire, unfettered, he cannot escape the yakuza and ultimately perishes at their hands. In addressing sexuality directly and in its conjunction with violence, Oshima invades the territory of Japan's sex industries, just as he competes with other directors such as Wakematsu and Tetuji Takechi in this market. *Etsuraku* might be seen as an acknowledgment of the danger posed by playing, even metaphorically, on the fringes of the yakuza, though economically it was a hit that turned Oshima's career around. Ironically, Oshima (1992: 255–262) will revisit it with regret that its sex remained too timid, that unlike his later *Realm of the Senses,* it failed to film "sex and sexual organs."

Another way to analyze Oshima's proximity to and embrace of pornography is to consider *The True Story of Abe Sada* by Tanaka Noburu (1975), which takes as its point of departure the same historical incident as Oshima's *Realm of the Senses* (1976). Tanaka's film may appear more standardly coded, more predictable, and less rich in innovation than Oshima's; it unfolds well within the codes of standard pornography, orchestrating its narrative to showcase sexual encounters and avoiding the kinds of challenges to its viewers that *Realm of the Senses* poses, challenges evident at screenings of the film in which audiences expecting something else simply leave, or else voice their dismay at several scenes (not just the ending). The comparison between the two films, though, shows that there is never any clear line between generic pornography and the sophisticated erotic text. Ironically, not even certain distinctions that some feminists make, distinctions that depend on female subjectivity in the portrayal of sexual desire, regarding eroticism and pornography will hold. The critique that heterosexually oriented pornography presents women as devoid of any meaningful subjectivity, rendering them only as fantasy objects opening unrestrictively to male projections, whatever its validity in terms of some films of marked objectification, fails to take into account how a film that does not challenge pornographic coding can be presented as a female diary, a story from her point of view. The Tanaka film seems to grant Abe Sada more subjectivity, more development as a character, than does Oshima's film. Oshima's Sada, as part of his overall strategy of undercutting the unity and fullness of character, has a much more opaque and contradictory representation. As I have tried to show in chapter 4, a larger consideration of textuality shows the Oshima film to be subversive on many theoretical questions, including those of gender, sexual difference, and desire, precisely because his formal structuration serves complex and multiple readings.

Many of Oshima's films then cross the very border posed by pornography, refusing to be simply inside or outside its territory. In treating explicit sexuality directly they lay a claim on pornography construed in a positive sense as the uncensored viewing of sex acts; however, in attempting to break down the taboos and the exploitation that have surrounded pornography as a genre, Oshima's films structure themselves in opposition to the expected coding of pornography, its potential complaisance with entertainment imperatives that make it lack subversion or resistance, that allow it to confirm restrictive gender roles and enforce power relations in its manner of presenting sexual imagery.

In his "Theory of Experimental Pornographic Film," Oshima suggests that the border surrounding pornography has been given geographic and historical dimensions, that it is conditioned by prohibitions against seeing what one desires to see.

> *In the Realm of the Senses* became the perfect pornographic film in Japan because it cannot be seen there. Its existence is pornographic—regardless of its content.
>
> Once it is seen, *In the Realm of the Senses* may no longer be a pornographic film. That may happen in Europe and the United States, where it can be seen in its entirety. (Oshima 1992: 253)

He begins to suggest here that *Realm of the Senses* entails a critique of its genre, insofar as that genre is defined by its patterns of exploitation (and release, but in a superficial sense) of a still-confined desire. To redefine pornography through its inscription of filmic textuality may ultimately be the goal of *Realm of the Senses.*

Many feminists have recently come to embrace pornography, sometimes retaining a sharp feminist critique of roles embodied in some pornography historically, though at other times, in a simple reversal aimed at overturning an association of feminism with antipornography, championing pornography and overlooking some of the ideological implications of its narratives (Gibson and Church 1993; Kipnis 1994; Williams 1989). I hold that Oshima's sexually explicit films should be seen as central to this endeavor. They point to a serious engagement with ideologies of sexual representation, but one that while aware of women's issues and able to use them is not yet free of exploitation of women. These films have contradictory impulses toward women, some inspired by a critique of patriarchy, others still a by-product of sexual liberation conceived from a male perspective.

Conclusion
Whither Oshima?

At the end of his 1974 essay, "Banishing Green," Oshima reflects that he may no longer be daring enough to banish green and negate sky, as I discussed in chapter 1. It is appropriate here to return to this reflection as prefiguring his current status as a film director who is now "no longer young." Oshima's poetic rhetoric repeatedly describes him as "the filmmaker" who is "on the threshold of old age," which allows him to set up a series of propositions that follow from his aging and his arriving at a certain stage in his career. He begins with, "If a film director thinks about the road his own work has traveled, he sees that with each new project the tendency to deny reality and play inside his own fantasies has grown stronger." The next proposition asks, given the camera's vocation for reality, "to what extent can the landscape be modified as landscape? And to what extent can the artist, using the camera as a medium, convert the landscape into fantasies?" It is at this point that he posits that even if the filmmaker is no longer as daring as he once was, "he will still strive to make his way into the endlessly minute aspects of reality to discover and abstract his own fantasies there. And he will try to use the fantastic to thoroughly negate reality" (Oshima 1992: 210).

Even so, he then describes a paradoxical aspect of Japan (which we might now term "postmodern") that makes his goal of negating reality extremely challenging. "Ambiguous Japan, where the instant anything is made it seems to be completely buried in reality" (p. 211), seems to indicate a process whereby what is fabricated can be incorporated into the real or "natural." This leads him to distrust "architects and others who create Japan's scenery" (p. 211) for they inevitably, it would seem, naturalize modernity and, we might add, create postmodernity, rendering new edifices as simply compatible with tradition or easily assimilated. No resistance, no contestatory disjuncture, remains in which any edifice, and by extension any text, stands out or points to alternative spaces and futures.

If this bleak perspective was already present in 1974, it did not stop Oshima from producing more films, from seeking to express fantasies in the myriad ways we have explored in this volume. Now, however, the filmmaker has reached a new juncture at which the predictions of the past have new urgency. Except for his new documentary, *Kyoto, My Mother's Place*, Oshima has not been able to produce a film since his last feature, *Max, Mon Amour*, though not for want of trying.

Hollywood Zen, begun in 1990, was to have been his next project. The British producer Jeremy Thomas invested in Oshima's desire to film his version of the life of the Japanese-American silent movie star Seshu Hayakawa. The biographical project promised an exploration of Hayakawa's relationship to Rudolph Valentino, and would provide a means to look at U.S., Japanese, and European relations during the years between the world wars as articulated by their film industries. Production of *Hollywood Zen* was blocked when a U.S. coproducer withdrew, according to Oshima.

In the meantime, Oshima has continued his work hosting and appearing on television talk shows. As he said in a November 1992 interview in *Le Monde*, "I try to bring the political significance of so-called societal problems to light. With all the scandals that Japan has experienced recently there has been a lot to do." He is often at the center of debates on Koreans living in Japan, on Japanese war crimes, on women's rights, on Japanese bureaucracies stifling artistic creativity, and, most recently, on the AUM Shin-Rikyo, the sect, led by Shoko Asahara, responsible for gassing the Tokyo subway. On the "Asa Made Nama Terebi" program broadcast on March 31, 1995, Oshima remarked that "AUM was created out of our society." For Oshima, such cults are a product of Japanese schools, homes, and society, a symptom requiring attention.

Oshima has also been active on film festival juries and most recently made a documentary commissioned as part of *The Century of Cinema*, a project planned by the television department of the British Film Institute. Oshima focuses on the history of Japanese cinema, paralleling documentaries made by Martin Scorcese on U.S. cinema, Jean-Luc Godard on French cinema, and Wim Wenders on German cinema.

Youth, significantly, was the theme Oshima chose to unify his overview of his nation's hundred years of cinema. Of course, this permitted him to introduce the impact his generation of filmmakers had when they first emerged at the end of the fifties as well as pay tribute to the genre of youth films of the early and mid-fifties that he wrote about as a film critic and that served as his inspiration, or point of departure. It also gave him a chance to present the work of his most famous predecessors in a new light and to turn toward a new generation producing films in Japan today. Oshima's segment of *The Century of Cinema* ends with a scene from a film by Sai Yoichi, *Tsuki wa dotchi ni dete iru* (All Under the Moon, 1993), which focuses on a second-generation North Korean resident living in Tokyo.

Earlier, even though he was largely discouraged by the demise of national cinemas in competition with violent U.S. action films, Oshima highlighted the global marketplace as opening new possibilities. He expressed hope that films such as his will continue to be made for small audiences all over the world. Oshima seemed entranced by an international artistic identity, one that was no longer completely and specifically Japanese. Ironically, his two recent projects, though supported by British commissions, sought Oshima's *Japanese* voice: *Kyoto, My Mother,* under the rubric of a series on film directors' biographies, and *The Century of Cinema,* as expert on his national cinema.

For this reason, Oshima's voice is all the more poignant in his recent role as Japanese spokesperson in an international protest of filmmakers against U.S. cinema's hegemony. Presiding over a conference in Tokyo, Oshima led the drafting of a communiqué to the European Federation of Audiovisual Directors. The communiqué supported another letter drafted by six European filmmakers, Pedro Almodovar, Bernardo Bertolucci, Stephen Frears, Emir Kusturica, Jeremy Thomas, and Wim Wenders, which was sent as an open letter to the U.S. directors Steven Spielberg and Martin Scorsese. It answered an earlier claim by the latter that the cinema needed to be given special consideration in the negotiation of the Global Agreement on Tariffs and Trade (GATT). The dispute in the GATT negotiations, led by the French, concerned the continuation of subsidies to national film industries and of laws restricting the percentage of U.S. films shown in theaters and on television. In original draft, GATT would have curtailed such government controls as unfair tariffs, restrictions, and subsidies. The Europeans presented themselves as the "dinosaurs of 1993," in danger of extinction and fighting for their lives.

One may have longed for *Hollywood Zen* as a response, however oblique, however set in history, to these present-day conditions in which cinematic innovation is ground to oblivion by a mass entertainment formula whose power overtakes most countervailing forces. If Oshima's writings display clear insights into the obstacles to cinematic expression now, those obstacles may keep those insights from finding filmic expression. *Hollywood Zen,* now shelved, remains as the trace of an alternative cinematic imagining, one that has given way to a newly announced alternative project.

Oshima has now undertaken a new film project, a samurai film, *Gohatto* (Taboo), to be produced at Shochiku by Okuyama Kazuyoshi, the son of an official at the studio at the time Oshima first began as an assistant director there. Okuyama is trying to revitalize Japanese production, and has reportedly given Oshima a free hand in his adaptation of a historical novel by Shiba Ryotaro, whose works have been extremely popular in Japan. Shiba, who died on February 12, 1996, was from Osaka and worked as a journalist as well as a novelist; he is often quoted for his opinion of contemporary Japan, as well as its relationship to the rest of East Asia, particularly Mongolia and Taiwan. *Gohatto* will tell of the Shinsengumi, a group of samurai active in the nineteenth century, the late Tokugawa era, just before the Meiji restoration. Oshima has announced his plan to highlight the homosexuality underlying their group identity, apparently continuing the exploration of homosexuality within a military context explored in *Merry Christmas, Mr. Lawrence.*

Yet this project also has been subject to delay, this time because of a minor stroke Oshima suffered which resulted in his hospitalization in London while on a speaking tour that was to take him next to Northern Ireland. Oshima was given time by Shochiku to recover; while spared any difficulties with speech and cognition, he did suffer paralysis on the right side of his body.

So we are left with an artist whose prophetic vision in the 1974 essay seems to be trying to catch up to him, as the obstacles to filmmaking become ever greater. Then Oshima saw such a circumstance in which one is overtaken by obstacles in individual terms, as "courage failing." Perhaps that faith in "courage" was the sign of a younger man who ultimately wanted to believe that personal commitment and strength of purpose could overcome systemic and institutional barriers. It seems far sadder to realize that both young and established older filmmakers in Japan have had great difficulty producing films that matter in Japan, in the ways Oshima's films mattered. Money is instead invested primarily in Japanese animation or in Hollywood studios, cultural products whose guaranteed high return is the object of financiers' desire. Films that interrogate the political unconscious as they extend film's formal vocabulary find no funds offered despite Japan's wealth. Then, just when Japanese financing is finally arranged for a new project, the delay is personal, but medical, rather than a question of will. As I said in chapter 6, among the recent Japanese films, comedies seem most likely to find funding and international distribution, most likely to achieve the stature Oshima's films once garnered. Oshima is often mysteriously silent about these comedies, choosing to discuss other films, particularly those by young Chinese and Korean filmmakers, as if he were granting his legacy.

If Oshima has generously praised recent films of young Chinese directors, such as Chén Kaige (*Huang tudi* [Yellow Earth], 1984; *Farewell, My Concubine,* 1993), it is perhaps because he sees in them one of his best hopes for a legacy with a younger generation. Kaige and others such as Zhang Yimóu (*Ju dou,* 1990; *Dàhóng denglóng gaogao guà* [Raise the Red Lantern], 1992) and Ho Ping (*Red Fireworks, Green Fireworks,* 1995) for the moment successfully market their films internationally, though they are censored in China. The current government has seen the eroticism of its young directors in economic terms. It promotes their production to ensure the balance of trade through a double mechanism, gaining through the investment in production by foreigners who coproduce these films (Hong Kong, Taiwan, Britain, and France), but also as revenues earned through foreign distribution. Their mixture of political allegory and sexual expression in many ways recalls Oshima's own, though they present little of the formal narrative difficulties, the philosophical experimentation with the means of expression that made Oshima's films so challenging.

Regardless of such questions of influence and legacy, regardless of whether Oshima is able to complete further projects, this book has argued for the continual significance of Oshima's body of work, argued that its significance changes and grows with time as we begin to see it historically and theoretically in new ways. I hold that these films still provide insights into Japan as they are reread today with greater attention to the specificity of that country's astounding, turbulent, and violent last century. As our vantage point changes, as it grows theoretically to embrace additional perspectives, such as feminism, or greater historical distance from the events depicted, these films will continue to be subject to different viewings and analysis. They will allow a view of the self, the subject, consciousness, and the unconscious whose fragmentation is always drawn in relation to social orders and historical junctures, but, it is hoped, we shall see these films anew, renewed.

"If I were asked, 'Whither have you been going?' I would probably respond 'Along the road to freedom,'" Oshima says in a 1965 essay. Then he adds, "We are free because freedom is not possible. Ending with that statement, I am left with a very heavy burden" (1992: 101). We have much to learn from the traces Oshima has left along that road.

FILMOGRAPHY

FEATURE FILMS

1959 *Ai to kobo no machi* (A Town of Love and Hope; original title: *The Boy Who Sells a Pigeon*)

Producer: Ikeda Tomio for Shochiku. Script: Oshima Nagisa. Cinematography: Kusuda Hiroshi (Shochiku Grandscope, B/W). Lighting: Iijima Hiroshi. Music: Manabe Riishiro. Assistant Director: Tamura Tsutomu. Sets: Uno Koji. Editing: Sugihara Yoshi. Sound: Shujuro Kurita. 63 min.

Cast: Fujikawa Hiroshi (Masuo), Mochizuki Yuko (Kuniko, Masuo's mother), Watanabe Fumio (Yuji, older brother of Kyoko), Chino Kakuko (Ms. Akiyama, schoolteacher), Tominaga Yuki (Kyoko), Suga Fujio (Hisahara, father of Yuji and Kyoko).

1960 *Seishun sankoku monogatari* (Cruel Story of Youth, aka *Cruel Tales of Youth*)

Producer: Ikeda Tomio for Shochiku. Script: Oshima Nagisa. Cinematography: Kawamata Ko (Shochiku Grandscope, Eastmancolor). Lighting: Sato Isamu. Music: Manabe Riishiro. Assistant Director: Ishido Toshiro. Sets: Uno Koji. Editing: Uraoko Keiichi. Sound: Kurita Shujuro. 96 min.

Cast: Kawasu Yusuke (Kiyoshi), Kuwano Miyuki (Makoto), Kuga Yoshiko (Yuki), Sato Kei (Matsuki Akira, the attacker), Watanabe Fumio (Akimoto, the doctor), Hanemura Jun (Shinjo Masahiro, father of Makoto and Yuki).

1960 *Taiyo no hakaba* (Burial of the Sun; literal Japanese translation: *The Sun's Grave*)

Producer: Ikeda Tomio for Shochiku. Script: Oshima Nagisa, Ishido Toshiro. Cinematography: Kawamata Ko (Shochiku Grandscope, Eastmancolor). Lighting: Sato Isumu. Music: Manabe Riishiro. Assistant Director: Ishido Toshiro. Sets: Uno Koji. Editing: Uraoko Keiichi. Sound: Kurita Shujuro. 87 min.

Cast: Honoo Kauoko (Hanako), Sasaki Isao (Takeshi), Tsugawa Masahiko (Shin), Toura Mutsuhiro (Masa), Watanabe Fumio (Yoshihei), Sato Kei (Sakaguchi, the doctor), Ben Junzaburo (Yosematsu, father of Hanako).

1960 *Nihon no yoru to kiri* (Night and Fog in Japan)

Producer: Ikeda Tomio for Shochiku. Script: Oshima Nagisa, Ishido Toshiro. Cinematography: Kawamata Ko (Shochiku Grandscope, Eastmancolor). Lighting: Sato Isumu. Music: Manabe Riishiro. Assistant Director: Ishido Toshiro. Sets: Uno Koji. Editing: Uraoko Keiichi. Sound: Kurita Shujuro. 107 min.

Cast: Watanabe Fumio (Nozawa, the journalist and bridegroom), Kuwano Miuki (Reiko, radical student and bride), Tsugawa Masahiko (Oto), Yoshizawa Takao (Nakayama, former radical in the fifties), Koyama Akiko (wife of Nakayama), Toura Mutsuhiro (Ura Higashi, another former radical in the fifties), Sakonjyo Hiroshi (Takao, radical from the fifties movement, disappeared), Hayami Ichiro (Takumi, radical from the fifties movement), Ajikoka Toru (Kitami, radical student and friend of Reiko).

1961 *Shiiku* (The Catch)

Producer: Tajima Saburo, Nakajima Masayuki for Palace Film. Script: Tamura Tsutomu, Matsumoto Toshio, Ishido Toshiro, Tomatsu Shomei from the Oe Kensaburo novel of the same name. Cinematography: Tonegawa Yoshitsugu (Scope, B/W). Lighting: Hishinuma Yokichi. Music: Manabe Riishiro. Assistant Director: Yanagida Hiromi. Sets: Hirata Isturo. Editing: Miyamori Miyuri. Sound: Okazaki Michio. 105 min.

Cast: Mikuni Rentaro (Kazumasa Takano, village chief), Koyama Akiko (Hiroko Ishii, refugee from Tokyo), Hugh Harj (U.S. pilot), Ishido Toshiro (Jito), Oshima Eiko (Mikiko, nephew of Kazumasa), Sazanka Kyu (Tsukada

Denmatsu), Kishi Teruko (Masu, wife of Tsukada), Toura Mutsuhiro (village official), Irizumi Toshiro (Hachiro).

Distributor: Taiho (Japan); Shibata (global).

1962 *Amakusa Shiro Tokisada* (Shiro Tokisada)

Producer: Okawa Hiroshi for Toei. Script: Oshima Nagisa, Ishido Toshiro. Cinematography: Kawasaki Shintaro (Scope, B/W). Lighting: Nakayana Hamo. Music: Manabe Riishiro. Sets: Kon Yasutaro. Editing: Miyamoto Shintaro. Sound: Sasaki Toshio. 100 min.

Cast: Ikawa Hashizo (Amakusa Shiro Tokisada), Oka Satomi (Sakura), Otomo Ryutaro, Oka Shinbe, Mikuni Tentaro (Emosaku, the painter), Tachikawa Sayuri (Okiku), Sato Kei (Mondo Taga), Toura Mutsuhiro (the ronin).

Distributor: Tori (Japan).

1964 *Esturaku* (Pleasures of the Flesh)

Producer: Nakajima Masayuki. Script: Oshima Nagisa from the novel *Kan no naka no esturuku* by Yamada Futaro. Cinematography: Takada Akira (Scope, color). Lighting: Koji Hirata. Music: Yuasa Joji. Sets: Kon Yasutaro. Editing: Uraoka Keiichi. Sound: Nishizaki Hideo. 90 min.

Cast: Katsuo Najamura (Wakisaki Atsushi), Kago Maiko (Inaba Shoko), Nogawa Yumiko (Hitomi, bar hostess), Yagi Masako (Shizuko), Higuchi Toshiko (Keiko, doctor), Shimizu (Hiroko Mari, prostitute), Osawa Shoichi (Hayami), Toura Mutsuhiro (Sakurai), Sato Kei (Inspector Keji), Hamada Akira (first gangster), Emori Toru (second gangster), Watanabe Fumio (third gangster).

Distributor: Shochiku (Japan).

1966 *Hakuchu no torima* (Violence at Noon)

Producer: Nakajima Masayuki for Sozosha. Script: Tsutomu Tamura, from the novel by Takeda Taijun. Cinematography: Takada Akira (Scope, B/W). Lighting: Miura Rei. Music: Hayashi Hikaru. Assistant Director: Sasaki Mamoru. Sets: Toda Jusho. Editing: Uraoka Keiichi. Sound: Nishizaki Hideo. 99 min.

Cast: Kawagushi Saeda (Shino, a maid and former peasant), Toura Mutsuhiro (Hiuga Genji), Sato Kei (Eisuke Oyamada), Koyama Akiko (high school teacher), Komatsu Hosei (father of Shino), Tonoyama Taiji (principal of the high school), Kanze Hideo (Inagaki, husband of woman who is raped and killed), Takahara Ryoki (woman who is raped and killed), Watanabe Fumio (Inspector Haraguchi).

Distributor: Shochiku (Japan).

1967 *Nihon sunka-ko* (A Treatise on Japanese Bawdy Song)

Producer: Nakajima Masayuki for Sozosha. Script: Tsutomu Tamura, Sasaki Mamoru, Tajima Toshio, Oshima Nagisa (title borrowed from scholarly book by Saeda Tomomichi). Cinematography: Takada Akira (Scope, color). Lighting: Nakamura Akira. Music: Hayashi Hikaru. Assistant Director: Sasaki Mamoru. Sets: Toda Jusho. Editing: Uraoka Keiichi. Sound: Nishizaki Hideo. 103 min.

Cast: Araki Ichiro (Nakamura Toyoaki, student), Yoshida Hideko (Kane Sachiko, student), Koyama Akiko (Tanigawa Takato), Itami Ichizo (Professor Otake), Tajima Kasuko (Fujiwara Mayuko), Miyamoto Nobuko (Satomi Sanae, student), Sato Hiroshi (Koji Maruyama, student), Iwabuchi Koji (Ueda Hideo, student), Kushida Kazumi (Hiroi Katsumi), Masuda Hiroko (Ikeda Tomoko, student).

Distributor: Shochiku (Japan).

1967 *Muri-shinju: Nihon no natsu* (Japanese Summer: Double Suicide)

Producer: Nakajima Masayuki for Sozosha. Script: Tsutomu Tamura, Sasaki Mamoru, Oshima Nagisa. Cinematography: Yoshioka Yasuhiro (Scope, B/W). Lighting: Sano Takeharu. Music: Hayashi Hikaru. Assistant Director: Yasui Osamu. Sets: Toda Jusho. Editing: Uraoka Keiichi. Sound: Hishizaki Hideo. 98 min.

Cast: Sakuai Keiko (Nejiko), Toura Mutsuhiro ("TV"), Sato Kei (man), Komatsu Hosei (ogre), Tonoyama Taiji (tinkerer), Tamura Masakazu (boy),

Kanze Hideo (bandit), Fukuda Yoshiyuki (Fukuda Yoshiyuki), Mizoguchi Sunryo (right hand of "TV"), T Clay (demon), Ashida Testuo (himejui), Ozawa Bunya (Matsuyama).

Distributor: Shochiku (Japan).

1968 *Koshikei* (Death by Hanging)

Producer: Nakajima Masayuki, Yamaguchi Takuji, Oshima Nagisa for Sozosha. Script: Tsutomu Tamura, Sasaki Mamoru, Michinori Kukao, Oshima Nagisa. Cinematography: Yoshioka Yasuhiro (Vistavision, B/W). Lighting: Sano Takeharu. Music: Hayashi Hikaru. Assistant Director: Ogasawara Kiyoshi. Sets: Toda Jusho. Editing: Uraoka Keiichi. Sound: Hishizaki Hideo. 117 min.

Cast: Yun Do Yun (R), Sato Kei (warden), Watanabe Fumio (education officer), Toura Mutsuhiro (doctor), Adachi Masao (chief guard), Komatsu Hosei (prosecutor), Matsuda (assistant prosecutor), Koyama Akiko (Korean woman).

Distributor: Art Theater Guild (Japan); Shibata (global); Argos (France).

1968 *Kaette kita yopparai* (Three Resurrected Drunkards)

Producer: Nakajima Masayuki for Sozosha. Script: Tsutomu Tamura, Sasaki Mamoru, Adachi Masao, Oshima Nagisa. Cinematography: Yoshioka Yasuhiro (Scope, color). Lighting: Sano Takeharu. Music: Hayashi Hikaru. Assistant Director: Ogasawara Kiyoshi, Yun Do Yun. Sets: Toda Jusho. Editing: Uraoka Keiichi. Sound: Hishizaki Hideo. 80 min.

Cast: Kato Kazuhiko (Big Boy), Kitayama Osamu (Run of the Mill), Hashida Norihiko (Pipsqueak), Sato Kei (the young man and the Korean soldier, I Chong Iru), Watanabe Fumio (pimp, "Poisonous Bug"), Midori Mako (adoptive daughter and mistress of "Poisonous Bug"), Toura Mutsuhiro.

Distributor: Shochiku (Japan).

1968 *Shinjuku dorobo nikki* (Diary of a Shinjuku Thief, aka *Diary of a Shinjuku Burglar*)

Producer: Nakajima Masayuki for Sozosha. Script: Tsutomu Tamura, Sasaki Mamoru, Adachi Masao, Oshima Nagisa. Cinematography: Yoshioka Yasuhiro, Sengen Seizo (Standard, B/W with color insert sequence). Sets: Toda Jusho. Editing: Oshima Nagisa. Sound: Hishizaki Hideo. 80 min.

Cast: Yokō Tadanori (Birdy Hilltop), Yokoyama Rie (Suzuki Umeko), Tanabe Moichi (himself, director of Kinokuniya), Takahashi Tetsu (himself, sexologist), Kara Juro (himself, director of Jokyo Theater Group), Sato Kei (himself), Watanabe Fumio (himself), Toura Mutsuhiro (man who makes love), Ri Reisen (wife of Kara Juro), members of the Jokyo Theater Group.

Distributor: Art Theater Guild (Japan); Shibata (global).

1969 *Shonen* (Boy)

Producer: Nakajima Masayuki, Yamaguchi Takuji for Art Theater Guild. Script: Tsutomu Tamura. Cinematography: Yoshioka Yasuhiro, Sengen Seizo (Scope, color). Music: Hayashi Hikaru. Sets: Toda Jusho. Editing: Uraoka Keiichi. Sound: Hishizaki Hideo. Sound Effects: Suzuki Akira. 97 min.

Cast: Koyama Akiko (the stepmother), Watanabe Fumio (the father), Abe Tetsuo (Toshio, the boy), Kinoshita Tsuyoshi (the little brother).

Distributor: Art Theater Guild (Japan); Shibata (global).

1970 *Tokyo senso sengo hiwa: Eiga de isho o nokoshite shinda otoko no monogatari* (The Battle of Tokyo, or the Story of the Young Man Who Left His Will on Film)

(Note the literal translation of the Japanese title: "He died after the Tokyo war." Note also the Japanese subtitle: *Eiga de isho o nokoshite shinda otoko no monogatari,* which translates "Story of a young man leaving a film as testament.")

Producer: Yamaguchi Takuji for Sozosha and Art Theater Guild. Script: Oshima Nagisa, Tsutomu Tamura. Cinematography: Narushima Toichiro (Standard, B/W). Music: Takemitsu Toru. Sets: Toda Jusho. Editing: Uraoka Keiichi. Sound: Hishizaki Hideo. Sound Effects: Suzuki Akira. 94 min.

Cast: Goto Kazuo (Shoichi Motoki), Iwasaki Emiko (Yasuko), Fukuoka Sugio (Tanizawa), Keiichi (Takagi), Horikoshi Kazuya (Endo), Oshima Tomoyo (Akiko).

Distributor: Art Theater Guild (Japan); Shibata (global).

1971 *Gishiki* (Ceremonies, aka *The Ceremony*)

Producer: Kuzui Kinshiro, Yamaguchi Takuji for Sozosha and Art Theater Guild. Script: Tsutomu Tamura, Oshima Nagisa, Sasaki Mamoru. Cinematography: Narushima Toichiro (Scope, color). Music: Takemitsu Toru. Sets: Toda Jusho. Editing: Uraoka Keiichi. Sound: Hishizaki Hideo. 124 min.

Cast: Kawarazaki Kenzo (Sakurada Masuo), Kaku Atsuko (Sakurada Ritsuko), Koyama Akiko (Sakurada Setsuko), Nakamura Atsuo (Tachibana Terumichi), Sato Kei (Sakurada Kazuomi), Tsuchiya Kiyoshi (Sakurada Tadashi), Watanabe Fumio (Sakurada Susumu), Otowa Nobuko (Sakurada Shizu), Takayama Mari (Sakurada Kiku), Mitobe Sue (Sakurada Chiyo), Komatsu Hosei (Sakurada Isamu), Tsubaki Koichi (Masuo as child), Narushima Yumi (Ritsuko as child), Ota Yochiaki (Terumichi as child), Tsubaki Yukihiro (Tadashi as child).

Distributor: Art Theater Guild (Japan); Shibata (global).

1972 *Natsu no imoto* (Dear Summer Sister)

Producer: Kuzui Kinshiro, Oshima Eiko for Sozosha and Art Theater Guild. Script: Tsutomu Tamura, Sasaki Mamoru, Oshima Nagisa. Cinematography: Yoshioka Yasuhiro (16 blown to 35 mm, Standard, Eastmancolor). Music: Takemitsu Toru. Sets: Toda Jusho. Editing: Uraoka Keiichi. Sound: Yasuda Tetsuo, supervision by Hishizaki Hideo. Sound effects: Honma Akira. 95 min.

Cast: Komatsu Hosei (judge, Kikushi Kosuke), Kurita Hiromi (Sunoko, daughter of Kosuke), Lily (Momoko, piano teacher of Sunoko), Koyama Akiko (Omura Tsuru), Ishibashi Shoji (Tsuruo, son of Tsuru), Sato Kei (commissioner), Taiji Tonoyama (Sakurada Takuzo), Toura Mutsuhiro (Teruya Rintoku, folk singer).

Distributor: Art Theater Guild (Japan); Shibata (global).

1976 *Ai no korida* (Realm of the Senses, aka *In the Realm of the Senses*)

Producer: Anatole Dauman for Argos Films (Paris), Oshima Productions

(Tokyo). Executive Producer: Wakamatsu Koji. Script: Oshima Nagisa. Lighting: Okamoto Kenichi. Cinematography: Ito Hideo (35 mm, Scope, color). Music: Minori Miki and traditional songs sung by Nippon Ongaku Shudan group. Sets and Costumes: Toda Jusho. Editing: Uraoka Keiichi. Sound: Yasuda Tetsuo. 104 min.

Cast: Matsuda Eiko (Sada Abe), Fuji Tatsuya (Kichi-zo), Nakajima Aoi (Toku, wife of Kichi), Taiji Tonoyama (beggar), Kobayashi Kanae (old geisha), Seri Meika (servant), Kokonoe Kyoji (professor), Koyama Akiko (geisha).

Distributor: Toho/Towa (Japan); Argos (global).

1978 *Ai no borei* (Empire of Passion)

Producer: Anatole Dauman for Argos Films (Paris), Oshima Productions (Tokyo). Script: Oshima Nagisa, from a story by Nakamura Itoko. Cinematography: Miyuajima Yoshio (Vistavision, 35 mm color). Lighting: Okamoto Kenichi. Music: Takemitsu Toru. Sets: Toda Jusho. Editing: Uraoka Keiichi. Sound: Yasuda Tetsuo. 105 min.

Cast: Tamura Takahiro (Tsukada Gisaburo), Yoshiyuki Kazuko (Seki), Fuji Tatsuya (Tanaka Toyoji, former soldier and Seki's lover), Hasagawa Masami (Oshin), Sugiura Takaaki (Denzo), Koyama Akiko.

Distributor: Toho/Towa (Japan): Argos (global).

1982 *Merry Christmas, Mr. Lawrence* (in Japan: *Senjo no merii kurisumasu;* in Europe: *Furyo*)

Producer: Jeremy Thomas for Cineventure Films (London), Oshima Productions (Tokyo). Script: Oshima Nagisa, Paul Mayersberg, based on the novel *The Sower and the Seed* by Laurens van der Post. Cinematography: Narushima Toichiro (Vistavision, 35 mm color). Music: Sakamoto Ryuichi. Sets: Toda Jusho. Editing: Oshima Tomoyo. Sound: Yasuda Tetsuo. 122 min.

Cast: David Bowie (Major Jack Celliers), Sakamoto Ryuichi (Captain Yonoi), Tom Conti (John Lawrence), Takeshi (Sergeant Hara Gengo), Jack Thompson (Major Hicksley), Johnny Okura (Kanemoto), Alistair Browing

(De Jong), James Malcolm (Celliers's brother), Chris Broun (Celliers at age 12).

1986 *Max, Mon Amour*

Producer: Serge Silberman for Greenwich Film Productions and A2 (Paris), Greenwich Films (U.S.). Script: Jean-Claude Carrière, Oshima Nagisa. Cinematography: Raoul Coutard. Music: Michel Portal. Sets: Pierre Guffroy. Editing: Helen Plemiannikov. 94 min.

Cast: Charlotte Rampling (Margaret), Anthony Higgins (Peter), Diana Quick (Camille), Christopher Hovik (Nelson), Milena Bukotic (maid), Victoria Abril (Maria), Pierre Etaix (detective).

SCENARIOS FOR FILMS

1956 *Shinkai Gyogun* (The Fish; published but never made into film)

1959 *Tsukimiso* (The Beautiful Plant)

Director: Iwaki Kimio. Script: Oshima Nagisa (original title: *Utsukushiki suisha goya no musume,* The Beautiful Mill Girl). Producer: Shochiku.

1959 *Donto okoze* (Let's Go)

Director: Nomura Yoshitaro. Script: Nomura Yoshitaro, Oshima Nagisa.

1959 *Jusan nichi no kinyobi* (Friday the 13th)

Director: Nomura Yoshitaro. Script: Oshima Nagisa. (Never made into film.)

1969 *Yoiyami semareba* (When Night Falls)

Director: Akio Jissoji. Script: Oshima Nagisa. Producer: Dan Toyoaki. 43 min. (released with *Diary of a Shinjuku Thief*).

SCENARIOS FOR TELEVISION

1960 *Satsui* (Volontary Homicide)

Director: Inoue Hiroshi. Producer: NHK Television. 60 min.

1961 *Seishun no fukaki fuchi yori* (The Deep Abyss of Youth)

Director: Hori Yasuo. Producer: KTV Kansai Television. 60 min.

1962 *Anato o yobu koe* (The Voice Which Calls Us)

Director: Jissoji Akio. Producer: TBS Television. 30 min.

1963 *Atsuki chishio ni* (Heated Blood)

Director: Nobuo Nakagewa from "Fuun Kodokan" (Tempest in the Judo House) by Ryutaro Kondo. 55 min.

1963 *Itsuka kyokio no kagayaku machini* (One Day in a City, Dawn)

Director: Akio Jissoji. Producer: TBS Television. 55 min.

1963 *Sakebi* (The Cry)

Director: Eto Jun. Producer: Kyushu Asahi for Hoso Television. 60 min.

1963 *Fufu hyakkei* (The Conjugal Views)

Director: Haruyama Kazunori. Producer: KTV. 30 min.

1964 *Maru to shikaku to* (The Circle or the Square)

Director: Yamamoto Kazuo. Producer: TBS Television. 56 min.

1964 *Anu nikushimi* (Hatred)

Director: Hiroshi Wakada. Producer: JOTX-TV

1964 *Katei no kofuku* (Family Happiness)

Director: Toru Shimku. Producer: NHK Television. 60 min.

1966 *Tsuyaku* (The Translator)

Director: Yssuo Hori. Producer: Kansai Television, from a novel by Matsumoto Seicho. 30 min.

SCENARIOS FOR RADIO

1964 *Gendai somon-ka* (Poems of Contemporary Love)

Director: Shinozaki Toshio. Producer: TBS. 30 min.

1964 *Ogon no toki wa sugiyuku* (Last Golden Summer)

Director: Mijagawa Shiro. Producer: TBS. 30 programs, 15 min. each, beginning June 29, 1964.

1964 *Heiwa no densetsu* (The Legend of Peace)

Director: Shinozaki Toshio. Producer: TBS. 60 min.

SHORT FILMS

1959 *Asu no taiyo* (Tommorrow's Sun)

Producer: Wakita Shigeru for Shochiku. Cinematography: Kawamata Ko. Sets: Uno Koji. Music: Ikeda Masayoshi. Editing: Habuto Mikiyo. Sound: Kurita Shujuro. Assistant Director: Tamura Tsutomu. 5 min.

Cast: Tsugawa Masahiko, Kuwano Miyuki, Tominaga Yuki, Toake Yukiyo.

1965 *Yunbogi no nikki* (Diary of Yunbogi)

Producer: Oshima Nagisa for Sozosha. Script, Commentary, Photographs: Oshima Nagisa, from *Yunbogi no nikki* (Yunbogi's Diary). Cinematography: Kawamata Ko (1 33 N/B). Music: Naito Takatoshi. Editing: Uraoko Keiichi. Collaboration: Shinozaki Toshio, Saki Mamoru, Yamaguchi Takuji, Yoshikawa Jun. Voice-over: Komatsu Hosei. 25 min.

Distributor: Sozosha (Japan); Shibata (global).

1991 *Kyoto, My Mother's Place*

Producer: Oshima Nagisa for the British Broadcasting Company. Script Voice-over: Oshima Nagisa. Cinematography: Yoshioka Yasuhiro. 51 min.

TELEVISION DRAMAS

1964 *Aisurebakoso* (Because I Love You)

Producer: Oshima Nagisa for NTV-Ginza (series *Musume no kekkon*, The Girl's Marriage). Script: Oshima Nagisa from a story by Yokota Masatoshi. Cinematography: Takada Akira. Sets: Kon Yesutaro. Assistant Director: Yanagida Hiromi. 56 min.

Cast: Saburi Shi (Wakita Masanori), Todoroki Yokiko (Atsuko, wife of Wakita Masanori), Yoshiko Ieda (Toshiko, daughter of Wakita Masanori), Yagyu Hiroshi (Hayano Toruo, friend of Toshiko), Suga Kentaro (Shima Yoichi, fiancée of Toshiko), Watanabe Fumio (Masaki, older son of Wakita Masanori), Toura Mutsuhiro (younger son of Wakita Masanori).

1964 *Aogeba totoshi* (Thinking Again of the Precious Lessons from My Teacher)

Producer: Wakaida Hisashi for JOTX-TV. Script, Editing: Oshima Nagisa. Music: Manabe Riichiro. 30 min.

Cast: Kuwayama Shoichi (Sueyoshi, teacher), Watanabe Fumio (Tanabe, hotel owner), Komatsu Hosei (Kato, son of construction company owner), Tomita Kotaro (Kojima, corporate head), Takagi Hitoshi (Matsuda, worker), Kobayashi Shoji (Furukawa, journalist), Hirata Mamoru (Iwasaki, employee), Hiano Akira (Nakatani, head of family enterprise), Tatakawa Danshi (Yagi, ex-con), Shiraishi Naomi (mother of Tanabe and daughter of hotel owner).

1964 *Ajia no akebono* (The Dawn of Asia)

Producer: Nakajima Masayuki, Shimamura Tatsuyoshi for Sozosha and Kokusai Hei-TBS. Script: Sasaki Mamoru, Tamura Tsutomu (episodes 1, 2, 3, 4, 5, 6, 10, 11, 13), Ishido Toshiro (episodes 7, 8, 9, 12) from the novel by Yamanaka Minetaro. Assistant Producer: Yamaguchi Takuji. Cinematography: Hishida Makoto (B/W). Lighting: Kume Shigeo. Sets: Kon Yasutaro, Kojima Hatsuo. Music: Tsukasa Ichiro, Asai Hinoshi. Assistant Director: Kataguri Naoki. 13 × 60 min.

Cast: Mikimoto Shinsuke (Nakayama Minetaro), Sato Kei (Rekkin Ri, Chinese man), Toura Mutsuhiro (Shu Ikuken, companion of Nakayama), Komatsu Hosei (Shikika, Chinese general), Kanze Hideo (Chinese general), Koyama Akiko (Yasuko, wife of Nakayama), Matsumoto Noriko (Saeki Yukiko, Chinese woman), Ari Roshimura (Ikuei, Chinese militant), Tachikawa Seyuri (Reirei), Shiihara Kunihiko (Osho Den), Hamada Torahiko (Oko).

TELEVISION DOCUMENTARIES

1962 *Kori no naka no seishun* (Youth on the Ice)

Producer: Yuki Toshizo for Nihon TV (series: Nonfiction Gekijyo). Script, Commentary: Oshima Nagisa. Cinematography: Tonegawa Yoshitsugu (B/W). Music: Manabe Riishiro. 2 parts, 30 min.

1963 *Wasurerareta kogun* (Forgotten Soldiers)

Producer: Ushiyama Junichi for Nihon TV (series: Nonfiction Gekijyo).

Script, Commentary: Oshima Nagisa. Voice-over: Komatsu Hosei. Cinematography: Shibata Sadanori, Suzawa Masaaki (B/W). Editing: Tamario Kurahei. Sound: Morimoto Takao. Collaboration: Noguchi Hideo, Hayasaka Akira. 30 min.

1964 *Aru kokutetsu jomuin: 4:17 suto chushi zengo* (An Engineer: Before and after the Work Stoppage of April 17)

Producer: Ushiyama Junichi for Nihon TV (series: Nonfiction Gekijyo). Script: Oshima Nagisa. Director: Tsuchimoto Noriaki, Hani Susumu, Tamura Tsutomu, Sekigawa Hideo, Onuma Tetsuro, Okamoto Yoshihiko, Shinkichi Noda. Commentary: Oshima Nagisa. Cinematography: Yoshitsugu Tonegawa, Kimura Akira. Voice-over: Toura Mutsuhiro. 27 min.

1964 *Gimai shojo* (The Girl under an Assumed Name)

Producer: Nihon TV (series: Nonfiction Gekijyo). Director: Oshima Nagisa, Ichioka Yasuko, Nakano Chiaki, Nakajima Tatsumi. Cinematography: Okada Tadao, Ichimuru Hiroshi, Kimura Akira. Voice-over: Komatsu Hosei, Sakaguchi Minako. 30 min.

1964 *Hahinosu-jo no kiroku* (A Rebel's Fortress, aka *Hidden Fortress*)

Producer: Ushiyama Junichi for Nihon TV (series: Nonfiction Gekijyo). Script, Commentary: Oshima Nagisa. Voice-over: Tokugawa Musei. Editing: Miyamoto Yusukei. Sound: Iwami Kiyoshi. B/W. 30 min.

1964 Chita Niseigo *Taiyeiyo Odan* (Crossing the Pacific on the *Chita Niseigo*)

Producer: Tamura Kazuye. Script, Commentary: Oshima Nagisa. Voice-over: Sano Asso. Cinematography: Kozo Itaya. Editing: Matsuno Yoshio. Sound: Iwami Kiyoshi. 2 × 30 min.

1964 *Seishun no ishibumi* (The Tomb of Youth)

Producer: Ushiyama Junichi for Nihon TV (series: Nonfiction Gekijyo). Script, Commentary: Oshima Nagisa. Voice-over: Akutagawa Hiroshi, Naraoka Tomoko. Collaboration: Makoto Murei. Cinematography: Komuro Yoshikazu. Music: Takemitsu Toru. Editing: Matsuno Yoshio. Sound: Iwami Kiyoshi. 45 min.

1965 *Gyosen sonansu: Wasurerareta taifu saigai* (The Forgotten Typhoon)

Producer: Ushiyama Junichi for Nihon TV (series: Nonfiction Gekijyo). Script: Oshima Nagisa. Collaboration: Toyotomi Yasushi, Ushiyama Junichi. 30 min.

1968 *Daitoasenso* (The Pacific War, aka *The Greater East Asian War*)

Producer: Ushiyama Junichi for the series Nijusseiki Hour. Commentary: Oshima Nagisa. Voice-over: Komatsu Hosei, Toura Mutsuhiro. Collaboration: Hoshino Toshiko, Shirai Tetsuro. Sound: Morimoto Takao. Editing: Oshima Nagisa. B/W. 2 × 60 min.

1969 *Moutakuto to Bunka Daikakumei* (Mao and the Cultural Revolution)

Producer: Ushiyama Junichi for the series Nijusseiki Hour. Script, Commentary: Oshima Nagisa. Voice-over: Toura Mutsuhiro, Kanze Hideo. Assistant Director: Toshiko Hoshino. Sound: Morimoto Takao. Music: Yamamoto Nozumi. Editing: Miyamoto Yusuke. 16 mm. B/W. 49 min.

1972 *Kyojin-gun* (Giants)

Producer: Goto Tasuhiko, Ushiyama Junichi for Nippon A.V. Productions. Commentary, Interview: Oshima Nagisa. Voice-over: Toura Mutsuhiro. Cinematography: Sengen Seizo. Editing: Hasagawa Yoshindo. Sound: Morimoto Takao, Kimura Tetsujin. Color. 73 min.

1972 *Joi Bengla!*

Producer: Ushiyama Junichi for Nippon A.V. Productions. Cinematography: Sengen Seizo. Sound: Morimoto Takao, Kimura Tetsujin, Ogasawara Kiyoshi. Music: Akiyama Michio. Sound: Kume Akira. Editing: Tomizuka Ryoichi. 24 min.

1972 *Goze-momoku no onna-tabigeinin* (The Village of the Blind Musicians)

Producer: Ushiyama Junichi for Nippon A.V. Productions. Codirector: Ogasawara Kiyoshi. Voice-over: Toura Mutsuhiro. Cinematography: Yoshioka Yasuhiro. Editing: Hiraga Kazuhiko. Sound: Nishizaki Hideo. Color. 24 min.

1973 *Bengal no chichi laman* (The Father of Bangladesh)

Producer: Ushiyama Junichi for Nippon A.V. Productions. Script, Interview: Oshima Nagisa. Cinematography: Sengen Seizo. Editing: Ikeda Ryuzo, Hiraga Kazuhiko. Sound: Ogasawara Kiyoshi. Voice-over: Toura Mutsuhiro. 16 mm. Color. 24 min.

1975 *Ikiteiru nihonkai kaisen* (The Battle of Tsushima)

Producer: Ushiyama Junichi for Nippon A.V. Productions. Interview: Oshima Nagisa. Cinematography: Tonegawa Yoshitsugu, Watanabe Yoshimune, Inaba Hisaichi. Editing: Hiraga Kazuhiko. Sound: Hiraga Hiroshi. Voice-over: Suzuki Mizuho. 16 mm. Color. 49 min.

1976 *Ogon no daichi Bengal* (The Golden Land of Bengal)

Producer: Ushiyama Junichi for Nippon A.V. Productions. Script: Oshima Nagisa. Codirector, Cinematography: Yamazaki Yuji. Editing: Ryuzo Ikeda. Sound: Ikeba Hiroshi. Voice-over: Suzuki Mizuho. 16 mm. Color. 49 min.

1976 *Denki-Moutakuto* (The Life of Mao)

Producer: Ushiyama Junichi for Nippon A.V. Productions. Editing: Tomizuka Ryoichi. Sound: Ikeba Hiroshi, Kimura Tetsujin. Voice-over: Oshima Nagisa. 16 mm. B/W and color. 65 min.

1976 *Ikiteiru umi no bohyo* (Graves at Sea, aka *The Sunken Tomb*)

Producer: Ushiyama Junichi for Nippon A.V. Productions. Cinematography: Masuda Hajime, Tonegawa Yoshitsugu. Editing: Tominaga Ryoichi. Sound: Ikeba Hiroshi. Voice-over: Suzuki Mizuho. Interviews: Oshima Nagisa. 16 mm. Color. 24 min.

1976 *Ikiteiru gyokusai no shima* (The Island of the Final Battle)

Producer: Ushiyama Junichi for Nippon A.V. Productions. Cinematography: Masuda Hajime, Tonegawa Yoshitsugu. Editing: Tominaga Ryoichi. Sound: Ikeba Hiroshi. Voice-over; Suzuki Mizuho. Interviews: Oshima Nagisa. 16 mm. Color. 24 min.

1977 *Yokoi Shoichi: Guam to 28 nen no nazo o ou* (Human Drama: 28 Years of Hiding in the Jungle)

Producer: Ushiyama Junichi, Noguchi Hideo for Nippon A.V. Productions. Cinematography: Matsushita Tokio, Tonegawa Yoshitsugu. Editing: Sato Koichi. Sound: Ikeba Hiroshi. Voice-over: Suzuki Mizuho. Interviews: Oshima Nagisa. 49 min.

1977 *Shisha wa itsumademo wakai* (The Dead Remain Young)

Producer: Ushiyama Junichi, Noguchi Hideo for Nippon A.V. Productions. Cinematography: Otsu Koshiro. Editing: Ikeda Ryuzo. Voice-over: Suzuki Mizuho. Interviews: Oshima Nagisa. 49 min.

1995 *100 Years of Japanese Cinema*

Producer: British Film Institue. The Century of Cinema Project. Script: Oshima Nagisa. 60 min.

BIBLIOGRAPHY

Akinari, Ueda. 1974. *Ugetsu Monogatari: Tales of Moonlight and Rain.* Trans. Leon Zolbrod. Tokyo: Tuttle.

Amakusu, Ken. 1978. "Aspects of Yayoi and Tumulus Art." In *The Beginnings of Japanese Art,* ed. Namio Egami. The Heibonsha Survey of Japanese Art. New York and Tokyo: Wetherhill/Heibonsha.

Anderson, Joseph, and Donald Richie. 1982. *The Japanese Film: Art and Industry.* Princeton: Princeton University Press.

Astruc, Alexandre. 1966. "What Is Mise-en-Scène?" *Cahiers du Cinéma in English,* no.1 (January): 53–55.

Aumont, Jacques. 1970. "A propos de petit garçon." *Cahiers du Cinéma* 218 (March): 30–34.

Barthes, Roland. 1970. *L'Empire des signes.* Paris: Skira.

———. 1977. "The Death of the Author." In *Image Music Text,* ed. and trans. Stephen Heath, 142–147. New York: Hill and Wang.

———. 1982. *Empire of Signs.* Trans. Richard Howard. New York: Hill and Wang.

Bataille, Georges. 1967. *Story of the Eye.* Trans. Joachim Neugroschel. New York: Urizen.

Bates, Tom. 1992. *Rads: The 1970 Bombing of the Army Math Research Center at the University of Wisconsin and Its Aftermath.* New York: HarperCollins.

Beauvoir, Simone de. 1953. *Must We Burn Sade?* Trans. Annette Michelson. London: Peter Neville.

Benayoun, Robert. 1976. "La Spiral de l'absolu." *Positif* 81 (May): 47–48.

Benjamin, Walter. 1966. *Versuch über Brecht.* Frankfurt am Main: Suhrkamp Verlag.

———. 1973. *Understanding Brecht.* Trans. Anna Bostock. London: New Left Books.

Binkin, Martin. 1982. *Blacks and the Military.* Washington, D.C.: Brookings Institution.

Blouin, Claude. 1982. *Le Chemin detourné: Essai sur Kobayashi et le cinéma japonais.* Quebec: Editions Hurtubise.

Bock, Audie. 1978. *Japanese Film Directors.* Tokyo, New York, and San Francisco: Kodansha.

Boland, Bernard. 1978. "Une Sourire pour les pauvres gens." *Cahiers du Cinéma* 292 (September): 50–51.

Bonitzer, Pascal. 1970. "Oshima et les corps-langages." *Cahiers du Cinéma* 218 (March): 30–34.

———. 1976a. "L'Empire des sens." *Cahiers du Cinéma* 265 (March/April): 65.

———. 1976b. "L'Essence du pire (L'Empire des sens)." *Cahiers du Cinéma* 270 (September/October): 48–52.

———. 1983. "La Bosse et la voix: Furyo de Nagisa Oshima." *Cahiers du Cinéma* 348–349 (June/July): 19–22.

Bonitzer, Pascal, ed. 1980. *Monstresses*. Paris: Cahiers du Cinéma.

Borch-Jacobson, Mikkel. 1991. *Lacan: The Absolute Master*. Trans. Douglas Brick. Stanford: Stanford University Press.

Bordwell, David. 1988. *Ozu and the Poetics of Cinema*. Princeton: Princeton University Press.

Bordwell, David, and Kristen Thompson. 1994. *Film History*. New York: McGraw-Hill.

Bowers, Fabion. 1982. *Japanese Theatre*. Rutland, Vt., and Tokyo: Tuttle.

Branigan, Edward. 1984. *Point of View in the Cinema: A Theory of Narration and Subjectivity in Classical Film*. Berlin, New York, and Amsterdam: Mouton.

Brecht, Bertolt. 1964. *Brecht on Theatre: The Development of an Aesthetic*. Trans. John Willet. New York: Hill and Wang.

———. 1975. *Collected Plays*. Trans. Ralph Manheim and John Willet. New York: Vintage.

———. 1993. *The Threepenny Opera. Baal the Mother*. Trans. Ralph Manheim and John Willett. New York: Arcade.

Brecht and East Asian Theatre: The Proceedings of a Conference on Brecht in East Asian Theatre. 1982. Hong Kong: Hong Kong University Press.

Burch, Noël. 1979. *To the Distant Observer: Form and Meaning in the Japanese Cinema*. Berkeley and Los Angeles: University of California Press.

Buscombe, Ed. 1981. "Ideas of Authorship." In *Theories of Authorship*, ed. John Caughie. BFI Readers in Film Studies. London: Routledge and Kegan Paul.

Callois, Roger. 1978. "Sur *L'Empire de la passion*." *Positif* 204 (November): 2–4.

Carter, Rose, and Lois Dilatush. 1976. "Office Ladies." In *Women in Changing Japan*, ed. Joyce Lebra, Joy Paulson, and Elizabeth Powers, 75–89. Stanford: Stanford University Press.

Caughie, John, ed. 1981. *Theories of Authorship*. BFI Readers in Film Studies. London: Routledge and Kegan Paul.

Cecchini, Rose Marie. 1976. "Women and Suicide." In *Women in Changing Japan*, ed. Joyce Lebra, Joy Paulson, and Elizabeth Powers, 263–296. Stanford: Stanford University Press.

Chapman, Seymour. 1978. *Story and Discourse*. Ithaca: Cornell University Press.

Coates, Paul. 1990. "Repetition and Contradiction in the Films of Oshima." *Quarterly Review of Film and Video* 11 (February): 65–71.

Daney, Serge. 1978. "Une Sourire pour les pauvres gens." *Cahiers du Cinéma* 292 (September): 50–51.

Danvers, Louis, and Charles Tatum, Jr. 1986. *Nagisa Oshima*. Paris: Cahiers du Cinéma.

Deleuze, Gilles. 1994. *Repetition and Difference*. Trans. Paul Patton. New York: Columbia University Press.

Deleuze, Gilles, and Felix Guattari. 1987. *A Thousand Plateaus: Capitalism and Schizophrenia*. Trans. Brian Mussumi. Minneapolis: University of Minnesota Press.

Derrida, Jacques. 1987. *The Post Card: From Socrates to Freud and Beyond.* Trans. Alan Bass. Chicago: University of Chicago Press.

———. 1988. "The Purveyor of Truth." In *The Purloined Poe: Lacan, Derrida and Psychoanalytic Reading,* trans. Alan Bass, ed. John P. Muller and William J. Richardson, 173–212. Baltimore: Johns Hopkins University Press.

———. 1994. *Politiques de l'amitié: Suivi de l'oreille de Heidegger.* Paris: Galilee.

Desser, David. 1988. *Eros plus Massacre: An Introduction to the Japanese New Wave Cinema.* Bloomington: Indiana University Press.

Desser, David, and Arthur Noletti, eds. 1992. *Reframing Japanese Cinema.* Bloomington: Indiana University Press.

Doi, L. Takeo. 1963. "Some Thoughts on Helplessness and the Desire to Be Loved." *Psychiatry* 26: 266–272.

Dorson, Richard. 1962. *Folk Legends of Japan.* Rutland, Vt., and Tokyo: Tuttle.

Eaton, Katherine Bliss. 1985. *The Theater of Meyerhold and Brecht.* Westport, Conn.: Greenwood Press.

Foucault, Michel. 1975. *Discipline and Punish: A History of the Prison.* Ithaca: Cornell University Press.

———. 1977. "What Is an Author?" *Language, Countermemory, Practice.* Ithaca: Cornell University Press.

Freud, Sigmund. 1900. *The Interpretation of Dreams.* Trans. James Strachey. *The Standard Edition of the Complete Psychological Works of Sigmund Freud.* London: Hogarth Press.

———. 1953. *Jokes and Their Relationship to the Unconscious.* Trans. James Strachey. *The Standard Edition of the Complete Psychological Works of Sigmund Freud.* London: Hogarth Press.

Gibson, Roma, and Pamela Church Gibson, eds. 1993. *Dirty Looks: Women, Pornography and Power.* London: British Film Institute Press.

Halford, Aubrey S., and Giovanna Halford. 1956. *The Kabuki Handbook.* Rutland, Vt., and Tokyo: Tuttle.

Hani, Mikiso. 1982. *Peasants, Outcasts and Rebels: The Underside of Modern Japan.* New York: Pantheon.

Harootunian, Harry, and Masao Miyoshi. 1989. *Postmodernism and Japan.* Durham, N.C.: Duke University Press.

Haver, William. 1996. *The Body of this Death: Historicity and Sexuality in the Time of AIDS.* Stanford: Stanford University Press.

Hayashi, Saburo. 1959. *Kōgun: The Japanese Army in the Pacific War.* Westport, Conn.: Greenwood Press.

Hearn, Lafcadio. 1984, *Glimpses of Unfamiliar Japan.* 2 vols. Boston: Houghton Mifflin.

Heath, Stephen. 1976–1977. "Anata mo." *Screen* 17(4): 49–66.

———. 1981. *Questions of Cinema.* Bloomington: Indiana University Press.

Hirano, Kyoko. 1992. *Mr. Smith Goes to Tokyo: Japanese Cinema under the American Occupation.* Washington, D.C.: Smithsonian Institution Press.

Hopkins, Jerry. 1985. *Bowie.* New York: Macmillan.

Irigaray, Luce. 1985. *Speculum of the Other Woman.* Trans. Gillian C. Gill. Ithaca: Cornell University Press.

Jackson, Laura. 1976. "Bar Hostesses." In *Women in Changing Japan,* ed. Joyce Lebra, Joy Paulson, and Elizabeth Powers, 133–156. Stanford: Stanford University Press.

Johnson, Barbara. 1988. "The Frame of Reference: Poe, Lacan, Derrida." In *The Purloined Poe: Lacan, Derrida, and Psychoanalytic Reading*, ed. John P. Muller and William J. Richardson. Baltimore: Johns Hopkins University Press.

Kafka, Franz. 1968. *The Trial*. New York: Alfred A. Knopf.

Karatani, Kijin. 1993. *Origins of Japanese Literature*. Trans. Brett de Bary. Durham, N.C.: Duke University Press.

Keene, Donald. 1988. *The Pleasures of Japanese Literature*. New York: Columbia University Press.

Kiebuzinska, Christine Olga. 1988. *Revolutionaries in the Theater: Meyerhold, Brecht, and Witkiewicz*. Ann Arbor: UMI Research Press.

Kipnis, Laura. 1994. *Ecstasy Unlimited: On Sex, Capital, Gender and Aesthetics*. Minneapolis: University of Minnesota Press.

Knee, Adam. 1987. "Criminality, Eroticism and Oshima." *Wide Angle* 9(2): 47–59.

Lacan, Jacques. [1973] 1977. *Le Séminaire livre XI: Les Quatres Concepts fondamentaux de la psychanalyse*. Translated as *Four Fundamental Concepts of Psychoanalysis*, by Alan Sheridan. New York: Norton.

———.1986. *Le Séminaire livre VII: L'Ethique de la psychanalyse*. Paris: Seuil.

———. 1988. "Seminar on 'The Purloined Letter.'" Trans. Jeffery Mehlman. In *The Purloined Poe: Lacan, Derrida, and Psychoanalytic Reading*, ed. John P. Muller and William J. Richardson, 28–54. Baltimore: Johns Hopkins University Press.

———. 1991. *Le Séminaire livre VIII: Le Transfert*. Paris: Seuil.

———. 1992. *The Seminar of Jacques Lacan, Book VII: The Ethics of Psychoanalysis, 1959–60*, New York: Norton.

Laplanche, J., and Pontalis, J.-B. 1973. *The Language of Psychoanalysis*, Trans. Donald Nicholson-Smith. New York: Norton.

Lebra, Joyce, Joy Paulson, and Elizabeth Powers, eds. 1976. *Women in Changing Japan*. Stanford: Stanford University Press.

Lehman, Peter. 1987. "Oshima: The Avant-Garde Artist Without an Avant-Garde Style." *Wide Angle* 9(2): 18–31.

———. 1993. *Running Scared: Masculinity and the Representation of the Male Body*. Philadelphia: Temple University Press.

Lellis, George. 1982. *Bertolt Brecht, Cahiers du Cinéma and Contemporary Film Theory*. Ann Arbor: UMI Research Press.

Lyotard, Jean-François. 1979. *Au juste: Conversations*. Paris: Bourgeois. [Translated as *Just Gaming*. Minneapolis: University of Minnesota Press, 1985.]

———. 1986. "Acinema." Trans. Paisley Livingston. In *Narrative, Apparatus, Technology*, ed. Phil Rosen, 349–359. New York: Columbia University Press, 1986.

———. 1988. *The Differend: Phrases in Dispute*. Minneapolis: University of Minnesota.

———. 1993. *Libidinal Economy*. Trans. Ian Hamilton Grant. Bloomington: Indiana University Press.

McCormick, Ruth. 1974. "Ritual, the Family and the State: A Critique of Nagisa Oshima's *The Ceremony*." *Cineaste* 6: 20–26.

McDonald, Keiko. 1983. *Cinema East: A Critical Study of Major Japanese Films*. East Brunswick, N.J.: Associated University Presses.

MacGregor, Morris J. 1981. *Integration of the Armed Forces, 1940–1965*. Washington, D.C.: Center of Military History, U.S. Army.

Martin, Marcel. 1983. "Furyo: L'Honneur d'un capitaine." *Revue du Cinéma; Image et Son* 385 (July/August): 19–20.

Masson, Alain. 1978. "Déchant du lendemain." *Positif* 206 (May): 8–10.

Matsumoto, Sheila. 1976. "Women in Factories." In *Women in Changing Japan,* ed. Joyce Lebra, Joy Paulson, and Elizabeth Powers, 51–74. Stanford: Stanford University Press.

Maxson, Mary Lou. 1976. "Women in Family Businesses." In *Women in Changing Japan,* ed. Joyce Lebra, Joy Paulson, and Elizabeth Powers, 89–106. Stanford: Stanford University Press.

Mellen, Joan. 1975. *Voices from the Japanese Cinema.* New York: Liveright.

———. 1976. *The Waves at Genji's Door: Japan Through Its Cinema.* New York: Pantheon.

Metz, Christian. 1974. *Language and Cinema.* The Hague: Mouton.

Michelson, Annette. 1992. "Introduction." In *Cinema, Censorship, and the State: The Writings of Nagisa Oshima,* trans. Dawn Lawson, Cambridge, Mass.: MIT Press, 1–5.

Mikami, Tsugio. 1981. *The Art of Japanese Ceramics.* Tokyo: Heibonsha.

Moullet, Luc. 1960. "Jean-Luc Godard." *Cahiers du Cinéma* 106: 25–36.

Muller, John P., and William J. Richardson, eds. 1988. *The Purloined Poe: Lacan, Derrida, and Psychoanalytic Reading.* Baltimore: Johns Hopkins University Press.

Munroe, Alexandra, ed. 1994a. *Japanese Art after 1945: Scream Against the Sky.* New York: Abrams.

———. 1994b. "Revolt of the Flesh: Ankoko Butoh and Obsessional Art." In *Japanese Art after 1945: Scream Against the Sky,* ed. Alexandra Munroe, 189–214. New York: Abrams.

———. 1994c. "To Challenge the Mid-Summer Sun: The Gutai Group." In *Japanese Art after 1945: Scream Against the Sky,* ed. Alexandra Munroe, 83–124. New York: Abrams.

Nichols, Bill. 1988. "The Voice of Documentary." In *New Challenges in Documentary,* ed. Alan Rosenthal, 48–63. Berkeley and Los Angeles: University of California Press.

Nygren, Scott. 1987. "The Pacific War: Reading, Contradiction, Denial." *Wide Angle* 9(2): 60–70.

Oe, Kenzaburo. 1981. *The Catch and Other War Stories.* Tokyo: Kodansha.

Ortolani, Benito. 1990. *The Japanese Theatre: From Shamanistic Ritual to Contemporary Pluralism.* Handbuch der Orientalistik. Fünfte Abteilung, *Japan.* 2. Bd., *Theater.* 1. Abschnitt. Leiden and New York: E. J. Brill.

Oshima, Nagisa. 1970. "Interview." *Cahiers du Cinéma* 218 (March): 30–34.

———. 1978a. "Interview." *Cahiers du Cinéma* 292 (September): 45–49.

———. 1978b. "La Revolution et l'état." *Positif* 207 (June): 5–7.

———. 1978c. "Ma profession, le crime, l'amour et la mort." *Positif* 206 (May): 11–13.

———. 1980. *Ecrits, 1956–1978: Dissolution et jaillissement.* Paris: Gallimard.

———. 1983a. "Entretien avec Nagisa Oshima sur Furyo." *Positif* 267 (May): 8–11.

———. 1983b. "Propos de Nagisa Oshima." *Revue de Cinéma: Image et Son* 385 (July/August): 20–21.

———. 1990. "Godard vu du Japon: Entretien avec Nagisa Oshima." *Cahiers du Cinéma* 437 (November): 26–27.

———. 1992. *Cinema, Censorship and the State: The Writings of Nagisa Oshima.* Trans. Dawn Lawson. Cambridge, Mass.: MIT Press.

Oudart, Jean-Pierre. 1971. "Le Hors-champ de l'auteur." *Cahiers du Cinéma* 236–237 (March/April): 86–89.

———. 1981. "The Absent Field of the Author." In *Theories of Authorship*, ed. John Caughie, 261–270. BFI Readers in Film Studies. London: Routledge and Kegan Paul.

Oudart, Jean-Pierre, and Serge Daney. 1971–1972. "Le Nom de l'auteur." *Cahiers du Cinéma* 234–235 (December/February): 79–93.

Ozaki, Yei Theodora. 1967. "The Mirror of Matsuyama." In *The Japanese Fairy Book*, 119–139. New York: Dover.

Polan, Dana. 1983. "Politics as Process in Three Films by Nagisa Oshima." *Film Criticism* 8, no. 1 (Fall): 35–41.

———. 1985. *The Political Language of Film and the Avant-Garde*. Ann Arbor: UMI Research Press.

Roland, Alan. 1988. *In Search of Self in India and Japan: Toward a Cross-Cultural Psychology*. Princeton: Princeton University Press.

Ronnell, Avital. 1989. *The Telephone Book: Technology, Schizophrenia, Electric Speech*. Lincoln: University of Nebraska Press.

Russell, Catherine. 1995. *Narrative Mortality: Death, Closure, and New Wave Cinemas*. Minneapolis: University of Minnesota Press.

Said, Edward. 1979. *Orientalism*. New York: Vintage.

Sakai, Naoki. 1992. *Voices of the Past: The Status of Language in Eighteenth-Century Japanese Discourse*. Ithaca: Cornell University Press.

Sato, Tadao. 1973. *Oshima Nagisa no sekai* (The World of Nagisa Oshima). Tokyo: Chikuma Shobo.

———. 1982. *Currents in Japanese Film*. Tokyo, New York, and San Francisco: Kodansha.

Sawicki, Jana. 1991. *Disciplining Foucault: Feminism, Power and the Body*. New York: Routledge.

Schefer, Jean-Louis. 1980. "C'est Polyxène." In *Monstresses*, ed. Pascal Bonitzer, 67. Paris: Cahiers du Cinéma.

Shochiku. 1960. Publicity brochure.

Sievers, Sharon. 1982. *Flowers in Salt: The Beginnings of Feminist Consciousness in Modern Japan*. Stanford: Stanford University Press.

Silverberg, Miriam. "The Modern Girl as Militant." In *Recreating Japanese Women, 1600–1945*, ed. Gail Lee Bernstein, 239–266. Berkeley and Los Angeles: University of California Press.

Silverman, Kaja. 1992. *Male Subjectivity at the Margins*. New York: Routledge.

Singer, Kurt. 1973. *Mirror, Sword and Jewel*. New York: George Braziller.

Song, Yun-Yeop. 1977. *Bertolt Brecht und die chinesische Philosophie*. Bonn: Bouvier.

Spence, Jonathan D. 1990. *The Search for Modern China*. New York: Norton.

Tatlow, Antony. 1977. *The Mask of Evil: Brecht's Response to the Poetry, Theatre and Thought of China and Japan. A Comparative and Critical Evaluation*. Europaische Hochschulschriften. Reihe I, Deutsche Literatur und Germanistik, v. 213. Bern: P. Lang.

Tayama, Rikiya. 1975. *Nihon no eiga sakka-tachi: Sosaku no himatsu*. Tokyo: Daviddosha.

Tessier, Max 1984. *Le Cinéma japonais au présent*. Paris: Pierre Lherminier.

———. 1981. *Images du cinéma japonais*. Paris: Henri Veyrier.

Tsurumi, Shunsuke. 1986. *An Intellectual History of Wartime Japan 1931–1945*. London: KPI.

————. 1987. "Trends in Popular Songs since the 60s." In *A Cultural History of Postwar Japan 1945–1980*, 79–102. London: KPI.

Turim, Maureen. 1976. *"Ecriture Blanche:* The Ordering of the Filmic Text in *The Chronicle of Anna Magdelena Bach."* In *Purdue Film Studies Annual*, 176–191. Lafayette, Ind.: Purdue University Press.

————. 1980. "Symmetry/Asymmetry and Visual Fascination." *Wide Angle* 4: 38–47.

————. 1981–1982. "Rituals, Desire, Death in Oshima's *Ceremonies." Enclitic* 5–6 (Fall/Spring): 181–189.

————. 1984. "Oblique Angles: The Film Projects of Jean-Marie Straub and Daniel Huillet." In *The New German Filmmaker*, ed. Klaus Phillips, 335–358. New York: Ungar.

————. 1986. "Textuality and Theatricality in Brecht and Straub/Huillet." In *German Film and Literature*, ed. Eric Rentschler, 231–245. New York: Methuen.

————. 1987. "Signs of Sexuality in Oshima's Tales of Passion." *Wide Angle* 9(2): 32–46.

————. 1989. *Flashbacks in Film: Memory and History.* New York: Routledge.

————. 1993. "The Erotic in Asian Cinema." In *Dirty Looks: Women, Pornography, Power*, ed. Pamela Church Gibson and Roma Gibson, 81–89. London: British Film Institute Press.

————. Forthcoming. "Looking Back at the Mirror." In *Psychoanalysis, Feminisms*, ed. Andrew Gorden and Peter Rudnytsky. Albany: State University of New York Press.

van der Post, Laurens. 1963. *The Sower and the Seed.* New York: W. Morrow.

Varley, H. Paul. 1984. *Japanese Culture.* Honolulu: University of Hawaii Press.

Walsh, Martin. 1981. *The Brechtian Aspect of Radical Cinema.* London: British Film Institute Press.

Weeks, Jeffrey. 1981. *Sex, Politics and Society: The Regulation of Sexuality since 1800.* London and New York: Longman.

Willett, John. 1984. *Brecht in Context: Comparative Approaches.* London and New York: Methuen.

Williams, Linda. 1989. *Hardcore: Power, Pleasure and the "Frenzy of the Visible."* Berkeley and Los Angeles: University of California Press.

Winston, Brian. 1988. "The Tradition of the Victim in Griersonian Documentary." In *New Challenges in Documentary*, ed. Alan Rosenthal, 21–33. Berkeley and Los Angeles: University of California Press.

Wittgenstein, Ludwig. 1958. *The Blue and Brown Books.* New York: Harper and Row.

Wylie, Philip. 1942. *A Generation of Vipers.* New York: Farrar and Rinehart.

Yanagita, Kunio. 1986. *The Yanagita Kunio Guide to the Japanese Folk Tale.* Trans. Fanny Hagin Mayer. Bloomington: Indiana University Press.

Yoshimoto, Mitsuhiro. 1993. "Logic of Sentiment: The Postwar Japanese Cinema and Questions of Modernity (Melodrama, Sentimentality, Kurosawa Akira, Masumura Yasuzo, Yasujiro Ozu, Oshima Nagisa)." Ph.D. dissertation, University of California, San Diego.

INDEX

Page references in italics refer to photographs.

Abe, Kobo, 25
Abe, Sada, 76, 267
Abe, Tetsuo, 89
Abortion: in *Boy*, 91–92; in *Burial of the Sun*,
    49; in *Cruel Story of Youth*, 41, 253
A Bout de souffle (Breathless), 13, 35
"Acting out" *(mise-en-acte, agieren)*, 74–75,
    114, 116, 123
Active involvement *(shutaiteki)*, 6
Activism. *See* Demonstrations
Aesthetics, 21–22
Agit-prop films, 88
Agit-prop theater, 44
Ai no borei. See *Empire of Passion*
Ai no korida. See *Realm of the Senses*
Ai to kibo no machi. See *Town of Love and
    Hope, A*
Ajioka, Toru, 56
Akasegawa, Genpei, 105
Akatsuki no dasso (Desertion at Dawn), 157
Akinari, Ueda, 145
Akutagwa, Hiroshi, 55
Ali, Muhammed, 86
Alienation. *See* Distanciation
Allegory: in *Burial of the Sun*, 51, 251; in
    The Catch, 163, 165, 168; in *Dear Summer
    Sister*, 204–5, 207; and feminist film
    theory, 261; in *Max, Mon Amour*, 209,
    213; in "The Purloined Letter," 32–33,
    106; in *Realm of the Senses*, 139–40; in
    Town of Love and Hope, 27–33; in *Violence
    at Noon*, 263

*All Under the Moon (Tsuki wa dotchi ni dete
    Iru)*, 270
Almodovar, Pedro, 271
Amaeru, 122
Amakasu, Ken, 24
Amakusa Shiro Tokisada (Shiro Tokisada), 183,
    215
AMPO demonstrations, 9–10, 39–40, 54–55,
    62, 122
Anderson, Joseph, 4, 11, 13, 216
Andersson, Harriet, 138
Androgyny, 88–89
Animal rights groups, 213
Animals, 162–63, 208–13
Animated films, 227, 229, 272
L'Année dernière à Marienbad (Robbe-Grillet),
    67
Anti-Semitism, 213–14
Antoine Bloyé (Nizan), 192
Apes, in films, 208–13
Ape Woman, The, 210
Araki, Ichiro, 187
Architecture, 22, 261
Arnaud, Jean-Jacques, 210
Art, 4, 62, 104–5
Art cinema, 61
Artisan families, 4
Asanuma, Inejiro, 59
Astruc, Alexandre, 53
ATG (film company), 66
Audience expectations, 96–98, 101
Au Juste (Lyotard), 67

Aumont, Jacques, 17, 90
AUM Shin Rikyo, 270
Auteurism, 2–6, 14–18, 159, 261, 272
Avant-garde artists *(zen'ei bijutsu)*, 105

Ban, Ho Chin, 223
Bando, Tomasaburo, 147
Bangladesh, 245
"Banish Green" (Oshima), 21–22, 269, 272
Bardeche, Maurice, 214
Bar hostesses, 250
Bars, 41
Barthes, Roland, 15–16, 126, 127–28, 129
Baseball, 116–18, 244
Bataille, Georges, 132–33, 142, 181, 183, 263
Battle of Tokyo, or the Story of the Young Man Who Left His Will on Film (Tokyo senso sengo hiwa): actions of protagonists in, 28; and art, 104–5; audience expectations undermined in, 96–98, 101; and auteurism, 15; comedy in, 105, 185; debate over theories of film in, *99*, 100–102, 217, 244, 245; dialogue in, 52, 96, 101, 103; documentary footage in, 99–102, 217, 244; film techniques in, 96–98, 103, 107; film-within-film in, 78, 97–103, 104, 105, 106, 107–9, 262; identity in, 26, 98–99, 102; intertitles in, 103–4; music in, 105; *Night and Fog in Japan* compared to, 52; political references in, *98*, 99–102, 104, 108–9; rape in, 107; repetitions in, 38, 76, 103; Sato on, 108–9; sexuality in, 102–3, 106; subjectivity in, 177; suicide in, 22, 100, 102, 107, 108; title of, 108, 126; voice-over in, 100; windows in, 22, 103
Battle of Tsushima, The (Ikiteiru nihonkai kaisen), 234–35
Bazin, André, 103
Beauty, 21
Beauvoir, Simone de, 258
Benjamin, Walter, 44
Bertolucci, Bernardo, 271
Bestiality, 208–9, 211–14
Betrothed, The (Nagasugita haru), 12, 33
"Beyond Endless Self-Negation" (Oshima), 6
Beyond the Pleasure Principle (Lacan), 136
Biao, Lin, 242–43
Bibliophilia, 82, 211
Bicycle Thief, The, 160
Biography, 3–4, 5–10, 15

Blanchot, Maurice, 136
Bloody May Day of 1953, 40
Bluestockings movement, 252
Bock, Audie, 7, 261
Bonitzer, Pascal, 70, 138–39, 180, 181, 182, 183
Bookstores, 81
Borch-Jacobson, Mikkel, 25
Boulle, Pierre, 210
Bouvard et Pécuchet (Flaubert), 86
Bowie, David, 169, 174, 178
Boy (Shonen): abortion in, 91–92; actions of protagonist in, 28; circulation metaphor in, 93; color in, 93–94; comedy in, 185; family in, 90–92; fantasy in, 94, 95; film techniques in, 89, 93, 95–96; flashbacks in, 95; humanism in, 89, 95–96; *Ikiru* compared to, 92; as inspired by actual event, 89–90; mirror metaphor in, 25; music in, 90; *One Wonderful Sunday* compared to, 92; psychoanalysis on, 89; repetitions in, 38, 93; scams in, 89–91, 92, 94, 95; voice-over in, 95
Brakhage, Stan, 97
Branigan, Edward, 98, 108
Brasillach, Robert, 214
Breathless (A Bout de souffle), 13, 35
Brecht, Bertolt: and Asian theater, 45; *Caucasian Chalk Circle*, 63–64; cinematic borrowing of, 45–46; and comedy, 185; and distanciation, 43–44, 45, 49, 63, 76, 89, 164; learning plays, 260; Oshima's films compared to, 2, 44–46, 49, 129, 158, 159, 164, 166–67, 251; and psychoanalysis, 123–24; reactions against, 45; *Rise and Fall of the City of Mahogany, The*, 45; *Threepenny Opera*, 45, 46, 63, 251
Brecht and East Asian Theater, 44
Bresson, Robert, 17
Breton, André, 191
Bride of Frankenstein, 138
Britain, 240; documentaries in, 217–18, 270
British Film Institute, 270
Buddhism, 6, 132, 154
Bungaku (masked dance), 129
Buñuel, Luis, 208
Burch, Noël, 11, 30, 46, 200, 263
Buren, Daniel, 104
Burial of the Sun (Taiyo no hakaba): abortion in, 49; allegory in, 51, 251; as Brechtian, 43–46, 49, 251; color in, 50–51; crimi-

nality in, 46; *Cruel Story of Youth* compared to, 41; film techniques in, 27, 46, *47,* 47–51; gangs in, 41, 47, 48–49, 251; gender in, 47–48, 246–48, *247,* 249–52; on humanism, 251; *Night and Fog in Japan* compared to, 14; Osaka in, 27, *28, 47,* 48, 51; political references in, 51, 247, 250–51; prostitution in, 47, 250, 251; publicity for, 246–47, *247;* rape in, 49–50, 251; repetitions in, 51; scams in, 47–48, 196, 250; sexuality in, 46, 47–48, 49–50, 246–48, *247,* 250–52; suicide in, 50; sun tribe films compared to, 50–51, 246–48; title of, 246, 247; violence in, 50; voyeurism in, 49, 50

Buscombe, Ed, 3

Butoh, 62, 135

Bye Bye Monkey, 210

Ça, 17

Cahiers du Cinéma, 3, 13, 17, 20–21, 138

Cain, James, 153

Camera-eye, 97

Camus, Albert, 67, 159

Cannes film festival, 210

Capital punishment, 65, 68–69, 80

Carné, Marcel, 214

Carrièrre, Jean-Claude, 208

Castration, 131, 137, 143, 181, 210

"Catch, The" (Oe), 158–63, 168

Catch, The (Shiiku), 164, 164–68, *167,* 183

Caucasian Chalk Circle (Brecht), *63–64*

Censorship: in China, 273; of *Desertion at Dawn,* 157; in France, 156; in Japan, 128, 157; of *Night and Fog in Japan,* 14, 52, 59, 60, 62; of *Realm of the Senses,* 45, 128, 156

Century of Cinema, The, 270, 271

Ceremonies (Gishiki): "acting out" in, 75, 114, 116, 123; comedy in, 185; family in, 109, 112, 113–14, 121, 260; fantasy in, 94, 95, 116, *117;* film techniques in, 113, *114,* 114–15, 118–19, *120;* flashbacks in, 110–12, 113, 116–17, 121, 122, 123; gender in, 118, 120–21, 254, *255;* incest in, 114, 206, 254; music in, 105, 112, 115; narrative sequences in, 110–12; obsession in, 115; patriarchal authority in, 118–22, *119,* 260; political references in, 122, 244; psychoanalysis on, 122–23; rape in, 119–20, 121, 185, 260–61; rituals in, 109, *116,* 116–18; sexuality in, 114, 117–22;

and subjectivity, 112–13; suicide in, 116, *117,* 120; voice-over in, 109, 114, 118; weddings in, 55, 121

Chabrol, Claude, 13

Chagall, Marc, 19

China: cultural revolution in, 9, 62, 240–44; documentaries on, 216; filmmakers in, 273; mirrors in, 24

Chinoise, La, 88

Christianity, 80, 182, 183

Cinemascope. *See* Wide-screen images

Cinémateque Française, 196

Cinema verité, 85–86, 97, 188, 201, 218, 221

Cinétheque, 17

Circularity, 22, 29, 80

Citizenship, in Japan, 72, 201

Class, 28–29, 30–32, 200, 235, 260

Coates, Paul, 31–32, 202

Color, 50–51, 93–94, 131

Comedy: absurd, 64–65, 208; in *Battle of Tokyo,* 105, 185; in *Boy,* 185; Brechtian, 185; in *Ceremonies,* 185; in *Dear Summer Sister,* 204–5, 208; in *Death by Hanging,* 78, 105; in fantasy, 208; in France, 212; in Japan, 185, 195, 214, 272; in *Max, Mon Amour,* 209–10, 211–12, 213; Oshima on, 185, 195, 214, 272; and repetitions, 202; song linked to, 185; in *Three Resurrected Drunks,* 196, 197, 202, 212; in *Treatise on Japanese Bawdy Song,* 186, 188, 190, 192–93, 194, 195

"Comfort women," 149, 193, 194, 222–23, 264

Communist party: in China, 62, 240–44; in Japan, 9, 44–45, 55, 243; *Night and Fog in Japan* on, 51, 59; and Nizan, 190; Oshima on, 9, 243

Conceptual art, 104–5

Conformity, 8, 23, 30, 177, 182

Confucious, 6

Cooper, Merrian C., 210

Coutard, Raoul, 212

Crazed Fruit (Kurutta kajitsu), 12, 33

Criminality, 46, 65–66

Crucified Lovers, 20

Cruel Story of Youth (Seishun sankoku monogatari): abortion in, 41, 253; *Breathless* cited in, 35; *Burial of the Sun* compared to, 41; *Crucified Lovers* compared to, 20; film techniques in, 42–43; gender in, 253–54; Ko cited in, 12, 13; as New Wave,

Cruel Story of Youth (continued)
5; political references in, 27, 39–40, 41–
42, 187; rape in, 36–37, 259; *Realm of the
Senses* compared to, 41; repetitions in,
38–39; scams in, 35–36, 42; sexuality in,
40–41; sun tribe films compared to, 33;
Town of Love and Hope compared to, 43;
voice-over in, 253
Currents in Japanese Cinema (Sato), 4

*Daàhóng denglóng gauogao guà (Raise the Red
Lantern)*, 273
Daiei, 12
Daito senso (The Pacific War), 216, 225–34,
228, 230, 232, 244
Dance, 62, 129, 135, 204
Danvers, Louis, 3, 7, 54
Dauman, Anatole, 125–26, 156
Dead Man, The (Bataille), *263*
*Dead Remain Young, The (Shisha wa itsuma
demo wakai–Okinaw gakudo sokai-sen no
higeki)*, 206, 235, *236, 237*
Dear Summer Sister (Natsu no imoto), 204–5,
207, 235
Death, 42–43, 140–43, 262–63. *See also*
Suicide
Death by Hanging (Koshikei): "acting out" in,
74–75; as Brechtian, 45, 62–65, 66–67,
70, 177; capital punishment in, 65, 68–
69, 80; comedy in, 78, 105; criticism
of, 65; dialogue in, 67, 70–71, 78–79,
80; documentary compared to, 68, 76;
dreams in, 79–81; "failed action" in, 70;
film techniques in, 69, 70, *73*, 74, *74,
75*–76, 77, 78, 80; as Freudian, 65–66;
gender in, 71–72, 77–78, 79; identity
in, 201; intertitles in, 66–67, 68, 69, 70;
Kafka compared to, 64; Korean issues in,
70; *Merry Christmas, Mr. Lawrence* compared to, 177; mirror metaphors in, 25;
psychoanalysis on, 66, 78–79, 80–81;
rape in, 66, 71–72, 76, 79, 259; reenactments in, 70–77; repetitions in, 71, 76–
77, 80; script of, 66; sound track in, 69,
80; *Three Resurrected Drunks* compared
to, 201; voice-over in, 69–70
Deleuze, Gilles, 136–37, 202
Demonstrations: AMPO (U.S. security pact
treaty), 9–10, 39–40, 54–55, 62, 122; in
Battle of Tokyo, 98, 99–100, 104, 108; in
Burial of the Sun, 51; bystanders in, 40;

in *Cruel Story of Youth,* 39–40; culture and
politics blended in, 62; Founder's Day,
186, 187; generational differences in, 40;
in Korea, 39, 40, 223; by Korean immigrants, *220,* 220–21; at Kyoto University,
9; in *Night and Fog in Japan,* 9–10, 55–
56; Okinawa Solidarity Day, 100; Oshima's involvement in, 9–10, 40, 251; political opposites of, 251; "Tokyo War," 108;
in *Treatise on Japanese Bawdy Song, 186,*
187, 189
"Densetsu" (Japanese folktale), 144
Depardieu, Gerard, 210
Derrida, Jacques, 32–33, 172–73
Desertion at Dawn (Akatsuki no dasso), 157
De Sica, Vittoria, 30–31, 160
Desire, displays of, 33–34. *See also* Sexuality
Desser, David, 5, 183, 202
*Deux ou trois choses que je sais d'elle (Two or
Three Things I Know about Her),* 86
Dialogue: in *Battle of Tokyo,* 52, 96, 101, 103;
in *The Catch,* 165, 166; in *Death by Hanging,* 67, 70–71, 78–79, 80; discussion-
drama, 52; in *Night and Fog in Japan,*
51–52; in *Realm of the Senses,* 140
*Diary of a Shinjuku Thief (Shinjuku dorobo
nikki):* "acting out" in, 75; bibliophilia
in, 211; cinema verité in, 85–86; film
techniques in, 81, 82, *84,* 85–86, *87,* 88;
gender in, 85–86; Godard's films compared to, 86, 88; Juro Karo Situation
Players in, 45, *87,* 87–88; mirror metaphors in, 85; *Night and Fog in Japan* compared to, 83; political references in, 45;
as postmodernist, 2; psychoanalysis on,
85; rape, 84; sexuality in, 84–89; Shinjuku district in, 81, 82; song in, 82, *84,*
88, 20; *Treatise on Japanese Bawdy Song*
compared to, 188; voice-over in, 86–87;
voyeurism in, 82, *84,* 85
Diary of Yunbogi (Yunbogi no nikki), 89, 223–
25, *224,* 225
Dietrich, Marlene, 138
Differend, The (Lyotard), 67
Discipline and Punish (Foucault), 68
Discussion drama (diskasshon-dorama), 52
Distanciation *(Verfremdung),* 43–44, 45, 49,
63, 76, 89, 164
Distribution. *See* International distribution
Docudrama, 76
Documentaries: about Korea, 223–25; Anglo-

American, 217–18; in *Battle of Tokyo*, 99–102, 217, 244; on cinema history, 270; as consciousness raising, 216–17; criticism of, 217–18; *Death by Hanging* compared to, 68, 76; film techniques in, 52–53, 217–19; Griersonian, 217–18; in Japan, 101, 215, 216–17, 218–19; during the Pacific War, 216, 218–19; post-war, 216–17; as propaganda, 216; television, 215, 218–19; voice-over in, 217. See also *specific documentaries*
Doi, L. Takeo, 122–23
Domestic dramas, 21
Don't Touch the White Woman (Ne Touchez pas aux femmes blanches), 209
Doro no kawa (Muddy River), 31, 32
Dorson, Richard, 132
Dostoyevsky, Fyodor, 81
Dreams, 28, 79–81, 146
Dreigroscher Oper, Die (Brecht), 45, 46, 63, 251
Drinking scenes, 41, 85–86
Drunken Angel (Yoidore tenshi), 31
Duras, Marguerite, 68

Ecrits (Lacan), 25
Edinburgh film festival, 208
Edo. *See* Tokyo
Eiga Hiho (Film Review), 12
Eisenstein, Sergei, 19, 45, 59, 74, 81
"Elegy of Seven-Mile Beach" (song), 188–89
Embryo Hunts in Secret (Taiiji ga mitsuryo suru toki), 263–64
L'Empire des signes (Barthes), 126
Empire of Passion (Ai no borei): dreams in, 146; film techniques in, 151, *152*, 154, 155–56; gender in, 149–50; ghosts in, 143–47, *147*, 151, 154–55; green in, 21; historical references in, 147–49; justice in, 153–55; as Nietzschean, 153–54; Oedipal mythology in, 151–52, 154; as pornography, 156; psychoanalysis on, 127; rape in, 259; *Realm of the Senses* compared to, 126, 143–44, 151, 155, 156; repetitions in, 154; sexuality in, 125, 147, 149–56; title of, 126–28; visual appeal of, 152–53, *153*, 155–56; voice-over in, 152; voyeurism in, 151–52
Equality, 30
Erinnern, 74
Eros plus Massacre (Desser), 5
Eroticism. *See* Sexuality
L'Etranger (Camus), 67

Etsuraku (Pleasures of the Flesh), 264–66, *265*
European Federation of Audiovisual Directors, 271

Face of Another, The (Abe), 25
Family: in *Boy*, 90–92; in *Ceremonies*, 109, 112, 113–14, 121, 260; in *Dear Summer Sister*, 204–5, 207; in Japan,, 4, 7–8, 122, 260; in Japanase arts, 4; in *Max, Mon Amour*, 213
Family dramas (Shomin-geki), 30, 89
Family Game, The (Kazoku geimu), 195
Fantasy: in *Boy*, 94, 95; in *Ceremonies*, 94, 95, 116, *117*; in comedy, 208; in *Realm of the Senses*, 142–43; in *Three Resurrected Drunks*, 201; in *Treatise on Japanese Bawdy Song*, 186–87, 188, 193, 194–95
Farewell My Concubine, 273
Fascism, 21, 23, 182
Fassbinder, Rainer Werner, 17, 45
Fatherhood, 7–8
"February 26 incident" of 1936, 173
Feminism: in Japan, 252; and Oshima, 249; "personal is political" slogan in, 56–57; on pornography, 267, 268; on rape, 258–59. *See also* Gender
Feminist film theory, 17–18, 249, 261
Ferreri, Marco, 209–10
Film Directors of the World (Sekkai no eiga sakka 6), 9
Film festivals, 62, 147, 208, 210
Film Review (Eiga Hiho), 12
Flaherty, Robert, 217
Flashbacks: in *Boy*, 95; in *Ceremonies*, 110–12, 113, 116–17, 121, 122, 123; in *Ikiru*, 92; in *Mao and the Cultural Revolution*, 241; in *Merry Christmas, Mr. Lawrence*, 170, 171, 179–81; in *Night and Fog in Japan*, 56, 57, *58*, 58–59; in *Violence at noon*, 257
Flashbacks in Film (Turim), 56, 179
Flaubert, Gustave, 86
Flower arranging (ikebana), 21
Fluctuating Equilibrium (Klee), 104
Folklore: female demons in, 137, 144–45, 155, 205; ghosts in, 144–46, 155; menstrual taboo in, 132; mirror metaphors in, 24–25, 145–46; and propaganda, 227, 229
Folk Parody Gang, 196
Forgotten Soldiers (Wasurerareta kogun), 219–23, *220*

Formalism, 112, 202

Forty-seven Ronin (Genroku chushingura), 11

Foucault, Michel, 15–16, 17, 68

Founder's Day (Kenkokubi), *186,* 187

France: anti-Semitism in, 214; auteurism in, 3, 15; censorship in, 156; comedy in, 212; infidelity drama in, 208; literature in, 67; screening archives in, 196

Frears, Stephen, 271

Free Theater (Joyu gekijo), 187

Freud, Sigmund: *Death by Hanging* on, 65–66; on dreams, 28; on "failed action," 70; on jokes, 187; Lacan on, 89, 136; on repetitions, 38; on repressed memories, 32, 106; and sex therapy, 85

Friendships, 172–74

"From an Endless Self-Negation" (Oshima), 6

Fukao, Michinori, 66

Furyo, 159. See *Merry Christmas, Mr. Lawrence*

Gangs *(shinai-kai),* 41, 47, 48–49, 251

Gangsters *(yakuza),* 33, 34–35, 47, 83, 196, 266

GATT (Global Agreement on Tarriffs and Trade), 271

Gender: and androgyny, 88–89; and author as subject, 17–18; in *Burial of the Sun,* 47–48, 246–48, *247,* 249–52; in *Ceremonies,* 118, 120–21, 254, *255;* in *Cruel Story of Youth,* 253–54; in *Death by Hanging,* 71–72, 77–78, 79; in *Diary of a Shinjuku Thief,* 85–86; in *Empire of the Passion,* 149–50; in *A Monument to Youth,* 223; in *Realm of the Senses,* 137–38, *138;* in *Treatise on Japanese Bawdy Song,* 188–89, 190, 192, 193; in *Violence at Noon,* 254–58, *256. See also* Feminism; Feminist film theory; Sexuality; Women

Generation of Vipers (Wylie), 8

Genet, Jean, 83, 86

Genre films, 19–20

Genroku chushingura (Forty-seven Ronin), 11

Germany, 44, 240

Ghosts: in *Empire of Passion,* 143–47, 151, 154–55; in folklore, 144–46, 155; in *Night and Fog in Japan,* 55; in *Violence at Noon,* 263

Giants (Kyojin-gur), 244

Gibson, Pamela Church, 268

Gibson, Roma, 268

Girardot, Annie, 210

Global Agreement on Tarriffs and Trade (GATT), 271

Global marketing. *See* International distribution

Godard, Jean-Luc, 13–14, 35, 45, 86, 88, 270

Gohatto (Taboo), 271–72

Golden Land of Bengal, The (Ougon no daichi Bengal), 245

Goldmann, Lucien, 18

Gombrowicz, Witold, 183

Goya, Lucientes, 195

Greater Pacific War, The (Daito senso), 216, 225–34, *228, 230, 232,* 244

Green: symbolism of, 21–22

Griersonian documentary, 217–18

Guam, 235, 237

Guattari, Felix, 136–37

Guillermin, John, 210

Guomindang, 241–42

Gutai art, 62, 105

Hagiwara, Sakutaro, 86

Hahinosu-jo kiroku (Hidden Fortress), 244

Hakucho-kao dance company, 204

Hamlet (Shakespeare), 177

Handa, Norihiku, 197

Haratsuka, Raicho, 252

Haru, Masato, 108

Haver, William, 154

Hawks, Howard, 17

Hayakawa, Seshu, 270

Hayami, Ichiro, 55

Hayashi, Saburo, 173

Hearn, Lafcadio, 145

Heath, Stephen, 75–76, 127, 129, 149, 208, 248

Helm, Brigitte, 138

Hidden Fortress (Hahinosu-jo kiroku), 244

Hirano, Kyoko, 157

Hi Red Center, 105

Hiroshima, 233

Hiroshima, Mon Amour, 68

L'Histoire d l'oeil (Bataille), 133, 142

Hitchcock, Alfred, 53, 93, 261

Hokkaido, 94

Hollywood: Japanese investment in, 272

Hollywood Zen, 270, 271

Homophobia, 213

Homosexuality: and bestiality, 212–13; in *The Catch,* 164, 165; in *Merry Christmas, Mr. Lawrence,* 165, 174–76, 179, 272; in *Realm of the Senses,* 134. *See also* Sexuality

Hotels: "love," 38, *265,* 265–66

Huang tudi (Yellow Earth), 273
Huillet, Danielle, 45, 54
Human Condition, The, 157
Human Drama: 28 Years of Hiding in the Jungle (Yokoi Shoichi: Guam to 28 nen nazo o on), 234, 235–40, *238, 239*
Humanism: in *Boy*, 31–32, 89, 95–96; *Burial of the Sun* on, 251; in *The Catch*, 165, 183; and Kurosawa, 58; Marxist, 31; in *Merry Christmas, Mr. Lawrence*, 182–84; *Night and Fog in Japan* on, 58; Oshima on, 22, 23, 43, 58, 67, 182–84, 223; *Town of Love and Hope* on, 28, 45, 183
Hurd, Hugh, 165

Ice fishing, 244
Ichikawa, Kon, 12
Iconoclasm, 14, 18–26, 83
Ikebana (flower arranging), 21
Ikiru, 21–22, 92
Ikiteiru nihonkai kaisen (Battle of Tsushima, The), 234–35
I Love You (Je t'aime), 209–10
Imamura, Shohei, 7, 222
Inagaki, Hiroshi, 146–47
Incest, 114, 143, 207, 254
Independent film making, 13–14
Indian films, 201
Infidelity drama, 208
Inns *(ryokan)*, *191*, 192
Intellectualization, 211
International Arbeiter Theatre Bund, 44
International distribution, 1–2, 62, 169, 208, 214, 223, 273
Intertitles, 66–67, 68, 69, 70, 103–4
Interview, 18, 20, 23
In the Realm of the Senses. See *Realm of the Senses*
Iriye, Akira, 229
Ishihara, Shintaro, 65
Ishodo, Toshiro, 59
"Is It a Breakthrough? The Modernists of Japanese Film" (Oshima), 12
Italian neorealism, 13, 30–31, 160
Izumi, Tatsu, 105

James, Henry, 17
Jansco, Miklos, 17
Japan: anticolonialism in, 227–29; architecture in, 22, 261; art in, 4, 62, 105; auteurism in, 4–5; beauty in, 21; capital punishment in, 68; censorship in, 128, 157; citizenship in, 71, 201; comedy in, 185, 195, 214, 272; Communist party in, 9, 44–45, 55, 243; conformity in, 8, 23, 30, 177, 182; corruption in, 251; documentaries in, 101, 215, 216–17, 218–19; economy of, 62; family in, 4, 7–8, 25, 122, 260; feminism in, 252; film industry in, 10–15, 20, 62, 248–49, 272; Korean immigrants in, 44, 72, 80, 201–202, 219–22, 220, 270; Meiji period in, 7, 105, 147–49, 161; mirrors in, 24; pornography in, 128, 263, 264–68; postmodernism in, 269; post-war Occupation, 8–9, 48, 122, 157, 158, 250–51; sex industry in, 4, 37, 250, 263–68; shoplifting in, 83; song in, 186–87; theater in, 44–45; Tokugawa period in, 4, 7, 21; victimization in, 158; Yayoi period in, 24
Japanese Culture (Varley), 148
Japanese Film (Anderson and Richie), 13
Japanese Film Directors (Bock), 261
Japan Motion Pictures Assocation, 11
Japan Proletariat Theater League, 44
Je t'aime (I Love You), 209–10
Jetée, La, 107
Jidai-geki (period dramas), 85
Johnson, Barbara, 32
Joi Bengla, 245
Jokes and Their Relationship to the Unconsious (Freud), 187
Journal d'un voleur (Genet), 83
Joyu gekijo (Free Theater), 187
Judaic iconoclasm, 18–19
Ju Duo, 273
Junan, Bok, 65, 77–78
Juro, Karo, 87–88
Juro Karo Situation Players, 45, 82, *87*, 87–88
Juvenile delinquency films, 50. *See also* Sun tribe *(taiyo-zoku)* films

Kabuki theater: familial system in, 4; female demons in, 137; ghosts in, 145; Juro on, 87–88; *nimaime* in, 188; *obi-hiki* in, 130–31; sexuality in, 128, 130–31; and Western theater, 45
Kaette kita yoppirai. See *Three Resurrected Drunks*
Kafka, Franz, 64
Kaige, Chén, 273

Kai-Shek, Chiang, 241
Karaoke, 186–87
Karatani, Kojin, 23
Karayuki-san, 222–23, 266
Karayuki-san: The Making of a Prostitute, 222
Kato, Kazuhiko, 197
Kawaguchi, Saeda, 255
Kawamata, Takashi, 59
Kazoku geimu (The Family Game), 195
Keene, Donald, 21
Kei, Kumio, 222
Kenkokubi (Founder's Day), *186*, 187
Kido, Shiro, 11, 13, 30
Kim, Fhu, 201
Kinema Junpo, 3
King Kong, 210, 211
Kinoshita, Keisuke, 11
Kipnis, Laura, 268
Kiss, The (Kuchisuke), 33
Kisses, 12
Kitayama, Osamu, 197
Klee, Paul, 104
Klossowski, Pierre, 136, 183
Kluge, Alexandre, 45
Knee, Adam, 46, 66
Ko, Nakahiro, 12, 33
Kobayshi, Setsuo, 157
Koda-ha faction, 173
Korea: ceramists in, 4; Christianity in, 80; colonial occupation of, 70–71, 221; documentaries about, 223–25; filmmaking in, 201, 272; immigrants in Japan, 44, 72, 80, 201–203, 219–22, 220, 270; political protest in, 39, 40, 223–24, 225; prostitution in, 223
Korean Proletariat Theater Group, 44
Korean War, 9, 162, 243
Kori no naka no seishun (Youth in the Ice), 244
Koshikei. See *Death by Hanging*
Koyama, Akiko, 55, 59, 206, 255
Koyoyashi, Masaki, 145
Krushchev, Nikita, 243
Kuchisuke (The Kiss), 33
"KU incident" (Kyoto University), 9
Kuroneko, 145
Kurosawa, Akira, 11; *Drunken Angel*, 31; *Ikiru*, 21–22, 92; *No Regrets for Our Youth*, 20–21, 58, 157; *One Wonderful Sunday*, 31, 93; Oshima on, 20–22; *Ran*, 208; *Rashomon*, 145; as realist, 259
Kurutta kajitsu (Crazed Fruit), 12, 33

Kusturica, Emir, 271
Kuwano, Miyuki, 55
Kwaidon, 145
Kyogen, 208
Kyojin-gur (Giants), 244
Kyosenyui, 21
Kyoto, 4, 27, 37, 51
Kyoto, My Mother's Place, 270, 271
Kyoto University, 9, 20, 51

Lacan, Jacques: and comedy, 208; on desire, 34, 135–36, 137, 139; English speakers on, 127; on Freud, 89, 136; on mirror-stage theory, 25, 85, 262; Nishida compared to, 154; on "The Purloined Letter," 32; on *stade*, 139–40; on the "touché," 80–81
Lady Chatterley's Lover (Lawrence), 189
Lake Hachiro, 244
Lambert, Christopher, 210
Lancaster, Elsa, 138
Language, 15, 67–68
Language and Cinema (Metz), 16
Laroche, Guy, 212
Last Woman, The (L'Ultima donna), 210
Lawrence, D. H., 189
"Laws of Self Negation, The" (Oshima), 6
Lean, David, 169
Lehman, Peter, 14–15
Lesbian sexuality, 134
Letters from Siberia, 220
Libidinal Economy (Lyotard), 136
Life of Matsu the Untamed (Muho matsu no issho), 146–47
Lipchitz, Jacques, 19
Literary adaptations, 158, 169–70
Literary criticism, 3, 15–16
Literature, 15–16, 23, 67, 161
Lodger, The, 261
Long takes, 20, 52, 53–54, 165. See also Mise-en-scène
"Love hotels," 38, 265, 265–66
Love of a Twenty-Year-Old, 65
Lyotard, Jean-François, 39, 67–68, 97, 100, 136

Macherey, Pierre, 18
Mahagony (Brecht), 46
Mako, Midori, 201
Male Subjectivity at the Margins (Silverman), 17–18

Mallarmé, Stéphane, 15
Malle, Louis, 13
Manabe, Riichiro, 59
Manchuria, 115, 193, 241
Mao, Zedong, 240–44
Mao and the Cultural Revolution (Moutakuto to Bunka Daikakumei), 240–44
Marker, Chris, 107, 220, 223
Marnie, 93
Martin, Marcel, 180
Marxism, 23, 44–45, 51
Masculin Feminin, 88
Masumura, Yasuzo, 12, 13, 33, 34
Max, Mon Amour, 208–14, 270
McCormick, Ruth, 122
McDonald, Keiko, 65
Meiji period, 7, 105, 147–49, 161
Mellen, Joan, 260–61
Melodramas, 11, 19–20, 21, 43, 45, 89, 166
Melville, Jean-Pierre, 13
Menstrual taboo, 132
Merry Christmas, Mr. Lawrence (Senjo no merii kurisumasu): as Brechtian, 177–78; *Bridge on the River Kwai* compared to, 169; casting of, 169, 174, 178; criticism of, 159; cultural references in, 168–69, 170–71, 177, 179; *Death by Hanging* compared to, 177; ending of, 182–83; film techniques in, 169, 176, 179; financing of, 170; flashbacks in, 170, 171, 179–81; friendships in, 172–74; homosexuality in, 165, 174–76, 179, 272; humanism in, 182–84; as literary adaptation, 158, 169–71; mirror metaphors in, 174, 181; Pacific War references in, 172; psychoanalysis on, 168, 181–82; rape in, 175; subjectivity in, 177
Metropolis, 138
Metz, Christian, 16
Meyerhold, Vsevolod, 44, 45
Michelson, Annette, 21, 22
Mifune, Toshiro, 147
Mighty Joe Young, 211
Mikami, Tsugio, 4
Militarism: sexual, 149
Military: blamed for war, 158; prisoners of war in, 78–79, 158, 166, 168, 169, 176–77; racial segregation in U.S., 161–62; service in, 7; stratification in Japanese, 173
Miller, Henry, 87, 161

"Minamata disease," 216
Minoru, Murata, 11
"Mirror Given by the Ghost, The," 145–46
Mirror metaphors: in *Boy*, 25; in *Death by Hanging*, 25; in *Diary of a Shinjuku Thief*, 85; in folklore, 24–25, 145–46; in *Merry Christmas, Mr. Lawrence*, 174, 181; in mirror-stage theory, 25, 85, 262; Oshima on, 23–24, 221; in *Realm of the Senses*, 141; repetitions of, 26; in *Violence at noon*, 262
"Mirror of Matsuyama, The" (folktale), 24–25
Mise-en-abîme, 103, 107
Mise-en-acte *(agieren)*, 74–75, 114, 116, 123
Mise-en-scène: in *Death by Hanging*, 73; in *Diary of a Shinjuku Thief*, 87; in *Empire of the Passion*, 151, 154; in *Night and Fog in Japan*, 59; in *Three Resurrected Drunks*, 201; in *Violence at Noon*, 262. See also Long takes
Mishima, Yukio, 122
Mizoguchi, Kenji: *Forty-Seven Ronin*, 11; long takes by, 53; Oshima compared to, 48, 53; Oshima on, 20; *Oskaka Elegy*, 188; as a realist, 259; *Ugetsu*, 145
"Modern Girl" (Moga), 250
Modernism, 1, 12, 82, 202, 249
Momotaro umi no shimpai, 227, 229
Monika, 138
Monstresses, 138, 139
Montage: in *Battle of Tokyo*, 98; in *Boy*, 89, 95; in *Cruel Story of Youth*, 42–43; in *Death by Hanging*, 74, 77, 78; in *Diary of a Shinjuku Thief*, 81, 82, 88; in documentaries, 53, 217; in *Forgotten Soldiers*, 219; and iconoclasm, 19; Lehman on, 14; in *Mao and the Cultural Revolution*, 243; in *Night and Fog in Japan*, 59; in *Pacific War*, 229, 231; and pyrotechnics, 39; in *Treatise on Japanese Bawdy Song*, 195; in *Violence at Noon*, 262
Monument to Youth, A (Seishun no ni), 223
Morita, Yoshimitsu, 195
Morris, Desmond, 210–11
Mort, La (Bataille), 263
Moses and Aaron, 54
Motherhood, 8
Moutakuto to Bunka Daikakumei (Mao and the Cultural Revolution), 240–44
Mr. Smith Goes to Tokyo (Kyoko), 157
Muddy River (Doro no kawa), 31, 32
Muho matsu no issho (Inagaki), 146–47

Music, 90, 105, 112, 115. *See also* Song
"My Adolescence Began with Defeat"
   (Oshima), 8
"My Father's Non-existence: A Determining
   Factor in My Existence" (Oshima), 7

Nadja (Breton), 191
Nagasaki, 233
Nakamura, Itoko, 144
Nakanishi, Natsuyuki, 105
Naked Ape, The (Morris), 211
Naniwa Ereji (Oskaka Elegy), 188
Nanking, 233, 241
Naruse, Mikio, 11, 253–54
National cinemas, 61–62, 270, 271
National identity, 21, 25, 170, 171, 205, 207
Natsu no imoto (Dear Summer Sister), 204–5,
   207, 207, 235
Nazi party, 44
Negation, 6, 22, 46, 269
Neorealism, 13, 30–32, 160
*Ne Touchez pas aux femmes blanches (Don't
   Touch the White Woman)*, 209
New Wave, 5, 10, 13, 62, 187
Nichols, Bill, 217–18
Nietzsche, Friederich, 2, 153–54
Night and Fog in Japan (Nihon no yoru to kiri):
   Battle of Tokyo compared to, 52; *Burial
   of the Sun* compared to, 14; censorship
   of, 14, 52, 59, 60, 62; dialogue in, 51–52;
   Diary of a Shinjuku Thief compared to, 83;
   film techniques in, 52–54, 53, 59; flash-
   backs in, 56, 57, 58, 58–59; ghosts in, 55;
   on humanism, 58; as New Wave, 5; *No
   Regrets for Our Youth* compared to, 58–59;
   October compared to, 59; political refer-
   ences in, 9–10, 27, 51–52, 54–59, 57, 187;
   title of, 52; voice-over in, 58; weddings
   in, 55, 57, 59
Night and Fog (Nuit et bruillard), 52–53
Nihilism, 108
*Nihon no yoru to kiri. See Night and Fog in
   Japan*
*Nihon sunka-ko. See Treatise on Japanese Bawdy
   Song, A*
Nihon University, 62
Nijushi no hitomi (Twenty-four Eyes), *11*
Nikkatsu, 12
Nimaime, 188
Nishida, Kitaro, 154
Nixon, Richard, 204

Nizan, Paul, 190–92
Noguchi, Yuichiro, 12–13
*No Regrets for Our Youth (Waga seishun ni kui
   nashi)*, 20–21, 58, 157
No theater, 4, 21, 137, 144, 145, 208
Nouvelle vague, 5, 10, 13, 62, 187
Nuit et bruillard (Night and Fog), 52–53
Nygren, Scott, 227–29

Obi-hiki, 130–31
Obsessions, 38–39, 115, 257
October, 59
Oe, Kenzaburo, 158–63, 168
Oedipal mythology, 151–52, 154
Ogawa, Shinsuke, 216–17, 223
Okinawa, 100, 204, 207, 235, 236, 237
Okuyama, Kazuyoshi, 271
One Wonderful Sunday (Subarashiki), 31, 93
Onibaba, 145
Origins of Modern Literature, The (Karatani), 23
Ortolani, Benito, 45
Osaka, 27, 28, 47, 48, 51
Osaka Elegy (Naniwa Ereji), 188
Osanai, Kaoru, 11
Oshima, Eiko, 165
Oshima, Nagisa: aging of, 269, 272; on the
   AUM Shin Rikyo, 270; and auteurism,
   2–5, 6, 14, 15, 159; biography of, 3–4, 5;
   as Brechtian, 44, 45–46, 129, 159; childhood of, 7–9, 159; on Chinese cinema,
   272–73; collaboration by, 2–3, 59–60,
   208; on comedy, 185, 195, 214, 272; commercial success of, 52; on the Communist party, 9, 243; criticism by, 5–9, 8,
   12–13, 17–22, 267–68, 269–72; education
   of, 9, 19; Ferrari compared to, 209–10;
   and fictionalization, 9–10; on genre
   films, 19–20, 193; Godard compared to,
   13–14, 35, 129; on humanism, 22, 23, 43,
   58, 67, 182–84, 223; as iconoclast, 18,
   19–26, 83; Imamura on, 7; as international director, 1–2, 61, 62, 125–26, 169,
   208, 214, 223; interviews with, 3, 5, 260–
   61, 270; on Japan's social problems, 270;
   on Korean cinema, 272; on Kurosawa,
   20–22; on Masumara, 33; on melodramas, 21; on Mizoguchi, 20; as New Wave
   director, 5, 10; Oe compared to, 158–59,
   168; on pornography, 267–68; as publicist, 5; Sade compared to, 258; on script
   writing, 12; on self-negation, 6; stroke

suffered by, 272; stylistic inconsistency of, 14–15; on subjectivity, 10–11; on sun tribe films, 12, 34–35, 46; and theater, 45, 51; on U.S. cinema, 271; Wakamatsu compared to, 263–64; wedding of, 59
Oshima Nagisa no Sekai (Sato), 4
Othon, 54
Oudart, Jean-Pierre, 17–18
Ougon no daichi Bengal (The Golden Land of Bengal), 245
Ozaki, Yei Theodora, 24
Ozu, Yasujiro, 11, 46, 93, 253–54

Pabst, Georg Willelm, 45
Pachinko (pinball), 128
Pacific War: in *The Catch,* 159–60, 161–62, 165; "comfort women" in, 149, 193, 194, 222–23, 264; documentaries during, 216, 218–19; fathers lost in, 7–8; Koreans recruited by Japan during, 219–22, *220;* in *Merry Christmas, Mr. Lawrence,* 172; political repression during, 8; propaganda during, 8, 225–34
Pacific War, The (Daito senso), 216, 225–34, *228, 230, 232,* 244
Paisa, 160
Park, Ok He, 223
Patriarchal authority, 118–22, *119,* 260
People's Liberation Army (PLA), 242
Performance art, 105
Period dramas (jidai-geki), 85
"Pillow shots," 46, 93
Pinball *(pachinko),* 128
Ping, Ho, 273
Planet of the Apes, 210
PLA (People's Liberation Army), 242
Pleasures in the Coffin (Yamada), 265
Pleasures of the Flesh (Etsuraku), 156, 264–66, *265*
Poe, Edgar Allen, 32–33, 106
Polan, Dana, 45–46, 54, 202
Political movements: in Japan, 62
Pornography: *Empire of Passion* as, 156; feminism on, 267, 268; in Japan, 128, 263, 264–68; and Oshima, 156; prostitution *vs.,* 266; *Realm of the Senses* as, 131, 156, 267–68
Postman Always Rings Twice (Cain), 153
Postmodernism, 2, 249, 269
Potemkin, 74
Prehistory of the Partisan Party, 216

Prevert brothers, 214
Prisoners of war, 78–79, 158, 166, 168–69, 176–77
Program pictures, 19–20
"Project for the Reconstruction of a New Japan," 121
Proletariat Theater League, 44
Propaganda, 8, 216, 225–34
Prostitution, 37; in *Burial of the Sun,* 47, 250, 251; "comfort" women in, 149, 193, 194, 222–23, 264; hotels for, 38, *265,* 265–66; in Korea, 223; pornography *vs.,* 266
Protests. *See* Demonstrations
Psychoanalysis, 123–24; on *Boy,* 89; on *Ceremonies,* 122–23; and comedy, 208; on *Death by Hanging,* 66, 78–79, 80–81; on *Diary of a Shinjuku Thief,* 85; on *Empire of Passion,* 127; on *Merry Christmas, Mr. Lawrence,* 168, 181–82; on *Realm of the Senses,* 127, 128, 131, 135–37, 139–40; on *Violence at Noon,* 262. *See also* Lacan, Jacques
Punishment, 65, 68–69
Punishment Room, 12
"Purloined Letter, The" (Poe), 32–33, 106
Pyromania, 38–39

Quest for Fire, 210
Quotations of Chairman Mao, 240

Racism, 23, 69, 71, 161–62, 163, 167–68, 171
Raise the Red Lantern (Daàhóng denglóng gauogao guà), 273
Rampling, Charlotte, 209, 213
Ran, 208
Rape: in *Battle of Tokyo,* 107; in *Burial of the Sun,* 49–50, 251; in *Ceremonies,* 119–20, 121, 185, 260–61; in *Cruel Story of Youth,* 36–37, 259; in *Death by Hanging,* 66, 71–72, 76, 79, 259; in *Diary of a Shinjuku Thief,* 84; in *Empire of Passion,* 259; feminism on, 258–59; in *Merry Christmas, Mr. Lawrence,* 175; in Oshima's films, 258–63; in *Realm of the Senses,* 134, 138, 143, 259; repetitions of, 259; in *Treatise on Japanese Bawdy Song,* 194; in *Violence at noon,* 255–56, 257
Rashomon, 145
Ray, Nicholas, 50
Realism, 30–31
Realm of the Senses (Ai no korida): on Abe

Sada, 76; allegory in, 139–40; Bataille compared to, 132–33, 142; castration in, 131, 137, 143, 210; censorship of, 45, 128, 156; color in, 131; confluence in, 34; critics on, 138–39; *Cruel Story of Youth* compared to, 41; on death, 140–43; dialogue in, 140; *Empire of Passion* compared to, 126, 143–44, 151, 155, 156; fantasy in, 142–43; film techniques in, 141, 142, 155–56; as French and Japanese film, 125–26; gender in, 137–38, *138;* incest in, 143; mirror metaphors in, 141; as Nietzschean, 153–54; as pornography, 131, 156, 267–68; psychoanalysis on, 127, 131, 135–37, 139–40; rape in, 134, 138, 143, 259; sadomasochism in, 129, 134–35; sexuality in, 41, 125, 128–43, *134,* 155; title of, 126–28; *True Story of Abe Sada* compared to, 266–67; voyeurism in, 49, 85, 129, 140–41, 142–43, 261–62

Rebel Without a Cause, 50

Red, 93, 94, 131

Red Fireworks, Green Fireworks, 273

Reflection theory, 23, 249

Reich, William, 2, 85

Repetition and Difference (Deleuze), 202

Repetitions: in *Battle of Tokyo,* 38, 76, 103; in *Boy,* 38, 93; in *Burial of the Sun,* 51; in *The Catch,* 166; Coates on, 202; and comedy, 202; in *Cruel Story of Youth,* 38–39; in *Death by Hanging,* 71, 76–77, 80; in *Empire of the Passion,* 154; Freud on, 38; of mirror metaphors, 26; and obsession, 38–39; of rape, 259; in *Three Resurrected Drunks,* 196–97, 202, 201–2, 207

Resnais, Alain, 52–53, 68

"Review of *Sleeping Lion:* Shochiku Ofuna, A" (Oshima), 12–13

Revolt of Shiro Takisada (Amakasu Shiro Toki-sada), 183, 215

Rhee, Syngman, 223, 224

Ri, Chin'u, 65–66, 77–78, 81

Richie, Donald, 4, 11, 13

Rikisha Man (Muho matsu no issho), 146–47

Rise and Fall of the City of Mahogany, The (Brecht), 45

River Kwai, 169

Robbe-Grillet, Alain, 67

Rocha, Glauber, 17

Rojo no reikon (Souls of the Road), 11

Romanticism, 35, 43, 65–66

Rope, 53

Rossellini, Roberto, 160

Russia, 9, 15, 19, 44, 62

Russo-Japanese War, 148–49, 234–35

Ryokans (inns), *191,* 192

Ryukyu islands, 204

Sade, Marquis de, 258

Sadomasochism, 129, 134–35

Sado no shima (Segawa), 132

Sai, Yoichi, 270

Said, Edward, 128

Saikaku, 128

Saipan, 231, 235

Sakai, Naoki, 21

Sakamoto, Riuichi, 169

Sakishima, 204

Sakonji, Hiroshi, 56

Samurai, 7, 173, 237, 272

Samurai films, 271–72

Sandakin No 8, 222–23

San-ichi Shabo press, 65

Sartre, Jean-Paul, 159, 191

Sasaki, Mamoru, 66

Sato, Kei, 201, 205, 215, 255

Sato, Tadao: on auteurism, 4; on *Battle of Tokyo,* 108–9; on *Death by Hanging,* 66; on discussion drama, 52; on *Night and Fog in Japan,* 54; on Ri-Chin'u, 81; on Shochiku Ofuna, 12–13; on *Town of Love and Hope,* 30; on *Treatise on Japanese Bawdy Song,* 187

Saturn Devouring His Son (Goya), 195

Scams: in *Boy,* 89–91, 92, 94, 95; in *Burial of the Sun,* 47–48, 196, 250; in *Cruel Story of Youth,* 35–36, 42; in *Three Resurrected Drunks,* 196; in *Town of Love and Hope,* 29–30

Scenography: in *Burial of the Sun,* 27, 46; *The Catch,* 165; in *Ceremonies,* 113; in *Death by Hanging,* 69; in *Empire of Passion,* 155–56; in *Realm of the Senses,* 155–56; in *Treatise on Japanese Bawdy Song,* 188

Schaffner, Frank, 210

Schefer, Jean-Louis, 138

Schoedsack, Ernest, 210, 211

Schwankendes Gleichgewicht (Klee), 104

Sciuscià (Shoeshine), 30–31

Scorsese, Martin, 270, 271

Script writing, 12

Sea of Youth (Seinen no umi), 216

Season of the Sun, 12
Security pact treaty (AMPO), 9–10, 39–40, 54–55, 122, 204
Segawa, Kiyoko, 132
Seinen no umi (Sea of Youth), 216
Seishun no ni (A Monument to Youth), 223
Seishun sankoku monogatari. See *Cruel Story of Youth*
Sekkai no eiga sakka 6 (Film Directors of the World), 9
Le Séminaire livre I (Lacan), 25
Le Séminaire livre XI (Lacan), 25
Senjo no merii kurisumasu. See *Merry Christmas, Mr. Lawrence*
Sensationalism, 46
Seppuku (suicide), 88
Sex industry, 4, 37, 250, 263–68. *See also* Pornography; Prostitution
Sex therapy, 85
"Sexual careerism," 149
Sexuality: in *Battle of Tokyo,* 102–3, 106; and bestiality, 208–9, 211–14; in *Burial of the Sun,* 46, 47–48, 49–50, 246–48, *247,* 250–52; in *Ceremonies,* 114, 117–22; in *Cruel Story of Youth,* 40–41; and death, 140–43; in *Diary of a Shinjuku Thief,* 84–89; in *Empire of Passion,* 125, 147, 149–56; exploitation of, 246–47; and intellectualization, 211; lesbian, 134; in Meiji Japan, 149; militarism *vs.,* 149; and orgasms, 135; Oshima *vs.* Oe on, 159; and pyromania, 38–39; in *Realm of the Senses,* 41, 125, 128–43, *134,* 155; sadomasochistic, 129, 134–35; taboos, 132, 209; in *Treatise on Japanese Bawdy Song,* 186, 187–88, 192–94. *See also* Gender; Homosexuality; Pornography; Rape
Shadow at Sunrise, The (Oe), 158
Shaka, Noboru, 204
Shanaghai Express, 138
Shanghai, 242
Shaoqui, Lin, 242–43
Shiba, Ryotaro, 271–72
"Shichiri ga Hama on Aika" (song), 188–89
"Shiiku" (Oe), 158–63, 168
Shiiku (The Catch), 164, 164–68, *167,* 183
Shimazu, Yasujiro, 30
Shimpa films (modern dramas), 253
Shinai-kai (gangs), 41, 47, 48–49, 251
Shindo, Kaneto, 145
Shingeki theater, 44

Shinjuku dorobo nikki. See *Diary of a Shinjuku Thief*
Shinsengumi, 272
Shinto, 24, 132, 246
Shirasaka, Yoshio, 12, 33
Shiro Tokisada (Amakusa Shiro Tokisada), 183, 215
Shisha wa itsuma demo wakai–Okinaw gakudo sokai-sen no higeki (The Dead Remain Young), 206, 235, *236, 237, 239*
Shochiku Ofuna: history of, 11–13; *Night and Fog in Japan* shelved by, 14, 52, 59, 60, 62; Oshima at, 10, 11–14, 27, 52, 59, 60, 204, 271; publicity tactics by, 34–35, 204, 246–47
Shoeshine (Sciuscià), 30–31
Shoko, Asahara, 270
Shomin-geki (family dramas), 30
Shonen. See *Boy*
Shoplifting, 83
Shutaiteki (active involvement), 6
Sight and Sound, 3
Silberman, Serge, 208, 214
Silverberg, Miriam, 250
Silverman, Kaja, 17–18
Singer, Kurt, 24
Sino-Japanese War, 148–49
Snow, Edgar, 241
Social commentary, 3, 31–32
Socialist party, 59
Song: American protest, 187, 194; comedy linked to, 185; in *Dear Summer Sister,* 204–5; in *Diary of a Shinjuku Thief,* 82, 84, 88, 205; in Japan, 186–87; karaoke, 186–87; Okinawan, 206; in *Three Resurrected Drunks,* 196; in *Treatise on Japanese Bawdy Song,* 186–87, 188–89, *190,* 190–91, 192, 193, 194
Song, Yun Yeop, 45
Souls of the Road (Rojo no reikon), 11
South Africa, 170, 171
South Korea. *See* Korea
Soutine, Chaim, 19
Soviet Union. *See* Russia
Sower and the Seed, The (van der Post), 158, 168, 169–71, 175, 181, 182, 183
Sozosha, 66
Speilberg, Steven, 271
Stalin, Joseph, 87, 243
Stalinism, 202
Story of the Eye (Bataille), 133, 142

Stranger, The (Camus), 67
Straub, Jean-Marie, 45, 54
Structuralism, 15, 112
Student demonstrations. *See* Demonstrations;
    Zengakuren
Subarashiki (One Wonderful Sunday), 31, 93
Subjectivity, 1, 5–11, 17–18, 21, 61, 112–13,
    177
Subtitles, 197
Suicide: in *Battle of Tokyo*, 22, 100, 102, 107,
    108; in *Burial of the Sun*, 50; in *Ceremonies*,
    116, *117*, 120; *seppuku*, 88; in *Violence at
    noon*, 257
*Summer that Was Too Long, The (Nagasugita
    haru)*, 33
Sung, Kim Il, 74
Sunset Boulevard, 138
Sun tribe *(taiyo-zoku)* films: *Burial of the Sun*
    compared to, 50–51, 246–48; *Cruel Story
    of Youth* compared to, 33; *Dear Summer
    Sister* compared to, 207; Oshima on, 12,
    34–35, 46
"Surprised Twice" (folktale), 146
Swanson, Gloria, 138

Tableaus, 27, 46, 59, 195
Taboo (Gohatto), 271–72
Taboos, 132, 209
*Taiiji ga mitsuryo suru toki (Embryo Hunts
    in Secret)*, 263–64
Taisho period, 105
Taiyo no hakaba. See Burial of the Sun
Taiyo-zoku. *See* Sun tribe *(taiyo-zoku)* films
Takamatsu, Jiro, 105
Takemitsu, Toro, 105
Takikawa, Professor, 20–21
Tamura, Takeshi, 66, 164–65
Tanaka, Noburu, 266–67
Tanigushi, Senkichi, 157
Tanin no kao (Abe), 25
Tatlow, Antony, 45
Tatum, Charles, Jr., 3, 7, 54
Tea ceremony, 23, 128
Television, 12; documentaries, 215, 218–19
Tendency films, 30
Teshigahara, Hiroshi, 25
Tessier, Ma, 144
Tetuji, Takechi, 266
Theater: of the absurd, 64–65, 208; agit-
    prop, 44; Butoh, 62; film *vs.*, 46; in
    Japan, 44–45; Kyogen, 208; and *Night*

and Fog in Japan, 51, 53–54; No, 4, 21,
    137, 144, 145, 208; oppositional, 51. *See
    also* Brecht, Bertolt; Kabuki theater
"Theory of Experimental Pornographic
    Film" (Oshima), 267–68
Therese Raquin (Zola), 153
Thomas, Jeremy, 270, 271
Thousand Plateaus, A (Deleuze and Guattari),
    136
Threepenny Opera, The (Brecht), 45, 46, 63, 251
Three Resurrected Drunks (Kaette kita yopparai):
    casting of, 197; comedy in, 196, 197, 202,
    212; *Death by Hanging* compared to, 202;
    fantasy in, 203; film techniques in, 197,
    198–99, 202, *200–1*; identity in, 202;
    political references in, 197, *198*, 202–
    203, *200–1*; publicity for, 204; repetitions
    in, 196–97, 202, *202*, scams in, 196; song
    in, 196
Tojo, Hideki, 227, 231
Tokugawa period, 4, 7, 21
Tokyo: architecture in, 22, *84;* bookstores
    in, 81; housing shortage in, 40; "Ochano-
    mizu Drop" in, 105; in Oshima's films,
    27, 188; sexual entertainment districts
    in, 4, 37; Shinjuku district in, 81, 82, 188;
    subway gassing, 270
Tokyo no, 202
*Tokyo senso sengo hiwa. See Battle of Tokyo, or
    the Story of the Young Man Who Left His Will
    on Film*
"Tokyo War" demonstration, 108
Tomioka, Taeko, 86
Tomomichi, Soeda, 187
Tosei group, 173
"To the Critics, mainly, from Future Artists"
    (Oshima), 19–20
To the Distant Observer (Burch), 202
Toura, Mutsuhiro, 257
Toura, Rokko, 206
Touvier, Paul, 213–14
Town of Love and Hope (Ai to kibo no machi):
    actions of protagonists in, 28; allegory in,
    27–33; class in, 28–29, 30–32; *Cruel Story
    of Youth* compared to, 43; on humanism,
    28, 31–32, 45, 183; neorealism in, 30–32;
    political references in, 27, 28, 30; scams
    in, 29–30; symbolism of pigeon in, 28–
    30, *31*, 32–33; title of, 28; violence in, 43
Toyotomi, Hideyoshi, 4
Translation, 126–27, 158, 197

Treatise on Japanese Bawdy Song, A (Nihon sunka-ko): casting of, 187; comedy in, 186, 188, 190, 192–93, 194, 195; *Diary of a Shinjuku Thief* compared to, 188; *Family Game* compared to, 195; fantasy in, 186–87, 188, 193, 194–95; film techniques in, 188, 189, 193–95; gender in, 188–89, 190, 192, 193; political references in, *186,* 187, 189, 190–91; rape in, 194; sexuality in, 186, 187–88, 192–94; song in, 186–87, 188–89, *190,* 190–91, 192, 193, 194; title of, 187; *Violence at Noon* compared to, 187

Trial, The (Kafka), 64

True Story of Abe Sada, The, 266–67

Tsuchimoto, Noriaki, 216, 217, 223

Tsugawa, Nasahiko, 55

Tsuki wa dotchi ni dete Iru (All Under the Moon), 270

Tsurumi, Shunsuke, 187, 188–89, 196

Tsushima-maru (ship), 235, *236,* 239

Turim, Maureen, 56, 179, 222

Tuskiji Little Theater Group, 44

Twenty-four Eyes (Nijushi no hitomi), 11

Two or Three Things I Know about Her (Deux ou trois choses que je sais d'elle), 86

Ugestu Monogatari, 145

Ugetsu, 145

Ukiyo-e, 4, 128, 156, 192

L'Ultima donna (The Last Woman), 210

United States: hegemony of cinema in, 271; racism in, 161–62

University of Tokyo, 62

Uno, Koji, 59

Ushiyama, Junichi, 215

U.S.S.R.. *See* Russia

Valentino, Rudolf, 270

Van der Post, Laurens, 158, 168, 169–70, 175, 181, 182, 183

Vanguard Trouipe, 44

Varley, H. Paul, 148

Venice film festival, 147

Verfremdung (distanciation), 43–44, 45, 49, 63, 76, 89, 164

Vertov, Dziga, 19

Victimization, 158

Vietnam, 203–4, 243

Vietnam War: French in, 9; protest against, 178, 179, 193, 194; references in Oshima's films on, 197, 234, 238–39

Violence: in *Burial of the Sun,* 50; in *Town of Love and Hope,* 43. *See also* Rape

Violence at Noon (Hakuchu no torima): allegory in, 263; film techniques in, 165, 256, 261–62; flashbacks in, 257; gender in, 254–58, *256;* ghosts in, 263; Hitchcock compared to, 261; mirror metaphors in, 262; obsession in, 257; and *Pleasures of the Flesh,* 264–65; psychoanalysis on, 262; rape in, 255–56, 257; suicide in, 257; *Treatise on Japanese Bawdy Song* compared to, 187; voyeurism in, 261–62

Voice-over: in *Battle of Tokyo,* 100; in *Boy,* 95; in *Ceremonies,* 109, 114, 118; in *Cruel Story of Youth,* 42, 253; in *Death by Hanging,* 69–70; in *Diary of a Shinjuku Thief,* 86–87; in documentaries, 217; in *Empire of Passion,* 152; in *Forgotten Soldiers,* 219–20, 221–22; in *Night and Fog in Japan,* 58; in *Pacific War,* 229

Voices of the Past (Sakai), 21

Voyeurism: in *Burial of the Sun,* 49, 50; in *Diary of a Shinjuku Thief,* 82, 84, 85; in *Empire of Passion,* 151–52; Heath on, 248; in *Max, Mon Amour,* 209; in *Realm of the Senses,* 49, 85, 129, 140–41, 142–43, 261–62; in *Violence at noon,* 261–62

Waga seishun ni kui nashi (No Regrets for Our Youth), 20–21, 58, 157

Wakamatsu, Koji, 263–64, 266

Watanabe, Fumio, 54, 203

War films, 157, 170

Wasurerareta kogun (Forgotten Soldiers), 219–22, *220,* 223

Weddings, 55, 57, 121

Wenders, Wim, 270, 271

Wide Angle, 3

Wide-screen images: in *Boy,* 93; in *Burial of the Sun,* 47, 47–48, 51; in *Ceremonies,* 115; in *Diary of a Shinjuku Thief,* 85; in Japan, 12; in *Merry Christmas, Mr. Lawrence,* 176; in *Night and Fog in Japan,* 52; Oshima's use of, 27, 59–60

Williams, Linda, 268

Windows, 22, 103

Winston, Brian, 218

Wittgenstein, Ludwig, 67

Women: as antiheroines, 247–52; as demons, 137–38, *138, 150;* in Korea, 223; and motherhood, 8; Oshima's pairing of, 252–

Women: *(continued)*
  58; Western *vs.* Japanese, 246. *See also*
  Feminism; Gender
Women's films, 11
World War II. *See* Pacific War
Wylie, Philip, 8

Xenophobia, 23. *See also* Racism

Yayoi period, 24
Yakuza (gangsters), 33, 34–35, 47, 83, 196, 266
Yamada, Futaro, 265
Yamamoto, Isoroku, 231
Yamazaki, Hiromi, 222, 266
Yanagida, Kunio, 86
Yanagita, Kunio, 24
Yat-sen, Sun, 241
Yellow Earth (Huang tudi), 273
Yimóu, Zhang, 273

Yoidore tenshi (Drunken Angel), 31
*Yokoi Shoichi: Guam to 28 nen nazo o on (Human
  Drama: 28 Years of Hiding in the Jungle),*
  234, 235–40, *238, 239*
Yoshida, Yajimi, 237
Yoshiimoto, Ryumei, 86
Yoshizawa, Takao, 55
Youth films. *See* Sun tribe *(taiyo-zoku)* films
Youth in the Ice (Kori no naka no seishun), 244
Yui shoshetsu, 87
Yunbogi no nikki (Diary of Yunbogi), 89, 223–
  25, *224, 225*

Zaibatsu, 29, 122
Zen Buddhism, 154
Zen'ei bijutsu (avante-garde artists), 105
Zengakuren (student organization), 40, 55,
  56, 216. *See also* Demonstrations
Zola, Emile, 153

Design: Ina Clausen
Composition: Integrated Composition Systems
Text: 10/12 Baskerville
Display: Baskerville
Printer and binder: BookCrafters, Inc.